Get the eBook FREE!

(PDF, ePub, Kindle, and liveBook all included)

We believe that once you buy a book from us, you should be able to read it in any format we have available. To get electronic versions of this book at no additional cost to you, purchase and then register this book at the Manning website.

Go to https://www.manning.com/freebook and follow the instructions to complete your pBook registration.

That's it!
Thanks from Manning!

Human-in-the-Loop Machine Learning

ACTIVE LEARNING AND ANNOTATION FOR HUMAN-CENTERED AI

ROBERT (MUNRO) MONARCH
FOREWORD BY CHRISTOPHER D. MANNING

MANNING
SHELTER ISLAND

For online information and ordering of this and other Manning books, please visit
www.manning.com. The publisher offers discounts on this book when ordered in quantity.
For more information, please contact

> Special Sales Department
> Manning Publications Co.
> 20 Baldwin Road
> PO Box 761
> Shelter Island, NY 11964
> Email: orders@manning.com

The figure on the cover is "Cephaloniene" (Woman from Cephalonia), an illustration by
Jacques Grasset de Saint-Sauveur from his 1797 book, *Costumes de Différents Pays*.

Manning Publications Co.
20 Baldwin Road
PO Box 761
Shelter Island, NY 11964

Development editor:	Susan Ethridge
Technical development editor:	Frances Buontempo
Review editor:	Ivan Martinović
Production editor:	Deirdre S. Hiam
Copy editor:	Keir Simpson
Proofreader:	Keri Hales
Technical proofreader:	Al Krinker
Typesetter:	Gordan Salinovic
Cover designer:	Marija Tudor

ISBN 9781617296741
Printed in the United States of America

brief contents

contents

v

foreword

With machine learning now deployed widely in many industry sectors, artificial intelligence systems are in daily contact with human systems and human beings. Most people have noticed some of the user-facing consequences. Machine learning can either improve people's lives, such as with the speech recognition and natural language understanding of a helpful voice assistant, or it can annoy or even actively harm humans, with examples ranging from annoyingly lingering product recommendations to résumé review systems that are systematically biased against women or under-represented ethnic groups. Rather than thinking about artificial intelligence operating in isolation, the pressing need this century is for the exploration of human-centered artificial intelligence—that is, building AI technology that effectively cooperates and collaborates with people, and augments their abilities.

This book focuses not on end users but on how people and machine learning come together in the production and running of machine learning systems. It is an open secret of machine learning practitioners in industry that obtaining the right data with the right annotations is many times more valuable than adopting a more advanced machine learning algorithm. The production, selection, and annotation of data is a very human endeavor. Hand-labeling data can be expensive and unreliable, and this book spends much time on this problem. One direction is to reduce the amount of data that needs to be labeled while still allowing the training of high-quality systems through active learning approaches. Another direction is to exploit machine learning and human–computer interaction techniques to improve the speed and accuracy of human annotation. Things do not stop there: most large, deployed systems also involve various kinds of human review and updating. Again, the machine learning can either be designed to leverage the work of people, or it can be something that humans need to fight against.

Robert Monarch is a highly qualified guide on this journey. In his work both before and during his PhD, Robert's focus was practical and attentive to people. He pioneered the application of natural language processing (NLP) to disaster-response-related messages based on his own efforts helping in several crisis scenarios. He started with human approaches to processing critical data and then looked for the best ways to leverage NLP to automate some of the process. I am delighted that many of these methods are now being used by disaster response organizations and can be shared with a broader audience in this book.

While the data side of machine learning is often perceived as mainly work managing people, this book shows that this side is also very technical. The algorithms for sampling data and quality control for annotation often approach the complexity of those in the downstream model consuming the training data, in some cases implementing machine learning and transfer learning techniques within the annotation process. There is a real need for more resources on the annotation process, and this book was already having an impact even as it was being written. As individual chapters were published, they were being read by data scientists in large organizations in fields like agriculture, entertainment, and travel. This highlights both the now-widespread use of machine learning and the thirst for data-focused books. This book codifies many of the best current practices and algorithms, but because the data side of the house was long neglected, I expect that there are still more scientific discoveries about data-focused machine learning to be made, and I hope that having an initial guidebook will encourage further progress.

—CHRISTOPHER D. MANNING

Christopher D. Manning is a professor of computer science and linguistics at Stanford University, director of the Stanford Artificial Intelligence Laboratory, and co-director of the Stanford Human-Centered Artificial Intelligence Institute.

preface

I am donating all author proceeds from this book to initiatives for better datasets, especially for low-resource languages and for health and disaster response. When I started writing this book, the example dataset about disaster response was uncommon and specific to my dual background as a machine learning scientist and disaster responder. With COVID-19, the global landscape has changed, and many people now understand why disaster response use cases are so important. The pandemic has exposed many gaps in our machine learning capabilities, especially with regard to access to relevant health care information and to fight misinformation campaigns. When search engines failed to surface the most up-to-date public health information and social media platforms failed to identify widespread misinformation, we all experienced the downside of applications that were not able to adapt fast enough to changing data.

This book is not specific to disaster response. The observations and methods that I share here also come from my experience building datasets for autonomous vehicles, music recommendations, online commerce, voice-enabled devices, translation, and a wide range of other practical use cases. It was a delight to learn about many new applications while writing the book. From data scientists who read draft chapters, I learned about use cases in organizations that weren't historically associated with machine learning: an agriculture company installing smart cameras on tractors, an entertainment company adapting face recognition to cartoon characters, an environmental company predicting carbon footprints, and a clothing company personalizing fashion recommendations. When I gave invited talks about the book in these data science labs, I'm certain that I learned more than I taught!

All these use cases had two things in common: the data scientists needed to create better training and evaluation data for their machine learning models, and almost nothing was published about how to create that data. I'm excited to share strategies and techniques to help systems that combine human and machine intelligence for almost any application of machine learning.

acknowledgments

I owe the most gratitude to my wife, Victoria Monarch, for supporting my decision to write a book in the first place. I hope that this book helps make the world better for our own little human who was born while I was writing the book.

Most people who have written technical books told me that they stopped enjoying the process by the end. That didn't happen to me. I enjoyed writing this book right up until the final revisions because of all the people who had provided feedback on draft chapters since 2019. I appreciate how intrinsic early feedback is to the Manning Publications process, and within Manning Publications, I am most grateful to my editor, Susan Ethridge. I looked forward to our weekly calls, and I am especially fortunate to have had an editor who previously worked as a "human-in-the-loop" in e-discovery. Not every writer is fortunate to have an editor with domain experience! I am also grateful for the detailed chapter reviews by Frances Buontempo; the technical review by Al Krinker; project editor, Deirdre Hiam; copyeditor, Keir Simpson; proofreader, Keri Hales; review editor, Ivan Martinović; and everyone else within Manning who provided feedback on the book's content, images, and code.

Thank you to all the reviewers: Alain Couniot, Alessandro Puzielli, Arnaldo Gabriel Ayala Meyer, Clemens Baader, Dana Robinson, Danny Scott, Des Horsley, Diego Poggioli, Emily Ricotta, Ewelina Sowka, Imaculate Mosha, Michal Rutka, Michiel Trimpe, Rajesh Kumar R S, Ruslan Shevchenko, Sayak Paul, Sebastián Palma Mardones, Tobias Bürger, Torje Lucian, V. V. Phansalkar, and Vidhya Vinay. Your suggestions helped make this book better.

Thank you to everyone in my network who gave me direct feedback on early drafts: Abhay Agarwa, Abraham Starosta, Aditya Arun, Brad Klingerberg, David Evans, Deba- jyoti Datta, Divya Kulkarni, Drazen Prelec, Elijah Rippeth, Emma Bassein, Frankie Li, Jim Ostrowski, Katerina Margatina, Miquel Àngel Farré, Rob Morris, Scott Cambo, Tivadar Danka, Yada Pruksachatkun, and everyone who commented via Manning's online forum. Adrian Calma was especially diligent, and I am lucky that a recent PhD in active learning read the draft chapters so closely!

I am indebted to many people I have worked with over the course of my career. In addition to my colleagues at Apple today, I am especially grateful to past colleagues at Idibon, Figure Eight, AWS, and Stanford. I am delighted that my PhD advisor at Stan- ford, Christopher Manning, provided the foreword for this book.

Finally, I am especially grateful to the 11 experts who shared anecdotes in this book: Ayanna Howard, Daniela Braga, Elena Grewal, Ines Montani, Jennifer Prendki, Jia Li, Kieran Snyder, Lisa Braden-Harder, Matthew Honnibal, Peter Skomoroch, and Radha Basu. All of them have founded successful machine learning companies, and all worked directly on the data side of machine learning at some point in their careers. If you are like most intended readers of this book—someone early in their career who is struggling to create good training data—consider them to be role mod- els for your own future!

about this book

This is the book that I *wish* existed when I was introduced to machine learning, because it addresses the most important problem in artificial intelligence: how should humans and machines work together to solve problems? Most machine learning models are guided by human examples, but most machine learning texts and courses focus only on the algorithms. You can often get state-of-the-art results with good data and simple algorithms, but you rarely get state-of-the-art results with the best algorithm built on bad data. So if you need to go deep in one area of machine learning first, you could argue that the data side is more important.

Who should read this book

This book is primarily for data scientists, software developers, and students who have only recently started working with machine learning (or only recently started working on the data side). You should have some experience with concepts such as supervised and unsupervised machine learning, training and testing machine learning models, and libraries such as PyTorch and TensorFlow. But you don't have be an expert in any of these areas to start reading this book.

When you become more experienced, this book should remain a useful quick reference for the different techniques. This book is the first to contain the most common strategies for annotation, active learning, and adjacent tasks such as interface design for annotation.

How this book is organized: A road map

This book is divided into four parts: an introduction; a deep dive on active learning; a deep dive on annotation; and the final part, which brings everything together with design strategies for human interfaces and three implementation examples.

The first part of this book introduces the building blocks for creating training and evaluation data: annotation, active learning, and the human–computer interaction concepts that help humans and machines combine their intelligence most effectively. By the end of chapter 2, you will have built a human-in-the-loop machine learning application for labeling news headlines, completing the cycle from annotating new data to retraining a model and then using the new model to help decide which data should be annotated next.

Part 2 covers active learning—the set of techniques for sampling the most important data for humans to review. Chapter 3 covers the most widely used techniques for understanding a model's uncertainty, and chapter 4 tackles the complicated problem of identifying where your model might be confident but wrong due to undersampled or nonrepresentative data. Chapter 5 introduces ways to combine different strategies into a comprehensive active learning system, and chapter 6 covers how the active learning techniques can be applied to different kinds of machine learning tasks.

Part 3 covers annotation—the often-underestimated problem of obtaining accurate and representative labels for training and evaluation data. Chapter 7 covers how to find and manage the right people to annotate data. Chapter 8 covers the basics of quality control for annotation, introducing the most common ways to calculate accuracy and agreement. Chapter 9 covers advanced strategies for annotation quality control, including annotations for subjective tasks and a wide range of methods to semi-automate annotation with rule-based systems, search-based systems, transfer learning, semi-supervised learning, self-supervised learning, and synthetic data creation. Chapter 10 covers how annotation can be managed for different kinds of machine learning tasks.

Part 4 completes the "loop" with a deep dive on interfaces for effective annotation in chapter 11 and three examples of human-in-the-loop machine learning applications in chapter 12.

Throughout the book, we continually return to examples from different kinds of machine learning tasks: image- and document-level labeling, continuous data, object detection, semantic segmentation, sequence labeling, language generation, and information retrieval. The inside covers contain quick references that show where you can find these tasks throughout the book.

About the code

All the code used in this book is open source and available from my GitHub account. The code used in the first six chapters of this book is at https://github.com/rmunro/pytorch_active_learning.

Some chapters also use spreadsheets for analysis, and the three examples in the final chapter are in their own repositories. See the respective chapters for more details.

liveBook discussion forum

Purchase of *Human-in-the-Loop Machine Learning* includes free access to a private web forum run by Manning Publications where you can make comments about the book, ask technical questions, and receive help from the author and from other users. To access the forum, go to https://livebook.manning.com/book/human-in-the-loop-machine-learning/welcome/v-11. You can learn more about Manning's forums and the rules of conduct at https://livebook.manning.com/#!/discussion.

Manning's commitment to our readers is to provide a venue where a meaningful dialogue between individual readers and between readers and the author can take place. It is not a commitment to any specific amount of participation on the part of the author, whose contribution to the forum remains voluntary (and unpaid). We suggest that you try asking the author some challenging questions lest his interest stray! The forum and the archives of previous discussions will be accessible from the publisher's website as long as the book is in print.

Other online resources

Each chapter has a "Further reading" section, and with only a handful of exceptions, all the resources listed are free and available online. As I say in a few places, look for highly cited work that cites the papers I referenced. It didn't make sense to include some influential papers, and many other relevant papers will be published after this book.

about the author

ROBERT MONARCH, PHD (formerly Robert Munro), is an expert in combining human and machine intelligence who currently lives in San Francisco and works at Apple. Robert has worked in Sierra Leone, Haiti, the Amazon, London, and Sydney, in organizations ranging from startups to the United Nations. He was the CEO and founder of Idibon, the CTO of Figure Eight, and he led Amazon Web Services's first natural language processing and machine translation services.

Part 1

First steps

Most data scientists spend more time working on the data than on the algorithms. Most books and courses on machine learning, however, focus on the algorithms. This book addresses this gap in material about the data side of machine learning.

The first part of this book introduces the building blocks for creating training and evaluation data: annotation, active learning, and the human–computer interaction concepts that help humans and machines combine their intelligence most effectively. By the end of chapter 2, you will have built a human-in-the-loop machine learning application for labeling news headlines, completing the cycle from annotating new data to retraining a model and then using the new model to decide which data should be annotated next.

In the remaining chapters, you will learn how you might extend your first application with more sophisticated techniques for data sampling, annotation, and combining human and machine intelligence. The book also covers how to apply the techniques you will learn to different types of machine learning tasks, including object detection, semantic segmentation, sequence labeling, and language generation.

Introduction to human-in-the-loop machine learning

This chapter covers

- Annotating unlabeled data to create training, validation, and evaluation data
- Sampling the most important unlabeled data items (active learning)
- Incorporating human–computer interaction principles into annotation
- Implementing transfer learning to take advantage of information in existing models

Unlike robots in the movies, most of today's artificial intelligence (AI) cannot learn by itself; instead, it relies on intensive human feedback. Probably 90% of machine learning applications today are powered by supervised machine learning. This figure covers a wide range of use cases. An autonomous vehicle can drive you safely down the street because humans have spent thousands of hours telling it when its

3

sensors are seeing a pedestrian, moving vehicle, lane marking, or other relevant object. Your in-home device knows what to do when you say "Turn up the volume" because humans have spent thousands of hours telling it how to interpret different commands. And your machine translation service can translate between languages because it has been trained on thousands (or maybe millions) of human-translated texts.

Compared with the past, our intelligent devices are learning less from programmers who are hardcoding rules and more from examples and feedback given by humans who do not need to code. These human-encoded examples—the training data—are used to train machine learning models and make them more accurate for their given tasks. But programmers still need to create the software that allows the feedback from nontechnical humans, which raises one of the most important questions in technology today: *What are the right ways for humans and machine learning algorithms to interact to solve problems?* After reading this book, you will be able to answer this question for many uses that you might face in machine learning.

Annotation and active learning are the cornerstones of human-in-the-loop machine learning. They specify how you elicit training data from people and determine the right data to put in front of people when you don't have the budget or time for human feedback on all your data. Transfer learning allows us to avoid a cold start, adapting existing machine learning models to our new task rather than starting at square one. We will introduce each of these concepts in this chapter.

1.1 The basic principles of human-in-the-loop machine learning

Human-in-the-loop machine learning is a set of strategies for combining human and machine intelligence in applications that use AI. The goal typically is to do one or more of the following:

- Increase the accuracy of a machine learning model.
- Reach the target accuracy for a machine learning model faster.
- Combine human and machine intelligence to maximize accuracy.
- Assist human tasks with machine learning to increase efficiency.

This book covers the most common active learning and annotation strategies and how to design the best interface for your data, task, and annotation workforce. The book gradually builds from simpler to more complicated examples and is written to be read in sequence. You are unlikely to apply all these techniques at the same time, however, so the book is also designed to be a reference for each specific technique.

Figure 1.1 shows the human-in-the-loop machine learning process for adding labels to data. This process could be any labeling process: adding the topic to news stories, classifying sports photos according to the sport being played, identifying the sentiment of a social media comment, rating a video on how explicit the content is, and so on. In all cases, you could use machine learning to automate some of the process of labeling or to speed up the human process. In all cases, using best practices means implementing the cycle shown in figure 1.1: sampling the right data to label, using that data to train a model, and using that model to sample more data to annotate.

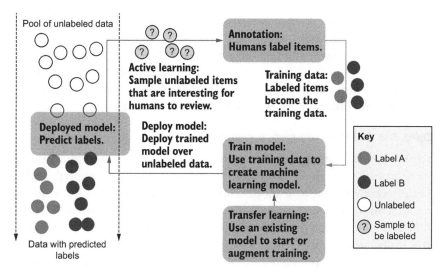

Figure 1.1 A mental model of the human-in-the-loop process for predicting labels on data

In some cases, you may want only some of the techniques. If you have a system that backs off to a human when the machine learning model is uncertain, for example, you would look at the relevant chapters and sections on uncertainty sampling, annotation quality, and interface design. Those topics still represent the majority of this book even if you aren't completing the "loop."

This book assumes that you have some familiarity with machine learning. Some concepts are especially important for human-in-the-loop systems, including deep understanding of softmax and its limitations. You also need to know how to calculate accuracy with metrics that take model confidence into consideration, calculate chance-adjusted accuracy, and measure the performance of machine learning from a human perspective. (The appendix contains a summary of this knowledge.)

1.2 *Introducing annotation*

Annotation is the process of labeling raw data so that it becomes training data for machine learning. Most data scientists will tell you that they spend much more time curating and annotating datasets than they spend building the machine learning models. Quality control for human annotation relies on more complicated statistics than most machine learning models do, so it is important to take the necessary time to learn how to create quality training data.

1.2.1 *Simple and more complicated annotation strategies*

An annotation process can be simple. If you want to label social media posts about a product as positive, negative, or neutral to analyze broad trends in sentiment about that product, for example, you could build and deploy an HTML form in a few hours. A simple HTML form could allow someone to rate each social media post according to the sentiment option, and each rating would become the label on the social media post for your training data.

An annotation process can also be complicated. If you want to label every object in a video with a bounding box, for example, a simple HTML form is not enough; you need a graphical interface that allows annotators to draw those boxes, and a good user experience might take months of engineering hours to build.

1.2.2 *Plugging the gap in data science knowledge*

Your machine learning algorithm strategy and your data annotation strategy can be optimized at the same time. The two strategies are closely intertwined, and you often get better accuracy from your models faster if you have a combined approach. Algorithms and annotation are equally important components of good machine learning.

All computer science departments offer machine learning courses, but few offer courses on creating training data. At most, you might find one or two lectures about creating training data among hundreds of machine learning lectures across half a dozen courses. This situation is changing, but slowly. For historical reasons, academic machine learning researchers have tended to keep the datasets constant and evaluated their research only in terms of different algorithms.

By contrast with academic machine learning, it is more common in industry to improve model performance by annotating more training data. Especially when the nature of the data is changing over time (which is also common), using a handful of new annotations can be far more effective than trying to adapt an existing model to a new domain of data. But far more academic papers focus on how to adapt algorithms to new domains *without* new training data than on how to annotate the right new training data efficiently.

Because of this imbalance in academia, I've often seen people in industry make the same mistake. They hire a dozen smart PhDs who know how to build state-of-the-art algorithms but don't have experience creating training data or thinking about the right interfaces for annotation. I saw exactly this situation recently at one of the world's largest auto manufacturers. The company had hired a large number of recent machine learning graduates, but it couldn't operationalize its autonomous vehicle technology because the new employees couldn't scale their data annotation strategy. The company ended up letting that entire team go. During the aftermath, I advised the company how to rebuild its strategy by using algorithms and annotation as equally-important, intertwined components of good machine learning.

1.2.3 *Quality human annotation: Why is it hard?*

To those who study it, annotation is a science that's tied closely to machine learning. The most obvious example is that the humans who provide the labels can make errors, and overcoming these errors requires surprisingly sophisticated statistics.

Human errors in training data can be more or less important, depending on the use case. If a machine learning model is being used only to identify broad trends in consumer sentiment, it probably won't matter whether errors propagate from 1% bad training data. But if an algorithm that powers an autonomous vehicle doesn't see 1% of pedestrians due to errors propagated from bad training data, the result will be disastrous. Some algorithms can handle a little noise in the training data, and random noise even helps some algorithms become more accurate by avoiding overfitting. But human errors tend not to be random noise; therefore, they tend to introduce irrecoverable bias into training data. No algorithm can survive truly bad training data.

For simple tasks, such as binary labels on objective tasks, the statistics are fairly straightforward for deciding which label is correct when different annotators disagree. But for subjective tasks, or even objective tasks with continuous data, no simple heuristics exist for deciding the correct label. Think about the critical task of creating training data by putting a bounding box around every pedestrian recognized by a self-driving car. What if two annotators have slightly different boxes? Which box is the correct one? The answer is not necessarily either box or the average of the two boxes. In fact, the best way to aggregate the two boxes is to use machine learning.

One of the best ways to ensure quality annotations is to ensure you have the right people making those annotations. Chapter 7 of this book is devoted to finding, teaching, and managing the best annotators. For an example of the importance of the right workforce combined with the right technology, see the following sidebar.

Human insights and scalable machine learning equal production AI

Expert anecdote by Radha Ramaswami Basu

The outcome of AI is heavily dependent on the quality of the training data that goes into it. A small UI improvement like a magic wand to select regions in an image can realize large efficiencies when applied across millions of data points in conjunction with well-defined processes for quality control. An advanced workforce is the key factor: training and specialization increase quality, and insights from an expert workforce can inform model design in conjunction with domain experts. The best models are created by a constructive, ongoing partnership between machine and human intelligence.

We recently took on a project that required pixel-level annotation of the various anatomic structures within a robotic coronary artery bypass graft (CABG) video. Our annotation teams are not experts in anatomy or physiology, so we implemented teaching sessions in clinical knowledge to augment the existing core skills in 3D spatial reasoning and precision annotation, led by a solutions architect who is a trained surgeon. The outcome for our customer was successful training and evaluation data. The outcome for us was to see people from under-resourced backgrounds in animated discussion about some of the most advanced uses of AI as they quickly became experts in one of the most important steps in medical image analysis.

Radha Basu is founder and CEO of iMerit. iMerit uses technology and an AI workforce consisting of 50% women and youth from underserved communities to create advanced technology workers for global clients. Radha previously worked at HP, took Supportsoft public as CEO, and founded the Frugal Innovation Lab at Santa Clara University.

1.3 Introducing active learning: Improving the speed and reducing the cost of training data

Supervised learning models almost always get more accurate with more labeled data. *Active learning* is the process of deciding which data to sample for human annotation. No one algorithm, architecture, or set of parameters makes one machine learning model more accurate in all cases, and no one strategy for active learning is optimal across all use cases and datasets. You should try certain approaches first, however, because they are more likely to be successful for your data and task.

Most research papers on active learning focus on the number of training items, but speed can be an even more important factor in many cases. In disaster response, for example, I have often deployed machine learning models to filter and extract information from emerging disasters. Any delay in disaster response is potentially critical, so getting a usable model out quickly is more important than the number of labels that need to go into that model.

1.3.1 Three broad active learning sampling strategies: Uncertainty, diversity, and random

Many active learning strategies exist, but three basic approaches work well in most contexts: uncertainty, diversity, and random sampling. A combination of the three should almost always be the starting point.

Random sampling sounds the simplest but can be the trickiest. What is random if your data is prefiltered, when your data is changing over time, or if you know for some other reason that a random sample will not be representative of the problem you are addressing? These questions are addressed in more detail in the following sections. Regardless of the strategy, you should always annotate some amount of random data to gauge the accuracy of your model and compare your active learning strategies with a baseline of randomly selected items.

Uncertainty and diversity sampling go by various names in the literature. They are often referred to as *exploitation* and *exploration,* which are clever names that alliterate and rhyme, but are not otherwise very transparent.

Uncertainty sampling is the set of strategies for identifying unlabeled items that are near a decision boundary in your current machine learning model. If you have a binary classification task, these items will have close to a 50% probability of belonging to either label; therefore, the model is called uncertain or confused. These items are most likely to be wrongly classified, so they are the most likely to result in a label that differs from the predicted label, moving the decision boundary after they have been added to the training data and the model has been retrained.

Diversity sampling is the set of strategies for identifying unlabeled items that are underrepresented or unknown to the machine learning model in its current state. The items may have features that are rare in the training data, or they might represent real-world demographics that are currently under-represented in the model. In either case, the result can be poor or uneven performance when the model is applied, especially when the data is changing over time. The goal of diversity sampling is to target new, unusual, or underrepresented items for annotation to give the machine learning algorithm a more complete picture of the problem space.

Although the term *uncertainty sampling* is widely used, *diversity sampling* goes by different names in different fields, such as representative sampling, stratified sampling, outlier detection, and anomaly detection. For some use cases, such as identifying new phenomena in astronomical databases or detecting strange network activity for security, the goal of the task is to identify the outlier or anomaly, but we can adapt them here as a sampling strategy for active learning.

Uncertainty sampling and diversity sampling have shortcomings in isolation (figure 1.2). Uncertainty sampling might focus on one part of the decision boundary, for example, and diversity sampling might focus on outliers that are a long distance from the boundary. So the strategies are often used together to find a selection of unlabeled items that will maximize both uncertainty and diversity.

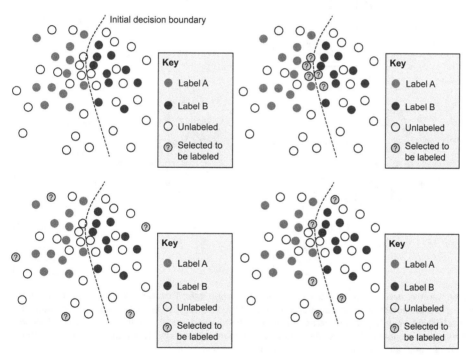

Figure 1.2   Pros and cons of different active learning strategies. *Top left:* The decision boundary from a machine learning algorithm between items, with some items labeled A and some labeled B. *Top right:* One possible result from uncertainty sampling. This active learning strategy is effective for selecting unlabeled items near the decision boundary. These items are the most likely to be wrongly predicted, and therefore, the most likely to get a label that moves the decision boundary. If all the uncertainty is in one part of the problem space, however, giving these items labels will not have a broad effect on the model. *Bottom left:* One possible result of diversity sampling. This active learning strategy is effective for selecting unlabeled items in different parts of the problem space. If the diversity is away from the decision boundary, however, these items are unlikely to be wrongly predicted, so they will not have a large effect on the model when a human gives them a label that is the same as the model predicted. *Bottom right:* One possible result from combining uncertainty sampling and diversity sampling. When the strategies are combined, items are selected that are near diverse sections of the decision boundary. Therefore, we are optimizing the chance of finding items that are likely to result in a changed decision boundary.

It is important to note that the active learning process is iterative. In each iteration of active learning, a selection of items is identified and receives a new human-generated label. Then the model is retrained with the new items, and the process is repeated. Figure 1.3 shows two iterations for selecting and annotating new items, resulting in a changing boundary.

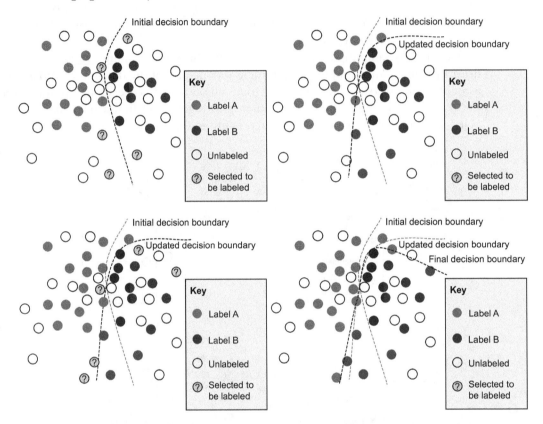

Figure 1.3   The iterative active learning process. *Top left to bottom right:* **Two iterations of active learning. In each iteration, items are selected along a diverse selection of the boundary, which in turn causes the boundary to move after retraining, resulting in a more accurate machine learning model. Ideally, we requested human labels for the minimum number of items as part of our active learning strategy. This request speeds the time to get an accurate model and reduces the overall cost of human annotation.**

Iteration cycles can be a form of diversity sampling in themselves. Imagine that you used only uncertainty sampling, and sampled from only one part of the problem space in an iteration. You might solve all uncertainty in that part of the problem space; therefore, the next iteration would concentrate somewhere else. With enough iterations, you might not need diversity sampling at all. Each iteration from uncertainty sampling would focus on a different part of the problem space, and together, the iterations are enough to get a diverse sample of items for training.

Implemented properly, active learning has this self-correcting function: each iteration finds new aspects of the data that are best for human annotation. If some part of your data space is inherently ambiguous, however, each iteration could keep bringing you back to the same part of the problem space with those ambiguous items. So it is generally wise to consider both uncertainty and diversity sampling strategies to ensure that you are not focusing all your labeling efforts on a part of the problem space that your model might not be able to solve.

Figures 1.2 and 1.3 give you good intuition about the process for active learning. As anyone who has worked with high-dimensional or sequence data knows, it is not always straightforward to identify distance from a boundary or diversity. At least, the process is more complicated than the simple Euclidean distance in figures 1.2 and 1.3. But the same idea still applies: we are trying to reach an accurate model as quickly as possible with as few human labels as possible.

The number of iterations and the number of items that need to be labeled within each iteration depend on the task. When you're working in adaptive machine+human translation, a single translated sentence is enough training data to require the model to update, ideally within a few seconds. It is easy to see why from a user-experience perspective. If a human translator corrects the machine prediction for some word, but the machine doesn't adapt quickly, the human may need to (re)correct that machine output hundreds of times. This problem is common when you're translating words that are highly context-specific. You may want to translate a person's name literally in a news article, for example, but translate it into a localized name in a work of fiction. The user experience will be bad if the software keeps making the same mistake so soon after a human has corrected it, because we expect recency to help with adaptation.

On the technical side, of course, it is much more difficult to adapt a model quickly. Consider large machine translation models. Currently, it takes a week or more to train these models. From the experience of the translator, a software system that can adapt quickly is employing continuous learning. In most use cases I've worked on, such as identifying the sentiment in social media comments, I needed to iterate only every month or so to adapt to new data. Although few applications have real-time adaptive machine learning today, more are moving this way.

1.3.2   *What is a random selection of evaluation data?*

It is easy to *say* that you should always evaluate on a random sample of held-out data, but in practical terms, it is rarely easy to ensure that you have a truly random sample of data. If you prefiltered the data that you are working with by keyword, time, or some other factor, you already have a nonrepresentative sample. The accuracy of that sample is not necessarily indicative of the accuracy on the data where your model will be deployed.

I've seen people use the well-known ImageNet dataset and apply machine learning models to a broad selection of data. The canonical ImageNet dataset has 1,000 labels, each of which describes the category of that image, such as "Basketball," "Taxi," or

"Swimming." The ImageNet challenges evaluated held-out data from that dataset, and systems achieved near-human-level accuracy within that dataset. If you apply those same models to a random selection of images posted on a social media platform, however, accuracy immediately drops to something like 10%.

In most applications of machine learning, the data will change over time as well. If you're working with language data, the topics that people talk about will change over time, and the languages themselves will innovate and evolve. If you're working with computer vision data, the types of objects that you encounter will change over time. Equally important, the images themselves will change based on advances and changes in camera technology.

If you can't define a meaningful random set of evaluation data, you should try to define a *representative* evaluation dataset. If you define a representative dataset, you are admitting that a truly random sample isn't possible or meaningful for your dataset. It is up to you to define what is representative for your use case, based on how you are applying the data. You may want to select data points for every label that you care about, a certain number from every time period or a certain number from the output of a clustering algorithm to ensure diversity. (I discuss this topic more in chapter 4.)

You may also want to have multiple evaluation datasets that are compiled through different criteria. One common strategy is to have one dataset drawn from the same data as the training data and at least one out-of-domain evaluation dataset drawn from a different source. Out-of-domain datasets are often drawn from different types of media or different time periods. If all the training data for a natural language processing (NLP) task comes from historical news articles, for example, an out-of-domain dataset might come from recent social media data. For most real-world applications, you should use an out-of-domain evaluation dataset, which is the best indicator of how well your model is truly generalizing to the problem and not simply overfitting quirks of that particular dataset. This practice can be tricky with active learning, however, because as soon as you start labeling that data, it is no longer out-of-domain. If doing so is practical, I recommend that you keep an out-of-domain dataset to which you *don't* apply active learning. Then you can see how well your active learning strategy is generalizing the problem, not simply adapting and overfitting to the domains that it encounters.

1.3.3 *When to use active learning*

You should use active learning when you can annotate only a small fraction of your data and when random sampling will not cover the diversity of data. This recommendation covers most real-world scenarios, as the scale of the data becomes an important factor in many use cases.

A good example is the amount of data present in videos. Putting a bounding box around every object in every frame of a video, for example, would be time-consuming. Suppose that this video is of a self-driving car on a street with about 20 objects you care about (cars, pedestrians, signs, and so on). At 30 frames a second, that's 30 frames * 60 seconds * 20 objects, so you would need to create *36,000* boxes for one minute of data! Even the fastest human annotator would need at least 12 hours to annotate one minute's worth of data.

If we run the numbers, we see how intractable this problem is. In the United States, people drive an average of 1 hour per day, which means that people in the United States drive 95,104,400,000 hours per year. Soon, every car will have a video camera on the front to assist with driving. So 1 year's worth of driving in the United States alone would take 60,000,000,000 (60 trillion) hours to annotate. There are not enough people on Earth to annotate the videos of drivers in the United States today, even if the rest of the world did nothing but annotate data all day to make U.S. drivers safer.

So any data scientists at an autonomous-vehicle company needs to answer a variety of questions about the annotation process. Is every *n*th frame in a video OK? Can we sample the videos so that we don't have to annotate them all? Are there ways to design an interface for annotation to speed the process?

The intractability of annotation is true in most situations. There will be more data to annotate than there is budget or time to put each data point in front of a human. That's probably why the task is using machine learning in the first place. If you have the budget and time to annotate all the data points manually, you probably don't need to automate the task.

You don't need active learning in every situation, although human-in-the-loop learning strategies might still be relevant. In some cases, humans are required by law to annotate every data point, such as a court-ordered audit that requires a human to look at every communication within a company for potential fraud. Although humans will ultimately need to look at every data point, active learning can help them find the fraud examples faster and determine the best user interface to use. It can also identify potential errors with human annotations. In fact, this process is how many audits are conducted today.

There are also some narrow use cases in which you almost certainly don't need active learning. If you are monitoring equipment in a factory with consistent lighting, for example, it should be easy to implement a computer vision model to determine whether a given piece of machinery is on or off from a light or switch on that machine. As the machinery, lighting, camera, and the like are not changing over time, you probably don't need to use active learning to keep getting training data after your model has been built. These use cases are rare, however. Fewer than 1% of the use cases that I have encountered in industry have no use for more training data.

Similarly, there might be use cases in which your baseline model is accurate enough for your business use case or the cost of more training data exceeds any value that a more accurate model might provide. This criterion could also be the stopping point for active learning iterations.

1.4   *Machine learning and human–computer interaction*

For decades, a lot of smart people failed to make human translation faster and more accurate with the help of machine translation. It seems obvious that it should be possible to combine human translation and machine translation. As soon as a human translator needs to correct one or two errors in a sentence from machine translation output, however, it would be quicker for the translator to retype the whole sentence from scratch. Using the machine translation sentence as a reference when translating makes little difference in speed, and unless the human translator takes extra care, they will end up perpetuating errors in the machine translation, making their translation less accurate.

The eventual solution to this problem was not in the accuracy of the machine translation algorithms, but in the user interface. Instead of requiring human translators to retype whole sentences, modern translation systems let them use the same kind of predictive text that has become common in phones and (increasingly) in email and document composition tools. Human translators type translations as they always have, pressing Enter or Tab to accept the next word in the predicted translation, increasing their overall speed every time the machine translation prediction is correct. So the biggest breakthrough was in human–computer interaction, not the underlying machine learning algorithm.

Human–computer interaction is an established field in computer science that has recently become especially important for machine learning. When you are building interfaces for humans to create training data, you are drawing on a field that is at the intersection of cognitive science, social sciences, psychology, user-experience design, and several other fields.

1.4.1   *User interfaces: How do you create training data?*

Often, a simple web form is enough to collect training data. The human–computer interaction principles that underlie interaction with web forms are equally simple: people are accustomed to web forms because they see them all day. The forms are intuitive because a lot of smart people worked on and refined HTML forms. You are building on these conventions: people know how a simple HTML form works, so you don't need to educate them. On the other hand, breaking these conventions would confuse people, so you are constrained to expected behavior. You might have some idea that dynamic text could speed some task, but that convention could confuse more people than it helps.

The simplest interface—binary responses—is also the best for quality control. If you can simplify or break your annotation project into binary tasks, it is a lot easier to design an intuitive interface and to implement the annotation quality control features covered in chapters 8–11.

When you are dealing with more complicated interfaces, the conventions also become more complicated. Imagine that you are asking people to put polygons around certain objects in an image, which is a common use case for autonomous-vehicle companies. What modalities would an annotator expect? Would they expect freehand, lines, paintbrushes, smart selection by color/region, or other selection tools? If people are accustomed to working on images in programs such as Adobe Photoshop, they might expect the same functionality when annotating images. In the same way that you are building on and constrained by people's expectations for web forms, you are also constrained by their expectations for selecting and editing images. Unfortunately, those expectations might require hundreds of hours of coding to build if you are offering full-featured interfaces.

For anyone who is undertaking a repetitive task such as creating training data, moving a mouse is inefficient and should be avoided if possible. If the entire annotation process can happen on a keyboard, including the annotation itself and any form submissions or navigations, the rhythm of the annotators will be greatly improved. If you have to include a mouse, you should be getting rich annotations to make up for the slower inputs.

Some annotation tasks have specialized input devices. People who transcribe speech to text often use foot pedals to navigate backward and forward in time in the audio recording. The process allows them to leave their hands on the keyboard. Navigating a recording with their feet is much more efficient than navigating the recording with a mouse.

Exceptions such as transcription aside, the keyboard is still king. Most annotation tasks haven't been popular for as long as transcription and therefore haven't developed specialized input devices. For most tasks, using a keyboard on a laptop or PC is faster than using the screen of a tablet or phone. It's not easy to type on a flat surface while keeping your eyes on inputs, so unless a task is a simple binary selection task or something similar, phones and tablets are not suited to high-volume data annotation.

1.4.2   *Priming: What can influence human perception?*

To get accurate training data, you have to take into account the focus of the human annotator, their attention span, and contextual effects that might cause them to make errors or to otherwise change their behavior. Consider a great example from linguistics research. In a study called "Stuffed toys and speech perception" (https://doi.org/10.1515/ling.2010.027), people were asked to distinguish between Australian and New Zealand accents. Researchers placed a stuffed toy kiwi bird or kangaroo (iconic animals for those countries) on a shelf in the room where participants undertook the study. The people who ran the study did not mention the stuffed toy to the participants; the toy was simply in the background. Incredibly, people interpreted an accent as sounding more New Zealand-like when a kiwi bird was present and more Australia-like when a kangaroo was present. Given this fact, it is easy to imagine that if you are building a machine learning model to detect accents (perhaps you are working on a smart home device that you want to work in as many accents as possible), you need to take context into account when collecting training data.

When the context or sequence of events can influence human perception, this phenomenon is known as *priming*. The most important type in creating training data is *repetition priming*, which occurs when the sequence of tasks can influence someone's perception. If an annotator is labeling social media posts for sentiment, for example, and they encounter 99 negative sentiment posts in a row, they are more likely to make an error by labeling the hundredth post as negative when it is positive. The post may be inherently ambiguous (such as sarcasm) or a simple error caused by an annotator's fading attention during repetitive work. In chapter 11, I talk about the types of priming you need to control for.

1.4.3 The pros and cons of creating labels by evaluating machine learning predictions

One way to combine machine learning and ensure quality annotations is to use a simple binary-input form to have people evaluate a model prediction and confirm or reject that prediction. This technique can be a nice way to turn a more complicated task into a binary annotation task. You could ask someone whether a bounding box around an object is correct as a simple binary question that doesn't involve a complicated editing/selection interface. Similarly, it is easier to ask an annotator whether some word is a location in a piece of text than it is to provide an interface to efficiently annotate phrases that are locations in free text.

When you do so, however, you run the risk of focusing on localized model uncertainty and missing important parts of the problem space. Although you can simplify the interface and annotation accuracy evaluation by having humans evaluate the predictions of machine learning models, you still need a diversity strategy for sampling, even if that strategy is merely ensuring that a random selection of items is also available.

1.4.4 Basic principles for designing annotation interfaces

Based on what I've covered so far, here are some basic principles for designing annotation interfaces. I'll go into more detail on these principles throughout the book:

- Cast your problems as binary choices wherever possible.
- Ensure that expected responses are diverse to avoid priming.
- Use existing interaction conventions.
- Allow keyboard-driven responses.

1.5 Machine-learning-assisted humans vs. human-assisted machine learning

Human-in-the-loop machine learning can have two distinct goals: making a machine learning application more accurate with human input and improving a human task with the aid of machine learning. The two goals are sometimes combined, and machine translation is a good example. Human translation can be made faster by using machine translation to suggest words or phrases that a human can choose to accept or reject, much as your smartphone predicts the next word as you are typing. This task is a machine-learning-assisted human processing task. I've also worked with customers who use machine translation when human translation would be too expensive. Because the content is similar across the human- and machine-translated data, the machine translation system gets more accurate over time from the data that is human-translated. These systems are hitting both goals, making the humans more efficient and making the machines more accurate.

Search engines are another great example of human-in-the-loop machine learning. People often forget that search engines are a form of AI despite being so ubiquitous for general search and for specific use cases such as e-commerce and navigation (online maps). When you search for a page online and click the fourth link that comes up instead of the first link, for example, you are probably training that search engine (information retrieval system) that the fourth link might be a better top response for your search query. There is a common misconception that search engines are trained only on feedback from end users. In fact, all the major search engines employ thousands of annotators to evaluate and tune their search engines. Evaluating search relevance is the single largest use case for human annotation in machine learning. Although there has been a recent rise in popularity of computer vision use cases, such as autonomous vehicles, and speech use cases, such as in-home devices and smartphones, search relevance is still the largest use case for professional human annotation.

However they appear at first glance, most human-in-the-loop machine learning tasks have some element of both machine-learning-assisted humans and human-assisted machine learning, so you need to design for both.

1.6 *Transfer learning to kick-start your models*

You don't need to start building your training data from scratch in most cases. Often, existing datasets are close to what you need. If you are creating a sentiment analysis model for movie reviews, for example, you might have a sentiment analysis dataset from product reviews that you can start with and then adapt to your use cases. This process—taking a model from one use case and adapting it to another—is known as transfer learning.

Recently, there has been a large increase in the popularity of adapting general pretrained models to new, specific use cases. In other words, people are building models *specifically* to be used in transfer learning for many use cases. These models are often referred to as *pretrained* models.

Historically, transfer learning has involved feeding the outputs of one process into another. An example in NLP might be

General part-of-speech tagger > Syntactic parser > Sentiment analysis tagger

Today, transfer learning typically means

Retraining part of a neural model to adapt to a new task (pretrained models) or using the parameters of one neural model as inputs to another

Figure 1.4 shows an example of transfer learning. A model can be trained on one set of labels and then retrained on another set of labels by keeping the architecture the same and freezing part of the model, retraining only the last layer in this case.

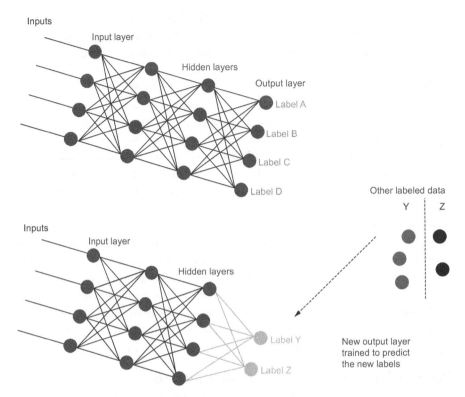

Figure 1.4   An example of transfer learning. A model was built to predict a label as "A," "B," "C," or "D." Retraining the last layer of the model and using far fewer human-labeled items than if we were training a model from scratch, the model is able to predict labels "Y" and "Z."

1.6.1   *Transfer learning in computer vision*

Transfer learning has seen the most progress recently in computer vision. A popular strategy is to start with the ImageNet dataset and build a model from the millions of examples to classify the 1,000 labels: sports, birds, human-made objects, and so on.

To learn to classify different types of sports, animals, and objects, the machine learning model is learning about the types of textures and edges that are needed to distinguish 1,000 types of items in images. Many of these textures and edges are more general than the 1,000 labels and can be used elsewhere. Because all the textures and edges are learned in the intermediate layers of the network, you can retrain only the last layer on a new set of labels. You may need only a few hundred or a few thousand examples for each new label, instead of millions, because you are already drawing on millions of images for the textures and edges. ImageNet has seen high success when people have retrained the final layer to new labels with little data, including objects such as cells in biology and geographic features from satellite views.

It is also possible to retrain several layers instead of the last one and to add more layers to the model from which you are transferring. Transfer learning can be used with many architectures and parameters to adapt one model to a new use case, but with the same goal of limiting the number of human labels needed to build an accurate model on new data.

Computer vision has been less successful to date for moving beyond image labeling. For tasks such as detecting objects within an image, it is difficult to create transfer learning systems that can adapt from one type of object to another. The problem is that objects are being detected as collections of edges and textures rather than as whole objects. Many people are working on the problem, however, so there is no doubt that breakthroughs will occur.

1.6.2 *Transfer learning in NLP*

The big push for pretrained models for NLP is even more recent than for computer vision. transfer learning of this form has become popular for NLP only in the past two or three years, so it is one of the most cutting-edge technologies covered in this text, but it also might become out of date quickly.

ImageNet-like adaptation does not work for language data. Transfer learning for one sentiment analysis dataset to another sentiment analysis dataset provides an accuracy increase of only ~2–3%. Models that predict document-level labels don't capture the breadth of human language to the extent that equivalent computer vision models capture textures and edges. But you can learn interesting properties of words by looking at the contexts in which they occur regularly. Words such as *doctor* and *surgeon* might occur in similar contexts, for example. Suppose that you found 10,000 contexts in which any English word occurs, looking at the set of words before and after. You can see how likely the word *doctor* is to occur in each of these 10,000 contexts. Some of these contexts will be medical-related, so *doctor* will have a high score in those contexts. But most of the 10,000 contexts will not be medical-related, so *doctor* will have a low score in those contexts. You can treat these 10,000 scores like a 10,000-long vector. The word *surgeon* is likely to have a vector similar to that of *doctor* because it often occurs in the same context.

The concept of understanding a word by its context is old and forms the basis of functional theories of linguistics:

> *You shall know a word by the company it keeps (Firth, J. R. 1957:11).*

Strictly, we need to go below the word to get to the most important information. English is an outlier in that words tend to make good atomic units for machine learning. English allows for complex words such as *un-do-ing*; it is obvious why we would want to interpret the separate parts (morphemes), but English does this much more rarely than a typical language. What English expresses with word order, such as subject-verb-object, is more frequently expressed with affixes that English limits to things such as present and past tense and singular/plural distinctions. So for machine learning tasks that are not biased toward a privileged language such as English, which is an outlier, we need to model subwords.

Firth would appreciate this fact. He founded England's first linguistics department at SOAS, where I worked for two years helping record and preserve endangered languages. It was clear from my time there that the full breadth of linguistic diversity means that we need more fine-grained features than words alone. Human-in-the-loop machine learning methods are necessary if we are going to adapt the world's machine-learning capabilities to as many of the 7,000 world languages as possible.

When transfer learning had its recent breakthrough moment, it followed the principle of understanding words (or word segments) in context. We can get millions of labels for our models for free if we predict the word from its context:

> *My ___ is cute. He ___ play-ing*

No human labeling is required. We can remove some percentage of the words in raw text and then turn the remaining text into a predictive machine-learning task. As you can guess, the first blank word might be *dog, puppy,* or *kitten,* and the second blank word is likely to be *is* or *was.* As with *surgeon* and *doctor,* we can predict words from context.

Unlike the early example in which transfer learning from one type of sentiment to another failed, these kinds of pretrained models have been widely successful. With only minor tuning from a model that predicts a word in context, it is possible to build state-of-the-art systems with small amounts of human labeling for language tasks such as question answering, sentiment analysis, and textual entailment. Unlike computer vision, transfer learning is quickly becoming ubiquitous for complicated NLP tasks such as summarization and translation.

The pretrained models are not complicated. The most sophisticated ones today are trained to predict a word in context, the order of words in a sentence, and the order of sentences. From that baseline model of three types of predictions that are inherent in the data, we can build almost any NLP use case with a head start. Because word order and sentence order are inherent properties of the documents, the pretrained models don't need human labels. They are still built like supervised machine learning tasks, but the training data is generated for free. The models might be asked to predict one in every ten words that have been removed from the data and to predict when certain sentences follow each other in the source documents, providing a powerful head start before any human labels are required for your task.

Pretrained models, however, are limited by how much unlabeled text is available. Much more unlabeled text is available in English than in other languages, even when you take the overall frequency of different languages into account. There will be cultural biases, too. The example *My dog is cute* might appear frequently in online text, which is the main source of data for pretrained models. But not everyone has a dog as a pet. When I briefly lived in the Amazon to study the Matsés language, monkeys were popular pets. The English phrase *My monkey is cute* rarely appears online, and the Matsés equivalent *Chuna bëdambo ikek* doesn't occur at all. Word vectors and the contextual models in pretrained systems do allow multiple meanings to be expressed by one word, so they could capture both *dog* and *monkey* in this context, but they are still biased toward the data on which they are trained, and the *monkey* context is unlikely to occur in large volumes in any language. We need to be aware that pretrained systems will tend to amplify cultural biases.

Pretrained models still require additional human labels to achieve accurate results in their tasks, so transfer learning does not change our general architecture for human-in-the-loop machine learning. It can give us a substantial head start in labeling, however, which can influence the choice of active learning strategy that we use to sample additional data items for human annotation and even the interface by which humans provide that annotation.

Transfer learning also forms the basis of some of the advanced active learning strategies discussed in chapter 5 and the advanced data annotation and augmentation strategies in chapter 9.

1.7   *What to expect in this text*

To think about how the pieces of this text fit together, it can be useful to think of the topics in terms of a knowledge quadrant (figure 1.5).

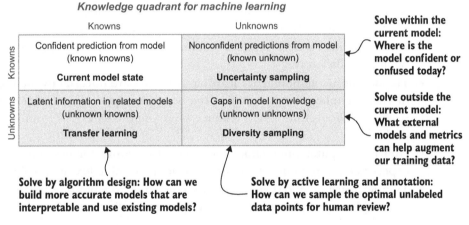

Figure 1.5   A machine learning knowledge quadrant, covering the topics in this book and expressing them in terms of what is known and unknown for your machine learning models

The four quadrants are

- *Known knowns*—What your machine learning model can confidently and accurately do today. This quadrant is your model in its current state.
- *Known unknowns*—What your machine learning model cannot confidently do today. You can apply uncertainty sampling to these items.
- *Unknown knowns*—Knowledge within pretrained models that can be adapted to your task. Transfer learning allows you to use this knowledge.
- *Unknown unknowns*—Gaps in your machine learning model. You can apply diversity sampling to these items.

The columns and rows are meaningful too, with the rows capturing knowledge of your model in its current state and the columns capturing the type of solutions needed:

- The top row captures your model's knowledge.
- The bottom row captures knowledge outside your model.
- The left column can be addressed by the right algorithms.
- The right column can be addressed by human interaction.

This text covers a wide range of technologies, so it might help to keep this figure handy to know where everything fits in.

The book has cheat sheets at the end of the first few chapters as a quick reference for the major concepts that were covered. You can keep these cheat sheets handy while reading later chapters.

Summary

- The broader human-in-the-loop machine learning architecture is an iterative process combining human and machine components. Understanding these components explains how the parts of this book come together.
- You can use some basic annotation techniques to start creating training data. Understanding these techniques ensures that you are getting annotations accurately and efficiently.
- The two most common active learning strategies are uncertainty sampling and diversity sampling. Understanding the basic principles of each type helps you strategize about the right combination of approaches for your particular problems.
- Human–computer interaction gives you a framework for designing the user-experience components of human-in-the-loop machine learning systems.
- Transfer learning allows us to adapt models trained from one task to another and build more accurate models with fewer annotations.

Getting started with human-in-the-loop machine learning

This chapter covers

- Ranking predictions by model confidence to identify confusing items
- Finding unlabeled items with novel information
- Building a simple interface to annotate training data
- Evaluating changes in model accuracy as you add more training data

For any machine learning task, you should start with a simple but functional system and build out more sophisticated components as you go. This guideline applies to most technology: ship the minimum viable product (MVP) and then iterate on that product. The feedback you get from what you ship first will tell you which pieces are the most important to build out next.

This chapter is dedicated to building your first human-in-the-loop machine learning MVP. We will build on this system as this book progresses, allowing you to learn about the different components that are needed to build more sophisticated data annotation interfaces, active learning algorithms, and evaluation strategies.

Sometimes, a simple system is enough. Suppose that you work at a media company, and your job is to tag news articles according to their topic. You already have topics such as sports, politics, and entertainment. Natural disasters have been in the news lately, and your boss has asked you to annotate the relevant past news articles as disaster-related to allow better search for this new tag. You don't have months to build out an optimal system; you want to get an MVP out as quickly as possible.

2.1   *Beyond hacktive learning: Your first active learning algorithm*

You may not realize it, but you've probably used active learning before. As you learned in chapter 1, active learning is the process of selecting the right data for human review. Filtering your data by keyword or some other preprocessing step is a form of active learning, although not an especially principled one.

If you have only recently started experimenting with machine learning, you have probably used common academic datasets such as ImageNet, the MNIST optical character recognition (OCR) dataset, and the CoNLL named entity recognition (NER) datasets. These datasets were heavily filtered with various sampling techniques before the actual training data was created. So if you randomly sample from any of these popular datasets, your sample is not truly random: it is a selection of data that conforms to whatever sampling strategies were used when these datasets were created. In other words, you unknowingly used a sampling strategy that was probably some handcrafted heuristic from more than a decade ago. You will learn more sophisticated methods in this text.

There is a good chance that you have used ImageNet, MNIST OCR, or the CoNLL NER datasets without realizing how filtered they are. Little formal documentation is available, and not mentioned in most that use these datasets, as I know by chance. ImageNet was created by colleagues when I was at Stanford; I ran one of the 15 research teams in the original CoNLL NER task; and I learned about the limitations of MNIST when it was mentioned in a now-famous foundational Deep Learning paper. It is obviously not ideal that piecing together how an existing dataset was created is so difficult and arbitrary, but until this book, there is no place telling you: *don't trust any existing dataset to be representative of data that you encounter in the real world.*

Because you are probably using filtered data by the time you build a machine learning model, it can be helpful to think of most machine learning problems as already being in the middle of the iteration process for active learning. Some decisions about data sampling have already been made; they led you to the current state of what data is annotated, and they probably weren't entirely optimal. So one of the first things you need to worry about is how to start sampling the right data as you move forward.

If you aren't explicitly implementing a good active learning strategy, instead employing ad hoc methods to sample your data, you are implementing *hacktive learning*.[1] It's fine to hack something together, but it is better to get the fundamentals right even if you are doing something quickly.

Your first human-in-the-loop machine learning system is going to look something like figure 2.1. For the remainder of this chapter, you will be implementing this architecture. This chapter assumes that you will be using the dataset introduced in section 2.2, but you can easily use your own data instead. Alternatively, you can build the system described here; then, by making changes in the data and annotation instructions, you should be able to drop in your own text annotation task.

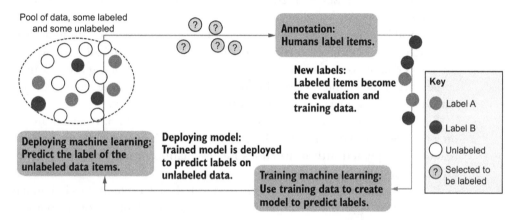

Figure 2.1   The architecture of your first human-in-the-loop machine learning system

2.2   *The architecture of your first system*

The first human-in-the-loop machine learning system that you will build in this text will label a set of news headlines as "disaster-related" or "not disaster-related." This real-world task could have many application areas:

- Using this dataset to build a machine learning model to help identify disaster-related news articles in real time to help with the response
- Adding a new "disaster-related" tag to news articles to improve the searchability and indexability of a database
- Supporting a social study about how disasters are reported in the media by allowing someone to analyze the relevant headlines

In global epidemic tracking, identifying news articles about outbreaks is an important task. H5N1 (bird flu) was reported openly weeks before it was identified as a new

---

[1] Thanks to Jennifer Prendki (one of the authors of an anecdote in this text) for the term *hacktive learning*. While working together, we misheard each other due to our different accents, and both of us understood *active learning* to be *hacktive learning*, accidentally inventing this useful phrase.

strain of the flu, and H1N1 (swine flu) was reported openly months in advance. If these reports had been put in front of virologists and epidemiologists sooner, they would have recognized the patterns of new strains of the flu and could have reacted sooner. Although this use case for your first human-in-the-loop machine learning system is simple, it is a real-world use case that could save lives.[2]

For data that you will be using throughout the book, you will use messages from several past disasters on which I worked as a professional disaster responder. In many of these cases, I ran the human-in-the-loop machine learning systems to process the data, so the examples are relevant to this text. The data includes messages sent following earthquakes in Haiti and Chile in 2010, floods in Pakistan in 2010, Hurricane Sandy in the United States in 2012, and a large collection of news headlines focused on disease outbreaks.

You will be joining students in NLP at Stanford, data science students at Udacity, and high-school students enrolled in AI for All (https://ai-4-all.org), who are also using this dataset as part of their courses today. You will be doing the task introduced at the start of the chapter: classifying news headlines. You can download the code and data at https://github.com/rmunro/pytorch_active_learning.

See the readme file for instructions on installing Python 3.6 or later and PyTorch on your machine. Versions of Python and PyTorch change rapidly, so I will keep the readme file updated with instructions for installation rather than try to include that information here.

If you are not familiar with PyTorch, start with the examples in this PyTorch tutorial: http://mng.bz/6gy5. The example in this chapter was adapted from a combination of this PyTorch example and the one in the PyTorch tutorial. If you become familiar with those two tutorials, all the code in this chapter should be clear to you. The data in the CSV files comprises two to five fields, depending on how processed it is, and looks something like the example in table 2.1.

Table 2.1   An example data file, with the ID, actual text, active learning sampling strategy chosen, and score for that sampling strategy

Text ID	Text	Label	Sampling strategy	Score
596124	Flood warning for Dolores Lake residents	1	Low confidence	0.5872
58503	First-aid workers arrive for earthquake relief	1	Random	0.6234
23173	Cyclists are lost trying to navigate new bike lanes	0	Random	0.0937

The data that you will be using in this chapter is from a large collection of news headlines. The articles span many years and hundreds of disasters, but most headlines *are not* disaster-related.

---

[2] For more on how we were tracking epidemics, see https://nlp.stanford.edu/pubs/Munro2012epidemics.pdf. Since I wrote this note in early 2019, COVID-19 has made the importance of this use case more obvious.

There are four locations for data in the repo:

- */training_data*—The data that your models will be trained on
- */validation_data*—The data that your models will be tuned with
- */evaluation_data*—The data that your models will be evaluated on for accuracy
- */unlabeled_data*—The large pool of data that you want to label

You will see the data in the CSV files in this repo, and they will have this format:

- 0. Text ID (a unique ID for this item)
- 1. Text (the text itself)
- 2. Label (the label: 1 = "disaster-related"; 0 = "not disaster-related")
- 3. Sampling strategy (the active learning strategy that we used to sample this item)
- 4. Confidence (the machine learning confidence that this item is "disaster-related")

(This list counts from 0 instead of 1 so that it will match the index of each field in the items/rows in the code).

These fields are enough information for you to build your first model. You will see that the unlabeled data in the example does not yet have a label, sampling strategy, or confidence, for obvious reasons.

If you want to jump in right away, you can run this script:

```
> python active_learning_basics.py
```

You will initially be prompted to annotate messages as "disaster-related" or "not disaster-related" to create the evaluation data. Then you will be prompted to do the same again for the initial training data. Only then will you see models start being built on your data and the active learning process beginning. We will return to the code later in this chapter and introduce the strategy behind it.

In an actual disaster, you would be classifying data into a large number of fine-grained categories. You might separate requests for food and water, for example, because people can go for much longer without food than without water, so requests for drinking water need to be responded to with more urgency than requests for food. On the other hand, you might be able to provide water locally with filtration, but food still needs to be shipped to the disaster-affected region for a longer period. As a result, different disaster relief organizations often focus on either food or water. The same is true for distinctions between types of medical aid, security, housing, and so on, all of which need fine-grained categories to be actionable. But in any of these situations, filtering between "relevant" and "not relevant" can be an important first step. If the volume of data is low enough, you might need machine learning assistance only to separate related from unrelated information; humans can take care of the rest of the categories. I have run disaster response efforts in which this was the case.

Also, in most disasters, you wouldn't be working in English. English makes up only about 5% of the world's conversations daily, so around 95% of communications about disasters are not in English. The broader architecture could be applied to any language, however. The biggest difference is that English uses whitespace to break sentences into words. Most languages have more sophisticated prefixes, suffixes, and compounds that make individual words more complicated. Some languages, such as Chinese, don't use whitespace between most words. Breaking words into their constituent parts (*morphemes*) is an important task in itself. In fact, this was part of my PhD thesis: automatically discovering word-internal boundaries for any language in disaster response communications. An interesting and important research area would be to make machine learning truly equal across the world, and I encourage people to pursue it!

It helps to make your data assumptions explicit so that you can build and optimize the architecture that is best for your use case. It is good practice to include the assumptions in any machine learning system, so here are ours:

- The data is only in English.
- The data is in different varieties of English (United Kingdom, United States, English as a second language).
- We can use whitespace-delimited words as our features.
- A binary classification task is sufficient for the use case.

It should be easy to see how the broader framework for human-in-the-loop machine learning will work for any similar use case. The framework in this chapter could be adapted to image classification almost as easily as to another text classification task, for example.

If you have already jumped in, you will see that you are asked to annotate some additional data before you can build a model. This is good practice in general: looking at your data will give you better intuitions for every part of your model. See the following sidebar to learn why you should look at your data.

Sunlight is the best disinfectant

Expert anecdote by Peter Skomoroch

You need to look at real data in depth to know exactly what models to build. In addition to high-level charts and aggregate statistics, I recommend that data scientists go through a large selection of randomly selected, granular data regularly to let these examples wash over them. As executives look at company-level charts every week, and network engineers look over stats from system logs, data scientists should have intuition about their data and how it is changing.

When I was building LinkedIn's Skill Recommendations feature, I built a simple web interface with a Random button that showed recommendation examples alongside the corresponding model inputs so that I could quickly view the data and get an intuition for the kinds of algorithms and annotation strategies that might be most successful. This approach is the best way to ensure that you have uncovered potential issues and obtained vital high-quality input data. You're shining a light on your data, and sunlight is the best disinfectant.

Peter Skomoroch, the former CEO of SkipFlag (acquired by WorkDay), worked as a principal data scientist at LinkedIn on the team that invented the title "data scientist."

2.3   *Interpreting model predictions and data to support active learning*

Almost all supervised machine learning models will give you two things:

- A predicted label (or set of predictions)
- A number (or set of numbers) associated with each predicted label

The numbers are generally interpreted as confidences in the prediction, although this can be more or less true depending on how the numbers are generated. If there are mutually exclusive categories with similar confidence, you have good evidence that the model is confused about its prediction and that human judgment would be valuable. Therefore, the model will benefit most when it learns to correctly predict the label of an item with an uncertain prediction.

Suppose that we have a message that might be disaster-related, and the prediction looks like this:

```
{
    "Object": {
        "Label": "Not Disaster-Related",
        "Scores": {
            "Disaster-Related": 0.475524352,
            "Not Disaster-Related": 0.524475648
        }
    }
}
```

In this prediction, the message is predicted to be "Not Disaster-Related." In the rest of supervised machine learning, this label is what people care about most: was the label prediction correct, and what is the overall accuracy of the model when predicting across a large held-out dataset?

In active learning, however, the numbers associated with the prediction typically are what we care about most. You can see in the example that "Not Disaster-Related" is predicted with a 0.524 score. This score means that the system is 52.4% confident that the prediction was correct.

From the perspective of the task here, you can see why you might want a human to review the result anyway: there is still a relatively high chance that this is disaster-related. If it *is* disaster-related, your model is getting this example wrong for some reason, so it is likely that you want to add it to your training data so that you don't miss similar examples.

In chapter 3, we will turn to the problem of how reliable a score of 0.524 is. Especially for neural models, these confidences can be widely off. For the sake of this chapter, we can assume that although the exact number may not be accurate, we can generally trust the relative differences in confidence across multiple predictions.

2.3.1 *Confidence ranking*

Suppose that we had another message with this prediction:

```
{
    "Object": {
        "Label": "Not Disaster-Related",
        "Scores": {
            "Disaster-Related": 0.015524352,
            "Not Disaster-Related": 0.984475648
        }
    }
}
```

This item is also predicted as "Not Disaster-Related" but with 98.4% confidence, compared with 52.4% confidence for the first item. So the model is more confident about the second item than about the first. Therefore, it is reasonable to assume that the first item is more likely to be wrongly labeled and would benefit from human review. Even if we don't trust the 52.4% and 98.4% numbers (and we probably shouldn't, as you will learn in later chapters), it *is* reasonable to assume that the rank order of confidence will correlate with accuracy. This will generally be true of almost all machine learning algorithms and almost all ways of calculating accuracy: you can rank-order the items by the predicted confidence and sample the lowest-confidence items. For a probability distribution over a set of labels y for the item x, the confidence is given by the equation, where y^* is the most confident (c) label:

$$\phi_c(x) = P_\theta(y^*|x)$$

For a binary prediction task like this example, you can simply rank by confidence and sample the items closest to 50% confidence. If you are attempting anything more complicated, however, such as predicting three or more mutually exclusive labels, labeling sequences of data, generating entire sentences (including translation and speech transcription), or identifying objects within images and videos, you have multiple ways to calculate confidence. We will return to other ways of calculating confidence in later chapters. The intuition about low confidence remains the same, and a binary task is easier for your first human-in-the-loop system.

2.3.2 *Identifying outliers*

As discussed in chapter 1, you often want to make sure that you are getting a diverse set of items for humans to label so that the newly sampled items aren't all like each other. This task can include making sure that you are not missing any important outliers. Some disasters are rare, such as a large asteroid crashing into the Earth. If a news headline says "Asteroid flattens Walnut Creek," and your machine learning model hasn't learned what an asteroid is or that Walnut Creek is a city, it is easy to see why your machine learning model might not have predicted this headline as being disaster-related. You could call this sentence an outlier in this regard: it lies farthest from anything you've seen before.

As with confidence ranking, we have many ways to ensure that we are maximizing the diversity of the content that is selected for human review. You will learn more about such approaches in later chapters. For now, we will focus on a simple metric: the average training data frequency of words in each unlabeled item. Here is the strategy that we will implement in this chapter:

1 For each item in the unlabeled data, count the average number of word matches it has with items already in the training data.
2 Rank the items by their average match.
3 Sample the item with the lowest average number of matches.
4 Add that item to the labeled data.
5 Repeat these steps until you have sampled enough for one iteration of human review.

Note that in step 4, when you have sampled the first item, you can treat that item as being labeled, because you know you are going to get a label for it later.

This method of determining outliers tends to favor small and novel headlines, so you will see that code adds 1 to the count as a smoothing factor. It also disfavors sentences with a lot of common words such as *the*, even if the other words are uncommon. So instead of using average matching, you could track the raw number of novel words to model the total amount of novel information in a headline instead of the overall average.

You could also divide the number of matches in the training data by the total number of times that word occurs across all the data and multiply each of these fractions, which would more or less give you the Bayesian probability of the element's being an outlier. Instead of using word matching, you could use more sophisticated edit-distance-based metrics that take the order of words within the sentence into account. Or you can use many other string-matching and other algorithms to determine outliers.

As with everything else, you can start by implementing the simple example in this chapter and experiment with others later. The main goal is an insurance policy: is there something completely different that we haven't seen yet? Probably not, but if there were, it would be the highest-value item to annotate correctly. We will look at ways of combining sampling by confidence and sampling by diversity in chapter 5.

We will also look at ways to combine your machine learning strategy with your annotation strategy. If you have worked in machine learning for a while but never in annotation or active learning, you have probably optimized models only for accuracy. For a complete architecture, you may want to take a more holistic approach in which your annotation, active learning, and machine learning strategies inform one another. You could decide to implement machine learning algorithms that can give more accurate estimates of their confidence at the expense of accuracy in label prediction. Or you might augment your machine learning models to have two types of inference: one to predict the labels and one to more accurately estimate the confidence of each prediction. If you are building models for more complicated tasks such as generating sequences of text (as in machine translation) or regions within images (as in object detection), the most common approach today is building separate inference capabilities for the task itself and interpreting the confidence. We will look at these architectures in chapters 9–11 of this book.

The process for building your first human-in-the-loop machine learning model is summarized in figure 2.2.

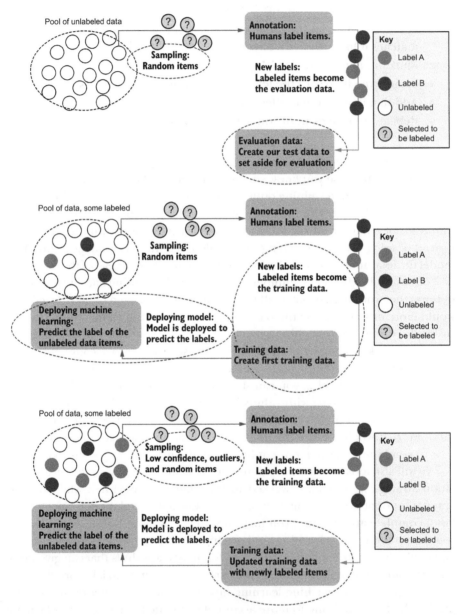

Figure 2.2   The iterative process in your first human-in-the-loop machine learning system. Initially (top), you are annotating a random sample of unlabeled items to set aside as your evaluation data. Then you are labeling the first items to be used for training data (middle), also starting with a random selection. After this point, you start using active learning (bottom) to sample items that are low-confidence or outliers.

2.3.3 *What to expect as you iterate*

In our example code, after we have enough evaluation and initial training data, we will iterate on active learning every 100 items. This number is probably a little small in terms of the number of items per iteration, as you'll be spending a lot of time waiting for the model to retrain for a relatively small number of new labeled items, but 100 is about right to get a feel for how much the sampled data changes in each iteration.

Here are some things you may notice as you iterate through the active learning process:

- *First iteration*—You are annotating mostly "not disaster-related" headlines, which can feel tedious. The balance will improve when active learning kicks in, but for now, it is necessary to get the randomly sampled evaluation data. You should also notice that this problem is not trivial because journalists often use disaster metaphors for nondisasters, especially sports teams (declaring war, a scoring drought, and so on). You will also be challenged by edge cases. Is a plane crash a disaster, for example, or does its status depend on the size of the plane and/or the cause? These edge cases will help you refine the definition of your task and create the right instructions for engaging a larger workforce to annotate your data at scale.

- *Second iteration*—You have created your first model! Your F-score is probably terrible, maybe only 0.20. Your area under the curve (AUC), however, might be around 0.75. (See the appendix for more on F-score and AUC.) So despite the bad accuracy, you can find disaster-related messages better than chance. You could fix the F-score by playing with the model parameters and architecture, but more data is more important than model architecture right now, as will become clear when you start annotating: you will immediately notice on your second iteration that a large number of items is disaster-related. In fact, most of the items may be. Early on, your model will still try to predict most things as "not disaster-related," so anything close to 50% confidence is at the "disaster-related" end of the scale. This example shows that active learning can be self-correcting: it is oversampling a lower-frequency label without requiring you to explicitly implement a targeted strategy for sampling important labels. You will also see evidence of overfitting. If your randomly selected items in the first iteration happened to have many headlines about floods, for example, you probably have *too* many headlines about floods and not enough about other types of disasters.

- *Third and fourth iterations*—You should start to see model accuracy improve, as you are now labeling many more "disaster-related" headlines, bringing the proposed annotation data closer to 50:50 for each label. If your model had overfitted some terms, such as the floods example, you should have seen some counterexamples, such as "New investment floods the marketplace," These counterexamples help push your models back to more accurate predictions for headlines with these terms. If the data was genuinely disaster-related for everything with *flood* in it, these items are now predicted with high confidence and are no longer near 50%. Either way, the problem self-corrects, and the diversity of the headlines you are seeing should increase.

- *Fifth to tenth iterations*—Your models start to reach reasonable levels of accuracy, and you should see more diversity in the headlines. As long as either the F-score or AUC goes up by a few percentage points for every 100 annotations, you are getting good gains in accuracy. You are probably wishing that you had annotated more evaluation data so that you could be calculating accuracy on a bigger variety of held-out data. Unfortunately, you can't. It's almost impossible to go back to truly random sampling unless you are prepared to give up a lot of your existing labels.

Although it feels simple, the system that you are building in this chapter follows the same strategy as the initial release of Amazon Web Services's (AWS) SageMaker Ground Truth in 2018 (less than a year before this chapter was written). In fact, in the first version, SageMaker sampled only by confidence and didn't look for outliers in that release. Although the system you are building is simple, it is beyond the level of algorithmic sophistication of an active learning tool that is currently offered by a major cloud provider. I worked briefly on SageMaker Ground Truth when I was at AWS, so this is not a criticism of that product or my colleagues who put much more work into it than I did. Although active learning is becoming part of large-scale commercial offerings for the first time, it is still in an early stage.

We will cover more sophisticated methods for sampling in part 2 of this book. For now, it is more important to focus on establishing the iterative process for active learning, along with the best practices for annotation and retraining and evaluating your models. If you don't get your iteration and evaluation strategies correct, you can easily make your model worse instead of better and not even realize it.

2.4 *Building an interface to get human labels*

To label your data, you need to start with the right interface. We'll cover what that looks like for our example data in this section.

The right interface for human labeling is as important as the right sampling strategy. If you can make your interface 50% more efficient, that's as good as improving your active learning sampling strategy by 50%. Out of respect for the people who are doing the labeling, you should do as much as you can to ensure that they feel they are as effective as possible. If you genuinely don't know whether an interface or algorithm improvement is the best thing to focus on next, start with the interface to improve the work of the humans, and worry about your CPU's feelings later.

Part 3 of this book is dedicated to data annotation, so we will make a few assumptions to keep the discussion in this chapter simple:

- Annotators aren't making a significant number of errors in the labels, so we don't have to implement quality control for annotations.
- Annotators understand the task and labels perfectly, so they aren't accidentally choosing the wrong labels.
- Only one annotator is working at a time, so we don't have to keep track of any labeling in progress.

These assumptions are big ones. In most deployed systems, you need to implement quality control to ensure that annotators are not making mistakes; you will most likely need several iterations of annotation to refine the definitions of the labels and instructions; and you will need a system to track work assigned to multiple people in parallel. A simple annotation interface like the one discussed here is enough if you want to annotate some data quickly for exploratory purposes, as you are doing here.

2.4.1 A simple interface for labeling text

The interface that you build is determined by your task and the distribution of your data. For a binary labeling task like the one we are implementing here, a simple command-line interface is enough (figure 2.3). You will see it immediately if you run the script that we introduced in this chapter:

```
> python active_learning_basics.py
```

```
Please type 1 if this message is disaster-related, or hit Enter if not.
Type 2 to go back to the last message, type d to see detailed
definitions, or type s to save your annotations.

Firefighting continues in Blue Mountains

> 1
```

Figure 2.3 The command-line interface annotation tool for the example in this chapter

As discussed in the introduction, many human–computer interaction factors go into making a good interface for annotation. But if you have to build something quickly, do the following:

1 Build an interface that allows annotators to focus on one part of the screen.
2 Allow hot keys for all actions.
3 Include a back/undo option.

Get those three things right first, and graphic design can come later.

To see exactly what the code is doing, look at the repo at https://github.com/rmunro/pytorch_active_learning, or clone it locally and experiment with it. Excerpts from that code will be shared in this book for illustrative purposes.

You can see the code to elicit annotations in the first 20 lines of the get_annotations() function in the following listing.

```
def get_annotations(data, default_sampling_strategy="random"):
    """Prompts annotator for label from command line and adds annotations to
      data

    Keyword arguments:
        data -- an list of unlabeled items where each item is
                [ID, TEXT, LABEL, SAMPLING_STRATEGY, CONFIDENCE]
        default_sampling_strategy -- strategy to use for each item if not
          already specified
    """

    ind = 0
    while ind <= len(data):
        if ind < 0:
            ind = 0 # in case you've gone back before the first
        if ind < len(data):
            textid = data[ind][0]
            text = data[ind][1]
            label = data[ind][2]
            strategy =  data[ind][3]

            if textid in already_labeled:
                print("Skipping seen "+label)
                ind+=1
            else:
                print(annotation_instructions)
                label = str(input(text+"\n\n> "))    ◁──── The input() function
                ...                                          prompts the user for input.
                ...
```

For our data, the labels are a little unbalanced because most headlines are not related to disasters. This fact has interface-design implications. It would be inefficient and boring for someone to continually select "Not Disaster-Related." You can make "Not Disaster-Related" the default option to improve efficiency so long as you have a back option when annotators inevitably get primed to select the default. You probably did this yourself: annotated quickly and then had to go back when you pressed the wrong answer. You should see this functionality in the next and final 20 lines of code of the get_annotations() function.

```
def get_annotations(data, default_sampling_strategy="random"):
            ...
            ...

            if label == "2":
```

```
                    ind-=1  # go back
            elif label == "d":
                    print(detailed_instructions) # print detailed
                    ⇨ instructions
            elif label == "s":
                    break  # save and exit
            else:
                    if not label == "1":
                        label = "0" # treat everything other than 1 as 0

                    data[ind][2] = label # add label to our data

                    if data[ind][3] is None or data[ind][3] == "":
                        data[ind][3] = default_sampling_strategy # default if
                        ⇨ none given
                    ind+=1

        else:
            #last one - give annotator a chance to go back
            print(last_instruction)
            label = str(input("\n\n> "))
            if label == "2":
                ind-=1
            else:
                ind+=1


    return data
```

2.4.2   *Managing machine learning data*

For a deployed system, it is best to store your annotations in a database that takes care of backups, availability, and scalability. But you cannot always browse a database as easily as you can files on a local machine. In addition to adding training items to your database, or if you are building a simple system, it can help to have locally stored data and annotations that you can quickly spot-check.

In our example, we will separate the data into separate files according to the label, for additional redundancy. Unless you are working in an organization that already has good data-management processes in place for annotation and machine learning, you probably don't have the same kind of quality control for your data as you do for your code, such as unit tests and good versioning. So it is wise to be redundant in how you store your data. Similarly, you will see that the code appends files but never writes over files. It also keeps the unlabeled_data.csv file untouched, checking for duplicates in the other datasets instead of deleting headlines from that file when the item has been labeled.

Redundancy in how you store labels and enforcing nondeletion of data will save you a lot of headaches when you start experimenting. I've never met a machine learning professional who hasn't accidentally deleted labeled data at some point, so follow this advice! Also remember that if you are storing data on your local machine, that data may belong to someone else or have sensitive content. Make sure that you have permission to store the data, and delete the data when you no longer need it.

Although the topic isn't covered in this book, version control for your data is also important, especially if you are updating your instructions as you go. Some older labels may be incorrect, and you want to be able to reproduce them if you want to re-create your active learning iterations later.

2.5 *Deploying your first human-in-the-loop machine learning system*

Now let's put all the pieces of your first human-in-the-loop system together! If you didn't do so earlier in the chapter, download the code and data from https://github .com/rmunro/pytorch_active_learning, and see the readme file for installation instructions.

You can run this code immediately, and it will start prompting you to annotate data and automatically train after each iteration. You should experience the changes in data at each iteration that you learned in section 2.3.3.

To see what is happening under the hood, let's go through the main components of this code and the strategies behind it. We use a simple PyTorch machine learning model for text classification. We will use a shallow model that can be retrained quickly to make our iterations fast. In PyTorch, this entire model definition is a dozen lines of code.

> ### Listing 2.3 Simple PyTorch text classification model with one hidden layer

```
class SimpleTextClassifier(nn.Module):  # inherit pytorch's nn.Module
    """Text Classifier with 1 hidden layer

    """

    def __init__(self, num_labels, vocab_size):
        super(SimpleTextClassifier, self).__init__() # call parent init
        # Define model with one hidden layer with 128 neurons
        self.linear1 = nn.Linear(vocab_size, 128)
        self.linear2 = nn.Linear(128, num_labels)

    def forward(self, feature_vec):
        # Define how data is passed through the model

        hidden1 = self.linear1(feature_vec).clamp(min=0) # ReLU
        output = self.linear2(hidden1)
        return F.log_softmax(output, dim=1)
```

Hidden layer with 128 neurons/nodes → `self.linear1 = nn.Linear(vocab_size, 128)`

Output layer predicting each label ← `self.linear2 = nn.Linear(128, num_labels)`

Using linear activation function for our output layer → `output = self.linear2(hidden1)`

Optimizing our hidden layer with a ReLU activation function ← `hidden1 = self.linear1(feature_vec).clamp(min=0) # ReLU`

Returning the log softmax of our linear output to optimize our model in training and to return as a probability distribution for prediction ← `return F.log_softmax(output, dim=1)`

Our input layer contains the one-hot encoding for every word in our feature set (thousands), our output layer is the two labels, and our hidden layer is 128 nodes.

For training, we know that the data is imbalanced between the labels initially, so we want to ensure that we select something closer to an even number of items for each label. This specification is set in these variables at the start of the code:

```
epochs = 10 # number of epochs per training session
select_per_epoch = 200  # number to sample per epoch per label
```

We are going to train our models for 10 epochs, and for each epoch, we are going to randomly select 200 items from each label. This approach won't make our model completely even, because we are still selecting from a bigger variety of not-disaster-related text across all the epochs, but it will be enough that we get some signal from our data even when we have only 100 or so disaster-related examples.

(The hidden neurons, epochs, and items selected per epoch are sensible but otherwise arbitrary starting points. You can experiment with different hyperparameters, but at the start of the annotation process, you should be concentrating on the data.)

The code to train our model is the `train_model()` function shown next.

Listing 2.4   Training the text classification model

```
def train_model(training_data, validation_data = "", evaluation_data = "",
➥ num_labels=2, vocab_size=0):
    """Train model on the given training_data

    Tune with the validation_data
    Evaluate accuracy with the evaluation_data
    """

    model = SimpleTextClassifier(num_labels, vocab_size)
    # let's hard-code our labels for this example code
    # and map to the same meaningful booleans in our data,
    # so we don't mix anything up when inspecting our data
    label_to_ix = {"not_disaster_related": 0, "disaster_related": 1}

    loss_function = nn.NLLLoss()
    optimizer = optim.SGD(model.parameters(), lr=0.01)

    # epochs training
    for epoch in range(epochs):
        print("Epoch: "+str(epoch))
        current = 0

        # make a subset of data to use in this epoch
        # with an equal number of items from each label

        shuffle(training_data) #randomize the order of the training data
        related = [row for row in training_data if '1' in row[2]]
        not_related = [row for row in training_data if '0' in row[2]]

        epoch_data = related[:select_per_epoch]
        epoch_data += not_related[:select_per_epoch]
        shuffle(epoch_data)
```

Select an equal amount of items with each label to effectively oversample the smaller label, especially in early iterations of labeling.

```
# train our model
for item in epoch_data:
    features = item[1].split()
    label = int(item[2])

    model.zero_grad()

    feature_vec = make_feature_vector(features, feature_index)
    target = torch.LongTensor([int(label)])

    log_probs = model(feature_vec)

    # compute loss function, do backward pass, and update the
    ➥ gradient
    loss = loss_function(log_probs, target)
    loss.backward()
    optimizer.step()
```

You can see that we are keeping our training hyperparameters constant, such as the learning rate and type of activation functions. For an actual system, you would probably want to experiment with training hyperparameters and also with architectures that better model the sequence of words or could better model clusters of pixels if you are doing image classification.

If you are doing any hyperparameter tuning at all, you should create validation data and use that data to tune your model, as you are already accustomed to doing in machine learning. In fact, you may want multiple kinds of validation datasets, including one drawn from your training data at each iteration, one drawn from your unlabeled data before you use active learning, and one drawn from the remaining unlabeled items at each iteration. We will return to validation data for active learning in chapter 3. For now, we save you the additional annotations. If you want to tune your model in the example in this chapter, pull a random selection of data from your training data set at each iteration.

The remainder of the train_model() function evaluates the accuracy of the new model and saves it to file in models/. I cover evaluation in the next section.

As stated earlier, you should become familiar with your data before you start building any machine learning system. Fortunately, this best practice applies to active learning too. You should select your evaluation data first, and you should be one of the people who labels it.

2.5.1 *Always get your evaluation data first*

Evaluation data is often called a test set or held-out data, and for this task, it should be a random sample of headlines that we annotate. We will always hold out these headlines from our training data so that we can track the accuracy of our model after each iteration of active learning.

It is important to get the evaluation data first, as there are many ways to inadvertently bias your evaluation data after you have started other sampling techniques. Here are some of the things that can go wrong if you don't pull out your evaluation data first:

- If you forget to sample evaluation data from your unlabeled items until after you have sampled by low confidence, your evaluation data will be biased toward the remaining high-confidence items, and your model will appear to be more accurate than it is.
- If you forget to sample evaluation data and you pull evaluation data from your training data after you have sampled by confidence, your evaluation data will be biased toward low-confidence items, and your model will appear to be less accurate than it is.
- If you have implemented outlier detection and later try to pull out evaluation data, it is almost impossible to avoid bias, as the items you pulled out have already contributed to the sampling of additional outliers.

What happens if you don't make evaluation data first?

It's difficult to know how accurate your model is if you don't remember to get evaluation data first. This mistake is one of the biggest ones I've seen people make. As soon as data scientists get any new human labels, they naturally want to add those labels to their training data to see how much more accurate their models get. But if your evaluation data is an afterthought, and you aren't careful about making it truly random, you won't know how accurate your model is. I have seen companies building self-driving cars, social media feeds, and dating apps get evaluation data wrong. Know that the car that swerved past you today, the news article that was recommended to you, and the person you might one day marry may all have been determined by machine learning models of uncertain accuracy.

If you want to start training right away, at least set the evaluation data aside first so that it doesn't factor into your analysis. You can return to annotate that data later or annotate in parallel with your training and validation data.

Finally, it may not be possible to select truly random data if you are applying your model to a continuously changing feed of information. In ongoing disaster-response situations, this will absolutely be the case, as new information is reported about the changing conditions and needs over time. For the example we are working on here, we are tasked with labeling a finite set of news headlines, so it is meaningful to select a random sample of the headlines to be in our training data. We will return to sampling strategies for evaluation data in more complicated contexts in chapter 3.

The code to evaluate the accuracy of your model at each iteration is the `evaluate_model()` function.

Listing 2.5   Evaluating the model on held-out data

```
def evaluate_model(model, evaluation_data):
    """Evaluate the model on the held-out evaluation data

    Return the f-value for disaster-related and the AUC
    """

    related_confs = [] # related items and their confidence of being related
    not_related_confs = [] # not related items and their confidence of
    being _related_

    true_pos = 0.0 # true positives, etc
    false_pos = 0.0
    false_neg = 0.0

    with torch.no_grad():
        for item in evaluation_data:
            _, text, label, _, _, = item

            feature_vector = make_feature_vector(text.split(), feature_index)
            log_probs = model(feature_vector)

            # get confidence that item is disaster-related
            prob_related = math.exp(log_probs.data.tolist()[0][1])        ◄────┐

            if(label == "1"):                                  The PyTorch tensors are
                # true label is disaster related                2D, so we need to pull
                related_confs.append(prob_related)             out only the predictive
                if prob_related > 0.5:                                  confidence.
                    true_pos += 1.0
                else:
                    false_neg += 1.0
            else:
                # not disaster-related
                not_related_confs.append(prob_related)
                if prob_related > 0.5:
                    false_pos += 1.0
                    ...
                    ...
```

This code gets the predicted confidence that each item is "disaster-related" and tracks whether each prediction was correct or incorrect. Raw accuracy would not be a good metric to use here. Because the frequency of the two labels is unbalanced, you will get almost 95% accuracy from predicting "not disaster-related" each time. This result is not informative, and our task is specifically to find the disaster-related headlines, so we will calculate accuracy as the F-score of the disaster-related predictions.

In addition to caring about the F-score, we care whether confidence correlates with accuracy, so we calculate the area under the ROC curve. A ROC (receiver operating characteristic) curve rank-orders a dataset by confidence and calculates the rate of true positives versus false positives.

See the appendix for definitions and discussions of precision, recall, F-score, and AUC, all of which are implemented in the evaluate_model() function of our code.

Listing 2.6 Calculating precision, recall, F-score, and AUC

```
def evaluate_model(model, evaluation_data):
                ...
                ...
    # Get FScore
    if true_pos == 0.0:
        fscore = 0.0
    else:                                             Harmonic mean of
        precision = true_pos / (true_pos + false_pos)  precision and recall
        recall = true_pos / (true_pos + false_neg)
        fscore = (2 * precision * recall) / (precision + recall)  ←

    # GET AUC
    not_related_confs.sort()
    total_greater = 0 # count of how many total have higher confidence
    for conf in related_confs:
        for conf2 in not_related_confs:
            if conf < conf2:        ←
                break                    For items with the label we care about
            else:                        ("related," in this case), we want to know
                total_greater += 1       how many are predicted to have that label
                                         with greater confidence than the items
                                         without that label.
    denom = len(not_related_confs) * len(related_confs)
    auc = total_greater / denom

    return[fscore, auc]
```

If you look at filenames for any models that you have built in the models directory, you will see that the filename includes a timestamp, the accuracy of the model by F-score and AUC, and the number of training items. It is good data-management practice to give your models verbose and transparent names, which will let you track accuracy over time with each iteration simply by looking at the directory listing.

2.5.2 *Every data point gets a chance*

By including new randomly sampled items in each iteration of active learning, you get a baseline in that iteration. You can compare the accuracy from training on the random items with your other sampling strategies, which can tell you how effective your sampling strategies are compared with random sampling. You will already know how many newly annotated items are different from your model's predicted label, but you won't know how much they will change the model for future predictions after they have been added to the training data.

Even if your other active learning strategies fail in the iteration, you will still get incremental improvement from the random sample, so random sampling is a nice fallback.

There is an ethical choice here too. We are acknowledging that all strategies are imperfect, so every data item still has some chance of being selected randomly and being reviewed by a human, even if none of the sampling strategies would have selected it. In an actual disaster scenario, would you want to eliminate the chance that someone would see an important headline because your sampling strategies would never select it? The ethical question is one you should ask yourself depending on the data and use case you are addressing.

2.5.3   *Select the right strategies for your data*

We know that disaster-related headlines are rare in our data, so the strategy of selecting outliers is not likely to select many disaster-related items. Therefore, the example code focuses on selecting by confidence and sampling data for each iteration according to the following strategy:

- 10% randomly selected from unlabeled items
- 80% selected from the lowest confidence items
- 10% selected as outliers

Assuming that the low-confidence items are truly 50:50 disaster-related and not disaster-related, the annotators should see a little more than 4/10 disaster-related messages when a large number of items have been annotated and our models are stable. This result is close enough to equal that we don't have to worry that ordering effects will prime the annotators in later iterations.

The following three listings contain the code for the three strategies. First, we get the low confidence predictions.

Listing 2.7   Sampling items with low confidence

```
def get_low_conf_unlabeled(model, unlabeled_data, number=80, limit=10000):
    confidences = []
    if limit == -1:
        print("Get confidences for unlabeled data (this might take a while)")
    else:
        # only apply the model to a limited number of items
        shuffle(unlabeled_data)
        unlabeled_data = unlabeled_data[:limit]

    with torch.no_grad():
        for item in unlabeled_data:
            textid = item[0]
            if textid in already_labeled:
                continue

            text = item[1]

            feature_vector = make_feature_vector(text.split(), feature_index)
            log_probs = model(feature_vector)
```

Get the probabilities for each label for the item.

```
prob_related = math.exp(log_probs.data.tolist()[0][1])

        if prob_related < 0.5:
            confidence = 1 - prob_related
        else:
            confidence = prob_related

        item[3] = "low confidence"
        item[4] = confidence
        confidences.append(item)

    confidences.sort(key=lambda x: x[4])
    return confidences[:number:]
```

Order the items by confidence.

Next, we get the random items.

Listing 2.8 Sample random items

```
def get_random_items(unlabeled_data, number = 10):
    shuffle(unlabeled_data)

    random_items = []
    for item in unlabeled_data:
        textid = item[0]
        if textid in already_labeled:
            continue
        random_items.append(item)
        if len(random_items) >= number:
            break

    return random_items
```

Finally, we get the outliers.

Listing 2.9 Sample outliers

```
def get_outliers(training_data, unlabeled_data, number=10):
    """Get outliers from unlabeled data in training data
    Returns number outliers

    An outlier is defined as the percent of words in an item in
    unlabeled_data that do not exist in training_data
    """
    outliers = []

    total_feature_counts = defaultdict(lambda: 0)

    for item in training_data:
        text = item[1]
        features = text.split()

        for feature in features:
            total_feature_counts[feature] += 1
```

Count all features in the training data.

```
while(len(outliers) < number):
    top_outlier = []
    top_match = float("inf")

    for item in unlabeled_data:
        textid = item[0]
        if textid in already_labeled:
            continue

        text = item[1]
        features = text.split()
        total_matches = 1 # start at 1 for slight smoothing
        for feature in features:
            if feature in total_feature_counts:
                total_matches += total_feature_counts[feature]

        ave_matches = total_matches / len(features)
        if ave_matches < top_match:
            top_match = ave_matches
            top_outlier = item

    # add this outlier to list and update what is 'labeled',
    # assuming this new outlier will get a label
    top_outlier[3] = "outlier"
    outliers.append(top_outlier)
    text = top_outlier[1]
    features = text.split()
    for feature in features:
        total_feature_counts[feature] += 1

return outliers
```

Add the number of times this feature in the unlabeled data item occurred in the training data.

Update the training data counts for this item to help with diversity for the next outlier that is sampled.

You can see that by default in the get_low_conf_unlabeled() function, we are predicting the confidence for only 10,000 unlabeled items, rather than from across the entire dataset. This example makes the time between iterations more manageable, as you would be waiting for many minutes or even hours for all predictions, depending on your machine. This example increases the diversity of the data too, as we are selecting low-confidence items from a different subset of unlabeled items each time.

2.5.4 *Retrain the model and iterate*

Now that you have your newly annotated items, you can add them to your training data and see the change in accuracy from your model. If you run the script that you downloaded at the start of this chapter, you will see that retraining happens automatically after you finish annotating each iteration.

   If you look at that code, you also see the controls that combine all the code that we went through in this chapter. This additional code is the hyperparameters, such as the number of annotations per iteration, and the code at the end of the file to make sure that you get the evaluation data first, train the models, and start iterating with active learning when you have enough evaluation data. The example in this chapter has fewer than 500 lines of unique code, so it is worth taking the time to understand what is going on in each step and thinking about how you might extend any part of the code.

If you come from a machine learning background, the number of features will probably jump out at you. You probably have more than 10,000 features for only 1,000 labeled training items. That is not what your model should look like if you are not labeling any more data: you would almost certainly get better accuracy if you reduced the number of features. But somewhat counterintuitively, you want a large number of features, especially in the early iterations of active learning, when you want to make every feature count for the rare disaster-related headlines. Otherwise, your early model would be even more biased toward the type of headlines that you happened to sample first randomly. There are many ways that you might want to combine your machine learning architecture and active learning strategies, and I will cover the major ones in chapters 9–11.

After you complete 10 or so iterations of annotation, look at your training data. You will notice that most of the items were selected through low confidence, which is not a surprise. Look for ones that are listed as selected by outlier, and you might be surprised. There will probably be a few examples with words that are obvious (to you) as being disaster-related, which means that these examples increased the diversity of your dataset in a way that might otherwise have been missed.

Although active learning can be self-correcting, can you see any evidence that it didn't self-correct some bias? Common examples include oversampling extra-long or extra-short sentences. The computer vision equivalent would be oversampling images that are extra-large or extra-small, or high- or low-resolution. Your choice of outlier strategy and machine learning model might oversample based on features like these, which are not core to your goal. You might consider applying the methods in this chapter to different buckets of data in that case: lowest-confidence short sentences, lowest-confidence medium sentences, and lowest-confidence long sentences.

If you like, you can also experiment with variations on your sampling strategies within this code. Try retraining on only the randomly selected items, and compare the resulting accuracy with another system retrained on the same number of items selected by low confidence and using outlier sampling. Which strategy has the greatest impact, and by how much?

You can also think about what you should develop next:

- A more efficient interface for annotation
- Quality controls to help stop errors in annotation
- Better active learning sampling strategies
- More sophisticated neural architectures for the classification algorithm

Your subjective experience might be different from mine, and trying this example on your own data instead of the example dataset provided here might have changed things, too. But chances are good that you identified one of the first three options as the most important component to build out next. If you come from a machine learning background, your first instinct may be to keep the data constant and start experimenting with more sophisticated neural architectures. That task can be the best next step, but it's rarely the most important one early on. Generally, you should get your data right first; tuning the machine learning architecture becomes more important later in the iterations.

The rest of this book helps you learn how to design better interfaces for annotation, implement better quality control for annotation, devise better active learning strategies, and arrive at better ways to combine these components.

Summary

- A simple human-in-the-loop machine learning system can cover the entire cycle, from sampling unlabeled data to updating the model. This approach lets you get started quickly with a complete MVP system that you can build out as needed.
- Two simple active learning strategies are easy to implement: sampling the least most confident items from predictions and sampling outliers. Understanding the basic goals of each of these strategies will help you dive deeper into uncertainty and diversity sampling later in this book.
- A simple command-line interface can allow humans to annotate data efficiently. Even a simple text-only interface can be efficient if it is built according to general human–computer interaction principles.
- Good data management, such as creating evaluation data as the first task, is important to get right. If you don't get your evaluation data right, you may never know how accurate your model is.
- Retraining a machine learning model with newly annotated data at regular iterations shows that your model gets more accurate over time. If designed correctly, the active learning iterations are naturally self-correcting, with overfitting in one iteration corrected by the sampling strategy in the following iterations.

Part 2

Active learning

Now that you have learned about human-in-the-loop architectures in the first two chapters, we will spend four chapters on active learning: the set of techniques for sampling the most important data for humans to review.

Chapter 3 covers *uncertainty sampling*, introducing the most widely used techniques for understanding a model's uncertainty. The chapter starts by introducing different ways to interpret uncertainty from a single neural model and then looks at uncertainty from different types of machine learning architectures. The chapter also covers how to calculate uncertainty when you have multiple predictions for each data item, such as when you are using an ensemble of models.

Chapter 4 tackles the complicated problem of identifying where your model might be confident but *wrong* due to undersampled or nonrepresentative data. It introduces a variety of data sampling approaches that are useful for identifying gaps in your model's knowledge, such as clustering, representative sampling, and methods that identify and reduce real-world bias in your models. Collectively, these techniques are known as *diversity sampling*.

Uncertainty sampling and diversity sampling are most effective when combined, so chapter 5 introduces ways to combine different strategies into a comprehensive active learning system. Chapter 5 also covers some advantage transfer learning techniques that allow you to adapt machine learning models to predict which items to sample.

Chapter 6 covers how the active learning techniques can be applied to different kinds of machine learning tasks, including object detection, semantic segmentation, sequence labeling, and language generation. This information, including the strengths and weaknesses of each technique, will allow you to apply active learning to any machine learning problem.

Uncertainty sampling

This chapter covers

- Understanding the scores of a model prediction
- Combining predictions over multiple labels into a single uncertainty score
- Combining predictions from multiple models into a single uncertainty score
- Calculating uncertainty with different kinds of machine learning algorithms
- Deciding how many items to put in front of humans per iteration cycle
- Evaluating the success of uncertainty sampling

The most common strategy that people use to make AI smarter is for the machine learning models to tell humans when they are uncertain about a task and then ask the humans for the correct feedback. In general, unlabeled data that confuses an algorithm is most valuable when it is labeled and added to the training data. If the algorithm can already label an item with high confidence, it is probably correct.

This chapter is dedicated to the problem of interpreting when our model is trying to tell us when it is uncertain about its task. But it is not always easy to know when a model is uncertain and how to calculate that uncertainty. Beyond simple binary labeling tasks, the different ways of measuring uncertainty can produce vastly different results. You need to understand and consider all methods for determining uncertainty to select the right one for your data and objectives.

For example, imagine that you are building a self-driving car. You want to help the car understand the new types of objects (pedestrians, cyclists, street signs, animals, and so on) that it is encountering as it drives along. To do that, however, you need to understand when your car is uncertain about what object it is seeing and how to best interpret and address that uncertainty.

3.1   *Interpreting uncertainty in a machine learning model*

Uncertainty sampling is a set of techniques for identifying unlabeled items that are near a decision boundary in your current machine learning model. Although it is easy to identify when a model is confident—there is one result with very high confidence—you have many ways to calculate uncertainty, and your choice will depend on your use case and what is the most effective for your particular data.

We explore four approaches to uncertainty sampling in this chapter:

- *Least confidence sampling*—Difference between the most confident prediction and 100% confidence. In our example, if the model was most confident that a pedestrian was in the image, least confidence captures how confident (or uncertain) that prediction was.
- *Margin of confidence sampling*—Difference between the two most confident predictions. In our example, if the model is most confident that a pedestrian was in the image and second most confident that the image contained an animal, margin of confidence captures the difference between the two confidences.
- *Ratio of confidence*—Ratio between the two most confident predictions. In our example, if the model is most confident that a pedestrian was in the image and the second most confident that the image contained an animal, ratio captures the *ratio* (not difference) between the two confidences.
- *Entropy-based sampling*—Difference between all predictions, as defined by information theory. In our example, entropy-based sampling would capture how much *every* confidence differed from every other.

We'll also look at how to determine uncertainty from different types of machine learning algorithms and how to calculate uncertainty when you have multiple predictions for each data item, such as when you are using an ensemble of models.

Understanding the strengths and weaknesses of each method requires going deeper into exactly what each strategy is doing, so this chapter provides detailed examples along with the equations and code. You also need to know how the confidences are generated before you can start interpreting them correctly, so this chapter starts with how to interpret your model's probability distributions, especially if they are generated by softmax, the most popular algorithm for generating confidences from neural models.

3.1.1   Why look for uncertainty in your model?

Let's return to our self-driving-car example. Suppose that your car spends most of its time on highways, which it is already good at navigating and which have a limited number of objects. You don't see many cyclists or pedestrians on major highways, for example. If you randomly selected video clips from the car's video cameras, your selections will mostly be from highways, where the car is already confident and driving well. There will be little that a human can do to improve the driving skills of the car if humans are mostly giving the car feedback about highway driving, on which the car is already confident.

Therefore, you want to know when your self-driving car is most confused as it is driving. So you decide to take video clips from where the car is most uncertain about the objects it is detecting and then have the human provide the *ground truth* (training data) for the objects in those video clips. The human can identify whether a moving object is a pedestrian, another car, a cyclist, or some other important object that the car's object detection system might have missed. Different objects can be expected to move at different speeds and to be more or less predictable, which will help the car anticipate the movements of those objects.

It might be the case, for example, that the car was most confused when driving through snowstorms. If you show video clips only from a snowstorm, that data doesn't help the car in the 99% of situations when it is not in a snowstorm. In fact, that data could make the car worse. The snowstorm will limit the visible range, and you could unintentionally bias the data so that the car's behavior makes sense only in a snowstorm and is dangerous elsewhere. You might teach the car to ignore all distant objects, as they simply cannot be seen when it is snowing; thus, you would limit the car's ability to anticipate objects at a distance in nonsnowing conditions. So you need different kinds of conditions in which your car is experiencing uncertainty.

Furthermore, it's not clear how to define uncertainty in the context of multiple objects. Is the uncertainty about the most likely object that was predicted? Was it between the two most likely predictions? Or should you take into account every possible object when coming up with an overall uncertainty score for some object that the car detected? When you drill down, deciding what objects from self-driving-car videos you should put in front of a human for review is difficult.

Finally, your model is not telling you in plain language when it is uncertain: even for a single object, the machine learning model gives you a number that might *correspond* to the confidence of the prediction but might not be a reliable measure of accuracy. Our starting point in this chapter is knowing when your model is uncertain. From that base, you will be able to build your broader uncertainty sampling strategies.

The underlying assumption of all active learning techniques is that some data points are more valuable to your model than others. (For a specific example, see the following sidebar.) In this chapter, we'll start with interpreting your model's outputs by taking a look at softmax.

Not all data is equal

Expert anecdote by Jennifer Prendki

If you care about your nutrition, you don't go to the supermarket and randomly select items from the shelves. You might eventually get the nutrients you need by eating random items from the supermarket shelves, but you will eat a lot of junk food in the process. I think it is weird that in machine learning, people still think it's better to sample the supermarket randomly than figure out what they need and focusing their efforts there.

The first active learning system I built was by necessity. I was building machine learning systems to help a large retail store make sure that when someone searched on the website, the right combination of products came up. Almost overnight, a company reorg meant that my human labeling budget was cut in half, and we had a 10x increase in inventory that we had to label. So my labeling team had only 5% the budget per item that we previously did. I created my first active learning framework to discover which was the most important 5%. The results were better than random sampling with a bigger budget. I have used active learning in most of my projects ever since, because not all data is equal!

Jennifer Prendki is the CEO of Alectio, a company that specializes in finding data for machine learning. She previously led data science teams at Atlassian, Figure Eight, and Walmart.

3.1.2   *Softmax and probability distributions*

As you discovered in chapter 2, almost all machine learning models give you two things:

- A predicted label (or set of predictions)
- A number (or set of numbers) associated with each predicted label

Let's assume that we have a simple object detection model for our self-driving car, one that tries to distinguish among only four types of objects. The model might give us a prediction like the following.

Listing 3.1   JSON-encoded example of a prediction

```
{
    "Object": {
        "Label": "Cyclist",
        "Scores": {
            "Cyclist": 0.9192784428596497,  ◁
            "Pedestrian": 0.01409964170306921,
            "Sign": 0.049725741147994995,
            "Animal": 0.016896208748221397
        }
    }
}
```

In this prediction, the object is predicted to be "Cyclist" with 91.9% accuracy. The scores will add to 100%, giving us the probability distribution for this item.

This output is most likely from *softmax*, which converts the logits to a 0–1 range of scores using the exponents. Softmax is defined as follows

$$\sigma(z_i) = \frac{e^{z_i}}{\sum_j e^{z_j}}$$

and as shown in figure 3.1.

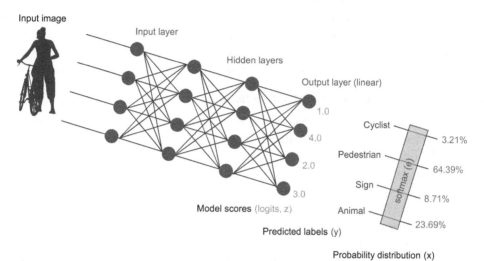

Figure 3.1   How softmax creates probability distributions. A linear activation function is used on the output layer, creating model scores (logits) that are then converted to probability distributions via softmax.

Because softmax divides by exponentials, it loses the scale of the logits. The logits in figure 3.1, for example, are [1, 4, 2, 1]. If the logits were [101, 104, 102, 101], softmax would produce the same probability distribution, so the level of activation in our model is lost in the output. We'll look at how to take activation into account in chapter 4. In this chapter, it's important to understand how some information is lost when only the probability distribution is used.

If you have only used the outputs of softmax in the past, I strongly recommend reading the appendix. As explained there, the softmax base (*e*) is arbitrary, and by changing the base, you can change the ranked order of confidence for predictions on different items. This fact isn't widely known and wasn't reported at all before this book. Rank order is important for uncertainty sampling, as you will see in this chapter, so for your own experiments, you might want to try changing the softmax base (or, equivalently, the temperature) in addition to employing the techniques described later in this chapter.

One common way to get more accurate confidences from your model is to adjust the base/temperature of softmax by using a validation dataset so that the probability distribution matches the actual accuracy as closely as possible. You might adjust the base/temperature of softmax so that a confidence score of 0.7 is correct 70% of the time, for example. A more powerful alternative to adjusting the base/temperature is using a local regression method such as LOESS to map your probability distributions to the actual accuracy on your validation data. Every stats package will have one or more local regression methods that you can experiment with.

If you are modeling uncertainty only so that you can sample the most uncertain items for active learning, however, it might not matter if the probability distributions are not accurate reflections of the accuracy. Your choice will depend on what you are trying to achieve, and it helps to know all the techniques that are available.

3.1.3   *Interpreting the success of active learning*

You can calculate the success of active learning with accuracy metrics such as F-score and AUC, as you did in chapter 2. If you come from an algorithms background, this technique will be familiar to you.

Sometimes, however, it makes more sense to look at the human cost. You could compare two active learning strategies in terms of the number of human labels that are required to get to a certain accuracy target, for example. This can be substantially bigger or smaller than comparing the accuracy with the same number of labels, so it can be useful to calculate both.

If you are not putting the items back into the training data, and therefore not implementing the full active learning cycle, it makes more sense to evaluate purely in terms of how many *incorrect* predictions were surfaced by uncertainty sampling. That is, when you sample the N most uncertain items, what percentage was incorrectly predicted by the model?

For more on human-centric approaches to evaluating quality, such as the amount of time needed to annotate data, see the appendix, which goes into more detail about ways to measure model performance.

3.2   *Algorithms for uncertainty sampling*

Now that you understand where the confidences in the model predictions come from, you can think about how to interpret the probability distributions to find out where your machine learning models are most uncertain.

Uncertainty sampling is a strategy for identifying unlabeled items that are near a decision boundary in your current machine learning model. If you have a binary classification task, like the one you saw in chapter 2, these items are predicted as being close to 50% probability of belonging to either label; therefore, the model is uncertain. These items are most likely to be classified wrongly; therefore, they are the most likely to result in a human label that is different from the predicted label. Figure 3.2 shows how uncertainty sampling should find items close to the decision boundary.

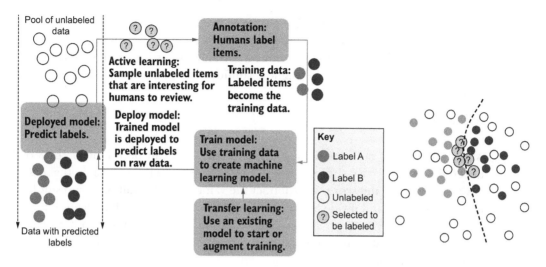

Figure 3.2 Uncertainty sampling is an active learning strategy that oversamples unlabeled items that are closer to the decision boundary (and sometimes to one another), and are therefore more likely to get a human label that results in a change in that decision boundary.

There are many algorithms for calculating uncertainty, some of which we will visit here. They all follow the same principles:

- Apply the uncertainty sampling algorithm to a large pool of predictions to generate a single uncertainty score for each item.
- Rank the predictions by the uncertainty score.
- Select the top N most uncertain items for human review.
- Obtain human labels for the top N items, retrain the model with those items, and iterate on the processes.

The three methods covered in this chapter are invariant of the data being predicted: a given item will get the same uncertainty score independent of the scores given to other items being predicted. This invariance helps with the simplicity and predictability of the approaches in this chapter: the rank order of uncertainty scores is enough to find the most uncertain across a set of predictions. Other techniques, however, can take the distribution of predictions to change the individual scores. We will return to this topic in chapters 5 and 6.

> **NOTE** For binary classification tasks, the strategies in this chapter are identical, but for three or more labels, the strategies diverge quickly.

3.2.1 Least confidence sampling

The simplest and most common method for uncertainty sampling takes the difference between 100% confidence and the most confidently predicted label for each item. You saw this implementation of active learning in chapter 2. Let's refer to the softmax result as the probability of the label given the prediction. We know that softmax isn't strictly giving us probabilities, but these equations are general equations that apply to probability distributions from any sources, not only from softmax. The basic equation is simply the probability of the highest confidence for the label, which you implemented in chapter 2:

$$\phi_{LC}(x) = P_\theta(y^*|x)$$

Although you can rank order by confidence alone, it can be useful to convert the uncertainty scores to a 0–1 range, where 1 is the most uncertain score. In that case, we have to normalize the score. We subtract the value from 1, multiply the result by the number of labels, and divide by the number of labels –1. We do this because the minimum confidence can never be less than the one divided by the number of labels, which is when all labels have the same predicted confidence. So least confidence sampling with a 0-1 range is

$$\phi_{LC}(x) = (1 - P_\theta(y^*|x)) \times \frac{n}{n-1}$$

The following listing has an implementation of least confidence sampling in PyTorch.

Listing 3.2 Least confidence sampling in PyTorch

```
def least_confidence(self, prob_dist, sorted=False):
    """
    Returns the uncertainty score of an array using
    least confidence sampling in a 0-1 range where 1 is most uncertain

    Assumes probability distribution is a pytorch tensor, like:
        tensor([0.0321, 0.6439, 0.0871, 0.2369])

    Keyword arguments:
        prob_dist -- a pytorch tensor of real numbers between 0 and 1 that
        ➥ total to 1.0
        sorted - if the probability distribution is pre-sorted from largest to
        ➥ smallest
    """
    if sorted:
        simple_least_conf = prob_dist.data[0]
    else:
        simple_least_conf = torch.max(prob_dist)

    num_labels = prob_dist.numel() # number of labels

    normalized_least_conf = (1 - simple_least_conf) *
    ➥ (num_labels / (num_labels - 1))

    return normalized_least_conf.item()
```

Let's apply least confidence to get an uncertainty score for our self-driving-car prediction. The confidence for "Pedestrian" is all that counts here. Using our example, this uncertainty score would be $(1 - 0.6439) * (4 / 3) = 0.4748$. Least confidence sampling, therefore, gives you ranked order of predictions where you will sample items with the lowest confidence for their predicted label. This method is sensitive to the values of the second, third, and so on only in that the sum of the other predictions will be the score itself: the amount of confidence that will go to labels other than the most confident.

Predicted label	Cyclist	Pedestrian	Sign	Animal
softmax	0.0321	0.6439	0.0871	0.2369

This method will not be sensitive to uncertainty between any of the other predictions: with the same confidence for the most confident, the second to nth confidences can take any values without changing the uncertainty score. If you care only about the most confident prediction for your particular use case, this method is a good starting point. Otherwise, you will want to use one of methods discussed in the following sections.

Least confidence is sensitive to the base used for the softmax algorithm. This example is a little counterintuitive, but recall the example in which softmax(base=10) gives ~0.9 confidence, which would result in an uncertainty score of 0.1—much less than 0.35 on the same data. For different bases, this score will change the overall ranking. Higher bases for softmax will stretch out the differences between the most confident label and the other labels; therefore, at higher bases, the difference between the label confidences will come to weigh more than the absolute difference between the most-confident label and 1.0.

3.2.2 Margin of confidence sampling

The most intuitive form of uncertainty sampling is the difference between the two most confident predictions. That is, for the label that the model predicted, how much more confident was it than for the next-most-confident label? This is defined as

$$\phi_{MC}(x) = P_\theta(y_1^* | x) - P_\theta(y_2^* | x)$$

Again, we can convert this to a 0–1 range. We have to subtract from 1.0 again, but the maximum possible score is already 1, so there is no need to multiply by any factor:

$$\phi_{MC}(x) = 1 - (P_\theta(y_1^* | x) - P_\theta(y_2^* | x))$$

Following is an implementation of margin of confidence sampling with PyTorch.

Listing 3.3 Margin of confidence sampling in PyTorch

```
def margin_confidence(self, prob_dist, sorted=False):
    """
    Returns the uncertainty score of a probability distribution using
```

```
    margin of confidence sampling in 0-1 range where 1 is most uncertain

    Assumes probability distribution is a pytorch tensor, like:
      tensor([0.0321, 0.6439, 0.0871, 0.2369])

    Keyword arguments:
      prob_dist -- a pytorch tensor of real numbers between 0 and 1 that
   ➥ total to 1.0
      sorted -- if the probability distribution is pre-sorted from largest to
   ➥ smallest
         """
    if not sorted:
      prob_dist, _ = torch.sort(prob_dist, descending=True)

    difference = (prob_dist.data[0] - prob_dist.data[1])
    margin_conf = 1 - difference

    return margin_conf.item()
```

Let's apply margin of confidence sampling to our example data. "Pedestrian" and "Animal" are the most-confident and second-most-confident prediction. Using our example, this uncertainty score would be 1.0 - (0.6439 - 0.2369) = 0.5930.

Predicted label	Cyclist	Pedestrian	Sign	Animal
softmax	0.0321	0.6439	0.0871	0.2369

This method will not be sensitive to uncertainty for any but the two most confident predictions: with the same difference in confidence for the most and second-most confident, the third to *nth* confidences can take any values without changing the uncertainty score.

If you care only about the uncertainty between the predicted label and the next-most-confident prediction for your particular use case, this method is a good starting point. This type of uncertainty sampling is the most common type that I've seen people use in industry.

Margin of confidence is less sensitive than least confidence sampling to the base used for the softmax algorithm, but it is still sensitive. Although softmax(base=10) would give a margin of confidence score of 0.1899 for our dataset, compared with 0.5930 with base *e*, all of the two most probable scores will move. Those scores will move at slightly different rates, depending on the total relative difference of all raw scores, but recall that we are sampling from when the model is most uncertain—that is, when the most-confident scores tend to be as low as possible and therefore most similar. For this reason, you might get a difference of only a few percentage points when you sample the most uncertain items by margin of confidence sampling under different bases of softmax.

3.2.3 *Ratio sampling*

Ratio of confidence is a slight variation on margin of confidence, looking at the ratio between the top two scores instead of the difference. It is the best uncertainty sampling method for improving your understanding of the relationship between confidence and softmax. To make the technique a little more intuitive, think of the ratio as capturing how many times more likely the first label was than the second-most-confident:

$$\phi_{RC}(x) = P_\theta(y_1^* | x) / P_\theta(y_2^* | x)$$

Now let's plug in our numbers again:

0.6439 / 0.2369 = 2.71828

We get back the natural log, $e = 2.71828$! Similarly, if we use base 10, we get

90.01% / 9.001% = 10

We get back 10—the base we used! This example is a good illustration of why e is an arbitrary base for generating confidences. (See the appendix for more on this topic.). Is "Pedestrian" really 2.71828 more likely as a prediction than "Animal" in this context? Probably not. It's doubtful that it's exactly 10 times more likely, either. The only thing that ratio of confidence is telling us is that the raw score from our models was "1" different between "Pedestrian" and "Animal"—nothing more. Ratio of confidence with a division can be defined in terms of the raw scores, in this case with softmax(base=), where is the base used for softmax (if not e):

$$\beta^{(z_1^* - z_2^*)}$$

Ratio of confidence is invariant across any base used in softmax. The score is determined wholly by the distance between the top two raw scores from your model; therefore, scaling by the base or temperature will not change the rank order. To give ratio of confidence a 0-1 normalized range, you can simply take the inverse of the preceding equation:

$$\phi_{RC}(x) = P_\theta(y_2^* | x) / P_\theta(y_1^* | x)$$

We used the noninverted version above so that it directly outputs their softmax base for illustrative purposes. The following listing has an implementation of ratio of confidence sampling using PyTorch.

Listing 3.4   Ratio of confidence sampling in PyTorch

```
def ratio_confidence(self, prob_dist, sorted=False):
    """
    Returns the uncertainty score of a probability distribution using
    ratio of confidence sampling in 0-1 range where 1 is most uncertain
```

```
    Assumes probability distribution is a pytorch tensor, like:
      tensor([0.0321, 0.6439, 0.0871, 0.2369])

    Keyword arguments:
      prob_dist -- pytorch tensor of real numbers between 0 and 1 that total
      ➥ to 1.0
      sorted -- if the probability distribution is pre-sorted from largest to
      ➥ smallest
      """
    if not sorted:
      prob_dist, _ = torch.sort(prob_dist, descending=True)

    ratio_conf = prob_dist.data[1] / prob_dist.data[0]

    return ratio_conf.item()
```

I hope that this example gives you another good way to intuit why margin of confidence sampling is relatively invariant: there's no big difference between subtracting your two highest values and dividing your two highest values when your goal is to rank them.

Happily, where margin of confidence with subtraction *does* differ from ratio of confidence, it does what we want by favoring the most uncertain. Although margin of confidence and ratio of confidence don't explicitly look at the confidences beyond the two most confident, they influence the possible values. If the third-most-confident value is 0.25, the first and second can differ by 0.5 at most. So if the third-most-confident prediction is relatively close to the first and second, the uncertainty score for margin of confidence increases. This variation is small and doesn't occur directly as a result of margin of confidence; it is a byproduct of the denominator in the softmax equation being larger as a result of the larger score for the third-most-confident value, which becomes disproportionately larger as an exponential. Nonetheless, this behavior is right; all else being equal, margin of confidence looks for uncertainty beyond the two most confident predictions in what would otherwise be a tie.

Unlike margin of confidence, in which the variation from the third to nth predictions is a lucky byproduct of softmax, our next-most-popular uncertainty sampling strategy explicitly models all the predictions.

3.2.4   *Entropy (classification entropy)*

One way to look at uncertainty in a set of predictions is by whether you expect to be surprised by the outcome. This concept underlies the entropy technique. How surprised would you be by each of the possible outcomes, relative to their probability?

It is intuitive to think about entropy and surprise in terms of a sporting team you supported for a long time even though it was on a losing streak. For me, that team is the Detroit Lions American football team. In recent years, even when the Lions are ahead early in a game, they still have only a 50% chance of winning that game. So even if the Lions are up early in the game, I don't know what the result will be, and there is an equal amount of surprise either way in every game. Entropy does not measure the emotional toll of losing—only the surprise. The entropy equation gives us a mathematically well-motivated way to calculate the surprise for outcomes, as shown in figure 3.3.

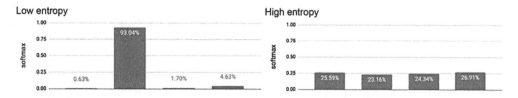

Figure 3.3 Example of low entropy (left) and high entropy (right). High entropy occurs when the probabilities are most like one another and there is the most surprise in any one prediction from the distribution. Entropy is sometimes a little counterintuitive, because the left graph has the most variability and three highly unlikely events. Those three unlikely events, however, are more than canceled by the one highly likely event. Four events at around equal likelihood will have greater total entropy, even if the three rarer events would have greater information on the rare times that they occur.

Entropy applied to a probability distribution involves multiplying each probability by its own log and taking the negative sum:

$$\phi_{ENT}(x) = -\sum_{y} P_\theta(y|x)\log_2 P_\theta(y|x)$$

We can convert the entropy to a 0–1 range by dividing by the log of the number of predictions (labels):

$$\phi_{ENT}(x) = \frac{-\sum_{y} P_\theta(y|x)\log_2 P_\theta(y|x)}{\log_2(n)}$$

The following listing shows an implementation of ratio of entropy score using Python and the PyTorch library.

Listing 3.5 Entropy-based sampling in PyTorch

```python
def entropy_based(self, prob_dist):
    """

    Returns uncertainty score of a probability distribution using entropy

    Assumes probability distribution is a pytorch tensor, like:
        tensor([0.0321, 0.6439, 0.0871, 0.2369])

    Keyword arguments:
        prob_dist -- a pytorch tensor of real numbers between 0 and 1 that
        ➡ total to 1.0
        sorted -- if the probability distribution is pre-sorted from largest to
        ➡ smallest
    """
```

```
log_probs = prob_dist * torch.log2(prob_dist)
raw_entropy = 0 - torch.sum(log_probs)
```
◁─── **Multiply each probability by its base 2 log.**

```
normalized_entropy = raw_entropy / math.log2(prob_dist.numel())

return normalized_entropy.item()
```

First, don't be scared by another arbitrary base, log(base=2), which is used for histori-cal reasons: the choice of base for entropy does not change the uncertainty sampling rank order. Unlike with softmax, calculating the entropy with different bases for uncertainty sampling does *not* change the rank order of scores across a dataset. You will get different entropy scores depending on the base, but the entropy scores will change monotonically for every probability distribution and therefore will not change the rank order for uncertainty sampling. Base 2 is used in entropy for historical rea-sons, as entropy comes from information theory, which deals with compressing data streams in binary bits. Let's calculate the entropy on our example data:

Predicted label	Cyclist	Pedestrian	Sign	Animal
P(y|x) aka softmax	0.0321	0.6439	0.0871	0.2369
log2(P(y|x))	−4.963	−0.635	−3.520	−2.078
P(y|x) log2(P(y|x))	−0.159	−0.409	−0.307	−0.492

Summing the numbers and negating them returns

$0 - \text{SUM}(-0.159, -0.409, -0.307, -0.492) = 1.367$

Dividing by the log of the number of labels returns

$1.367 \, / \, \log_2(4) = 0.684$

Note that the $P(y|x) \log(P(y|x))$ step is not monotonic with respect to the probability dis-tribution given by softmax. "Pedestrian" returns −0.409, but "Animal" returns −0.492. So "Animal" contributes most to the final entropy score even though it is neither the most-confident or least-confident prediction.

Data ranked for uncertainty by entropy is sensitive to the base used by the softmax algorithm and about equally sensitive as least confidence. It is intuitive why this is the case: entropy *explicitly* uses every number in the probability distribution, so the further these numbers are spread out via a higher base, the more divergent the result will be.

Recall our example in which softmax(base=10) gives ~0.9% confidence, which would result in an uncertainty score of 0.1—much less than 0.35 on the same data. For different bases, this score will change the overall ranking. Higher bases for soft-max will stretch out the differences between the most-confident label and the other labels.

3.2.5   *A deep dive on entropy*

If you want to get deeper into entropy, you can try plugging different confidences into the inner part of the equation where each confidence is multiplied by its own log, such as $0.3 * \log(0.3)$. For this measure of entropy, the per-prediction score of $P(y|x)$ $\log(P(y|x))$ will return the largest (negative) numbers for confidences of around 0.3679. Unlike in softmax, Euler's number is special, as $e^{-1} = 0.3679$. The formula used to derive this result is known as *Euler's Rule*, itself a derivation of the *Thâbit ibn Kurrah Rule*, created sometime in the ninth century to generate amicable numbers. The largest (negative) numbers for each prediction will be around 0.3679 no matter which base you use for entropy, which should help you understand why the base doesn't matter in this case.

You will encounter entropy in a few places in machine learning and signal processing, so this equation is a good one to get your head around. Fortunately, you don't need to derive Euler's Rule or the Thâbit ibn Kurrah Rule to use entropy for uncertainty sampling. The intuition that 0.3679 (or a number near it) contributes most to entropy is fairly simple:

- If the probability is 1.0, the model is completely predictable and has no entropy.
- If the probability is 0.0, that data point provides no contribution to entropy, as it is never going to happen.
- Therefore, some number between 0.0 and 1.0 is optimal for entropy on a per-prediction basis.

But 0.3679 is optimal only for individual probabilities. By using 0.3679 of the probability for one label, you are leaving only 0.6431 for every other label. So the highest entropy for the entire probability distribution, not individual values alone, will always occur when each probability is identical and equal to one divided by the number of labels.

3.3   *Identifying when different types of models are confused*

You are most likely using neural models in machine learning, but there are many different architectures for neural models and many other popular types of supervised machine learning algorithms. Almost every machine learning library or service will return some form of scores for the algorithms in them, and these scores can be used for uncertainty sampling. In some cases, you will be able to use the scores directly; in other cases, you will have to convert the scores to probability distributions using something like softmax.

Even if you are using only predictive models from neural networks or the default settings on common machine learning libraries and services, it is useful to understand the full range of algorithms and how uncertainty is defined in different kinds of machine learning models. Some are much different from the interpretations that we make from neural network models, but not necessarily any better or worse, so it will help you appreciate the strengths and weaknesses of different common approaches. The strategies for determining uncertainty for different types of machine learning algorithms are summarized in figure 3.4 and expanded on in more detail in this section.

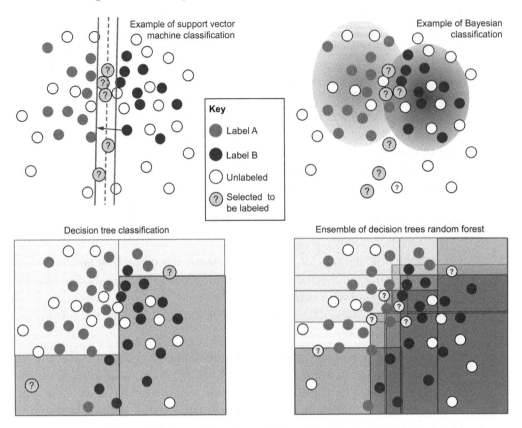

Figure 3.4   Uncertainty sampling from different supervised machine learning algorithms.

Top left: The decision boundary from a support vector machine (SVM). A discriminative learner, like a neural model, attempts to find a way to divide the data optimally. Unlike neural classifiers, SVMs are also trying to maximize the width of the boundary. This is how an SVM decides which of multiple possible central lines is the best division: it has the widest boundary. Note that the distance from the divider (the *hyperplane* for SVMs) is from the far side of the divider, not the middle line.

Top right: A potential Bayesian model. This model is a *generative* supervised learning model, trying to model the distribution of each label rather than model the boundary between them. The confidence on a per-label basis can be read directly as a probability of being that label.

Bottom left: The division that a decision tree might provide, dividing and recursively subdividing the data one feature at time. The confidence is defined by the percentage of a label in the final bucket (leaf), The bottom-left leaf, for example, has one Label A and three Label Bs, so a prediction in that leaf would be 25% confidence in Label A and 75% confidence in Label B. Decision trees are sensitive to how far you let them divide—they could keep dividing to leaves of one item—so probabilities tend not to be reliable.

Bottom right: An ensemble of decision trees, of which the most well-known variant is a random forest. Multiple decision trees are trained. The different trees are usually achieved by training on different subsets of the data and/or features. The confidence in a label can be the percentage of times an item was predicted across all models or the average confidence across all predictions.

3.3.1 Uncertainty sampling with logistic regression and MaxEnt models

For interpreting model confidence, you can treat logistic regression and MaxEnt (maximum entropy) models the same as neural models. There is little difference (sometimes none) between a logistic regression model, a MaxEnt model, and a single-layer neural model. Therefore, you can apply uncertainty sampling in the same way that you do for neural models: you might get softmax outputs, or you might get scores to which you can apply softmax. The same caveats apply: it is not the job of a logistic regression or MaxEnt model to calculate the confidence of a model accurately, as the model is trying to distinguish optimally between the labels, so you may want to experiment with different bases/temperatures for softmax if that is how you are generating your probability distribution.

3.3.2 Uncertainty sampling with SVMs

Support vector machines (SVMs) represent another type of discriminative learning. Like neural models, they are attempting to find a way to divide the data optimally. Unlike neural classifiers, SVMs are also trying to maximize the width of the boundary and decide which of the multiple possible divisions is the right one. The optimal boundary is defined as the widest one—more specifically, the one that optimally models the greatest distance between a label and the far side of the dividing boundary. You can see an example of SVMs in figure 3.5. The support vectors themselves are the data points that define the boundaries.

SVMs also differ in how they model more complicated distributions. Neural networks use hidden layers to discover boundaries between labels that are more complicated than simple linear divisions. Two hidden layers are enough to define any

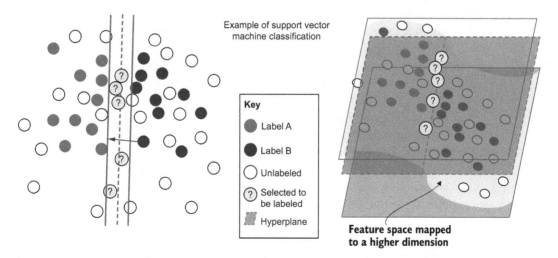

Figure 3.5 SVM projecting our example 2D dataset (top) into 3D (bottom) so that a linear plane can separate the two sets of labels: Label A is above the plane, and Label B is below the plane. The sampled items are the least distance from the plane. If you want to learn from some of the important early active learning literature, you need to understand how SVMs work at this high level.

function. SVMs more or less do the same thing, but with predefined functions that map the data into higher dimensions. In figure 3.5, our 2D example data is projected into a third dimension that raises items on one side of that function and lowers them on the other. With the projection into a higher dimension, the data is linearly separable, and a plane divides the two labels.

It is many orders of magnitude more efficient to train a model when you've predefined the type of function (as in SVMs) rather than let your model find the function itself among all possible alternatives (as in neural models). The chance of predefining the correct function type is low, however, and the cost of hardware is coming down while speed is going up, so SVMs are rarely used today, compared with their earlier popularity.

3.3.3   *Uncertainty sampling with Bayesian models*

Bayesian models are generative supervised learning models, which means that they are trying to model the distribution of each label and the underlying samples rather than model the boundary between the labels. The advantage of Bayesian models is that you can read the probabilities straight off the model:

$$P_\theta(x|y) \;=\; \frac{P_\theta(y|x)P_\theta(x)}{P_\theta(y)}$$

You don't need a separate step or specific activation function to convert arbitrary scores to a probability distribution; the model is explicitly calculating the probability of an item's having a label. Therefore, confidence on a per-label basis can be read directly as a probability of that label.

Because they are not trying to model the differences between labels, Bayesian models tend not to be able to capture more complicated decision boundaries without a lot more fine-tuning. The Naive Bayes algorithm gets the *Naive* part of its name from not being able to model linear relationships between features, let alone more complicated ones, although it can be retrained almost instantly with new training data, which is appealing for human-in-the-loop systems.

Bayesian models also have to make assumptions about data distributions, such as real values falling within a normal distribution, which may not necessarily hold up in your actual data. These assumptions can skew the probabilities away from the true values if you are not careful. They will still tend to be better than probabilities from discriminative models, but you can trust them blindly without understanding their assumptions about the data.

Therefore, although Bayesian models aren't always as likely to get the same accuracy as discriminative models, they typically produce more reliable confidence scores, so they can be used directly in active learning. If you trust your confidence score, for example, you can sample based on that score: sample 90% items with 0.9 uncertainty, sample 10% of items with 0.1 uncertainty, and so on. Beyond simple labeling tasks, however, when people talk about Bayesian methods for active learning, they typically mean predictions over ensembles of discriminative models, which is covered in section 3.4 later in this chapter.

3.3.4 *Uncertainty sampling with decision trees and random forests*

Decision trees are discriminative learners that divide the data one feature at a time, recursively subdividing the data into buckets until the final bucket—the leaves—has only one set of labels. The trees are often stopped early (*pruned*) so that the leaves ultimately have some diversity of labels and the models don't overfit the data. Figure 3.4, earlier in this chapter, shows an example.

The confidence is defined by the percentage of a label in the leaf for that prediction. The bottom-left leaf in figure 3.4, for example, has one Label A and three Label Bs, so a prediction in that leaf would be 25% confidence in Label A and 75% confidence in Label B.

Decision trees are sensitive to how far you let them divide; they could keep dividing to leaves of one item. By contrast, if they are not deep enough, each prediction will contain a lot of noise, and the bucket will be large, with relatively distant training items in the same bucket erroneously contributing the confidence. So probabilities tend not to be reliable.

The confidence of single decision trees are rarely trusted for this reason, and they are not recommended for uncertainty sampling. They can be useful for other active learning strategies, as we will cover later, but for any active learning involving decision trees, I recommended that you use multiple trees and combine the results.

Random forests are the best-known ensemble of decision trees. In machine learning, an *ensemble* means a collection of machine learning models that are combined to make a prediction, which we cover more in section 3.4.

For a random forest, multiple different decision trees are trained, with the goal of getting slightly different predictions from each one. The different trees are usually achieved by training on different subsets of the data and/or features. The confidence in a label can be the percentage of times an item was predicted across all models or the average confidence across all predictions.

As figure 3.4 shows with the combination of four decision trees in the bottom-right diagram, the decision boundary between the two labels is starting to become more gradual as you average across multiple predictions. Therefore, random forests make a good, useful approximation confidence along the boundary between two labels. Decision trees are fast to train, so there is little reason not to train many trees in a random forest if they are your algorithm of choice for active learning.

3.4 *Measuring uncertainty across multiple predictions*

Sometimes, you have multiple models built from your data. You may already be experimenting with different types of models or hyperparameters and want to combine the predictions into a single uncertainty score. If not, you may want to experiment with a few different models on your data to look at the variance. Even if you are not using multiple models for your data, looking at the variation in predictions from different models will give you an intuition for how stable your model is today.

3.4.1 Uncertainty sampling with ensemble models

Similar to how a random forest is an ensemble of one type of supervised learning algorithm, you can use multiple types of algorithms to determine uncertainty and aggregate across them. Figure 3.6 shows an example. Different classifiers have confidence scores that are unlikely to be directly compatible because of the different types of statistics used.

The simplest way to combine multiple classifiers is to rank-order the items by their uncertainty score for each classifier, give each item a new score based on its rank order, and then combine those rank scores into one master rank of uncertainty.

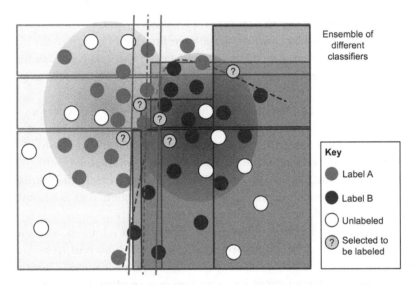

Figure 3.6 An ensemble model that combines predictions from different types of machine learning algorithms: neural models, SVMs, Bayesian models, and decision trees (decision forest). The predictions can be combined in various ways (max, average, and so on) to find the joint uncertainty of each unlabeled item.

You can calculate uncertainty by how often different models agree on the label of an item. The items with the most disagreement are the ones to sample. You can also take the probability distributions of the predictions into account. You can combine the predictions from different models in multiple ways:

- Lowest maximum confidence across all models
- Difference between minimum and maximum confidence across models
- Ratio between minimum and maximum confidence across models
- Entropy across all confidences in all models
- Average confidence across all models

You probably noticed that the first four methods are the same algorithms we used for uncertainty sampling within a single prediction, but in this case across multiple predictions. So you should already be able to implement these methods.

3.4.2 *Query by Committee and dropouts*

Within active learning, the ensemble-based approach is sometimes known as *Query by Committee*, especially when only one type of machine learning algorithm is used for the ensemble. You could try the ensemble approach with neural models: train a model multiple times and look at the agreement on the unlabeled data across the predictions from each neural model. If you're already retraining your model multiple times to tune hyperparameters, you might as well take advantage of the different predictions to help with active learning.

Following the random forest method, you could try retraining your models with different subsets of items or features to force diversity in the types of models that are built. This approach will prevent one feature (or a small number of features) from dominating the final uncertainty score.

One recently popular method for neural models uses dropouts. You are probably familiar with using dropouts when training a model: you remove/ignore some random percentage of neurons/connections while training the model to avoid overfitting your model to any specific neuron.

You can apply the dropout strategy to predictions: get a prediction for an item multiple times, dropping out a different random selection of neurons/connections each time. This approach results in multiple confidences for an item, and you can use these confidences with the ensemble evaluation methods to sample the right items, as shown in figure 3.7.

You will see more examples throughout the book of using the neural architecture itself to help with active learning. Chapter 4, which covers diversity sampling, begins with a similar example that uses model activation to detect outliers, and many of the advanced techniques later in the book do the same thing.

It is an exciting time to be working in human-in-the-loop machine learning. You get to work with the newest architectures for machine learning algorithms *and* think about how they relate to human–computer interaction.

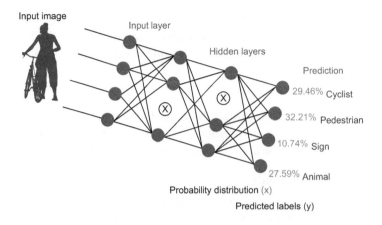

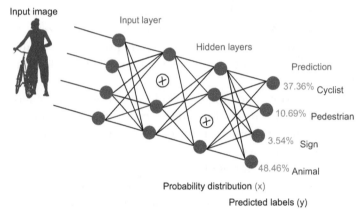

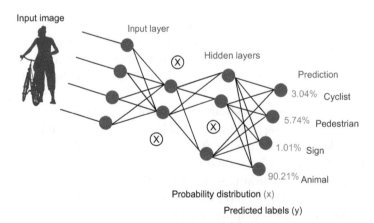

Figure 3.7 Applying dropout to a model to get multiple predictions for a single item. In each prediction, a random set of neurons is dropped (ignored), resulting in different confidences and (possibly) different predicted labels. Then the uncertainty can be calculated as the variation across all predictions: the higher the disagreement, the more uncertainty. This approach to getting multiple predictions from a single model is known as *Monte Carlo dropouts*.

3.4.3   *The difference between aleatoric and epistemic uncertainty*

The terms *aleatoric uncertainty* and *epistemic uncertainty*, from the philosophy literature, are popular among machine learning scientists who have never read the philosophy literature. In the machine learning literature, the terms typically refer to the methods used. *Epistemic uncertainty* is uncertainty within a single model's predictions, and *aleatoric uncertainty* is uncertainty across multiple predictions (especially Monte Carlo dropouts in the recent literature). *Aleatoric* historically meant inherent randomness, and *epistemic* meant lack of knowledge, but these definitions are meaningful only in machine learning contexts in which no new data can be annotated, which is rare outside academic research.

Therefore, when reading machine learning literature, assume that the researchers are talking only about the methods used to calculate uncertainty, not the deeper philosophical meanings. Figure 3.8 illustrates the differences.

Figure 3.8 shows how multiple predictions allows you to predict uncertainty in terms of variance from multiple decision boundaries in addition to distance from a single decision boundary. For a neural model, the variation in distance from the decision boundary can be calculated as the variation in the labels predicted, the variation in any of the uncertainty sampling metrics covered in section 3.2, or variation across the entire probability distribution for each prediction.

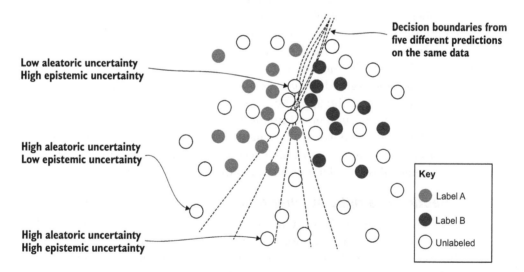

Figure 3.8 Differences between aleatoric and epistemic uncertainty, according to the definitions that are most widely used in machine learning literature. The first highlighted item is near the decision boundary of all five predictions, so it has high epistemic uncertainty, but the decision boundaries are clustered together, so it has low aleatoric uncertainty. The second highlighted item has low epistemic uncertainty because it is not near most decision boundaries, but its distance from the decision boundaries has a large amount of variation, so it has high aleatoric uncertainty. The final item is near the average decision boundary and has great variance in the distance between all boundaries, so it has high uncertainty for both types.

See section 3.8 for further reading on starting places, as this area of research is an active one. The literature on aleatoric uncertainty tends to focus on the optimal types of ensembles or dropouts, and the literature on epistemic uncertainty tends to focus on getting more accurate probability distributions from within a single model.

3.4.4   *Multilabeled and continuous value classification*

If your task is multilabeled, allowing multiple correct labels for each item, you can calculate uncertainty by using the same aggregation methods as for ensembles. You can treat each label as though it is a binary classifier. Then you can decide whether you want to average the uncertainty, take the maximum uncertainty, or use one of the other aggregation techniques covered earlier in this chapter.

When you treat each label as a binary classifier, there is no difference among the types of uncertainty sampling algorithms (least confidence, margin of confidence, and so on), but you might try the ensemble methods in this section *in addition* to aggregating across the different labels. You can train multiple models on your data and then aggregate the prediction for each label for each item, for example. This approach will give you different uncertainty values for each label for an item, and you can experiment with the right methods to aggregate the uncertainty per label in addition to across labels for each item.

For continuous values, such as a regression model that predicts a real value instead of a label, your model might not give you confidence scores in the prediction. You can apply ensemble methods and look at the variation to calculate the uncertainty in these cases. In fact, Monte Carlo dropouts were first used to estimate uncertainty in regression models in which no new data needed to be labeled. In that controlled environment, you could argue that *epistemic uncertainty* is the right term.

Chapter 6 covers the application of active learning to many use cases, and the section on object detection goes into more detail about uncertainty in regression. Chapter 10 has a section devoted to evaluating human accuracy for continuous tasks that may also be relevant to your task. I recommend that you read those two chapters for more details about working with models that predict continuous values.

3.5   *Selecting the right number of items for human review*

Uncertainty sampling is an iterative process. You select some number of items for human review, retrain your model, and then repeat the process. Recall from chapter 1 the potential downside of sampling for uncertainty without also sampling for diversity, as shown in figure 3.9.

The most uncertain items here are all near one another. In a real example, thousands of examples might be clustered together, and it would not be necessary to sample them all. No matter where the item is sampled from, you can't be entirely sure what the influence on the model will be until a human has provided a label and the model is retrained.

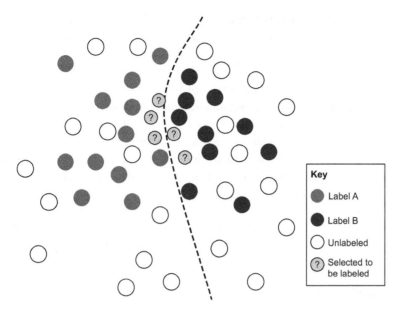

Figure 3.9 **A selection of uncertain items that are all from the same region of the feature space, and therefore lack diversity**

Retraining a model can take a long time, however, and it can be a waste of time to ask the human annotators to wait during that period. Two competing forces are at work:

- Minimizing the sample size will ensure that the most benefit is gained from each data point at each iteration.
- Maximizing the sample size will ensure that more items get labeled sooner and the model needs to be retrained less often.

As you saw in chapter 2, there was low diversity in the early iterations of your model, but this situation self-corrected in later iterations as the model was retrained. The decision ultimately comes down to a business process. In recent work in translation, we wanted our models to adapt in a few seconds so that they seemed to be responsive in real time to our translators while they worked. I've also seen companies being happy with about one iteration per year to adapt to new data.

3.5.1 *Budget-constrained uncertainty sampling*

If you have a fixed budget for labels, you should try to get as many iterations as possible. The number of possible iterations will depend on whether you are compensating annotators per label (as with many crowdsourced worker models) or per hour (as with many expert human models).

If your budget is per label, meaning that you are paying a fixed price per label no matter how long the gap is between getting those labels, it is best to optimize for the maximum number of iterations possible. People do tend to get bored waiting for their models to train. When retraining a model takes more than a few days, I've seen people max out at about 10 iterations and plan accordingly. There's no particular reason to choose 10: it's an intuitive number of iterations to monitor for changes in accuracy.

If your budget is per-hour, meaning that you have a set number of people labeling a set number of hours per day, it is best to optimize for always having data available to label. Have annotators gradually work through the rank order of unlabeled items by uncertainty, and retrain a model at regular intervals, subbing out an old uncertainty ranking for a new one whenever a new model is ready. If you are using uncertainty sampling and want to avoid oversampling from only one part of the problem space, you should replace models regularly. Realistically, if people are working full time to label data for you, you owe them the respect of implementing multiple active learning sampling strategies from this book and sampling from all those strategies, so that those people feel that they are contributing the greatest value possible. You are also less likely to introduce bias that could result from implementing only one of the algorithms, so both humans and machines score a win. We will return to strategies for different kinds of annotation workforces in chapter 7.

3.5.2   *Time-constrained uncertainty sampling*

If you are time-constrained and need to get an updated model out quickly, you should consider strategies to retrain the models as quickly as possible, as in chapter 2. The quickest way is to use simple models. A model with only one or two layers (or, better yet, a Naive Bayes model) can be retrained incredibly quickly, allowing you to iterate quickly. Further, there is some evidence that uncertainty sampling from a simpler model can be as effective as sampling from a more complicated model. Remember that we're looking for the most confusion, not the most accuracy. Provided that a simple model is the most confused about the same items as a more complicated model, both models will sample the same items.

A more advanced way is to retrain only the final layer(s) of a much larger model. You can retrain your model quickly by retraining only the last layer with new data, compared with retraining the whole model. This process can take a matter of seconds instead of weeks. The retrained model will not necessarily be as accurate, but it may be close. As with choosing a simpler model, this small loss in accuracy may not matter if the goal is to look for more uncertainty. The faster iteration may even result in a more accurate model than if you'd waited a long time to retrain the entire model with fewer iterations.

One advanced method is to have the best of both worlds: use methods to discover which parameters are the most important to retrain across your entire model, and retrain only them. This approach can give you the same accuracy as retraining the entire model, but in a fraction of the time.

Another advanced method that can be easier to implement is to have two models: an incremental model that is updated immediately with every new training item and a second model that is retrained from scratch at regular intervals. One of the example implementations in chapter 12 uses this architecture.

3.5.3　*When do I stop if I'm not time- or budget-constrained?*

Lucky you! You should stop when your model stops getting more accurate. If you have tried many strategies for uncertainty sampling and are not getting any more gains after a certain accuracy is reached, this condition is a good signal to stop and think about other active learning and/or algorithmic strategies if your desired accuracy goal hasn't been met.

You will ultimately see diminishing returns as you label more data; no matter what strategy you use, the learning rate will decrease as you add more data. Even if the rate hasn't plateaued, you should be able to run a cost-benefit analysis of the accuracy you are getting per label versus the cost of those labels.

3.6　*Evaluating the success of active learning*

Always evaluate uncertainty sampling on a randomly selected, held-out test set. If the test data is selected randomly from your training data after each iteration, you won't know what your actual accuracy is. In fact, your accuracy is likely to appear to be lower than it is. By choosing items that are hard to classify, you are probably oversampling inherently ambiguous items. If you are testing more on inherently ambiguous items, you are more likely to see errors. (We covered this topic in chapter 2, but it is worth repeating here.) Therefore, don't fall into the trap of forgetting to sample randomly in addition to using uncertainty sampling: you won't know whether your model is improving!

3.6.1　*Do I need new test data?*

If you already have test data set aside, and you know that the unlabeled data is from more or less the same distribution as your training data, you do not need additional test data. You can keep testing on the same data.

If you know that the test data has a different distribution from your original training data, or if you are unsure, you should collect additional labels through random selection of unlabeled items and add them to your test set or create a second, separate test set.

> **TIP**　Create your new test set before your first iteration of uncertainty sampling.

As soon as you have removed some unlabeled items from the pool via uncertainty sampling, that pool is no longer a random selection. That pool is now biased toward *confidently* predicted items, so a random selection from this pool is likely to return erroneously high accuracy if it is used as a test set.

Keep your test set separate throughout all iterations, and do not allow its items to be part of any sampling strategy. If you forget to do this until several iterations in, and your random sample includes items that were selected by uncertainty sampling, you will need to go back to the first iteration. You can't simply remove those test items from the training data going forward, as they were trained on and contributed to selections in the interim uncertainty sampling strategies.

It is also a good idea to see how well your uncertainty sampling technique is performing next to a baseline of random sampling. If you aren't more accurate than random sampling, you should reconsider your strategy! Choose randomly selected items for which you know the comparison will be statistically significant: often, a few hundred items are sufficient. Unlike the evaluation data for your entire model, these items can be added to your training data in the next iteration, as you are comparing the sampling strategy at each step, given what is remaining to be labeled.

Finally, you may want to include a random sample of items along with the ones chosen by uncertainty sampling. If you are not going to implement some of the diversity sampling methods in chapter 4, random sampling will give you the most basic form of diversity sampling and ensure that every data point has a chance of getting human review.

3.6.2   *Do I need new validation data?*

You should also consider up to four validation sets at each iteration, with data drawn from

- The same distribution as the test set
- The remaining unlabeled items in each iteration
- The same distribution as the newly sampled items in each iteration
- The same distribution as the total training set in each iteration

If you are tuning the parameters of your model after each addition of data, you will use a validation set to evaluate the accuracy. If you tune a model on the test set, you won't know whether your model has truly generalized or you have simply found a set of parameters that happen to work well with that specific evaluation data.

A validation set will let you tune the accuracy of the model without looking at the test set. Typically, you will have a validation set from the outset. As with your test set, you don't need to update/replace it if you think that the unlabeled items come from the same distribution as your initial training data. Otherwise, you should update your validation data before the first iteration of your uncertainty sampling, as with your test data.

You may want to use a second validation set to test how well your active learning strategy is doing within each iteration. After you start active learning iterations, the remaining unlabeled items will no longer be a random sample, so this distribution will not be the same as your existing test set and validation set. This dataset acts as a baseline for each iteration. Is uncertainty sampling still giving you better results than selecting from random among the remaining items? Because this dataset set is useful for only one iteration, it is fine to add these items to the training data at the end of each iteration; these labels aren't human labels that get discarded.

If you want to evaluate the accuracy of the human-labels created in each iteration, you should do this on a third validation data set drawn from the same distribution as the newly sampled data. Your newly sampled data may be inherently easier or harder for humans to label, so you need to evaluate human accuracy on that same distribution.

Finally, you should consider a fourth validation set drawn randomly from the training data at each iteration. This validation data can be used to ensure that the model is not overfitting the training data, which a lot of machine learning libraries will do by default. If your validation data and training data are not from the same distribution, it will be hard to estimate how much you are overfitting, so having a separate validation set to check for overfitting is a good idea.

The downside is the human-labeling cost for up to four validation data sets. In industry, I see people using the wrong validation dataset more often than not, typically letting one validation set be used in all cases. The most common reason is that people want to put as many labeled items as possible into their training data to make that model more accurate sooner. That's also the goal of active learning, of course, but without the right validation data, you won't know what strategic direction to take next to get to greater accuracy.

3.7 Uncertainty sampling cheat sheet

Our example data in this text has only two labels. Uncertainty sampling algorithms will return the same samples with two labels. Figure 3.10 shows an example of target areas for the different algorithms when there are three labels. The figure shows that margin of confidence and ratio sample some items that have only pairwise confusion, which reflects the fact that the algorithms target only the two most likely labels. By contrast, entropy maximizes for confusion among all labels, which is why the highest concentration is between all three labels.

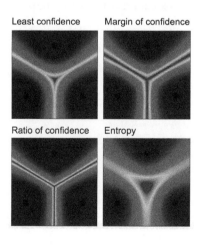

Figure 3.10 A heat map of the four main uncertainty sampling algorithms and the areas that they sample for a three-label problem. In this example, each dot is an item with a different label, and the heat of each pixel is the uncertainty. The hottest (most uncertain) pixels are the lightest pixels (the red pixels, if you're viewing in color). Top left is least confidence sampling, top right is margin of confidence sampling, bottom left is ratio sampling, and bottom right is entropy-based sampling. The main takeaway is that margin of confidence and ratio sample some items that have only pairwise confusion and entropy maximizes for confusion among all labels.

Notice that the difference between the methods becomes even more extreme with more labels. Figure 3.11 compares configurations to highlight the differences among the methods.

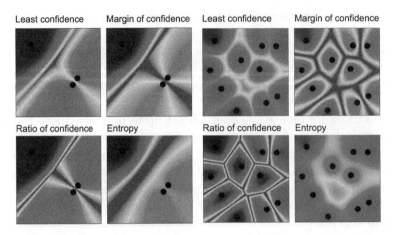

Figure 3.11   A comparison of methods. The four left images show that a lot of the uncertainty space for margin of confidence and ratio is between two of the labels, which is ignored entirely by entropy because it is not ambiguous for the third label. The four right images show that especially in more complicated tasks, the items that will be sampled by different uncertainty sampling algorithms will be different.[1]

TIP You can play around with interactive versions of figure 3.10 and figure 3.11 at http://robertmunro.com/uncertainty_sampling_example.html. The source code for the interactive example has implementations of the uncertainty sampling algorithms in JavaScript, but you're more likely to want the Python examples in the code repository associated with this chapter in PyTorch and in NumPy.

Figure 3.12 summarizes the four uncertainty sampling algorithms that you've implemented in this chapter.

---

[1] Thank you, Adrian Calma, for suggesting the left images as a great way to highlight the differences.

Uncertainty sampling cheat sheet

When a supervised machine learning model makes a prediction, it often gives a confidence in that prediction. If the model is uncertain (low confidence), human feedback can help. Getting human feedback when a model is uncertain is a type of *active learning* known as *uncertainty sampling*.

This cheat sheet has four common ways to calculate uncertainty, with examples, equations, and Python code.

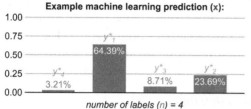

Example machine learning prediction (x):

The predictions are a probability distribution (x), meaning that every prediction is between 0 and 1 and the predictions add to 1. y^*_1 is the most confident, y^*_2 is the second-most-confident, and so on for n predicted labels.

This example can be expressed as a PyTorch tensor:
```
prob = torch.tensor ([0.0321, 0.6439, 0.0871,
0.2369]).
```

Least confidence: Difference between the most confident prediction and 100% confidence

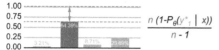

$$\frac{n\,(1-P_\theta(y^*_1 \mid x))}{n-1}$$

```
most_conf = torch.max(prob)
num_labels = prob.numel ()
numerator = (num_labels * (1 - most_conf))
denominator = (num_labels - 1)

least_conf = numerator/denominator
```

Margin of confidence: Difference between the two most confident predictions

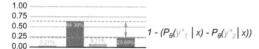

$$1 - (P_\theta(y^*_1 \mid x) - P_\theta(y^*_2 \mid x))$$

```
prob, _  = torch.sort (prob, descending=True)
difference = (prob.data [0] - prob.data[1])

margin_conf = 1 - difference
```

Ratio of confidence: Ratio between the two most confident predictions

$$\frac{P_\theta(y^*_2 \mid x)}{P_\theta(y^*_1 \mid x)}$$

```
prob, _  = torch.sort (prob, descending=True)

ratio_conf = (prob.data [1] / prob.data [0])
```

Entropy: Difference between all predictions, as defined by information theory

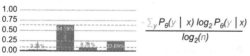

$$\frac{-\sum_y P_\theta(y \mid x) \log_2 P_\theta(y \mid x)}{\log_2(n)}$$

```
prbslogs  = prob * torch.log2 (prob)
numerator = 0 - torch.sum(prbslogs)
denominator = torch.log2(prob.numel ())

entropy = numerator / denominator
```

Robert (Munro) Monarch. *Human-in-the-Loop Machine Learning*, Manning Publications. http://bit.ly/huml_book See the book for more details on each method and for more sophisticated problems like sequence models and semantic segmentation, plus other sampling strategies like diversity sampling. robertmunro.com I @WWRob

Figure 3.12 Uncertainty sampling cheat sheet

3.8   *Further reading*

Uncertainty sampling has been around for a long time, and a lot of good literature has been written about it. For the most cutting-edge research on uncertainty sampling, look for recent papers that are frequently cited themselves.

Note that most of the papers do not normalize the scores to a [0, 1] range. If you're going to deploy your models for real-world situations, I highly recommend that you normalize the outputs. Even if normalizing the outputs won't change the accuracy, it will make spot checks easier and prevent problems with downstream processing, especially for advanced methods that you will learn in later chapters.

3.8.1   *Further reading for least confidence sampling*

A good early paper on least confidence is "Reducing labeling effort for structured prediction tasks," by Aron Culotta and Andrew McCallum (http://mng.bz/opYj).

3.8.2   *Further reading for margin of confidence sampling*

A good early paper on margin of confidence is "Active Hidden Markov Models for Information Extraction," by Tobias Scheffer, Christian Decomain, and Stefan Wrobel (http://mng.bz/nMO8).

3.8.3   *Further reading for ratio of confidence sampling*

I'm not aware of papers on ratio of confidence, although I've taught the subject in classes on active learning. The relationship between ratio and softmax base/temperature was new when it was presented in this book. As ratio of confidence is similar to margin of confidence, in that both look at the relationship between the two most confident predictions, the literature for margin of confidence should be mostly relevant.

3.8.4   *Further reading for entropy-based sampling*

A good early paper on entropy-based sampling is "Committee-Based Sampling For Training Probabilistic Classifiers," by Ido Dagan and Sean P. Engelson (http://mng.bz/vzWq).

3.8.5   *Further reading for other machine learning models*

A foundational paper for uncertainty sampling more generally is "A Sequential Algorithm for Training Text Classifiers," by David D. Lewis and William A. Gale (http://mng.bz/4ZQg). This paper uses a Bayesian classifier. If you look at highly cited texts from the following decade, you will find that SVMs and linear models are common. For the reasons mentioned in this chapter, I do not recommend that you try to implement uncertainty sampling with decision trees.

3.8.6   *Further reading for ensemble-based uncertainty sampling*

The Dagan and Engelson paper (section 3.8.4) covers the use case of multiple classifiers (Query by Committee), so it is a good starting point for ensemble models. For more recent work focused on neural models, including dropouts and Bayesian approaches to better uncertainty estimates, a good entry point is "Deep Bayesian Active Learning for Natural Language Processing: Results of a Large-Scale Empirical Study," by Zachary C. Lipton and Aditya Siddhant (http://mng.bz/Qmae).

You will see random dropouts called Monte Carlo dropouts and Bayesian (deep) active learning in academic literature. Regardless of the name, the strategy is still randomly selecting neurons/connections to ignore during prediction. The term *Monte Carlo* was a joke made by the physicist who invented the term. The term *Bayesian* comes from the fact that if you squint at the variation, it looks like a Gaussian distribution; it is not an actual Bayesian classifier. On the positive side of understanding the terminology, by passing one extra parameter to your model during prediction, you can impress your friends by telling them that you just implemented *Monte Carlo dropouts for Bayesian deep active learning*.

Summary

- Four common algorithms are used for uncertainty sampling: least confidence, margin of confidence, ratio of confidence, and entropy. These algorithms can help you understand the different kinds of "known unknowns" in your models.
- You can get different samples from each type of uncertainty sampling algorithm. Understanding why will help you decide which one is the best way to measure uncertainty in your models.
- Different types of scores are output by different supervised machine learning algorithms, including neural models, Bayesian models, SVMs, and decision trees. Understanding each score will help you interpret them for uncertainty.
- Ensemble methods and dropouts can be used to create multiple predictions for the same item. You can calculate uncertainty by looking at variation across the predictions from different models.
- There is a trade-off between getting more annotations within each active learning cycle and getting fewer annotations with more cycles. Understanding the trade-offs will let you pick the right number of cycles and size of each cycle when using uncertainty sampling.
- You may want to create different kinds of validation data to evaluate different parts of your system. Understanding the different types of validation data will let you choose the right one to tune each component.
- The right testing framework will help you calculate the accuracy of your system, ensuring that you are measuring performance increases correctly and not inadvertently biasing your data.

Diversity sampling

This chapter covers

- Using outlier detection to sample data that is unknown to your current model
- Using clustering to sample more diverse data before annotation starts
- Using representative sampling to target data most like where your model is deployed
- Improving real-world diversity with stratified sampling and active learning
- Using diversity sampling with different types of machine learning architectures
- Evaluating the success of diversity sampling

In chapter 3, you learned how to identify where your model is uncertain: what your model "knows it doesn't know." In this chapter, you will learn how to identify what's missing from your model: what your model "doesn't know that it doesn't know" or the "unknown unknowns." This problem is a hard one, made even harder because what your model needs to know is often a moving target in a constantly changing world. Just like humans are learning new words, new objects, and new behaviors every day in response to a changing environment, most machine learning algorithms are deployed in a changing environment.

For example, if we are using machine learning to classify or process human language, we typically expect the applications to adapt to new words and meanings, rather than remain stale and understand the language only up to one historical point in time. We'll explore a couple of use cases in speech recognition and computer vision in the upcoming chapters to illustrate the value of diversity sampling for different kinds of machine learning problems.

Imagine that your job is to build a voice assistant that can be successful for as many users as possible. Your company's leaders expect your machine learning algorithms to have much broader knowledge than any one human. A typical English speaker knows about 40,000 words of English's 200,000-word vocabulary, which is only 20% of the language, but your model should have closer to 100% coverage. You have a lot of unlabeled recordings that you can label, but some of the words that people use are rare. If you randomly sampled the recordings, you would miss the rare words. So you need to explicitly try to get training data covering as many different words as possible. You might also want to see what words are most commonly used when people speak to their voice assistants and sample more of those words.

You are also worried about demographic diversity. The recordings are predominantly from one gender and from people living in a small number of locations, so resulting models are likely to be more accurate for that gender and for only some accents. You want to sample as fairly as possible from different demographics to make the model equally accurate for all demographics.

Finally, many people don't speak English and would like a voice assistant, but you have little non-English data. You may have to be open and honest about this limitation in diversity.

This problem is harder than simply knowing when your model is confused, so the solutions for diversity sampling are themselves more algorithmically diverse than those for uncertainty sampling.

4.1 Knowing what you don't know: Identifying gaps in your model's knowledge

We explore four approaches to diversity sampling in this chapter:

- *Model-based outlier sampling*—Determining which items are unknown to the model in its current state (compared with uncertain, as in chapter 3). In our voice assistant example, model-based outlier sampling would help identify words that our voice assistant hasn't encountered before.
- *Cluster-based sampling*—Using statistical methods independent of your model to find a diverse selection of items to label. In our example, cluster-based sampling would help identify natural trends in the data so we can make sure that we don't miss any rare but meaningful trends.
- *Representative sampling*—Finding a sample of unlabeled items that look most like your target domain, compared with your training data. In our example, let's

imagine that people used your voice assistant mostly to request songs. Representative sampling, therefore, would target examples of song requests.

- *Sampling for real-world diversity*—Ensuring that a diverse range of real-world entities are in our training data to reduce real-world bias. In our example, this approach could include targeting recordings for as many accents, ages, and genders as possible.

As you learned in the book's introduction, the phrase *uncertainty sampling* is widely used in active learning, but *diversity sampling* goes by different names in different fields, often tackling only part of the problem. You may have seen diversity sampling referred to as stratified sampling, representative sampling, outlier detection, or anomaly detection. A lot of the time, the algorithms that we use for diversity sampling are borrowed from other use cases. Anomaly detection, for example, is primarily used for tasks such as identifying new phenomena in astronomical databases or detecting strange network activity for security.

So as not to confuse the non-active learning use cases and to provide consistency, we'll use the phrase *diversity sampling* in this text. This phrase intentionally invokes diversity in the sense of the demographics of people represented in the data. Although only the fourth kind of diversity sampling that we look at explicitly targets demographic diversity, the other three types correlate with real-world diversity. Chances are that your unlabeled data is biased toward the most privileged demographics: languages from the wealthiest nations, images from the wealthiest economies, videos created by the wealthiest individuals, and other biases that result from power imbalances. If you build models only on randomly sampled raw data, you could amplify that bias. Any method that increases the diversity of the items that you sample for active learning will likely increase the diversity of the people who can benefit from models built from that data.

Even if you are not worried about biases in demographics of people, you probably still want to overcome sample bias in your data. If you are processing images from agriculture and happen to have one type of crop overrepresented in your raw data, you probably want a sampling strategy that will rebalance the data to represent many types of crops. Also, there may be deeper biases related to people. If you have more examples of one type of crop, is that crop more common in wealthier countries, and do you have more photographs because tractors in wealthier countries are more likely to have cameras? Data bias and real-world bias tend to be closely related when we dig deep. Figure 4.1 repeats the example of diversity sampling that you saw in chapter 1.

For uncertainty sampling, you want to see only what is near your current decision boundary or what varies most across multiple predictions—a relatively small and well-defined feature space. For diversity sampling, you want to explore the much larger problem of every corner of the feature space and expand the decision boundary into new parts of that space. Needless to say, the set of algorithms that you can use are more diverse and sometimes more complicated than those used for uncertainty sampling.

You may not need to worry about every data point if you are looking only at academic datasets, but the problem of diversity is much more common in real-world

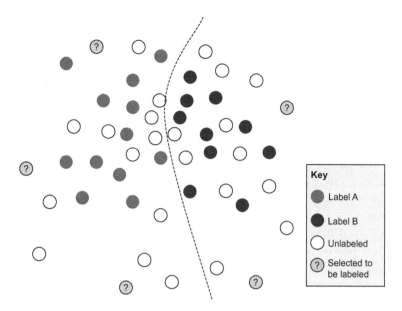

Figure 4.1 Diversity sampling, showing items selected to be labeled that are maximally different from the existing training items and from one another. You want to sample items that are not like the items that are currently in your training data and are also not like one another.

datasets. See the following sidebar for more information about the difference between real-world and academic datasets.

The difference between academic and real-world data labeling
Expert anecdote by Jia Li

It is much harder to deploy machine learning in the real world than for academic research, and the main difference is the data. Real-world data is messy and often hard to access due to institutional hurdles. It is fine to conduct research on clean, unchanging datasets, but when you take those models into the real world, it can be hard to predict how they will perform.

When I was helping to build ImageNet, we didn't have to worry about every possible image class that we might encounter in the real world. We could limit the data to images that were a subset of concepts in the WordNet hierarchy. In the real world, we don't have that luxury. For example, we can't collect large amounts of medical images related to rare diseases. Labeling of such images further requires domain expertise, which poses even more challenges. Real-world systems need both AI technologists and domain experts collaborating closely to inspire research, provide data and analysis, and develop algorithms to solve the problem.

Jia Li is CEO and co-founder of Dawnlight, a health-care company that uses machine learning. She previously led research divisions at Google, Snap, and Yahoo!, and has a PhD from Stanford.

4.1.1   *Example data for diversity sampling*

In this chapter, we will build on our example from chapter 2 with disaster response messages. Recall from chapter 2 that we wanted to label news headlines as disaster-related or not disaster-related. We implemented a basic outlier detection algorithm in that chapter, which we will now expand on with more sophisticated diversity sampling algorithms. The code is in the same library that you used for chapter 2: https://github .com/rmunro/pytorch_active_learning. The code that we will use in this chapter is in these two files: diversity_sampling.py and active_learning.py.

We will cover many types of diversity sampling strategies in this chapter. For our example data, you can imagine that a machine learning model could be useful for tracking disasters as they are being reported and to distinguish eyewitness reports from secondhand (or thirdhand) information. If you want to deploy this kind of system to track disasters in real time, you want as diverse a set of past training data items as possible. Only one or two news articles about floods might have been reported in your past training data, for example, which could easily have been missed if you chose items at random for humans to label.

You can also imagine new types of disasters, such as disease outbreaks that have a pattern of infection that hasn't been observed before. If people are talking about these new disasters in new ways, you want to ensure that you aren't missing these items and that the items get human labels as quickly as possible.

Finally, you might want to start incorporating new sources of data. If some of the new sources are US English instead of UK English, if they use different slang, or if they are not in English, your model will not be accurate on those new sources of information. You want to make sure that your model can adapt to these new data sources and their stylistic differences as quickly as possible, as it is adapting to new types of information in the text itself.

It is important to reduce bias at every step. If you use your model predictions to find more examples of floods, but your existing model only has data from floods in Australia, you might get more examples from floods in Australia for human review and from no other part of the world, so you would never get away from the initial bias in your model. For that reason, most diversity sampling algorithms are independent of the model we are using.

4.1.2   *Interpreting neural models for diversity sampling*

For some of the sampling strategies in this chapter, we will need new ways to interpret our models. If you access the raw outputs of a linear activation function in your final layer instead of the softmax output, you can more accurately separate true outliers from items that are the result of conflicting information. An activation function that also includes a negative range, like Leaky ReLU, is ideal; otherwise, you might end up with a lot of zeroed-out scores with no way to determine which is the biggest outlier.

You will learn how to access and interpret the different layers of a PyTorch model in section 4.1.3. But you may not have a say about the architecture of the activation function in the final layer. Softmax may the most accurate activation function for predicting labels precisely because it can ignore the absolute values of its inputs. In these cases, you may still be able to persuade your algorithms team to expose other layers for analysis.

What if I don't control my model architecture?

If you don't have a say on the architecture of the predictive algorithm, you might be able to convince your algorithms team to expose the logits or retrain only the final layer of the model with a Leaky ReLU activation function. Retraining the last layer of the model will be orders of magnitude faster than retraining an entire model. This approach should appeal to someone who is worried about the cost of retraining: they are supporting a new use case for not much extra work with a fun parallel architecture. If you are using Transformer models, the same concept applies, but you would train a new Attention head. (Don't worry if you are not familiar with Transformer models; they are not important for this chapter.)

If you encounter resistance to the idea of retraining the last layer, or if there are technical barriers, your next-best option is to use the second-to-last layer of the model. Regardless, it might be interesting to compare outlier sampling methods on different layers of the model to see what works best with your particular data and model architecture. These kinds of model analytics are some of the most exciting areas of machine learning research today and also allow for transfer learning, which is used in techniques in most of the upcoming chapters.

In this chapter, we will limit ourselves to simple but effective ways to interpret your model. The two scenarios in figure 4.2 interpret the last layer or the second-to-last layer.

The second method, using the second-to-last layer, work bests on deeper networks in which the second-to-last layer more closely resembles the last layer and there are fewer neurons in that layer. More neurons will introduce more random variability that can be more difficult to overcome, statistically.

Regardless of which architecture you use, you are left with a set (vector/tensor) of numbers representing a level of activation at/near the output of your predictive model. For simplicity, we'll refer to either vector as z even though z is typically reserved to mean only the logits from the last layer. We will also use n to indicate the size of that vector (the number of neurons), regardless of whether it happens to be the final layer and therefore also the number of labels or a middle layer.

Low activation means that this item is more likely to be an outlier. Mathematically, an outlier could be any unusual vector, atypically high or atypically low. But when we are interpreting model predictions to find outliers, we are concerned only with the low-activation items—the items that the model has little information about today.

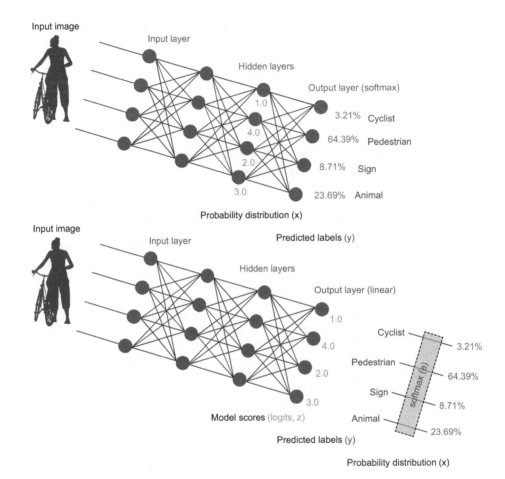

Figure 4.2 Two neural architectures and how you can interpret them for outlier detection. In the top example, you can use the model scores (known as *z* or *logits*), which retain their absolute values before they are normalized via softmax. In the bottom example, you have lost the absolute values in the final layer because of the softmax function, so you can use the activation in the second-to-last layer to determine whether an item is an outlier.

4.1.3 *Getting information from hidden layers in PyTorch*

To get the z values (logits) of the values from hidden layers in the model, we will need to modify our code so that we can access this information. Fortunately, the code is simple in PyTorch. First, as a reminder, here's the code from chapter 2 that you used for the feed-forward steps in training and for generating the confidences and label predictions in inference:

```
def forward(self, feature_vec):
    # Define how data is passed through the model

    hidden1 = self.linear1(feature_vec).clamp(min=0) # ReLU
    output = self.linear2(hidden1)
    return F.log_softmax(output, dim=1)
```

You can see that the middle layer and outputs are variables (`hidden1` and `output`) that hold the activation from each layer (PyTorch tensors in this case, which will be 1D arrays). So we can simply add a parameter to return all layers, modifying the code accordingly.

Listing 4.1 Allowing our model to return hidden layers in addition to softmax values

```
def forward(self, feature_vec, return_all_layers=False):
    # Define how data is passed through the model and what is returned

    hidden1 = self.linear1(feature_vec).clamp(min=0) # ReLU
    output = self.linear2(hidden1)
    log_softmax = F.log_softmax(output, dim=1)

    if return_all_layers:
        return [hidden1, output, log_softmax]
    else:
        return log_softmax
```

Same as the return function but pulled out into a variable → points to `log_softmax = F.log_softmax(output, dim=1)`

The only real new line, returning all the layers when return_all_layers=True → points to `return [hidden1, output, log_softmax]`

That's it! You'll see this modified code in active_learning.py. Now we can use any part of our model to find outliers within the model. Also, we have other ways to query our model's hidden layers.[1] I prefer encoding the option explicitly in the inference function, as with the `forward()` function. We are going to query our model in many ways in future chapters, and this approach makes the simplest code to build on.

Good coding practices for active learning

As a note on good coding practices, you may want to change the `return log_softmax` line in your `forward()` function to also return an array: `return [log_softmax]`. That way, your function is returning the same data type (an array) no matter what parameters are passed to it, which is a better software development practice. The downside is that it's not backward-compatible, so you'll have to change every piece of code that is calling the function. If you're an experienced PyTorch user, you may be accustomed to using a feature in the function that knows when it is in training mode or evaluation mode. This feature can be handy for some common machine learning strategies, such as masking neurons in training but not when predicting. But resist the temptation to use this feature here; it is bad software development in this context because global variables make unit tests harder to write and will make your code harder to read in isolation. Use named parameters like `return_all_layers=True/False`; you want to extend code in the most transparent way possible.

With the addition of code to access all layers of the model in inference, we can use that code to determine outliers. Recall that in chapter 2, you got the log probabilities from your model with this line:

```
log_probs = model(feature_vec)
```

---

[1] An alternative way to get hidden layers in PyTorch are the `hook()` methods. See the documentation at http://mng.bz/XdzM.

Now you can choose which layer of the model you want to use by calling the function with this line:

```
hidden, logits, log_probs = model(feature_vector, return_all_layers=True)
```

You have the hidden layer, the logits (z), and the log_probabilities of the model for your item.

Recall from chapter 3 and the appendix that our logits (scores from the last layer) lose their absolute values when converted to probability distributions via softmax. Figure 4.3 reproduces some of these examples from the expanded section on softmax in the appendix.

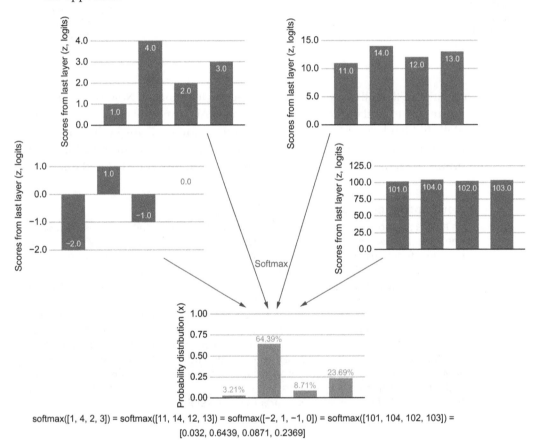

softmax([1, 4, 2, 3]) = softmax([11, 14, 12, 13]) = softmax([−2, 1, −1, 0]) = softmax([101, 104, 102, 103]) =
[0.032, 0.6439, 0.0871, 0.2369]

Figure 4.3   Four identical probability distributions that are derived from different inputs via softmax with base e

Our probability distributions, therefore, don't tell us the difference between uncertainty that derives from the lack of information (as in the left example in figure 4.3) and uncertainty due to conflicting but highly confident information (as in the right example in figure 4.3). So it is better to use the logits (scores from the last layer) to differentiate the two types of uncertainty.

Beyond uncertainty, we can find outliers that were certain but wrong. The most valuable unlabeled items to label are those that were incorrectly predicted and far from the decision boundary—that is, items that the current model is predicting confidently but incorrectly. Low activation across all neurons is often a good signal that there is not yet enough training data with the features found in that item.

4.2 *Model-based outlier sampling*

Now that we can interpret our model, we can query our model to find outliers. A *model outlier* in a neural model is defined as the item with the lowest activation in a given layer. For our final layer, this activation is the logits.

The biggest barrier to choosing the right metric for determining an outlier is knowing the distribution of values from your neurons. You were taught in high school that any data point greater than three standard deviations from the mean is an outlier, but this is true only for normal distributions. Unfortunately, your linear activation functions are not creating normal distributions: they should be bimodally distributed if they are modeling your task accurately. If you've investigated models in the past, you'll also know that some of the neurons might be modeling noise or simple passing through values and can vary even when you train a model twice on identical data. Furthermore, unless you have a simple architecture, you will have different activation functions for different parts of your network, so they will not be directly comparable.

Just like we couldn't trust the absolute values for confidence for uncertainty sampling, we can't trust the absolute values of our neurons to determine outliers. But just like we could trust the ranked order confidence to find the most uncertain predictions, we can trust the ranked order of neuron activation to find the least activated. Rank order is a robust method that lets us avoid determining the actual distribution of activation in every neuron.

Here's a simple example of ranked order for determining how much of an outlier some item is. Let's assume that we have made predictions for 10 items and that these predictions were the result from a neuron, ordered (ranked) from largest to smallest:

```
[2.43, 2.23, 1.74, 1.12, 0.89, 0.44, 0.23, -0.34, -0.36, -0.42]
```

The item with an activation of –0.36 (underlined) is the ninth-lowest of the 10 items, so we can give it an outlier score of $9/10 = 0.9$. At either end of the scale, an item with –0.42 activation would have a score of 1.0, and an item with 2.43 activation would have a score of 0. So we can convert this ranked order of activation for each neuron into a scale. The question, then, is what data to use to generate the ranking.

4.2.1 *Use validation data to rank activations*

We can't use the training data for our rankings, because the model has trained on that data and some neurons will have overfit that data more than others, so we have to use data from the same distribution as our training data. That is, we have to use a validation data set drawn from the same distribution as our training data. This is not a big difference from an implementation point of view: we simply calculate the rankings on the validation data and then use that ranking to get the outlier score on our unlabeled data, as you'll see in this section.

The main difference is that we will get values from the unlabeled data that are between two values in the rankings. We can use simple linear interpolation to calculate these values. Suppose that our validation data consists of only 10 items, which happen to be the same as in section 4.2:

```
[2.43, 2.23, 1.74, 1.12, 0.89, 0.44, 0.23, -0.34, (-0.35) -0.36, -0.42]
```

Now imagine an unlabeled item with a value of –0.35 (above where it would fall in the ranking). That value is halfway between the eighth- and ninth-lowest items, so we can give the item an outlier score of 8.5/10 = 85%. Similarly, if the unlabeled item has a value of –0.355, which is three-quarters of the distance between the eighth and ninth item, the score would be 87.5%. We treat values above the first item as 1 and values below the last item as 0, giving us a [0–1] range in which the biggest outlier has a value of 100%.

There are different ways to combine the scores across the neurons for each item. It is statistically safest to take the average activation across all the neurons for each item. Especially if you are using activation from one of the hidden layers, you may have some neurons that are essentially spitting out random values and therefore generating a falsely high maximum for what would otherwise be an outlier. Your logits are more likely to be reliable for every value, so you could experiment with the equivalent of least confidence for logits: the lowest maximum score across all neurons. To see the results of model-based outlier sampling, run

```
> python active_learning.py --model_outliers=95
```

As in chapter 2, the code will choose this sampling strategy and select 95 unlabeled items for you to annotate, along with 5 randomly selected items from remaining unlabeled items. As in chapter 2, you always want to include a small number of random items as a safety net. If you don't want to evaluate any random items, you can add a random=0 option:

```
> python active_learning.py --model_outliers=95 --random_remaining=0
```

You can play around with other numbers to see and/or annotate more or less than 95, too. If you skipped chapter 2, you will first be asked to annotate a purely random sample until you have enough initial training and test options. This time spent annotating will be important for evaluating accuracy and understanding the data, so please do these annotations now if you didn't previously!

The code for calculating the rank model outlier score is broken into four chunks of code. The model outlier function takes the current model, the unlabeled data, and held-out validation data taken from the same distribution as the training data. First, we

create the rankings on our held-out validation data, which you can see within diversity_
sampling.py.

Listing 4.2   Get activation rankings using validation data

```
def get_validation_rankings(self, model, validation_data, feature_method):
    """Get activation rankings using validation data

    Keyword arguments:
        model -- current machine learning model for this task
        validation_data -- held out data drawn from the same distribution as
        ➥ the training data
        feature_method -- the method to create features from the raw text

    An outlier is defined as
    unlabeled_data with the lowest average from rank order of logits
    where rank order is defined by validation data inference

    """


    validation_rankings = [] # 2D array, every neuron by ordered list of
    ➥ output on validation data per neuron

    # Get per-neuron scores from validation data
    if self.verbose:
        print("Getting neuron activation scores from validation data")

    with torch.no_grad():
        v=0
        for item in validation_data:
            textid = item[0]
            text = item[1]

            feature_vector = feature_method(text)
            hidden, logits, log_probs = model(feature_vector,
            ➥ return_all_layers=True)

            neuron_outputs = logits.data.tolist()[0] #logits

            # initialize array if we haven't yet
            if len(validation_rankings) == 0:
                for output in neuron_outputs:
                    validation_rankings.append([0.0] * len(validation_data))

            n=0
            for output in neuron_outputs:
                validation_rankings[n][v] = output
                n += 1

            v += 1

    # Rank-order the validation scores
    v=0
    for validation in validation_rankings:
```

We get the results from all model layers here.

We store the logit score for each validation item and each neuron.

```
        validation.sort()
        validation_rankings[v] = validation
        v += 1
```

Rank-order each neuron
according the scores from
the held-out validation data.

```
    return validation_rankings
```

In the second step, we order each unlabeled data item according to each neuron.

Listing 4.3   Code for model-based outliers in PyTorch

```
def get_model_outliers(self, model, unlabeled_data, validation_data,
➥ feature_method, number=5, limit=10000):
    """Get model outliers from unlabeled data

    Keyword arguments:
        model -- current machine learning model for this task
        unlabeled_data -- data that does not yet have a label
        validation_data -- held out data drawn from the same distribution
        ➥ as the training data
        feature_method -- the method to create features from the raw text
        number -- number of items to sample
        limit -- sample from only this many items for faster sampling
        ➥ (-1 = no limit)

    An outlier is defined as
    unlabeled_data with the lowest average from rank order of logits
    where rank order is defined by validation data inference

    """

    # Get per-neuron scores from validation data
    validation_rankings = self.get_validation_rankings(model,
    ➥ validation_data, feature_method)

    # Iterate over unlabeled items
    if self.verbose:
        print("Getting rankings for unlabeled data")

    outliers = []
    if limit == -1 and len(unlabeled_data) > 10000 and self.verbose:
        # we're drawing from *a lot* of data this will take a while
        print("Get rankings for a large amount of unlabeled data: this
        ➥ might take a while")
    else:
        # only apply the model to a limited number of items
        shuffle(unlabeled_data)
        unlabeled_data = unlabeled_data[:limit]

    with torch.no_grad():
        for item in unlabeled_data:
            text = item[1]

            feature_vector = feature_method(text)
```

Call to get the activation
on validation data.

```
                        hidden, logits, log_probs = model(feature_vector,
                        ➥ return_all_layers=True)
```

We get the results from all model layers here.

```
                        neuron_outputs = logits.data.tolist()[0] #logits

                        n=0
                        ranks = []
                        for output in neuron_outputs:
                            rank = self.get_rank(output, validation_rankings[n])
                            ranks.append(rank)
                            n += 1
```

We get the rank order for each unlabeled item.

```
                        item[3] = "logit_rank_outlier"

                        item[4] = 1 - (sum(ranks) / len(neuron_outputs)) # average
                        ➥ rank

                        outliers.append(item)

                    outliers.sort(reverse=True, key=lambda x: x[4])
                    return outliers[:number:]
```

The ranking function takes the activation value for one unlabeled item for one neuron and the rankings for that neuron that were calculated on the validation data. Use the following code for ordering each unlabeled item according to the validation rankings.

Listing 4.4 Return the rank order of an item in terms of validation activation

```
    def get_rank(self, value, rankings):
        """ get the rank of the value in an ordered array as a percentage

        Keyword arguments:
            value -- the value for which we want to return the ranked value
            rankings -- the ordered array in which to determine the value's
            ➥ ranking

        returns linear distance between the indexes where value occurs, in the
        case that there is not an exact match with the ranked values
        """

        index = 0 # default: ranking = 0

        for ranked_number in rankings:
            if value < ranked_number:
                break #NB: this O(N) loop could be optimized to O(log(N))
            index += 1

        if(index >= len(rankings)):
            index = len(rankings) # maximum: ranking = 1

        elif(index > 0):
            # get linear interpolation between the two closest indexes
```

```
        diff = rankings[index] - rankings[index - 1]
        perc = value - rankings[index - 1]
        linear = perc / diff
        index = float(index - 1) + linear

    absolute_ranking = index / len(rankings)

    return(absolute_ranking)
```

This listing is simply the implementation of the ranked-ordering example. Don't worry too much about the linear interpolation part; the code is a little opaque when implemented, but it is not capturing anything more complicated than you saw in the examples.

4.2.2   *Which layers should I use to calculate model-based outliers?*

You may want to try outlier detection on different layers of your model to see whether they produce better outliers for sampling. In general, the earlier the layer, the closer the neurons will be to the raw data. If you chose the input layer from the model, which is the feature vector, outliers from the input layer are almost identical to the outlier detection method that you implemented in chapter 2. Any hidden layer is going to fall somewhere between representing the raw data (early layers) and representing the predictive task (later layers).

You could also choose to look at multiple layers within the same sample. This approach is used in transfer learning with pretrained models; the model is "flattened" to create one single vector combining all the layers. You could use a flattened model for outlier detection too, but you may want to normalize by the amount of neurons per layer. In our model, the 128 neurons in the hidden layer would become the main contributor to an outlier detection algorithm that also included the 2 neurons from the final layer, so you might want to calculate the outlier ranking for the layers independently and then combine the two results.

Alternatively, you could sample from both, taking half your model-outliers from the logits and half from the hidden layer. Note that the 128 neurons in the hidden layer probably aren't too informative if you still have only 1,000 or so training items. You should expect the hidden layers to be noisy and some neurons to be random until you have many more labeled training items than neurons in your hidden layer—ideally, two or more orders of magnitude more training items than neurons in the layer (more than 10,000 labeled items).

If you are using layers near the input, be careful when your feature values don't represent activation. For our text example, the inputs *do* represent a form of activation, because they represent how often a word occurs. For computer vision, however, a higher input value may simply represent a lighter RGB color. In these cases, the layers toward the output of the model and the logits will be more reliable.

4.2.3 *The limitations of model-based outliers*

Here is a summary of the main shortcomings of using your model for sampling outliers:

- The method can generate outliers that are similar and therefore lack diversity within an active learning iteration.
- It's hard to escape some statistical biases that are inherent in your model, so you may continually miss some types of outliers.
- You still need a model in place before you start, and this approach gets better with more training data, so model-based outlier sampling is not suited to a cold start.
- We are determining an outlier by using our unlabeled data. It is easy to accidentally sample the opposite of what we want—things that look least like the data that we are trying to adapt to with new labels. For this reason, we use validation data to get our rankings, and you should follow this practice for any other kind of model-based outlier detection.

We will cover some solutions to the first issue in chapter 5, with algorithms that combine outlier detection and transfer learning. The second, third, and fourth issues are harder to overcome. Therefore, if you are sampling model-based outliers, you should consider using other methods of diversity sampling at the same time, including the methods that you can use from a cold start, such as clustering, which we cover next.

4.3 *Cluster-based sampling*

Clustering can help you target a diverse selection of data from the start. The strategy is fairly straightforward: instead of sampling training data randomly to begin with, we also divide our data into a large number of clusters and sample evenly from each cluster.

The reason why this works should be equally straightforward. By now, you have probably noticed that there are tens of thousands of news articles about local Australian sports teams in the headlines. If we randomly sample the data for human review, we are going to spend a lot of time manually annotating similar headlines about the results of sporting matches. If we precluster our data, however, these headlines are likely to end up together in one cluster, so we will need to annotate only a handful of examples from this sports-related cluster. This approach will save a lot of time, which we can instead spend annotating data from other clusters. Those other clusters may represent rarer types of headlines that are important but so rare that they would have been missed with random sampling. So clustering is saving time and increasing diversity.

Clustering is by far the most common method used for diversity sampling in real-world machine learning. It is the second method discussed in this chapter because it fit the flow of the book better. In practice, you will probably try this method of diversity sampling first.

You have probably encountered unsupervised learning, and you're most likely familiar with k-means, the clustering algorithm that we will be using. The approaches to unsupervised clustering and clustering for active learning are the same, but we will

be using the clusters to sample items for human review for labeling instead of interpreting the clusters or using the clusters themselves in downstream processing.

4.3.1   *Cluster members, centroids, and outliers*

The item that is closest to the center of a cluster is known as the *centroid*. In fact, some
clustering algorithms explicitly measure the distance from the centroid item rather
them from the cluster properties as a whole.

   You calculated outliers from the entire dataset in chapter 2, and you can also calculate outliers when using clustering. Outliers are the statistical counterpoint of the centroid: they are farthest from the center of any cluster.

   Figure 4.4 shows an example with five clusters, with a centroid and outlier for two
of the clusters indicated. The majority of items in figure 4.4 are in one cluster: the
large one in the middle. So if we sampled randomly instead of by clustering, we would
end up spending most of the time labeling similar items. By clustering first and sampling from each cluster, we can ensure more diversity.

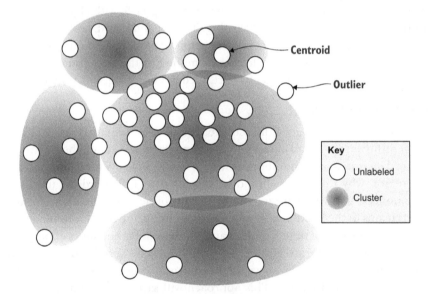

**Figure 4.4   An example clustering algorithm applied to the data, splitting it into five
separate clusters. For each cluster, the most central item is known as the *centroid*,
and the items farthest from the centers are *outliers*.**

We will sample from clusters in three ways:

- *Random*—Sampling items at random from each cluster. This strategy is close to
  random sampling but will spread out our selection across our feature space
  more evenly than purely random sampling.
- *Centroids*—Sampling the centroids of clusters to represent the core of significant trends within our data.

- *Outliers*—Sampling the outliers from our clustering algorithm to find potentially interesting data that might have been missed in the clusters. Outliers within clustering are sometimes known as *proximity-based* outliers.

Within a single cluster, the ranked centroids are likely to be similar. That is, the item that is the closest to the center is likely to be similar to that item that is second-closest to the center. So we sample randomly within the cluster or chose only the centroid.

Similarly, we probably need to sample only a small number of outliers per cluster. It's possible that the outliers are meaningful trends that the algorithm is missing, but it is more likely that they are genuinely rare: repeated rare words in the case of text or noisy/corrupted images in the case of computer vision. Typically, you need to sample only a small number of outliers, perhaps only one outlier from each cluster if you have a large number of clusters.

To keep the example simple, assume that we are sampling the centroid of each cluster, the single biggest outlier from each cluster, and three additional randomly sampled items within each cluster. To use cluster-based sampling, run

```
> python active_learning.py --cluster_based=95 --verbose
```

This command samples 95 unlabeled items via cluster-based sampling for you to annotate, along with 5 randomly selected items from remaining unlabeled items. I recommend running the code with the `verbose` flag, which prints three random items from each cluster as the code runs. You can get an idea of how well the clusters are capturing meaningful differences by examining whether the items in the cluster seem to be semantically related. In turn, this approach will give you an idea of how many meaningful trends in the data are being surfaced for human annotation.

4.3.2 Any clustering algorithm in the universe

As far as I know, no one has studied in depth whether one clustering algorithm is consistently better than another for active learning. Many pairwise studies look at variations on particular clustering algorithms, but no comprehensive broad study exists, so if you are interested in this topic, this situation would make a great research study.

Some clustering algorithms need only a single pass over the data, and some can be $O(N^3)$ complexity or worse. Although the more compute-intensive algorithms reach more mathematically well-motivated clusters within your data, the distribution of information across clusters won't necessarily be any better or worse for sampling items that need to be labeled.

For the system we will implement here, we don't want to make the people using the system wait a long time for the clustering algorithm to find the best clusters, so we'll choose an efficient clustering algorithm. We are going to use a variation of k-means that uses cosine similarity as the distance measure rather than the more typical Euclidean distance (figure 4.5). We have high-dimensional data, and Euclidean distance doesn't work well in high dimensions. One way to think about this problem is to think

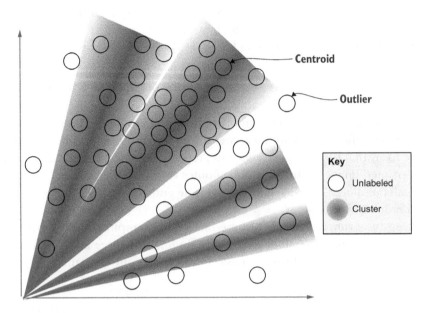

Figure 4.5   An example clustering algorithm using cosine similarity. For each cluster, the center is defined as a vector from 0, and the membership of that cluster is the angle between the vector representing the cluster and the vector representing the item. Note that although this example looks less like real clusters than the spheroidal clusters in figure 4.4, it is limited by being 2D. For higher-dimensional sparse data, which you are more likely to be using with your models, this kind of clustering is often better than the spheroid type shown here.

of many corners in your data. Almost all clustering algorithms are prone to producing unreliable results with high-dimensional data. In figure 4.4, we have examples in two dimensions and only four corners where outliers can hide from the center of the data distributions. If we had features in three dimensions, outliers could occupy eight corners. (Think of the eight corners of a cube.) By the time we get to 300 features, the data has 10^90 corners, and 10^90 is more than the number of atoms in the observable universe. You will certainly have more than 300 features in almost any natural language processing (NLP) task, so outliers can occur in a lot of corners of the space. For data with more than 10 dimensions, more than 99% of the space is in the corners, so if the data is uniformly distributed or even a Gaussian distribution, you will be measuring an artifact of the corners more than the distance, which can be unreliable.

You can think of cosine similarity in terms of looking at stars in the night sky. If you drew a straight line from yourself toward two stars and measured the angle between those lines, that angle would give you the cosine similarity. In the night-sky example, you have only three physical dimensions, but your data has one dimension for each feature. Cosine similarity is not immune to the problems of high dimensionality, but it tends to perform better than Euclidean distance especially for sparse data, such as our text encodings.

Cosine similarity measures whether two vectors are pointing in the same direction but does not measure the distance. There might be a small angle between two stars in the sky, but one happens to be much farther away. Because you are measuring only the angle, you are treating the stars as being equally far away. For this reason, cosine similarity is sometimes called *spherical k-means,* with all data points treated as though they were the same distance from 0 on a multidimensional sphere. This example does bring up an issue: data points can accidentally be in the same direction and therefore erroneously seem to be similar. The chance that this issue will occur in high-dimensional data is low, however, so high dimensions help (and make our calculations simpler). We can calculate a cluster's vector as the sum of all the vectors (features) of the items in that cluster and not worry about normalizing by the number of items, because cosine is not sensitive to the absolute values of the distance function.

4.3.3 *K-means clustering with cosine similarity*

Given two feature-vectors of the same size, v_1 and v_2, you can calculate the cosine of the angle between those vectors as

$$\phi_{CS}(v_1, v_2) = (v_1 \cdot v_2)/(\|v_1\|_2 \cdot \|v_2\|_2)$$

Cosine similarity is a native function in PyTorch, so we won't go too deeply into the implementation here. The double-line notation indicates the norm of the vector. The intuition of angles between stars in the night sky and the example in figure 4.5 (section 4.3.2) should be enough for you to understand what is going on. (If you are interested in reading more about cosine similarity or looking at other distance functions in PyTorch, you can start with the documentation at http://mng.bz/XdzM.)

Other popular machine learning libraries also have a lot of implementations of clustering algorithms. These other algorithms could work as well as the example that you are implementing here. There is a commonly held belief that clustering algorithms shouldn't be used for datasets with more than 10,000 items, but it isn't true. There have always been clustering algorithms that work reasonably well with a single pass of the data, so you shouldn't think of any limitation according to dataset size unless you are trying to trim your processing time to a few seconds. Even with compute-intensive clustering algorithms, you can often build the clusters in smaller subsets (batches) of the data to build clusters, and using the resulting clusters will be almost as good as using the entire dataset.

The general strategy for k-means is as follows:

1 Select the number of clusters you want by working backward from the number of annotations that you need.
2 Randomly add the data items to one of the initial clusters.
3 Iterate through the items and move them to another cluster if they are closer to that cluster.
4 Repeat step 3 until there are no more items to move or you have reached some predefined limit on the number of epochs through the data.

> ## Cosine similarity and cosine distance are the same thing
> You might see cosine similarity referred to as *cosine distance* in the literature. These terms mean the same thing. In general, clustering algorithms are more likely to use the term *distance* than *similarity*, and in the strictest definitions, distance = 1 – similarity. Cosine similarity does not follow the strict definition of the triangle inequality property (Schwarz inequality), however, so cosine similarity does not meet the formal definition of a distance metric—hence the name *similarity*. The terminology is confusing enough in this chapter when we are treating centroids and outliers as complements to get our [0, 1] range for every sampled item, so don't let this add to your confusion!

As noted in step 1, you should work backward and choose the number of clusters that makes the most sense given how many items you want to sample from each cluster. If you want to sample 5 items per cluster (1 centroid, 1 outlier, and 3 randomly chosen), and you want to annotate 100 items in this active learning iteration through this sampling strategy, you would select 20 clusters, as $20 \times 5 = 100$.

For completeness, the full code for k-means clustering with cosine similarity was implemented in the example code for this book, and you can see it at http://mng .bz/MXQm. This k-means strategy is the same regardless of the distance measure. The k-means function takes only two arguments: the data, which can be unlabeled or labeled (in which case the labels are ignored), and the number of clusters you want. You can see the k-means strategy in diversity_sampling.py with the main function in the following listing.

Listing 4.5   Cluster-based sampling in PyTorch

```
def get_cluster_samples(self, data, num_clusters=5, max_epochs=5,
    limit=5000):
    """Create clusters using cosine similarity

    Keyword arguments:
        data -- data to be clustered
        num_clusters -- the number of clusters to create
        max_epochs -- maximum number of epochs to create clusters
        limit -- sample only this many items for faster clustering (-1 = no
            limit)

    Creates clusters by the k-means clustering algorithm,
    using cosine similarity instead of more common euclidean distance

    Creates clusters until converged or max_epochs passes over the data

    """

    if limit > 0:
        shuffle(data)
        data = data[:limit]
```

```
cosine_clusters = CosineClusters(num_clusters)

cosine_clusters.add_random_training_items(data)

for i in range(0, max_epochs):
    print("Epoch "+str(i))
    added = cosine_clusters.add_items_to_best_cluster(data)
    if added == 0:
        break

    centroids = cosine_clusters.get_centroids()
    outliers = cosine_clusters.get_outliers()
    randoms = cosine_clusters.get_randoms(3, verbose)

    return centroids + outliers + randoms
```

Initialize clusters with random assignments.

Move each item to the cluster that it is the best fit for, and repeat.

Sample the biggest outlier in each cluster.

Sample the best-fit (centroid) from each cluster.

Sample three random items from each cluster, and pass the verbose parameter to get an idea of what is in each cluster.

You could substitute cosine for any other distance/similarity measure, and it might work equally well. One tactic that you may want to try to speed the process is to create the clusters on a subset of the data and then assign the rest of the data to its clusters. That approach gives you the best of both worlds: creating clusters quickly and sampling from the entire dataset. You may also want to experiment with a different number of clusters and a different number of random selections per cluster.

You'll remember from high school mathematics that $\cosine(90°) = 0$ and $\cosine(0°) = 1$. This makes our goal of a $[0,1]$ range easy, because cosine similarity already returns values in a $[0,1]$ range when calculated only on positive feature values. For our centroids, we can take the cosine similarity directly as our diversity score for each item. For the outliers, we will subtract the values from 1 so that we are consistent in our active learning ranking strategies and always sampling the highest numbers. As we said in chapter 3, consistency is important for downstream tasks.

4.3.4 *Reduced feature dimensions via embeddings or PCA*

Clustering works better for text than for images. If you come from a computer vision background, you know this already. When you looked at the clusters in your examples in this chapter, you could see semantic relationships between items in each cluster. All the clusters contain news headlines with similar topics, for example. But the same wouldn't be true if cosine similarity were applied to images, because individual pixels are more abstracted from the content of the images than sequences of characters are from the content of the text. If you applied cosine similarity to images, you might get a cluster of images that are landscapes, but that cluster might also erroneously include an image of a green car in front of a blue wall.

The most common method for reducing the dimensionality of data is principal component analysis (PCA). PCA reduces the dimensionality of a dataset by combining highly-correlated features. If you have been doing machine learning for some time, you probably thought that PCA was your first option to reduce the dimensionality of the data. PCA was common for early non-neural machine learning algorithms that degraded in quality more when there was a high number of dimensions (features) with correlations between features. Neural model-based embeddings are more common in academia today, but PCA is more common in industry.

Implementing PCA is outside the scope of this book. It's a good technique to know in machine learning regardless, so I recommend reading more about it so that you have several tools for dimensionality reduction. PCA is not a native function in PyTorch (although I would not be surprised if it were added fairly soon), but the core operation of PCA is singular value decomposition (SVD), which is covered at https://pytorch.org/docs/stable/torch.html#torch.svd.

As an alternative to PCA, you can use embeddings from your model—that is, use the hidden layers of your model or from another model that has been trained on other data. You can use these layers as representations for modeling directly. Alternatively, you can use model distillation to lower the dimensionality within the clustering process, as follows:

1 Select the number of clusters you want.
2 Cluster the items according to your existing (high-dimensional) feature space.
3 Treat each cluster as a label, and build a model to classify items into each cluster.
4 Using the hidden layer from your new middle as your new feature set, continue the process of reassigning items to the best cluster.

Model design is important here. For text data, your architecture from section 4.2 is probably enough: a single hidden layer with 128 neurons. For image data, you probably want to have more layers and to use a convolutional neural network (CNN) or a similar network to help generalize away from specific pixel locations. In either case, use your intuition from building models for the amount of data you have and the chosen number of clusters (labels).

Note that if you have negative values in your vector, as you would if you are clustering on a hidden layer with LeakyReLU as the activation function, cosine similarity will return values in a [–1,1] range instead of a [0,1] range. For consistency, therefore, you would want to normalize by adding 1 and halving the result of cosine similarity to get a [0,1] range.

For a denser feature vector, whether from a model or from PCA, you might also consider a distance function other than cosine. Cosine similarity is best for large, sparse vectors, such as our word representations. You may not want to treat activations of [0.1, 0.1] the same as activations of [10.1,10.1], as cosine similarity does. PyTorch also has a built-in distance function for pairwise distance, which might be more appropriate in that case. You can see this function commented out where the cosine function now exists in the pytorch_clusters.py file. You can experiment with different distance functions to see whether you get more meaningful clusters. As the code says, you may need to normalize your cluster vectors according to the number of items in that cluster; otherwise, you should be able to sub in other distance functions without making other changes to the code.

As one final point on advanced clustering for computer vision, if you are clustering for diversity sampling, it may not matter if the clusters aren't semantically meaningful. From a sampling point of view, you might get good diversity of images from across your clusters even if the clusters themselves aren't semantically consistent. That is, you might be able to ignore embeddings and PCA, and cluster directly on the pixel values. This approach might give you equal success. Cosine similarity will create identical vectors for RGB = (50,100,100) and RGB = (100,200,200), so lighter, more saturated versions of the same image may be identical, but this may not matter. I'm not aware of any in-depth research on whether pixel-level clustering for images is always worse than using a reduced dimension when sampling for active learning, so this research topic would be a valuable topic for anyone who's interested in pursuing it.

4.3.5 *Other clustering algorithms*

In addition to other variations of k-means, you may want to experiment with other clustering algorithms and related unsupervised machine learning algorithms. It is beyond the scope of this book to talk about every popular clustering algorithm; many good books have been written on clustering. In this book, however, we will take a high-level look at three algorithms:

- Proximity-based clustering, such as k-nearest neighbors (KNN) and spectral clustering
- Gaussian mixture models (GMM)
- Topic modeling

You are probably familiar with KNN algorithms. KNN forms clusters based on proximity between a small number of items in that cluster (k items, instead of that cluster as a whole. A strength and limitation of k-means is that all clusters have a meaningful center: the mean itself. You can imagine L-shape clusters or other patterns that have no meaningful center; KNN allows you to capture these kinds of clusters. The same is true of spectral clustering, which is a vector-based clustering method that can also discover more complicated cluster shapes by representing the feature space in new vectors.

There is no clear evidence, however, that proximity-based clustering is consistently better than k-means clustering for active learning. You may want to capture data points separately at two different extremes in an L-shape because they are sufficiently different even if there is an unbroken link of items between them. Furthermore, your k-means algorithms will be discovering different kinds of shapes in your features if you build your clusters on hidden layers or PCA-derived vectors, as you learned earlier. Your k-means algorithm will discover simple spheroid clusters only in the vectors that it learns from, but if those vectors are abstracted from a greater number of features, your clusters would be more complicated if they are mapped back into those features. In fact, applying k-means to a vector from a hidden layer is similar using spectral clustering to discover different cluster shapes. So there is no clear advantage for spectral clustering for active learning—at least, no one has yet researched this topic in depth, to the point that one method is clearly better in most active learning use cases.

A GMM allows an item to be a member of multiple clusters at the same time. This algorithm can lead to more mathematically well-motivated clusters compared with k-means, which tries to force a cluster boundary where two clusters naturally overlap. You may see GMMs and related algorithms referred to as soft versus hard clustering or as fuzzy clustering. As with proximity-based clustering, there's no strong evidence that GMMs produce better samples for active learning than k-means. Early in my career, I worked with mixture models and active learning at the same time but never combined the two; I never felt that other active learning techniques fell short in a way that needed GMMs or similar algorithms to overcome them. So from practical experience, I can report that I never found it necessary to try to combine the two, but I haven't tested GMMs for active learning in depth either. This topic is another potentially exciting research area.

Topic modeling is used almost exclusively for text. Topic models explicitly discover sets of related words in a topic and the distributions of those topics across documents. The most popular algorithm is Latent Dirichlet Allocation (LDA), and you might see topic modeling referred to as LDA in the literature. Unlike GMMs, topic modeling is used a lot in practice, and it is especially common in social media monitoring tools. The related words in a single topic are often semantically related, so an expert user can generate topics and then select the most interesting ones for further analysis. This approach is a form of light supervision, an important human-in-the-loop strategy that we will return to in chapter 9. Within diversity sampling, you could generate clusters as topics and sample items from each topic as you would with any other clustering mechanism.

Although any clustering algorithm may not be *better* than k-means for modeling the data, it will be *different*, which will increase diversity. So if you have multiple clustering algorithms producing samples for active learning, you are less likely to have biases resulting from the mathematical assumptions of any one clustering method. If you're already using clustering algorithms on your data for some other reason, try them out as a sampling strategy.

4.4   Representative sampling

Representative sampling refers to explicitly calculating the difference between the training data and the application domain where we are deploying the model. In the model-based outliers and cluster-based sampling methods, we did not explicitly try to model the gap between our model and the data where we are evaluating our model's accuracy. So the natural next step is to try to find items that fit this profile: what unlabeled data looks most like the domain where we are deploying our model? This step can be as useful for you as a data scientist as it is for your model: learning what data looks most like where you are adapting it will give you good intuition about that dataset as a whole and the problems you might face. An example is shown in figure 4.6.

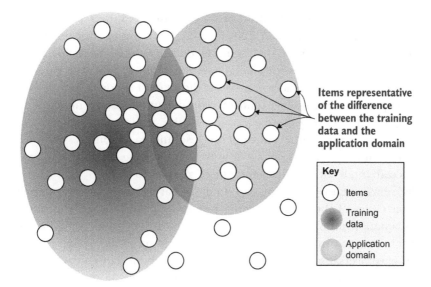

Figure 4.6 An example of representative sampling, showing that the current training data is from a different distribution of the data from the application domain. Representative sampling maximizes sampling of items that look the most like the application domain relative to the current training data.

4.4.1 *Representative sampling is rarely used in isolation*

It would be understandable if you assumed that representative sampling is the best method for active learning. If we can sample data that looks the most like where we want to deploy our models, doesn't this solve most of our diversity problems? While the general intuition is correct and representative sampling is one of the most powerful active learning strategies, it also one of the most prone to errors and overfitting. So, we will cover some of the limitations before jumping into the implementation.

For one thing, in most real-world scenarios, your unlabeled data is not from the domain where you will deploy your model. If you are deploying a model to identify future news headlines (as in our example) or to help autonomous vehicles navigate on the road at some point in the future, you do not have a sample of data from your target domain; you have a sample from an earlier intermediate time. This fact will be true of most real-world scenarios: you are deploying your model in the future. So if you tune your training data too closely to your unlabeled data, your model will be stuck in the past when it is deployed to future data.

In some deployment scenarios, such as a centralized model processing news headlines, you may be able to adapt to new data in near real time, so you won't have a big problem. In other use cases, such as autonomous vehicles, adapting the model in near real time and deploying it to every vehicle will be impossible. In either case, you still need a greater diversity of training items than only those that look the most like your current unlabeled data.

Representative sampling is the most prone to noise of all the active learning strategies in this book. If you have clean training data, the noise in your unlabeled data is often the most different from that training data. In NLP tasks, this noise would include corrupted text, text from a language that is not part of your target domain, text that came from a list of places names that didn't exist in your training data, and so on. For computer vision, noise would include corrupted image files; photos taken accidentally (while pointing the camera lens at the ground, for example); and artifacts that arise from using different cameras, resolutions, or compression techniques. Chances are that none of these types of noise is interesting for your task, so they will not produce an interesting or diverse range of samples to label.

Finally, representative sampling can do more harm than good if you apply it only during later cycles of the active learning process, especially when you don't have a domain adaptation problem. Suppose that you used uncertainty sampling for a few iterations of active learning and then applied representative sampling for later iterations. You have oversampled items *near* the decision boundary in early iterations, so representative sampling will oversample items *away* from the decision boundary in later iterations. This method will be worse than random sampling if you implement it this way.

For these reasons, representative sampling is rarely used in isolation; it is most often used in algorithms or processes that combine representative sampling with uncertainty sampling. You might use representative sampling only for items that are also near the decision boundary, for example. In some of the foundational academic papers on representative sampling, you might see that what they mean by *representative sampling* is a combination of diversity and uncertainty. We will return to combinations of approaches in chapter 5, which is where we will get the most out of all the sampling techniques. In this chapter, we'll introduce representative sampling in isolation so that you understand the basic principles before learning how to combine it with other methods.

With these caveats, representative sampling can be useful for domain adaptation. In academic research, there is a focus on domain adaptation without any additional labels, which is often called *discrepancy* rather than *representation*. In industry, I have yet to encounter domain adaptation without additional human intervention, so it should become an important tool in your belt.

4.4.2 *Simple representative sampling*

As with our clustering example in section 4.4.1, we can use many algorithms for representative sampling. We mentioned one in chapter 2, in which a small modification to our outlier detection method calculated whether something was an outlier for the training data but not an outlier for the unlabeled data. Here, we'll step up the sophistication a little and use cosine similarity from our training data to our unlabeled data, as follows:

1 Create one cluster containing the training data.
2 Create a second cluster containing the unlabeled data.
3 Sample items that have the greatest outlier score from the training relative to their outlier score from the unlabeled data.

To try representative sampling, run

```
> python active_learning.py --representative=95
```

This command samples 95 unlabeled items using representative sampling for you to annotate, along with 5 randomly selected items from remaining unlabeled items. The representative sampling function takes the training data and unlabeled data as arguments to find the unlabeled data items that are the most representative of the unlabeled data relative to the training data. Using our existing implementation for clustering, we can see that this is only a few lines of additional code.

Listing 4.6 Representative sampling in PyTorch

```
def get_representative_samples(self, training_data, unlabeled_data,
    number=20, limit=10000):
    """Gets the most representative unlabeled items, compared to training data
    Keyword arguments:
        training_data -- data with a label, that the current model is trained
        ➥ on
        unlabeled_data -- data that does not yet have a label
        number -- number of items to sample
        limit -- sample from only this many items for faster sampling (-1 =
        ➥ no limit)
    Creates one cluster for each data set: training and unlabeled

    """

    if limit > 0:
        shuffle(training_data)
        training_data = training_data[:limit]
        shuffle(unlabeled_data)
        unlabeled_data = unlabeled_data[:limit]

    training_cluster = Cluster()                    ⟵——— Create a cluster for
    for item in training_data:                            the training data.
        training_cluster.add_to_cluster(item)

    unlabeled_cluster = Cluster()                   ⟵——— Create a cluster for
    for item in unlabeled_data:                           the unlabeled data.
        unlabeled_cluster.add_to_cluster(item)

                                                    For each unlabeled item, calculate how
                                                    close it is to the unlabeled data relative
                                                    to the labeled data.
    for item in unlabeled_data:                     ⟵———
        training_score = training_cluster.cosine_similary(item)
        unlabeled_score = unlabeled_cluster.cosine_similary(item)

        representativeness = unlabeled_score - training_score
```

```
    item[3] = "representative"
    item[4] = representativeness


unlabeled_data.sort(reverse=True, key=lambda x: x[4])
return unlabeled_data[:number:]
```

As with the clustering code, if you are applying this sampling strategy to images, you might want to use a lower-dimension vector that has abstracted the image away from individual pixels. Nothing in the code needs to change if you are using a different dimensionality of features; you are only plugging that new data vector directly into the algorithm.

4.4.3   *Adaptive representative sampling*

A small change to our code means that we can make our representative sampling strategy adaptive within each active learning iteration. When we have sampled the most representative item, we know that the item will get a label later, even if we don't know yet what that label will be. So we can add that single item to the hypothetical training data and then run representative sampling again for the next item. This approach will help prevent representative sampling from sampling only similar items. To try adaptive representative sampling, run

```
> python active_learning.py --adaptive_representative=95
```

This command samples 95 unlabeled items using adaptive representative sampling for you to annotate, along with 5 randomly selected items from remaining unlabeled items. The new code is even shorter, taking the same arguments and calling the representative sampling function once for each new item.

Listing 4.7   Adaptive representative sampling in PyTorch

```
def get_adaptive_representative_samples(self, training_data, unlabeled_data,
➥ number=20, limit=5000):
    """Adaptively gets the most representative unlabeled items, compared to
    ➥ training data

    Keyword arguments:
        training_data -- data with a label, that the current model is trained on
        unlabeled_data -- data that does not yet have a label
        number -- number of items to sample
        limit -- sample from only this many items for faster sampling (-1 =
        ➥ no limit)

    Adaptive variant of get_representative_samples() where the training_data
    ➥ is updated
    after each individual selection in order to increase diversity of samples

    """

    samples = []
```

```
for i in range(0, number):
    print("Epoch "+str(i))
    representative_item = get_representative_samples(training_data,
    ➥ unlabeled_data, 1, limit)[0]
    samples.append(representative_item)
    unlabeled_data.remove(representative_item)

return samples
```

With our building blocks of clusters and representative sampling, it is a small extension codewise to start implementing more sophisticated active learning strategies. We will cover more of these advanced techniques in detail in chapter 5. The code will be as short in most cases, but it is important to know the building blocks.

Note that this function takes a while to run because it needs to reevaluate the representative score for every unlabeled data point you are sampling. So if you are running this code on a smaller server or personal computer, you may want to lower the number of items to sample or the `limit` on items to consider so that you can see the results of this sampling strategy without waiting a long time.

4.5 *Sampling for real-world diversity*

Strategies for identifying and reducing bias are complicated and could fill a book of their own. In this text, we will concentrate on the data annotation problem: ensuring that training data represents real-world diversity as fairly as possible. As you read in the introduction to this chapter, we expect more from machine learning in some cases than we do from people. We expect many models to include something closer to English's 200,000-word vocabulary than the ~40,000 words known by a typical fluent human, for example. Therefore, this section covers the current best practice for ensuring that models are fair from an active learning point of view, knowing that measuring and reducing real-world bias is a complicated field that is far from solved.

The demographics for real-world diversity can be any real-world division that is meaningful for your data. Here is a (nonexhaustive) list of the kind of demographics that we might care about for our disaster-response examples:

- *Language*—Can we more accurately identify disaster-related content written in certain languages? There is an obvious bias here, as the data is mostly English.
- *Geography*—Can we more accurately identify disaster-related content from/about some countries? There is a high chance of bias here, as some countries will have more media reporting their disasters, and there will also be country-level population biases.
- *Gender*—Can we more accurately identify disaster-related content from/about people of one gender? It is possible that more males are writing the content than other genders, and this could be reflected in the style of writing.
- *Socioeconomics*—Can we more accurately identify disaster-related content from/about people with different incomes? There is often more reporting about wealthy nations, so perhaps this situation leads to bias in the data and models.

- *Race and ethnicity*—Can we more accurately identify disaster-related content from/about people of certain races or ethnicity? The media articles often portray the same type of event, such as a shooting by a lone man, as part of a war of terror for some ethnicities (and therefore disaster-related) but as an individual crime for other ethnicities (and therefore not disaster-related).
- *Date and time*—Can we more accurately identify disaster-related content at certain times of the day, days of the week, or months of the year? Fewer articles are published on weekends, and those articles tend to be more human-interest focused.

The biases may be different in combination, a situation known as *intersectional bias*. A bias toward people of a certain gender might be better, worse, or even inverted for some races and ethnicities, for example.

Depending on where you deploy your model, you may need to conform to local laws. In California, for example, labor laws prevent discrimination in several demographics, including many of the ones in the preceding list, as well as age, immigration status, sexual orientation, and religion. In some cases, solving the problem by encoding the data to change the sampling strategy may not be the right choice; instead, you need to solve the problem while you are collecting the data.

4.5.1 *Common problems in training data diversity*

Three common problems for fairness in data are summarized in figure 4.7. Each of the three demographics in figure 4.7 shows common problems that you will find when trying to create training data:

- A demographic that is overrepresented in your training data but not from the same distribution as your training data (X)
- A demographic that is from a distribution similar to the overall data distribution but not yet represented in a balanced way in the training data (O)
- A demographic that is underrepresented in the training data in such a way that the resulting model might be worse than if random sampling were used (Z)

Machine learning algorithms themselves are not prone to many inherent biases that are not already in the data, although those biases are possible. Most of the time, when an algorithm shows bias, it is reflecting or amplifying a bias that comes from the training data or the way that the training data is represented as features for the model. Even if bias comes solely from the model itself, you are probably responsible for creating the evaluation data to detect and measure that bias. If the source of data leads to poor results, you are also responsible for identifying that fact when you start to annotate the data. So if you are responsible for annotating the data, you may have more influence on model fairness than anyone else in your organization.

Note that many researchers in AI ethics use a broader definition of *algorithm* than most computer scientists do, including the treatment of the data for the machine learning models and the interpretation of the output. This definition is not inherently better or worse—only different. Be mindful about exactly which parts of an application using machine learning are being referred to when you read about algorithms in the AI ethics literature.

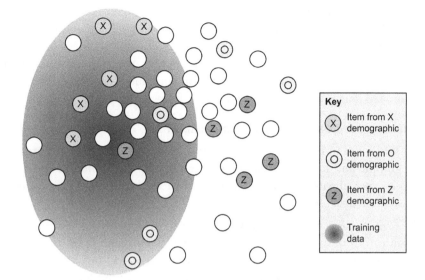

Figure 4.7 An example of the problems that diversity sampling tries to address. Here, we have items mapped to three real-world demographics that we're calling X, O, and Z.

Demographic X looks pretty good. All the examples we have so far are within the current training data. X is not the same distribution as the training data as a whole. This problem isn't typical of neural models, but it could be a problem with simpler models such as Naive Bayes. X is typical of a privileged demographic with a positive bias, such as standard English data within a multilingual dataset.

Demographic O is partially in the training data today and partially outside it. O is distributed across the entire feature range fairly evenly. So if we can collect training data that is representative of the entire feature space, we are least worried about O. O is typical of a demographic with minimal bias (positive or negative), such as time-based demographics, in which each item was collected carefully over a certain period.

By contrast, demographic Z is clustered outside the current training data. Even worse, a Z data point inside the current training data appears to be an outlier for Z. The model may not have information about Z and may actually be modeling Z incorrectly. Z is typical of an underrepresented demographic, such as an underrepresented ethnicity that does not appear in the dataset except when that person happens to share features with a more privileged demographic.

4.5.2 *Stratified sampling to ensure diversity of demographics*

Without a reference data set of unlabeled items from each demographic, you need to apply active learning strategies that you have applied before, but now in a stratified manner across all your data:

1. Apply least confidence sampling for every demographic, selecting an equal number of items in each demographic where that demographic was the most-confident prediction.
2. Apply margin of confidence sampling for every demographic, selecting an equal number of items in each demographic where that demographic was the most-confident or second-most-confident. Recall that margin of confidence is explicitly looking at the two most confident.)
3. Apply model-based outlier detection for each demographic.
4. Apply cluster-based sampling within each demographic.

Basically, in the same way that we wanted the best possible dataset from our unlabeled data as a whole, we want to do this for each demographic, being careful to stratify the sampling across those demographics.

There is no separate code for this task in this chapter. You should be able to divide up the data according to demographics that you care about and apply the sampling strategies only to data for each demographic.

4.5.3 *Represented and representative: Which matters?*

There is a subtle but important difference between having data that is representative of a demographic and having the demographic be well-represented in the data. The distinction is especially important depending on the type of model you are using, so we will tease them apart here:

- *Representative demographic data*—Your data is representative of a demographic if it is drawn from the same distribution as that demographic. In statistical terms, your labeled data is representative if it is independent and identically distributed (IDD) from a data that is randomly drawn from that demographic.
- *A demographic that is well-represented*—A demographic is well-represented if there is sufficient data representing that demographic for your model to perform fairly, but the data is not required to be IDD.

If you know that your unlabeled data fairly represents the demographic you care about and it is accurately encoded for that demographic, you can create an additional evaluation data set that draws randomly from within each demographic. If your demographics are not equally frequent, this approach will be faster than creating evaluation data by randomly sampling from across the entire data set. But you can use this dataset only for evaluating your per-demographic accuracy (section 4.5.4).

Remember that your unlabeled data may *not* be representative of each demographic. Data in this chapter that comes from an Australian media organization focuses on news within Australia and countries that are geographically or politically close to Australia. Articles about Uganda, for example, are not going to be representative of actual events in Uganda; the data will be biased toward events that are perceived as more important for Australia. It is not possible to get representative data for Uganda in this case. Instead, you should use clustering to get as diverse a set of articles about Uganda as possible so that at very least, articles about Uganda are well-represented.

If you are using a neural model, you might be OK if you have well-represented data that is *not* representative. Provided that there is enough data, a neural model can be accurate for all items in a given demographic, even if it was trained on data that was imbalanced within that demographic. The Uganda news articles, for example, might be balanced too much toward sports-related articles. Provided there are sufficient examples of the other types of news from Uganda for your model to be accurate on those topics, it won't matter that sports-related news is overrepresented; your model can be equally accurate on all types of news from Uganda.

If you are using generative models, however, especially a simpler one like Naive Bayes, your model is explicitly trying to model the classification task by assuming representative data. In this case, you need to work harder to ensure that your data is representative or to try to encode representativeness in your model by manipulating parameters such as the prior probability of certain data types.

This approach separates sampling for real-world diversity from stratified sampling. In the social sciences, *stratified sampling* is a technique for ensuring that data is as representative as possible and for weighting the results of activities such as surveys to account for demographic imbalances. Depending on the neural model, it might be enough that the data exists in the training data and the bias won't be perpetuated. On the other hand, a model might amplify any bias. So, the situation becomes a little more complicated and needs to be tackled holistically, taking into account the machine learning architecture. If you care about the real-world diversity of your models, the literature on stratified sampling is still a good place to start, knowing that this sampling strategy will not necessarily be the only solution to the problem.

4.5.4 *Per-demographic accuracy*

If we have real-world demographics in our data, we can calculate a variation of macro accuracy according to those demographics. For each item belonging to a certain demographic, how many of those were predicted correctly for their given labels? Note that each "error" will be both a false positive and a false negative. So unless you are excluding certain labels from your accuracy or are setting a threshold for trusted predictions, you will have identical precision and recall values for per-demographic accuracy (the same situation as for micro precision and recall). Let d indicate membership in each demographic. Precision and recall, therefore, are

$$P_{demographic} = \frac{\sum_d P_d}{d}$$

$$R_{demographic} = \frac{\sum_d R_d}{d}$$

I haven't seen this technique used often in industry, but that doesn't mean that it shouldn't be adopted. Most studies of demographic inequality tend to be ad-hoc. For face recognition, for example, there are many examples of popular media organizations selecting a small number of images of people who represent different ethnicities and looking for different levels of accuracy across those ethnicities. In those use cases, the media organizations are testing precision only, and on a small (and possibly nonrepresentative) sample. That approach works for a media story, but it won't work if we are serious about improving the fairness of our models.

If you are responsible for building the model and ensuring that it is as fair as possible, you should look at a broader range of ways to measure accuracy. You may want to refine demographic-based accuracy further, according to your use case. Here are some options:

- *Minimum accuracy*—The lowest precision, recall, and/or F-score of any demographic. If you want to treat your model as being only as strong as its weakest link in terms of fairness across demographics, you should take the minimum accuracy. You could take the minimum F-score from one demographic. For a harsher metric, take the minimum precision and minimum recall, possibly from different labels, and apply the F-score to those.
- *Harmonic accuracy*—The harmonic mean of the per-demographic accuracy, which will be harsher than the average demographic accuracy but not as harsh as taking the minimum (unless there are 0 values). As we take the harmonic mean of precision and recall to get the F-score, instead of the arithmetic mean, we could also take the harmonic mean. The harmonic mean will punish outlier low accuracies more than it rewards outlier high accuracies, but not as much as taking the minimum.

4.5.5   Limitations of sampling for real-world diversity

The biggest shortcoming of sampling for real-world diversity is that you have no way to guarantee that the model will be perfect, but you can measure the bias more accurately and ensure that your models will be much fairer than if you used only random sampling. Sometimes, you won't be able to make up for the bias, simply because not enough unlabeled data is available. I have worked in disaster response in languages such as Haitain Kreyol and Urdu, where there simply wasn't enough available data to cover the same breadth of potential disasters that we have for the English headlines. There is no way to fix this problem with labeling alone. Data collection is outside the scope of this book, but we will return to some other relevant techniques in chapter 9, when we cover methods for creating synthetic data.

4.6   Diversity sampling with different types of models

You can apply diversity sampling to any type of model architecture. Similar to what we learned in chapter 3 for uncertainty sampling, sometimes diversity sampling for other models is the same as for neural models, and sometimes diversity sampling is unique to a given type of model.

4.6.1   Model-based outliers with different types of models

For models that use linear regression, you can calculate model outliers in the same way as for a neural model: which items have the least activation across all labels? Use the prenormalized prediction scores, if you have access to them, as you did with the logits in this chapter.

In the case of Bayesian models, a model-based outlier has the lowest overall probability of each label. As with our neural models here, you could calculate lowest overall as the lowest average or the lowest maximum, depending on what makes the most sense for your use case.

In the case of SVMs, you can look for predictions that are near the hyperplane (decision boundary) but are the maximal distance from the support vectors themselves: the training items that determine the decision boundary. These items will be the equivalent of the model outliers that have high uncertainty in neural models.

4.6.2 Clustering with different types of models

You can use the unsupervised clustering methods in this chapter, such as k-means, to sample for any supervised machine learning algorithm. There is no need to change the k-means approach for different types of supervised machine learning algorithms, so you can start with the ones in this chapter and then think about refining them based on your model and data.

If you want to go deeper into cluster-based sampling, a lot of research was done on diversity sampling in the early 2000s. SVMs were at their peak popularity at the same time, so you will need to brush up on your SVM knowledge to get the most out of the research done at that time.

4.6.3 Representative sampling with different types of models

As mentioned earlier in the chapter, you could use Naive Bayes or Euclidean distance for representative sampling instead of cosine similarity. Any distance function could be as good for your particular data; we used cosine similarity in this book only because of the continuity from section 4.3 on clustering. If you changed the distance function in the clustering algorithm from cosine similarity to the probability of cluster membership, this edit of a few lines of code would be enough to you to try Bayesian clustering.

Decision trees offer a unique type of diversity sampling. You can look at where the number of predictions in different leaves differs from training to evaluation data. Suppose that your decision tree has 10 leaves, and all 10 leaves have an equal number of items when predicting your validation data. Now imagine that when you apply the model to your unlabeled data, 90% of that data ends up in one leaf. That leaf obviously represents the type of data in your target domain much better than your training data so far. So you should sample more items from within the leaf with 90% of the data, knowing that the data is more important for where you will deploy your model.

4.6.4 Sampling for real-world diversity with different types of models

The strategies for improving diversity in your neural models can be applied to other types of machine learning models. You want to ensure that you are optimizing for the same number of labels for each demographic and for equal accuracy for each demographic.

4.7 Diversity sampling cheat sheet

Figure 4.8 is a cheat sheet for the four diversity sampling approaches that you implemented in this chapter. If you are confident about these strategies, keep this cheat sheet handy as a quick reference.

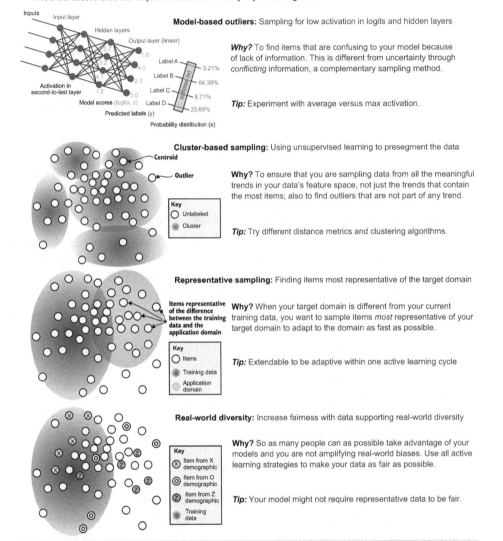

Diversity sampling cheat sheet

Supervised machine learning models are limited by their data. For example, a chat bot will not support diversity if trained only on one variety of English. For many tasks, you need to find data that represents diversity in the data and diversity in the real-world. This is a form of *active learning* known as *diversity sampling*.

This cheat sheet shares four ways to increase the diversity of your training data.

Model-based outliers: Sampling for low activation in logits and hidden layers

Why? To find items that are confusing to your model because of lack of information. This is different from uncertainty through *conflicting* information, a complementary sampling method.

Tip: Experiment with average versus max activation.

Cluster-based sampling: Using unsupervised learning to presegment the data

Why? To ensure that you are sampling data from all the meaningful trends in your data's feature space, not just the trends that contain the most items; also to find outliers that are not part of any trend.

Tip: Try different distance metrics and clustering algorithms.

Representative sampling: Finding items most representative of the target domain

Why? When your target domain is different from your current training data, you want to sample items *most* representative of your target domain to adapt to the domain as fast as possible.

Tip: Extendable to be adaptive within one active learning cycle

Real-world diversity: Increase fairness with data supporting real-world diversity

Why? So as many people can as possible take advantage of your models and you are not amplifying real-world biases. Use all active learning strategies to make your data as fair as possible.

Tip: Your model might not require representative data to be fair.

Robert (Munro) Monarch. *Human-in-the-Loop Machine Learning*, Manning Publications. http://bit.ly/huml_book
See the book for more details on each method and other active learning strategies like uncertainty sampling, with open source implementations in PyTorch. robertmunro.com | @WWRob

Figure 4.8   Cheat sheet for the types of diversity sampling covered in this chapter: model-based outlier sampling, cluster-based sampling, representative sampling, and sampling for real-world diversity. These four strategies ensure diversity and representation in your data—respectively, items that are unknown to your model in its current state; items that are statistically representative of the entire distribution of your data; items that are maximally representative of where you are going to deploy your model; and items that are most representative of real-world demographics.

4.8   Further reading

You will have to go outside of the machine learning literature for many of the most important papers related to diversity sampling. If you are focused on collecting the right data, then the language documentation and archiving literature starting in the early 2000s is the best starting place. If you are focused on stratified sampling within your data, then there is a century of social science literature that is relevant in fields as varied as education and economics. This section limits the further reading to the machine learning literature, so keep in mind that the best papers are building on advances in other fields.

4.8.1   Further reading for model-based outliers

The model-based outlier algorithms are ones that I've personally developed and have not yet published outside this book except in informal presentations and classes. The literature on neural-based methods for determining outliers is growing but tends to focus on statistical outliers not low activation.

The practice of investigating a neural model to determine its knowledge (or lack thereof) is sometimes called *probing*. While there aren't yet papers on probing to discover outliers for active learning, there are no doubt some good techniques in the broader model probing literature that could be adapted for this purpose.

4.8.2   Further reading for cluster-based sampling

For cluster-based sampling, the best starting point is "Active Learning Using Pre-clustering," by Hieu T. Ngyuen and Arnold Smeulders (http://mng.bz/ao6Y). For the most cutting-edge research on cluster-based sampling, look for papers that cited these authors recently and are themselves highly cited.

Note that Ngyuen and Smeulders used an active learning metric that combines clustering with uncertainty sampling. As noted earlier in this chapter, this combination is the most common way to use clustering within active learning. The topics are taught separately in this text so you can understand them in isolation before learning how to combine them. Before jumping into the research, you may want to read chapter 5, in which you combine clustering and uncertainty sampling.

The earliest papers that look at clustering for active learning came from scientists in Russia. The first English version of these papers that I'm aware of is Novosibirk Zagoruiko's "Classification and Recognition" (http://mng.bz/goXn). If you can read Russian, you can find even earlier papers from scientists who were thinking about this problem more than 50 years ago!

4.8.3   Further reading for representative sampling

The principles of representative sampling were first explored in "Employing EM and Pool-Based Active Learning for Text Classification," by Andrew Kachites McCallum and Kamal Nigam (http://mng.bz/e54Z). For the most cutting-edge research on representative sampling, look for papers that cited these authors recently and are themselves highly cited.

4.8.4   *Further reading for sampling for real-world diversity*

Here are two good papers on machine learning for real-world diversity, one each in computer vision and NLP. Both find that popular models are more accurate for people from wealthier backgrounds and that training data is biased toward the object seen by wealthier people and the languages spoken by wealthier/majority populations:

- "Does Object Recognition Work for Everyone?", by Terrance DeVries, Ishan Misra, Changhan Wang, and Laurens van der Maaten (http://mng.bz/pVG0).
- "Incorporating Dialectal Variability for Socially Equitable Language dentification," by David Jurgens, Yulia Tsvetkov, and Dan Jurafsky (http://mng.bz/OEyO).

For a critical review of bias in the language technology literature, including how inconsistently the term bias is used, I recommend Su Lin Blodgett, Solon Barocas, Hal Daumé III, and Hanna Wallach's paper "Language (Technology) Is Power: A Critical Survey of 'Bias' in NLP" (http://mng.bz/Yq0Q).

Summary

- This chapter covered four common approaches to diversity sampling: model-based outlier sampling, cluster-based sampling, representative sampling, and sampling for real-world diversity. These techniques can help you understand the kinds of "unknown unknowns" in your models.
- Model-based outlier sampling allows you to sample items that are unknown to your model in its current state, helping you expand your model's knowledge where there are currently gaps.
- Cluster-based sampling allows you to sample items that are statistically representative of the entire distribution of your data, helping you expand your model's knowledge to capture all the meaningful trends in your data, including the rarer ones that would likely be missed with random sampling.
- Representative sampling can be used to sample items that are maximally representative of where you are going to deploy your model, helping you adapt your model to domains that are different from your current training data, which is a common problem in real-world machine learning.
- To support real-world diversity, you need to deploy all your techniques from uncertainty sampling and diversity sampling to make your applications more accurate across a diverse set of users and, therefore, more fair.
- Accuracy metrics such as micro and macro F-score can be applied across real-world demographics as one way to measure potential biases in a model.
- Interpreting the layers of a neural model for diversity sampling lets you access as much information as possible for active learning, giving you more options for calculating model outliers and providing a building block for advanced transfer learning techniques.

- The strategies for deciding how many items should be reviewed by humans when implementing diversity sampling is different from uncertainty sampling, because in some cases, they can be adaptive within each iteration of active learning. Adaptive sampling methods allow you to make the human-in-the-loop machine learning feedback loop more efficient because you don't have to wait for your model to retrain.
- Implementing diversity sampling is possible with any supervised machine learning algorithm, including neural models, Bayesian models, SVMs, and decision trees. You can implement active learning with any type of machine learning algorithm that you are currently using; you don't need to switch to the neural models that are the focus of the examples in this book. You might even decide to try some of these additional algorithms for active learning to take advantage of their unique properties.

Advanced active learning

In chapters 3 and 4, you learned how to identify where your model is uncertain (what your model knows it doesn't know) and what is missing from your model (what your model doesn't know that it doesn't know). In this chapter, you learn how to combine these techniques into a comprehensive active learning strategy. You also learn how to use transfer learning to adapt your models to predict which items to sample.

5.1 Combining uncertainty sampling and diversity sampling

This section explores ways to combine all the active learning techniques that you have learned up to this point so that you can use them effectively them for your particular use cases. You will also learn one new active learning strategy: expected error reduction, which combines principles of uncertainty sampling and diversity sampling. Recall from chapter 1 that an ideal strategy for active learning tries to sample items that are near the decision boundary but are distant from one another, as shown in figure 5.1.

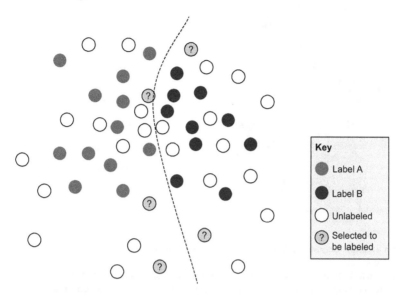

Figure 5.1   One possible result of combining uncertainty sampling and diversity sampling. When these strategies are combined, items near diverse sections of the decision boundary are selected. Therefore, we are optimizing the chance of finding items that are likely to result in a changed decision boundary when they're added to the training data.

You have learned to identify items that are near the decision boundary (uncertainty sampling) and distant from one another (cluster-based sampling and adaptive representative sampling). This chapter shows you how to sample items that are both near the decision boundary and diverse, like those shown in figure 5.1.

5.1.1   *Least confidence sampling with cluster-based sampling*

The most common way that uncertainty sampling and diversity sampling are combined in industry is takes a large sample from one method and further filter the sample with another method. This technique has no common name, despite its ubiquity, probably because so many companies have invented it independently by necessity.

If you sampled the 50% most uncertain items with least confidence sampling and then applied cluster-based sampling to sample 10% of those items, you could end up with a sample of 5% of your data more or less like those in figure 5.1: a near-optimal combination of uncertainty and diversity. Figure 5.2 represents this result graphically. First, you sample the 50% most uncertain items; then you apply clustering to ensure diversity within that selection, sampling the centroid of each cluster.

With the code you have already learned, you can see that combining least confidence sampling and clustering is a simple extension in advanced_active_learning.py

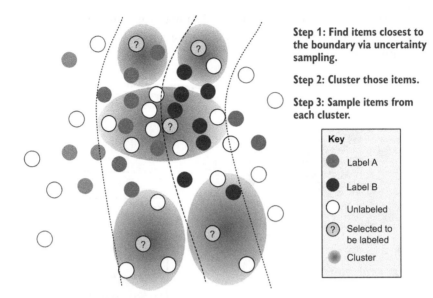

Step 1: Find items closest to the boundary via uncertainty sampling.

Step 2: Cluster those items.

Step 3: Sample items from each cluster.

Key

Label A

Label B

Unlabeled

Selected to be labeled

Cluster

Figure 5.2 An example combining least confidence and clustering-based sampling. First, uncertainty sampling finds items near the decision boundary; then clustering ensures diversity within that selection. In this figure, the centroids from each cluster are sampled. Alternatively, or in addition, you could select random members of outliers.

within the same code repository that we have been using (https://github.com/rmunro/pytorch_active_learning), as shown in the following listing.

Listing 5.1 Combining least confidence sampling and clustering

```
def get_clustered_uncertainty_samples(self, model, unlabeled_data, method,
    feature_method, perc_uncertain = 0.1, num_clusters=20, max_epochs=10,
    limit=10000):

    if limit > 0:                                    Get a large sample of the
      shuffle(unlabeled_data)                        most uncertain items.
      unlabeled_data = unlabeled_data[:limit]
    uncertain_count = math.ceil(len(unlabeled_data) * perc_uncertain)

    uncertain_samples = self.uncertainty_sampling.get_samples(model,
        unlabeled_data,
        method, feature_method, uncertain_count, limit=limit)   ◄──────────┐
    samples = self.diversity_sampling.get_cluster_samples(uncertain_samples,
        num_clusters=num_clusters)                              ◄──────┐

    for item in samples:
      item[3] = method.__name__+"_"+item[3] # record the sampling method

    return samples                           Within those uncertain items, use
                                             clustering to ensure a diverse sample.
```

Only two new lines of code are needed to combine the two approaches: one to get the most uncertain items and one to cluster them. If you are interested in the disaster-response text classification task, try it with this new command:

```
> python active_learning.py --clustered_uncertainty=10 --verbose
```

You'll immediately see that data tends to fall near the divide of text that may or not be disaster-related and that the items are a diverse selection. You have many options for using uncertainty sampling to find items near the decision boundary and then apply cluster-based sampling to ensure diversity within those items. You can experiment with different types of uncertainty sampling, different thresholds for your uncertainty cutoff, and different parameters for clustering. In many settings, this combination of clustering and uncertainty sampling will be the fastest way to drill down on the highest-value items for active learning and should be one of the first strategies that you try for almost any use case.

The simple methods of combining strategies rarely make it into academic papers; academia favors papers that combine methods into a single algorithm rather than chaining multiple simpler algorithms. This makes sense, because combining the methods is easy, as you have already seen; there is no need to write an academic paper about something that can be implemented in a few lines of code. But as a developer building real-world active learning systems, you should always implement the easy solutions before attempting more experimental algorithms.

Another reason to try simple methods first is that you might need to keep supporting them in your applications for a long time. It will be easier to maintain your code if you can get 99% of the way there without having to invent new techniques. See the following sidebar for a great example of how early decisions matter.

Your early data decisions continue to matter
Expert anecdote by Kieran Snyder

The decisions that you make early in a machine learning project can influence the products that you are building for many years to come. This is especially true for data decisions: your feature-encoding strategies, labeling ontologies, and source data will have long-term impacts.

In my first job out of graduate school, I was responsible for building the infrastructure that allowed Microsoft software to work in dozens of languages around the world. This job included making fundamental decisions such as deciding on the alphabetical order of the characters in a language—something that didn't exist for many languages at the time. When the 2004 tsunami devastated countries around the Indian Ocean, it was an immediate problem for Sinhalese-speaking people in Sri Lanka: there was no easy way to support searching for missing people because Sinhalese didn't yet have standardized encodings. Our timeline for Sinhalese support went from several months to several days so that we could help the missing-persons service, working with native speakers to build solutions as quickly as possible.

(continued)
The encodings that we decided on at that time were adopted by Unicode as the official encodings for the Sinhalese language and now encode that language forever. You won't always be working on such critical timelines, but you should always consider the long-term impact of your product decisions right from the start.

Kieran Snyder is CEO and co-founder of Textio, a widely used augmented writing platform. Kieran previously held product leadership roles at Microsoft and Amazon and has a PhD in linguistics from the University of Pennsylvania.

Don't assume that a complicated solution is necessarily the best; you may find that a simple combination of least confidence and clustering is all you need for your data. As always, you can test different methods to see which results in the biggest change in accuracy against a baseline of random sampling.

5.1.2   *Uncertainty sampling with model-based outliers*

When you combine uncertainty sampling with model-based outliers, you are maximizing your model's current confusion. You are looking for items near the decision boundary and making sure that their features are relatively unknown to the current model. Figure 5.3 shows the kinds of samples that this approach might generate.

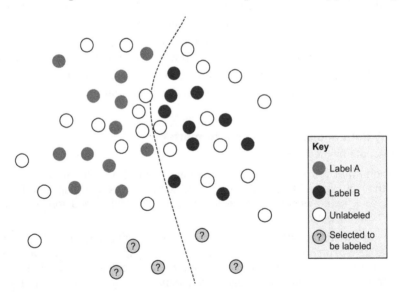

Key

● Label A

● Label B

○ Unlabeled

⑦ Selected to be labeled

Figure 5.3   This example of combining uncertainty sampling with model-based outliers selects items that are near the decision boundary but that are different from the current training data items and, therefore, different from the model.

Listing 5.2   Combining uncertainty sampling with model-based outliers

```
def get_uncertain_model_outlier_samples(self, model, outlier_model,
    unlabeled_data, training_data, validation_data, method, feature_method,
    perc_uncertain = 0.1, number=10, limit=10000):
    if limit > 0:                                              Get the most
      shuffle(unlabeled_data)                                  uncertain items.
      unlabeled_data = unlabeled_data[:limit]
    uncertain_count = math.ceil(len(unlabeled_data) * perc_uncertain)

    uncertain_samples = self.uncertainty_sampling.get_samples(model,
      unlabeled_data, method, feature_method, uncertain_count, limit=limit)

    samples = self.diversity_sampling.get_model_outliers(outlier_model,
      uncertain_samples, validation_data,feature_method,
      number=number, limit=limit)                    Apply model-based outlier
    for item in samples:                             sampling to those items.
      item[3] = method.__name__+"_"+item[3]

    return samples
```

As in the example in listing 5.1, you need only two lines of code here to pull everything together. Although combining uncertainty sampling with model-based outliers is optimal for targeting items that are most likely to increase your model's knowledge and overall accuracy, it can also sample similar items. You can try this technique with this command:

```
> python active_learning.py --uncertain_model_outliers=100 --verbose
```

5.1.3   *Uncertainty sampling with model-based outliers and clustering*

Because the method in section 5.1.2 might oversample items that are close to one another, you may want to implement this strategy first and then apply clustering to ensure diversity. It takes only one line of code to add clustering to the end of the previous method, so you could implement it easily. Alternatively, if you have quick active learning iterations, this approach ensures more diversity when you combine uncertainty sampling and model-based outliers; you can sample a small number of items in each iteration.

5.1.4   *Representative sampling cluster-based sampling*

One shortcoming of the representative sampling technique that you learned in chapter 4 is that it treats the training data and target domain as single clusters. In reality, your data will often be multinodal in a way that a single cluster cannot optimally capture.

   To capture this complexity, you can combine representative sampling and cluster-based sampling in a slightly more complicated architecture. You can cluster your training data and your unlabeled data independently, identify the clusters that are most representative of your unlabeled data, and oversample from them. This approach gives you a more diverse set of items than representative sampling alone (figure 5.4).

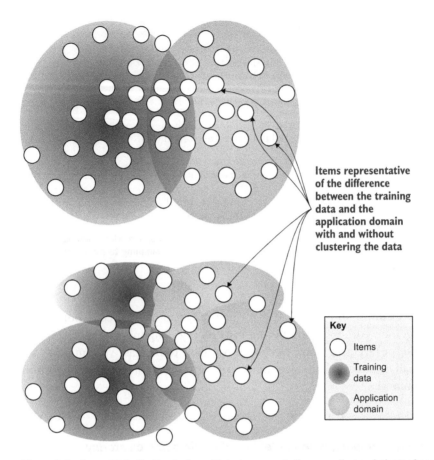

Items representative
of the difference
between the training
data and the
application domain
with and without
clustering the data

Key

◯ Items

⬤ Training
    data

⬤ Application
    domain

Figure 5.4   An example (bottom) of combining representative sampling and cluster-based sampling. This method samples items that are most like your application domain relative to your current training data and also different from one another. By comparison, the simpler representative sampling method in chapter 4 treats each distribution as a single distribution.

As you can see in figure 5.4, your current training data and target domains may not be uniform distributions within your feature space. Clustering the data first will help you model your feature space more accurately and sample a more diverse set of unlabeled items. First, create the clusters for the training data and unlabeled data from the application domain.

Listing 5.3   Combining representative sampling and clustering

```
def get_representative_cluster_samples(self, training_data, unlabeled_data,
➥ number=10, num_clusters=20, max_epochs=10, limit=10000):
    """Gets the most representative unlabeled items, compared to training data,
    ➥ across multiple clusters
```

```
Keyword arguments:
  training_data -- data with a label, that the current model is trained on
  unlabeled_data -- data that does not yet have a label
  number -- number of items to sample
  limit -- sample from only this many items for faster sampling (-1 =
➥ no limit)
  num_clusters -- the number of clusters to create
  max_epochs -- maximum number of epochs to create clusters

"""

if limit > 0:
  shuffle(training_data)
  training_data = training_data[:limit]
  shuffle(unlabeled_data)
  unlabeled_data = unlabeled_data[:limit]

# Create clusters for training data

training_clusters = CosineClusters(num_clusters)
training_clusters.add_random_training_items(training_data)

for i in range(0, max_epochs):
  print("Epoch "+str(i))
  added = training_clusters.add_items_to_best_cluster(training_data)
    if added == 0:
      break

# Create clusters for unlabeled data

unlabeled_clusters = CosineClusters(num_clusters)
unlabeled_clusters.add_random_training_items(training_data)

for i in range(0, max_epochs):
  print("Epoch "+str(i))
  added = unlabeled_clusters.add_items_to_best_cluster(unlabeled_data)
    if added == 0:
      Break
```

> **Create clusters within the existing training data.**

> **Create clusters within the unlabeled data.**

Then iterate each cluster of unlabeled data, and find the item in each cluster that is closest to the centroid of that cluster relative to training data clusters.

Listing 5.4 Combining representative sampling and clustering, continued

```
most_representative_items = []

# for each cluster of unlabeled data
for cluster in unlabeled_clusters.clusters:
    most_representative = None
    representativeness = float("-inf")
```

```
                    # find the item in that cluster most like the unlabeled data
                    item_keys = list(cluster.members.keys())

                    for key in item_keys:
                        item = cluster.members[key]

                        _, unlabeled_score =
                        unlabeled_clusters.get_best_cluster(item)
                        _, training_score = training_clusters.get_best_cluster(item)

                        cluster_representativeness = unlabeled_score - training_score

                        if cluster_representativeness > representativeness:
                            representativeness = cluster_representativeness
                            most_representative = item

                    most_representative[3] = "representative_clusters"
                    most_representative[4] = representativeness
                    most_representative_items.append(most_representative)

            most_representative_items.sort(reverse=True, key=lambda x: x[4])
            return most_representative_items[:number:]
```

Find the best-fit cluster within the unlabeled data clusters. (annotation pointing to `unlabeled_clusters.get_best_cluster(item)`)

Find the best-fit cluster within the training data clusters. (annotation pointing to `_, training_score = training_clusters.get_best_cluster(item)`)

Record the difference between the two as our representativeness score. (annotation pointing to `cluster_representativeness = unlabeled_score - training_score`)

In design, this code is almost identical to the representative sampling method that you implemented in chapter 4, but you are asking the clustering algorithm to create multiple clusters for each distribution instead of only one for training data and one for unlabeled data. You can try this technique with this command:

```
> python active_learning.py --representative_clusters=100 --verbose
```

5.1.5   *Sampling from the highest-entropy cluster*

If you have high entropy in a certain cluster, a lot of confusion exists about the right labels for items in that cluster. In other words, these clusters have the highest average uncertainty across all the items. These items, therefore, are most likely to change labels and have the most room for changes in label.

The example in figure 5.5 is the opposite of clustering for diversity in some ways, as it deliberately focuses on one part of the problem space. But sometimes, that focus is exactly what you want.

Note that this approach works best when you have data with accurate labels and are confident that the task can be solved with machine learning. If you have data that has a lot of inherent ambiguity, this method will tend to focus in those areas. To solve this problem, see how much of your existing training data falls into your high-entropy clusters. If the cluster is already well represented in your training data, you have good

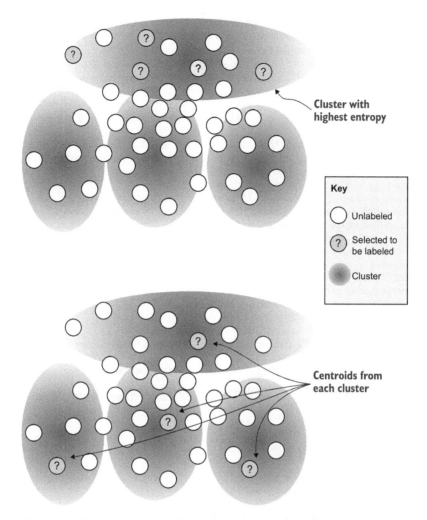

Figure 5.5 This example of combining cluster-based sampling with entropy (bottom) samples items within the cluster that show the most confusion. You might think of this cluster as being the one that straddles the decision boundary most closely. In this example, random items are sampled in the cluster, but you could experiment by sampling the centroid, outliers, and/or oversampling items within the cluster that have the highest entropy. By comparison, simple clustering (top) samples items from every cluster.

evidence that it is an inherently ambiguous part of your feature space and that additional labels will not help. The following listing shows the code for selecting the cluster with the highest average entropy.

Listing 5.5 Sampling from the cluster with the highest entropy

```
def get_high_uncertainty_cluster(self, model, unlabeled_data, method,
➡ feature_method, number=10, num_clusters=20, max_epochs=10, limit=10000):
    """Gets items from the cluster with the highest average uncertainty

    Keyword arguments:
      model -- machine learning model to get predictions from to determine
      ➡ uncertainty
      unlabeled_data -- data that does not yet have a label
      method -- method for uncertainty sampling (eg: least_confidence())
      feature_method -- the method for extracting features from your data
      number -- number of items to sample
      num_clusters -- the number of clusters to create
      max_epochs -- maximum number of epochs to create clusters
      limit -- sample from only this many items for faster sampling
      ➡ (-1 = no limit)
    """

    if limit > 0:
      shuffle(unlabeled_data)
      unlabeled_data = unlabeled_data[:limit]

    unlabeled_clusters = CosineClusters(num_clusters)
    unlabeled_clusters.add_random_training_items(unlabeled_data)

    for i in range(0, max_epochs):       ◄──── Create the clusters.
      print("Epoch "+str(i))
      added = unlabeled_clusters.add_items_to_best_cluster(unlabeled_data)
      if added == 0:
        break

    # get scores

    most_uncertain_cluster = None
    highest_average_uncertainty = 0.0

    # for each cluster of unlabeled data
    for cluster in unlabeled_clusters.clusters:
      total_uncertainty = 0.0
      count = 0

      item_keys = list(cluster.members.keys())

      for key in item_keys:
        item = cluster.members[key]
        text = item[1] # the text for the message

        feature_vector = feature_method(text)
        hidden, logits, log_probs = model(feature_vector,
        ➡ return_all_layers=True)

        prob_dist = torch.exp(log_probs) # the probability distribution of
        ➡ our prediction
```

```
        score = method(prob_dist.data[0]) # get the specific type of
    ➥ uncertainty sampling

        total_uncertainty += score                    Calculate the average uncertainty (using
        count += 1                                     entropy) for the items in each cluster.

    average_uncertainty = total_uncertainty / count
    if average_uncertainty > highest_average_uncertainty:
        highest_average_uncertainty = average_uncertainty
        most_uncertain_cluster = cluster

samples = most_uncertain_cluster.get_random_members(number)

return samples
```

In this code example, we are taking the average entropy of all items in a cluster. You can try different aggregate statistics based on your sampling strategy. If you know that you are sampling only the top 100 items, for example, you could calculate the average entropy across the 100 most uncertain items in each cluster rather than across every item in the cluster. You can try this technique with this command:

```
> python active_learning.py --high_uncertainty_cluster=100 --verbose
```

5.1.6 *Other combinations of active learning strategies*

There are too many possible combinations of active learning techniques to cover in this book, but by this stage, you should have a good idea of how to combine them. Here are some starting points:

- *Combining uncertainty sampling and representative sampling*—You can sample items that are most representative of your target domains and are also uncertain. This approach will be especially helpful in later iterations of active learning. If you used uncertainty sampling for early iterations, your target domain will have items that are disproportionately far from the decision boundary and could be selected erroneously as representative.
- *Combining model-based outliers and representative sampling*—This method is the ultimate method for domain adaptation, targeting items that are unknown to your model today but are also relatively common in your target domain.
- *Combining clustering with itself for hierarchical* clusters—If you have some large clusters or want to sample for diversity within one cluster, you can take the items from one cluster and use them to create a new set of clusters.
- *Combining sampling from the highest-entropy cluster with margin of confidence sampling (or some other uncertainty metrics)*—You can find the cluster with the highest entropy and then sample all the items within it that fall closest to a decision boundary.
- *Combining ensemble methods or dropouts with individual strategies*—You may be building multiple models and decide that a Bayesian model is better for determining

uncertainty, but a neural model is better for determining model-based outliers. You can sample with one model and further refine with another. If you're clustering based on hidden layers, you could adapt the dropout method from uncertainty sampling and randomly ignore some neurons while creating clusters. This approach will prevent the clusters from overfitting to the internal representation of your network.

5.1.7 *Combining active learning scores*

An alternative to piping the output from one sampling strategy to another is taking the scores from the different sampling strategies and finding the highest average score, which makes mathematical sense for all methods other than clustering. You could average each item's score for margin of confidence, model-based outliers, and representative learning, for example, and then rank all items by that single aggregate score.

Although all the scores should be in a [0–1] range, note that some of them may be clustered in small ranges and therefore not contribute as much to the average. If this is the case with your data, you can try converting all your scores to percentiles (quantiles), effectively turning all the sampling scores into stratified rank orders. You can use built-in functions from your math library of choice to turn any list of numbers into percentiles. Look for functions called `rank()`, `percentile()`, or `percentileofscore()` in various Python libraries. Compared with the other methods that you are using for sampling, converting scores to percentiles is relatively quick, so don't worry about trying to find the most optimal function; choose a function from a library that you are already using.

You could also sample via the union of the methods rather than filtering (which is a combination via intersection). This approach can be used for any methods and might make the most sense when you are combining multiple uncertainty sampling scores. You could sample the items that are in the most 10% uncertain by any of least confidence, margin of confidence, ratio of confidence, or entropy to produce a general "uncertain" set of samples, and then use those samples directly or refine the sampling by combining it with additional methods. There are many ways to combine the building blocks that you have learned, and I encourage you to experiment with them.

5.1.8 *Expected error reduction sampling*

Expected error reduction is one of a handful of active learning strategies in the literature that aim to combine uncertainty sampling and diversity sampling into a single metric. This algorithm is included here for completeness, with the caveat that I have not seen it implemented in real-world situations. The core metric for expected error reduction sampling is how much the error in the model would be reduced if an unlabeled item were given a label.[1] You could give each unlabeled item the possible labels that it could have, retrain the model with those labels, and then look at how the

---

[1] "Toward Optimal Active Learning through Sampling Estimation of Error Reduction," by Nicholas Roy and Andrew McCallum (https://dl.acm.org/doi/10.5555/645530.655646).

model accuracy changes. You have two common ways to calculate the change in model accuracy:

- *Overall accuracy*—What is the change in number of items predicted correctly if this item had a label?
- *Overall entropy*—What is the change in aggregate entropy if this item had a label? This method uses the definition of entropy that you learned in the uncertainty sampling chapter in sections 3.2.4 and 3.2.5. It is sensitive to the confidence of the prediction, unlike the first method, which is sensitive only to the predicted label.

The score is weighted across labels by the frequency of each label. You sample the items that are most likely to improve the model overall. This algorithm has some practical problems, however:

- Retraining the model once for every unlabeled item multiplied by every label is prohibitively expensive for most algorithms.
- There can be so much variation when retraining a model that the change from one additional label could be indistinguishable from noise.
- The algorithm can oversample items a long way from the decision boundary, thanks to the high entropy for the labels that are a diminishingly small likelihood.

So there are practical limitations to using this method with neural models. The original authors of this algorithm used incremental Naive Bayes, which can be adapted to new training items by updating the counts of a new item's features, and is deterministic. Given this fact, expected error reduction works for the authors' particular algorithm. The problem of oversampling items away from the decision boundary can be addressed by using the predicted probability of each label rather than the label frequency (prior probability), but you will need accurate confidence predictions from your model, which you may not have, as you learned in chapter 3.

If you do try to implement expected error reduction, you could experiment with different accuracy measures and with uncertainty sampling algorithms other than entropy. Because this method uses entropy, which comes from information theory, you might see it called *information gain* in the literature on variations of this algorithm. Read these papers closely, because *gain* can mean *lower* information. Although the term is mathematically correct, it can seem counterintuitive to say that your model knows more when the predictions have less information.

As stated at the start of this section, no one has (as far as I know) published on whether expected error reduction is better than the simple combination of methods through the intersection and/or union of sampling strategies. You could try implementing expected error reduction and related algorithms to see whether they help in your systems. You may be able to implement them by retraining only the final layer of your model with the new item, which will speed the process.

If you want to sample items with a goal similar to expected error reduction, you can cluster your data and then look at clusters with the highest entropy in the predictions, like the example in figure 5.4 earlier in this chapter. Expected error reduction has a problem, however, in that it might find items in only one part of the feature space, like the uncertainty sampling algorithms used in isolation. If you extend the example in figure 5.4 to sample items from the *N* highest entropy clusters, not only the single highest entropy cluster, you will have addressed the limitations of expected error reduction in only a few lines of code.

Rather than try to handcraft an algorithm that combines uncertainty sampling and diversity sampling into one algorithm, however, you can let machine learning decide on that combination for you. The original expected error reduction paper was titled "Toward Optimal Active Learning through Sampling Estimation of Error Reduction" and is 20 years old, so this is likely the direction that the authors had in mind. The rest of this chapter builds toward machine learning models for the sampling process itself in active learning.

5.2   *Active transfer learning for uncertainty sampling*

The most advanced active learning methods use everything that you have learned so far in this book: the sampling strategies for interpreting confusion that you learned in chapter 3, the methods for querying the different layers in your models that you learned in chapter 4, and the combinations of techniques that you learned in the first part of this chapter.

Using all these techniques, you can build a new model with the task of predicting where the greatest uncertainty occurs. First, let's revisit the description of transfer learning from chapter 1, shown here in figure 5.6.

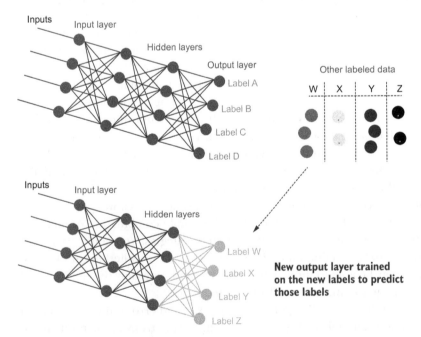

Figure 5.6 We have a model that predicts a label as "A," "B," "C," or "D" and a separate dataset with the labels "W," "X," "Y," and "Z." When we retrain only the last layer of the model, the model is able to predict labels "W," "X," "Y," and "Z," using far fewer human-labeled items than if we were training a model from scratch.

New output layer trained on the new labels to predict those labels

In the example in figure 5.6, you can see how a model can be trained on one set of labels and then retrained on another set of labels by keeping the architecture the same and freezing part of the model, retraining only the last layer in this case. There are many more ways to use transfer learning and contextual models for human-in-the-loop machine learning. The examples in this chapter are variations on the type of transfer learning shown in figure 5.6.

5.2.1 Making your model predict its own errors

The new labels from transfer learning can be any categories that you want, including information about the task itself. This fact is the core insight for active transfer learning: you can use transfer learning to ask your model where it is confused by making it predict its own errors. Figure 5.7 outlines this process.

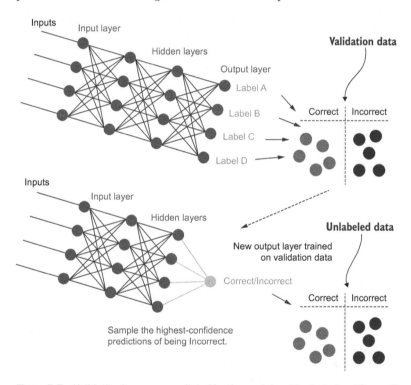

Figure 5.7 Validation items are predicted by the model and bucketed as "Correct" or "Incorrect" according to whether they were classified correctly. Then the last layer of the model is retrained to predict whether items are "Correct" or "Incorrect," effectively turning the two buckets into new labels.

As figure 5.7 shows, this process has several steps:

1 Apply the model to a validation dataset, and capture which validation items were classified correctly and incorrectly. This data is your new training data. Now your validation items have an additional label of "Correct" or "Incorrect."

2 Create a new output layer for the model, and train that new layer on your new training data, predicting your new "Correct" and "Incorrect" labels.

3 Run your unlabeled data items through the new model, and sample the items that are predicted to be "Incorrect" with the highest confidence.

Now you have a sample of items that are predicted by your model as the most likely to be incorrect and therefore will benefit from a human label.

5.2.2 *Implementing active transfer learning*

The simplest forms of active transfer learning can be built with the building blocks of code that you have already learned. To implement the architecture in figure 5.7, you can create the new layer as its own model and use the final hidden layer as the features for that layer.

Here are the three steps from section 5.2.1, implemented in PyTorch. First, apply the model to a validation dataset, and capture which validation items were classified correctly and incorrectly. This data is your new training data. Your validation items have an additional label of "Correct" or "Incorrect," which is in the (verbosely but transparently named) get_deep_active_transfer_learning_uncertainty_samples() method.

Listing 5.6 Active transfer learning

```
correct_predictions = [] # validation items predicted correctly
incorrect_predictions = [] # validation items predicted incorrectly
item_hidden_layers = {} # hidden layer of each item, by id

for item in validation_data:

    id = item[0]
    text = item[1]
    label = item[2]

    feature_vector = feature_method(text)
    hidden, logits, log_probs = model(feature_vector, return_all_layers=True)

    item_hidden_layers[id] = hidden         Store the hidden layer for this item
                                            to use later for our new model.
    prob_dist = torch.exp(log_probs)
    # get confidence that item is disaster-related
    prob_related = math.exp(log_probs.data.tolist()[0][1])

    if item[3] == "seen":                   The item was correctly predicted, so it
        correct_predictions.append(item)    gets a "Correct" label in our new model.

    elif(label=="1" and prob_related > 0.5) or (label=="0" and prob_related
➥       <= 0.5):
        correct_predictions.append(item)    The item was incorrectly predicted,
    else:                                   so it gets an "Incorrect" label in our
        incorrect_predictions.append(item)  new model.
```

Second, create a new output layer for the model trained on your new training data, predicting your new "Correct" and "Incorrect" labels.

Listing 5.7 Creating a new output layer

```
correct_model = SimpleUncertaintyPredictor(128)
loss_function = nn.NLLLoss()
optimizer = optim.SGD(correct_model.parameters(), lr=0.01)

for epoch in range(epochs):        ◁─────┐  The code for training is similar to
    if self.verbose:                      │  the other examples in this book.
        print("Epoch: "+str(epoch))
    current = 0

    # make a subset of data to use in this epoch
    # with an equal number of items from each label

    shuffle(correct_predictions) #randomize the order of the validation data
    shuffle(incorrect_predictions) #randomize the order of the validation data

    correct_ids = {}
    for item in correct_predictions:
        correct_ids[item[0]] = True
    epoch_data = correct_predictions[:select_per_epoch]
    epoch_data += incorrect_predictions[:select_per_epoch]
    shuffle(epoch_data)

    # train the final layers model
    for item in epoch_data:
        id = item[0]
        label = 0
        if id in correct_ids:
            label = 1
                                                Here, we use the hidden layer from
        correct_model.zero_grad()               the original model as our feature
                                                vector.
        feature_vec = item_hidden_layers[id]  ◁──┘
        target = torch.LongTensor([label])

        log_probs = correct_model(feature_vec)

        # compute loss function, do backward pass, and update the gradient
        loss = loss_function(log_probs, target)
        loss.backward(retain_graph=True)
        optimizer.step()
```

Finally, run your unlabeled data items through the new model, and sample the items that are predicted to be incorrect with the highest confidence.

Listing 5.8 Predicting "Incorrect" labels

```
deep_active_transfer_preds = []
                                       The code for evaluation is similar
with torch.no_grad():          ◁──────┘ to the others in this book.
    v=0
```

```
for item in unlabeled_data:
    text = item[1]

    # get prediction from main model
    feature_vector = feature_method(text)      ◁
    hidden, logits, log_probs = model(feature_vector,
    ⤳ return_all_layers=True)

    # use hidden layer from main model as input to model predicting
    ⤳ correct/errors
    logits, log_probs = correct_model(hidden, return_all_layers=True)  ◁

    # get confidence that item is correct
    prob_correct = 1 - math.exp(log_probs.data.tolist()[0][1])

    if(label == "0"):
        prob_correct = 1 - prob_correct

    item[3] = "predicted_error"
    item[4] = 1 - prob_correct
    deep_active_transfer_preds.append(item)


deep_active_transfer_preds.sort(reverse=True, key=lambda x: x[4])

return deep_active_transfer_preds[:number:]
```

First, we need to get the hidden layer from our original model.

Then we use that hidden layer as the feature vector for our new model.

If you are interested in the disaster-response text classification task, try it with this new method for active transfer learning:

```
> python active_learning.py --transfer_learned_uncertainty=10 --verbose
```

As you can see in this code, we are not altering our original model for predicting whether a message is related to disaster response. Instead of replacing the final layer of that model, we are effectively adding a new output layer over the existing model. As an alternative, you could replace the final layer with the same result.

This architecture is used in this book because it is nondestructive. The old model remains. This architecture prevents unwanted errors when you still want to use the original model, either in production or for other sampling strategies. You also avoid needing the extra memory to have two copies of the full model in parallel. Building a new layer or copying and modifying the model are equivalent, so choose whichever approach is right for your codebase. All this code is in the same file as the methods discussed earlier in this chapter: advanced_active_learning.py.

5.2.3   *Active transfer learning with more layers*

You don't need to limit active transfer learning to a single new layer or build on only the last hidden layer. As figure 5.8 shows, you can build multiple new layers, and they can connect directly with any hidden layer.

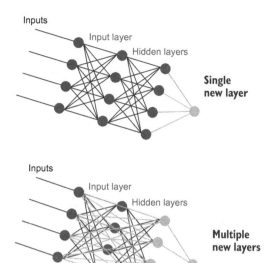

Figure 5.8 More-complicated active transfer learning architectures, using active transfer learning to create a prediction. The top example has a single neuron in the new output layer. The bottom example is a more-complicated architecture, with a new hidden layer that connects with multiple existing hidden layers.

The extension to the more-complicated architecture in figure 5.8 requires only a few lines of extra code. First, the new model to predict "Correct" or "Incorrect" needs a hidden layer. Then that new model will take its features from multiple hidden layers. You can append the vectors from the different layers to one another, and this flattened vector becomes the features for the new model.

If you are familiar with contextual models for natural language processing (NLP) or convolutional models for computer vision, this process is a familiar one; you are extracting the activations of neurons from several parts of your network and flattening into one long feature vector. The resulting vector is often called a *representation* because you are using the neurons from one model to represent your features in another model. We will return to representations in chapter 9, where they are also important for some semi-automated methods for creating training data.

The fact that you *can* build a more complicated model, however, doesn't mean that you *should* build it. If you don't have a lot of validation data, you are more likely to overfit a more-complicated model. It is a lot easier to avoid training errors if you are training only a single new output neuron. Use your instincts about how complicated your model needs to be, based on what you would normally build for that amount of data for a binary prediction task.

5.2.4 The pros and cons of active transfer learning

Active transfer learning has some nice properties that make it suitable for a wide range of problems:

- You are reusing your hidden layers, so you are building models directly based on your model's current information state.

- You don't need too many labeled items for the model to be effective, especially if you are retraining only the last layer (handy if your validation data is not large).
- It is fast to train, especially if you are retraining only the last layer.
- It works with many architectures. You may be predicting labels at document or image level, predicting objects within an image, or generating sequences of text. For all these use cases, you can add a new final layer or layers to predict "Correct" or "Incorrect." (For more on active learning use cases, see chapter 6.)
- You don't need to normalize the different ranges of activation across different neurons, because your model is going to work out that task for you.

The fifth point is especially nice. Recall that with model-based outliers, you need to quantize the activation with the validation data because some of the neurons could be arbitrarily higher or lower in their average activation. It is nice to be able to pass the information to another layer of the neurons and tell that new layer to figure out exactly what weight to apply to the activation of each existing neuron. Active transfer learning also has some drawbacks:

- Like other uncertainty sampling techniques, it can focus too much on one part of the feature space; therefore, it lacks diversity.
- You can overfit your validation data. If there aren't many validation items, your model for predicting uncertainty may not generalize beyond your validation data to your unlabeled data.

The first problem can be partially addressed without additional human labels, as you see later in this chapter in section 5.3.2. This fact is one of the biggest strengths of this approach compared with the other uncertainty sampling algorithms.

The overfitting problem can be diagnosed relatively easily too, because it manifests itself as high confidence that an item is an error. If you have a binary prediction for your main model, and your error-prediction model is 95% confident that an item was classified incorrectly, your main model should have classified that item correctly in the first place.

If you find that you are overfitting and that stopping the training earlier doesn't help, you can try to avoid overfitting by getting multiple predictions, using the ensemble methods from section 3.4 of chapter 3. These methods include training multiple models, using dropouts at inference (Monte Carlo sampling), and drawing from different subsets of the validation items and features.

5.3   *Applying active transfer learning to representative sampling*

We can apply the same active transfer learning principles to representative sampling. That is, we can adapt our models to predict whether an item is most like the application domain of our model compared with the current training data.

This approach will help with domain adaptation, like the representative sampling methods that you learned in chapter 4. In fact, representative sampling is not too different. In both chapter 4 and the example in the following sections, you are building a new model to predict whether an item is most representative of the data to which you are trying to adapt your model.

5.3.1   *Making your model predict what it doesn't know*

In principle, you don't need your existing model to predict whether an item is in your training data or in your unlabeled data. You can build a new model that uses both your training data and your unlabeled data as a binary prediction problem. In practice, it is useful to include features that are important for the machine learning task that you are trying to build.

Figure 5.9 shows the process and architecture for representative active transfer learning, showing how you can retrain your model to predict whether unlabeled items are more like your current training data or more like the application domain for your model.

As figure 5.9 shows, there are few differences from active transfer learning for uncertainty sampling. First, the original model predictions are ignored. The validation and

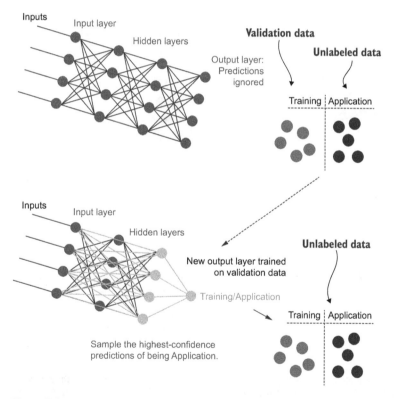

Figure 5.9   We can build a model to sample the items that are most unlike the current training data. To begin, we take validation data from the same distribution as the training data and give it a "Training" label. Then we take unlabeled data from our target domain and give it an "Application" label. We train a new output layer to predict the "Training" and "Application" labels, giving it access to all layers of the model. We apply the new model to the unlabeled data (ignoring the unlabeled items that we trained on), and sample the items that are most confidently predicted as "Application."

unlabeled data can be given labels directly. The validation data is from the same distribution as the training data, so it is given a "Training" label. The unlabeled data from the target domain is given an "Application" label. Then the model is trained on these labels.

Second, the new model should have access to more layers. If you are adapting to a new domain, you may have many features that do not yet exist in your training data. In such a case, the only information that your existing model contains is the fact that these features exist in the input layer as features but have not contributed to any other layer in the previous model. The more-complicated type of architecture will capture this information.

5.3.2   *Active transfer learning for adaptive representative sampling*

Just like representative sampling (chapter 4) can be adaptive, active transfer learning for representative sampling can be adaptive, meaning that you can have multiple iterations within one active learning cycle, as shown in figure 5.10.

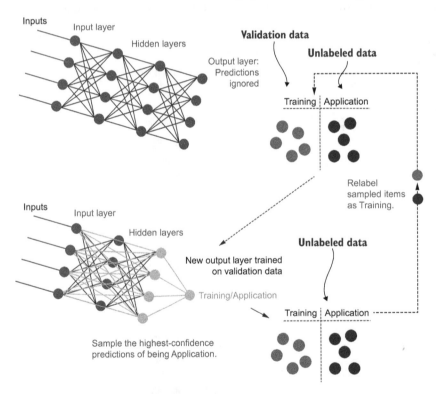

Figure 5.10   Because our sampled items will get a human label later, we can assume that they become part of the training data without needing to know what the label is. To begin, we take validation data from the same distribution as the training data and give it a "Training" label. We take unlabeled data from our target domain and give it an "Application" label. We train a new output layer to predict the "Training" and "Application" labels, giving it access to all layers of the model. We apply the new model to the unlabeled data (ignoring the unlabeled items that we trained on) and sample the items that are most confidently predicted as "Application." We can assume that those items will later get labels and become part of the training data. So we can take those sampled items, change their label from "Application" to "Training," and retrain our final layer(s) on the new dataset.

The process in figure 5.10 starts like the non-adaptive version. We create new output layers to classify whether an item is in the existing training data or in the target domain, sampling the items that are most confidently predicted as "Application." To extend the process to the adaptive strategy, we can assume that the sampled items will later get a label and become part of the training data. So we can take those sampled items, change their label from "Application" to "Training," and retrain our final layer(s) on the new dataset. This process can be repeated until there are no more confident predictions for "Application" domain items, or until you reach the maximum number of items that you want to sample in this iteration of active learning.

5.3.3 *The pros and cons of active transfer learning for representative sampling*

The pros and cons of active transfer learning for representative sampling are the same as for the simpler representative sampling methods in chapter 4. Compared with those methods, the pros can be more positive because you are using more powerful models, but some of the cons, such as the danger of overfitting, become bigger potential errors.

To summarize those strengths and weaknesses again: representative sampling is effective when you have all the data in a new domain, but if you're adapting to future data that you haven't sampled yet, your model can wind up being stuck in the past. This method is also the most prone to noise of all the active learning strategies in this book. If you have new data that is corrupted text—text from a language that is not part of your target domain, corrupted image files, artifacts that arise from using different cameras, and so on—any of these factors could look different from your current training data, but not in an interesting way. Finally, active transfer learning for representative sampling can do more harm than good if you apply it in iterations after you use uncertainty sampling, because your application domain will have more items away from the decision boundary than your training data. For these reasons, I recommended that you deploy active transfer learning for representative sampling only in combination with other sampling strategies, as you learned in section 5.1.

5.4 *Active transfer learning for adaptive sampling*

The final algorithm for active learning in this book is also the most powerful; it is a form of uncertainty sampling that can be adaptive within one iteration of active learning. All the uncertainty sampling techniques that you learned in chapter 3 were nonadaptive. Within one active learning cycle, all these techniques risk sampling items from only one small part of the problem space.

Active transfer learning for adaptive sampling (ATLAS) is an exception, allowing adaptive sampling within one iteration without also using clustering to ensure diversity. ATLAS is introduced here with the caveat that it is the least-tested algorithm in this book at the time of publication. I invented ATLAS in late 2019 when I realized that active transfer learning had certain properties that could be exploited to make it adaptive. ATLAS has been successful on the data that I have been experimenting with, but it has not yet been widely deployed in industry or tested under peer review in academia. As you would with any new method, be prepared to experiment to be certain that this algorithm is right for your data.

5.4.1   *Making uncertainty sampling adaptive by predicting uncertainty*

As you learned in chapter 3, most uncertainty sampling algorithms have the same problem: they can sample from one part of the feature space, meaning that all the samples are similar in one iteration of active learning. You can end up sampling items from only one small part of your feature space if you are not careful.

As you learned in section 5.1.1, you can address this problem by combining clustering and uncertainty sampling. This approach is still the recommended way to think about beginning your active learning strategy; you can try ATLAS after you have that baseline. You can exploit two interesting properties of active transfer learning for uncertainty sampling:

- You are predicting whether the model is correct, not the actual label.
- You can generally expect to predict the labels of your training data items correctly.

Taken together, these two items mean that you can assume that your sampled items will be correct later, even if you don't yet know the labels (figure 5.11).

The process in figure 5.11 starts like the non-adaptive version. We create new output layers to classify whether an item is "Correct" or "Incorrect," sampling the items that are most confidently predicted as "Incorrect." To extend this architecture to the adaptive strategy, we can assume that those sampled items will be labeled later and become part of the training data, and that they will be predicted correctly after they receive a label (whatever that label might be). So we can take those sampled items, change their label from "Incorrect" to "Correct," and retrain our final layer(s) on the new dataset. This process can be repeated until we have no more confidence predictions for "Incorrect" domain items or reach the maximum number of items that we

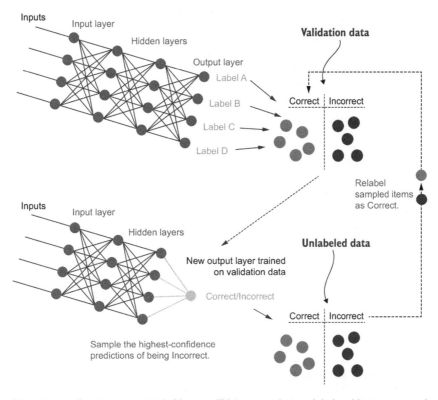

Figure 5.11 Because our sampled items will later get a human label and become part of the training data, we can assume that the model will later predict those items correctly, because models are typically the most accurate on the actual items on which they trained. To begin, validation items are predicted by the model and bucketed as "Correct" or "Incorrect," according to whether they were classified correctly. The last layer of the model is retrained to predict whether items are "Correct" or "Incorrect," effectively turning the two buckets into new labels. We apply the new model to the unlabeled data, predicting whether each item will be "Correct" or "Incorrect." We can sample the most likely to be "Incorrect." Then we can assume that those items will get labels later and become part of the training data, which will be labeled correctly by a model that predicted on that same data. So we can take those sampled items, change their label from "Incorrect" to "Correct," and retrain our final layer(s) on the new dataset.

want to sample in this iteration of active learning. It takes only 10 lines of code to implement ATLAS as a wrapper for active learning for uncertainty sampling.

Listing 5.9   Active transfer learning for adaptive sampling

```
def get_atlas_samples(self, model, unlabeled_data, validation_data,
⇒ feature_method, number=100, limit=10000, number_per_iteration=10,
⇒ epochs=10, select_per_epoch=100):
"""Uses transfer learning to predict uncertainty within the model

Keyword arguments:
    model -- machine learning model to get predictions from to determine
    ⇒ uncertainty
    unlabeled_data -- data that does not yet have a label
    validation_data -- data with a label that is not in the training set, to
    ⇒ be used for transfer learning
    feature_method -- the method for extracting features from your data
    number -- number of items to sample
    number_per_iteration -- number of items to sample per iteration
    limit -- sample from only this many items for faster sampling (-1 = no
    ⇒ limit)
"""

if(len(unlabeled_data) < number):
    raise Exception('More samples requested than the number of unlabeled
    ⇒ items')

atlas_samples = [] # all items sampled by atlas

while(len(atlas_samples) < number):
    samples =
    ⇒ self.get_deep_active_transfer_learning_uncertainty_samples(model,
    ⇒ unlabeled_data, validation_data, feature_method,
    ⇒ number_per_iteration, limit, epochs, select_per_epoch)

    for item in samples:
        atlas_samples.append(item)
        unlabeled_data.remove(item)

        item = copy.deepcopy(item)
        item[3] = "seen" # mark this item as already seen

        validation_data.append(item) # append so that it is in the next
        ⇒ iteration

return atlas_samples
```

The key line of code adds a copy of the sampled item to the validation data after each cycle. If you are interested in the disaster-response text classification task, try it with this new method for an implementation of ATLAS:

```
> python active_learning.py --atlas=100 --verbose
```

Because you are selecting 10 items by default (`number_per_iteration=10`) and want 100 total, you should see the model retrain 10 times during the sampling process. Play around with smaller numbers per iteration for a more diverse selection, which will take more time to retrain.

Although ATLAS adds only one step to the active transfer learning for uncertainty sampling architecture that you first learned, it can take a little bit of time to get your head around it. There aren't many cases in machine learning in which you can confidently give a label to an unlabeled item without human review. The trick is that we are not giving our items an actual label; we know that the label will come later.

5.4.2 *The pros and cons of ATLAS*

The biggest pro of ATLAS is that it addresses both uncertainty sampling and diversity sampling in one method. This method has another interesting advantage over the other methods of uncertainty sampling: it won't get stuck in inherently ambiguous parts of your feature space. If you have data that is inherently ambiguous, that data will continue to have high uncertainty for your model. After you annotate the data in one iteration of active learning, your model might still find the most uncertainty in that data in the next iteration. Here, our model's (false) assumption that it will get this data right later helps us. We need to see only a handful of ambiguous items for ATLAS to start focusing on other parts of our feature space. There aren't many cases in which a model's making a mistake will help, but this case is one of them.

The biggest con is the flip side: sometimes, you won't get enough labels from one part of your feature space. You won't know for certain how many items you need from each part of your feature space until you get the actual labels. This problem is the equivalent of deciding how many items to sample from each cluster when combining clustering and uncertainty sampling. Fortunately, future iterations of active learning will take you back to this part of your feature space if you don't have enough labels. So it is safe to underestimate if you know that you will have more iterations of active learning later.

The other cons largely come from the fact that this method is untested and has the most complicated architecture. You may need a fair amount of hyperparameter tuning to build the most accurate models to predict "Correct" and "Incorrect." If you can't automate that tuning and need to do it manually, this process is not an automated adaptive process. Because the models are a simple binary task, and you are not retraining all the layers, the models shouldn't require much tuning.

5.5 *Advanced active learning cheat sheets*

For quick reference, figures 5.12 and 5.13 show cheat sheets for the advanced active learning strategies in section 5.1 and the active transfer learning techniques in sections 5.2, 5.3, and 5.4.

Advanced active learning cheat sheet

Supervised machine learning models have two types of errors that can be fixed with more labeled data: errors that the models know about and errors that the models don't yet know about. *Uncertainty sampling* is the *active learning* strategy to find the known errors, and *diversity sampling* is the strategy to find the unknown errors. This cheat sheet has 10 common methods to combine uncertainty sampling and diversity sampling. See my cheat sheets on each for background: http://bit.ly/uncertainty_sampling | http://bit.ly/diversity_sampling

1. Least confidence sampling with clustering-based sampling: Sample items that are confusing to your model and then cluster those items to ensure a diverse sample.

2. Uncertainty sampling with model-based outliers: Sample items that are confusing to your model and within those find items with low activation in the model.

3. Uncertainty sampling with model-based outliers and clustering: Combine methods 1 and 2.

4. Representative cluster-based sampling: Cluster your data to capture multinodal distributions and sample items that are most like your target domain.

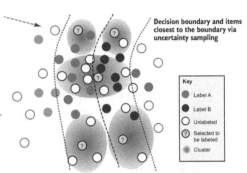

5. Sampling from the highest-entropy cluster: Cluster your unlabeled data and find the cluster with the highest average confusion for your model.

6. Uncertainty sampling and representative sampling: Sample items that are both confusing to your current model and the most like your target domain.

7. Model-based outliers and representative sampling: Sample items that have low activation in your model but are relatively common in your target domain.

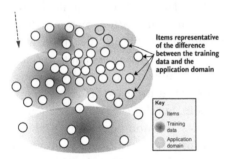

8. Clustering with itself for hierarchical clusters: Recursively cluster to maximize the diversity.

9. Sampling from the highest-entropy cluster with margin of confidence sampling: Find the cluster with the most confusion and then sample for the maximum pairwise label confusion within that cluster.

10. Combining ensemble methods and dropouts with individual strategies: Aggregate results that come from multiple models or multiple predictions from one model via Monte Carlo dropouts aka Bayesian deep learning.

Tip: Treat the individual active learning methods as building blocks to be combined:

Uncertainty sampling and diversity sampling work best in combination.

While academic papers about combining uncertainty sampling and diversity sampling focus on single metrics that combine the two, in practice you can simply chain the methods: apply one method to get a large sample and then refine that sample with another method.

Robert (Munro) Monarch. *Human-in-the-Loop Machine Learning,* Manning Publications. http://bit.ly/huml_book See the book for more details on active learning building blocks and advanced methods for combining them, with open source implementations in PyTorch. robertmunro.com | @WWRob

Figure 5.12 Advanced active learning cheat sheet

Active transfer learning cheat sheet

Supervised machine learning models can combine active learning and transfer learning to sample the optimal unlabeled items for human review. Transfer learning tells us whether our model will correctly predict the label of an item and which item looks most like data from our application domain. This cheat sheet builds on principles of uncertainty sampling and diversity sampling: http://bit.ly/uncertainty_sampling | http://bit.ly/diversity_sampling

Active transfer learning for uncertainty sampling:
Validation items are predicted by the model and relabeled as Correct or Incorrect according to whether they were predicted correctly. The last layer of the model is then retrained to predict whether items are Correct or Incorrect. Unlabeled items can now be predicted by the new model as to whether our initial model will give Correct or Incorrect predictions, and we sample the most likely to be Incorrect.

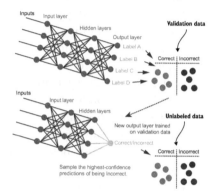

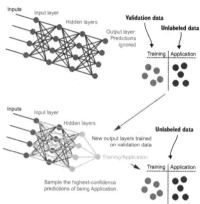

Active transfer learning for representative sampling:
To adapt to new domains, we retrain our model to predict whether an unlabeled item looks more like validation data from the distribution of our current training data or data from our application domain. *Tip:* Allow the new model to see all layers to minimize bias from your current model state.

Active transfer learning for adaptive sampling (ATLAS): We can make our models adaptive by assuming that our items will get a human label later, even if we don't yet know what that label will be. We assume that our model will predict items like these correctly after it has been trained on them. So we can continually retrain our model with our samples. ATLAS therefore addresses both uncertainty sampling and diversity sampling in a single adaptive system.

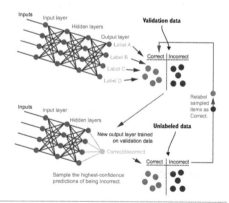

Robert (Munro) Monarch. *Human-in-the-Loop Machine Learning*, Manning Publications. http://bit.ly/huml_book See the book for more details on active learning advanced active learning, and Active transfer learning, with open source implementations in PyTorch. robertmunro.com | @WWRob

Figure 5.13   Active transfer learning cheat sheet

5.6 *Further reading for active transfer learning*

As you learned in the chapter, there is little existing work on the advanced active learning techniques in which one method is used to sample a large number of items and a second method is used to refine the sample. Academic papers about combining uncertainty sampling and diversity sampling focus on single metrics that combine the two methods, but in practice, you can simply chain the methods: apply one method to get a large sample and then refine that sample with another method. The academic papers tend to compare the combined metrics to the individual methods in isolation, so they will not give you an idea of whether they are better than chaining the methods together (section 5.1).

The active transfer learning methods in this chapter are more advanced than the methods currently reported in academic or industry-focused papers. I have given talks about the methods before publishing this book, but all the content in those talks appears in this chapter, so there is nowhere else to read about them. I didn't discover the possibility of extending active transfer learning to adaptive learning until late 2019, while I was creating the PyTorch library to accompany this chapter. After this book is published, look for papers that cite ATLAS for the up-to-date research.

If you like the fact that ATLAS turns active learning into a machine learning problem in itself, you can find a long list of interesting research papers. For as long as active learning has existed, people have been thinking about how to apply machine learning to the process of sampling items for human review. One good recent paper that I recommend is "Learning Active Learning from Data," by Ksenia Konyushkova, Sznitman Raphael, and Pascal Fua (http://mng.bz/Gxj8). Look for the most-cited works in this paper and more recent work that cites this paper for approaches to active learning that use machine learning. For a deep dive, look at the PhD dissertation of Ksenia Konyushkova, the first author of the NeurIPS paper, which includes a comprehensive literature review.

For an older paper that looks at ways to combine uncertainty and representative sampling, I recommend "Optimistic Active Learning Using Mutual Information," by Yuhong Guo and Russ Greiner (http://mng.bz/zx9g).

Summary

- You have many ways to combine uncertainty sampling and diversity sampling. These techniques will help you optimize your active learning strategy to sample the items for annotation that will most help your model's accuracy.
- Combining uncertainty sampling and clustering is the most common active learning technique and is relatively easy to implement after everything that you have learned in this book so far, so it is a good starting point for exploring advanced active learning strategies.
- Active transfer learning for uncertainty sampling allows you to build a model to predict whether unlabeled items will be labeled correctly, using your existing

model as the starting point for the uncertainty-predicting model. This approach allows you to use machine learning within the uncertainty sampling process.

- Active transfer learning for representative sampling allows you to build a model to predict whether unlabeled items are more like your target domain than your existing training data. This approach allows you to use machine learning within the representative sampling process.

- ATLAS allows you to extend active transfer learning for uncertainty sampling so that you are not oversampling items from one area of your feature space, combining aspects of uncertainty sampling and diversity sampling into a single machine learning model.

Applying active learning to different machine learning tasks

6

This chapter covers

- Calculating uncertainty and diversity for object detection
- Calculating uncertainty and diversity for semantic segmentation
- Calculating uncertainty and diversity for sequence labeling
- Calculating uncertainty and diversity for language generation
- Calculating uncertainty and diversity for speech, video, and information retrieval
- Choosing the right number of samples for human review

In chapters 3, 4, and 5, the examples and algorithms focused on document-level or image-level labels. In this chapter, you will learn how the same principles of uncertainty sampling and diversity sampling can be applied to more complicated computer vision tasks such as object detection and semantic segmentation (pixel labeling) and more complicated natural language processing (NLP) tasks such as sequence labeling and natural language generation. The general principles are the same, and in many cases, there is no change at all. The biggest difference is how you sample the items selected by active learning, and that will depend on the real-world problem that you are trying to solve.

Most real-world machine learning systems use tasks that are more complicated than document-level or image-level label predictions. Even problems that sound simple tend to require advanced active learning techniques when you dive into them. Imagine that you are building a computer vision system to help with agriculture. You have smart tractors with cameras that need to distinguish seedlings from weeds so that the tractors can efficiently and accurately apply fertilizer and herbicides. Although weeding fields is one of the most common and repetitive tasks in human history, you need object detection within an image, not image-level labels, to automate this task.

Also, your model has different kinds of confusion. In some cases, your model knows that an object is a plant but can't decide whether that plant is a seedling or a weed. In other cases, your model isn't certain whether some new object is a plant because all kinds of small objects can find their way onto a field. You need uncertainty sampling for the seedling/weed distinction combined with diversity sampling to identify new objects.

Finally, your camera is capturing up to 100 plants in every image, so you have to decide how to resolve the image-level confusion with the object-level confusion. Do you prioritize human review when one object in the image is very confusing or when 100 objects are a little confusing? Do you prioritize the correct label for the type of object or the accuracy of the object outline? Any of these types of error could be the most important for the problem you are addressing, so you need to decide how to map your real-world problem to the right sampling and evaluation strategy. Therefore, even though you are automating one of the most common and repetitive tasks in history, you need advanced active learning techniques to solve the problem.

6.1 Applying active learning to object detection

Until now, we have looked at relatively simple machine learning problems: making predictions about whole images (image labeling) or whole pieces of text (document labeling). For many problems, however, more fine-grained predictions are needed.

You may want to identify only certain objects within an image, for example, so you care more about uncertainty and diversity in the objects than in the backgrounds. Our example at the start of the chapter is like this: you care about identifying weeds more than identifying the field that surrounds them. To the extent that you care about the background, you care only so that you can distinguish the weeds from different backgrounds.

For these examples, you want to employ active learning strategies that also focus on the areas that you care about. Sometimes, you get this focus for free; your models are concentrating on the areas that you care about, so you won't often need to change anything in the approaches that you learned for image and document labeling. In other cases, you need to crop/mask your data to the areas that you care about and be careful that you are not introducing bias in that process. For the next few sections of this chapter, we will go over some kinds of machine learning problems and see how the active learning strategies that you have already learned can be adapted to them.

Figure 6.1 illustrates a problem for identifying uncertainty and diversity in object detection tasks. Assume that this task uses the same example image from chapter 3, but whereas in chapter 3, we wanted only to predict a label for the image, now we want to identify specific objects within an image and place a bounding box around those images. As figure 6.1 shows, the object we care about—the bicycle—is only a tiny fraction of the pixels in the bounding box that surrounds it.

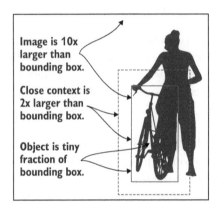

Image is 10x larger than bounding box.

Close context is 2x larger than bounding box.

Object is tiny fraction of bounding box.

Figure 6.1   An illustration of the problem of identifying uncertainty and diversity in object detection tasks. The object we care about—the bicycle—is a small percentage of the pixels in the bounding box that surrounds it. Even a modest amount of context is twice the number of pixels, and the image as a whole is 10 times the number of pixels of the bounding box. Therefore, if we tried to calculate uncertainty or diversity across the whole image, we would risk focusing on a lot of irrelevant information.

The edge of an object is often where the most information is, but increasing the context by 20% will almost double the total amount of pixels at which we are looking. The image as a whole is 10 times the number of pixels of the bounding box. Therefore, if we tried to calculate uncertainty or diversity across the whole image, we would risk focusing on a lot of irrelevant information. Although we can use the uncertainty sampling and diversity sampling techniques that we learned in chapters 4 and 5, we want to focus that uncertainty and diversity on the areas about which we care most.

The rest of this section will cover how to calculate uncertainty and diversity. You get uncertainty fairly easily from your models; the highest uncertainty will tend to be in your objects, not in the background. For diversity, you want to focus primarily on diversity in areas that are also uncertain.

6.1.1   *Accuracy for object detection: Label confidence and localization*

You have two tasks here: object detection and object labeling. You should apply different types of uncertainty and diversity to both tasks:

- Labeling each object (bicycle, human, pedestrian, and so on)
- Identifying the boundaries of objects in an image

The confidence for each task is

- Object label confidence (confidence that the label is correct)
- Object localization confidence (confidence that the bounding box is correct)

If you get a confidence score from your object detection algorithm, your confidence score is most likely *only* the object label confidence. The majority of object detection algorithms used today use convolutional neural networks (CNNs) and rely on regression to arrive at the right bounding box. All these algorithms return the label confidence, but few return a score from the regression that arrived at the bounding box itself.

You can determine label accuracy the same way that you determine image-and document-level accuracy: by looking at some variation on F-score or area under the curve (AUC), as you learned in earlier chapters and the appendix. Intersection over union (IoU) is the most common metric for determining localization accuracy. If you've worked in computer vision before, you are aware of IoU already. Figure 6.2 shows an example of IoU, calculating accuracy as the area where the predicted and actual bounding box intersect, divided by the total area covered by those two boxes.

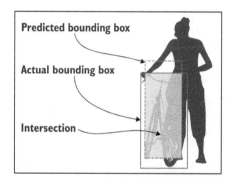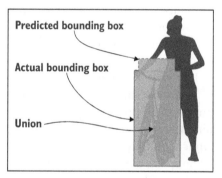

Figure 6.2 An example of IoU for measuring the accuracy of a bounding box. The accuracy is calculated as the area that intersects the predicted bounding box with the actual bounding box, divided by the area that is the union of the two boxes.

IoU is also used in active learning for object detection, so it's important to learn (or refresh your knowledge) before you jump into uncertainty sampling and diversity sampling for object detection. In terms of the accuracy metrics that we've already looked at, IoU is more strict in that it tends to have lower values over the same data. Think of IoU in terms of the amount of area (or pixels) that is correct or incorrectly predicted:

$$\text{precision} = \frac{\text{true positives}}{\text{true positives} + \text{false positives}}$$

$$\text{recall} = \frac{\text{true positives}}{\text{true positives} + \text{false positives}}$$

$$\text{F-score} = \frac{2 \cdot \text{precision} \cdot \text{recall}}{\text{precision} + \text{recall}}$$

$$\text{IoU} = \frac{\text{true positives}}{\text{true positives} + \text{false positives} + \text{false negatives}}$$

Like F-score, IoU combines both types of errors: false positives and false negatives. IoU is always lower than F-score except in the trivial case of 100% accuracy. F-score tends to be more popular in NLP, and IoU is used almost exclusively in computer vision. You'll see AUC in the literature for most machine learning fields, although AUC is not used as often as it should be in NLP and computer vision.

You will also see mean average precision (mAP) in the computer vision literature. mAP is a different kind of curve from AUC, but with a similar idea. For mAP, you rank the items by precision and then plot by recall, creating a precision-recall curve, and the average precision is the area under that curve. This application of mAP requires a threshold at which an object is "correct"—often, an IoU of 0.5 or 0.75. The exact threshold calculation of mAP tends to vary and is often defined specifically for different datasets and use cases. For a highly calibrated task such as autonomous driving, you obviously want much more than 0.50 IoU to call the prediction correct. It is not important to know any of the mAP calculations for this book; it is sufficient to be aware of this other, common accuracy metric that will be task-specific.

For active learning, you generally want to employ a strategy that samples from both localization confidence and label confidence. You need to determine how much you want to focus on each type. Although your label and IoU accuracy will help you determine where you need to focus the most attention, your focus will also depend on the application that you are building.

Suppose that you are deploying our example model to detect pedestrians, cars, bicycles, and other objects on roads. If your application is designed to predict collisions, localization is most important; it doesn't matter whether you get the label wrong as much as it matters whether your object boundaries are off. If your application is meant to identify different traffic volumes, however, the exact boundaries of the objects aren't important, but the labels are important because you want to be precise about knowing exactly how many cars, pedestrians, and other objects are seen.

So you could have the same model deployed in the same place, but depending on the use case, you might focus your active learning and data annotation strategies on either localization or confidence. Determine what is most important for your use case, and focus your active learning strategy accordingly.

6.1.2 Uncertainty sampling for label confidence and localization in object detection

You can use label confidence for uncertainty sampling, as you did for image-level labels in chapter 3. Your object detection model will give a probability distribution, and you can apply least confidence, margin of confidence, ratio of confidence, entropy, or an ensemble model to determine your uncertainty for the label prediction.

For localization confidence, an ensemble model is your best option, combining multiple deterministic predictions into a single one that can be interpreted as confidence. Figure 6.3 shows an example. You can use either of two approaches: a true ensemble or dropouts within one model, both of which you learned in chapter 3.

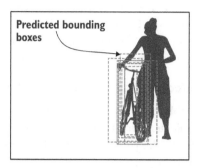
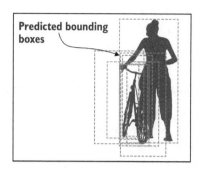
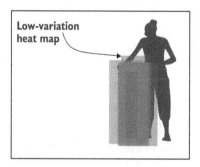
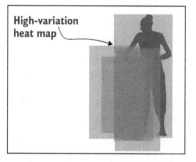

Figure 6.3 An example prediction heat map for an object, showing low variation (left) and high variation (right). The high variation is evidence of more uncertainty in the model; therefore, the right example is a good candidate for human evaluation. You can generate multiple predictions by using ensemble models, getting predictions from multiple models and changing the parameters, using a subset of features or a subset of items, or introducing random variation into your models in some other way. Within a single model, you can generate multiple predictions for a single item by using a dropout over a random selection of neurons for each prediction (known as Monte Carlo dropouts). You can also combine both methods: create an ensemble of models, and use dropouts for multiple predictions per model.

For a true ensemble, you get predictions from multiple models and ensure that those predictions will vary by using different hyperparameters for different models, training on a subset of features for each model, training on a subset of items for each model, or introducing random variation into your training runs in other ways, such as shuffling the order of training items.

For a single model, you can generate multiple predictions by using a dropout over a random selection of neurons for each prediction (aka Monte Carlo dropout). This approach is faster and easier than building multiple models and surprisingly effective for how simple it is. You could also combine both methods: train a handful of models with different parameters and then apply dropouts to each model.

The uncertainty is calculated from the average IoU across all predictions. This calculation naturally gives a [0, 1] range, so there is no need to normalize it. Divide by the number of models, not predictions. Some models may not make a prediction, and this information is important: treat all nonpredictions as IoU=0.

Now that you have an uncertainty score for each bounding box, you can sample the bounding boxes with the greatest uncertainty for human review. If you are using ensemble methods or dropouts for localization, you can use them for label confidence, in place of or in addition to the other uncertainty sampling methods.

6.1.3   *Diversity sampling for label confidence and localization in object detection*

For diversity sampling, we need to solve the problem that we introduced at the start of this chapter: we care about diversity in the objects more than diversity in the background. The simplest solution is to crop images to the predicted bounding boxes and then apply diversity sampling, but there are more sophisticated variations, which we'll cover in this section. Chapter 4 introduced three types of diversity sampling:

- Model-based outlier sampling
- Cluster-based sampling
- Representative sampling
- Sampling for real-world diversity

For model-based outliers and real-world diversity, you don't necessarily need to do anything beyond what you've already learned for image-level labels:

- You can apply model-based outlier detection to an object detection problem in the same way that you apply it to an image labeling problem.
- You can sample for real-world diversity in an object detection problem in the same way that you sample for an image labeling problem.

For model-based outliers, the hidden layers focus on both the labeling and localization problems, so your neurons will be capturing information primarily about the objects and labels. You can crop the images to the predicted objects and then look for model-based outliers, but the small amount of neurons dedicated to the background might be interesting for diversity, so you could lose something in this case.

For diversity sampling, the principles from chapter 4 also apply. You need to combine all the active learning methods to ensure fair data across real-world demographics. The background can matter in this case too, because you can erroneously model the context of objects rather than the objects themselves if you are not careful. (See the following sidebar.) For object detection, you may want to ensure that your data tries to balance each type of object across factors including the type of camera, zoom, time of day, and weather. Even for highly controlled settings, such as medical imaging, I've seen systems limited by training on data from only a small number of patients and only one type of imaging machine, introducing unwanted real-world bias.

Is your model really ignoring the background?

This book assumes that your model focuses on the objects and not the background. Sometimes, however, your model might be using background information erroneously. If you took photographs of bicycles only in bicycle lanes, for example, your model might be predicting bicycle lanes and be essentially blind to bicycles in other contexts. Or it might rely on bicycle lanes only when the lanes are present, which is still non-ideal, as the model is not generalizing its knowledge of bikes in those contexts to other backgrounds.

An influential recent paper on model interpretability presents another example. The authors created what looked like an accurate model for distinguishing wolves from huskies,[a] but used only photos of wolves in snow and huskies not in snow. They showed that the model was predicting whether snow was in the background, not the actual animals! This problem is a bigger one with image-level labeling, because with object detection, you are also explicitly forcing the model to learn the outline of the object itself, making it hard for your model to focus on the background. But the problem can occur to some degree in any machine learning problem in which context needs to be controlled for.

The solution is better sampling for real-world diversity, ensuring that the contexts are as diverse as possible across all the labels and objects that you care about. If you are worried about this problem with your model, here is how to diagnose it: use a method to find out which pixels are important features for your predictions (such as LIME, the method in the huskies/wolves paper, or the Captum interpretability library, which is in PyTorch as of October 2019) and then measure what percentage of the pixels fall outside the bounding boxes on your validation data. The images with the highest scores are the most likely to be problematic. Look at these images to identify any patterns in what the model is focusing on outside your bounding boxes.

[a] "Why Should I Trust You?": Explaining the Predictions of Any Classifier," by Marco Tulio Ribeiro, Sameer Singh, and Carlos Guestrin (https://www.kdd.org/kdd2016/papers/files/rfp0573-ribeiroA .pdf).

For cluster-based sampling and representative sampling, the focus should be on the objects themselves, not the backgrounds. If your background makes up 90% of your images, such as the example in figure 6.1 (repeated in figure 6.4), it will make up 90% of the influence on what determines a cluster or is representative. Figure 6.1 also contains a relatively large object that takes up half of the height of the frame. But in many cases, the example is more like the second image in figure 6.4, in which the object takes up fewer than 1% of the pixels.

In figure 6.4, the bicycle itself and immediate context are enough to identify the object as a bicycle. Some information outside the box probably can help determine the scale and context in which bicycles appear more often, but not much.

Therefore, the area around each predicted object should be cropped. Because your model isn't 100% accurate, you need to ensure that you are capturing the object.

Figure 6.4   An example of an object—a bicycle—in an image in which 99% of the image is not the bicycle. The bicycle and immediate context captured by the dotted line should be enough for identifying that the object is a bicycle. With some strategies, such as representative sampling and clustering, we need to crop or mask the image to target these areas.

Use your method from uncertainty sampling (ensembles or dropout) to make multiple predictions. Then do either of the following:

- *Crop at a given threshold.* You might create the smallest cropping that captures 90% of the predicted bounding boxes for an object, for example.
- *Use every predicted box for the same object, and weight the boxes.* You might apply representative sampling to every predicted box and then average across all the representative sampling in which the weighted average is determined by the average IoU of each box to all others.

As an alternative to cropping the image, you can ignore the pixels outside your contextual box—a process called *masking*. You can think of a mask for a model trained on pixel inputs as being a dropout on the first layer because you are ignoring some input neurons (pixels).

How important is context?

There are a few exceptions in computer vision in which the context *is* important. I've encountered only one of these exceptions on multiple occasions: identifying empty supermarket shelves to help restocking. An empty space (the object) also needed context such as adjacent items and a price tag beneath the empty shelf. Otherwise, it wasn't clear to the model whether the shelf was meant to be empty or whether there were meant to be products on the shelf.

Unless you have a use case like this one, essentially labeling a hole according to context, keep the boxes as tight as possible for clustering and representative sampling. You can capture broader diversity in contexts by using some diversity sampling for entire images.

Depending on your use case, you also want to resize the images. If you've worked in computer vision, you already have your tools of choice for resizing programmatically. It's probably not important that our bicycle is at the bottom of the photo, for example, so you can normalize your data by cropping each prediction to be the entire image and then normalize further by scaling all your sample images to be the same dimensions. As a general rule, make the crop/mask decision based on how you want to encode data for clustering and representative sampling:

- If you are using pixels as features or a separate tool to create features, crop the images, and consider whether you should also resize them.
- If you are using the hidden layer(s) from the *same* model that you are using for object detection, you can mask the images and not move or resize them. Your features can capture the similarities in objects at different locations and scales.

Now you have cropped or masked images that you can use for clustering and representative sampling! With each cropped or masked object in an image, you can apply clustering or representative sampling. You apply cluster-based sampling and representative sampling as you learned in chapter 4.

Make sure that you are sampling images with a different number of objects per image. If you find that you are sampling only images with a small or large number of objects, you are inadvertently introducing bias into your process. In such a case, stratify your sampling. You might sample 100 images that have 1 predicted object, 100 images that have 2 predicted objects, and so on.

6.1.4 *Active transfer learning for object detection*

You can apply active transfer learning to object detection in the same way that you apply it to image-level labels. You can also apply active transfer learning for adaptive sampling (ATLAS), adapting within one active learning cycle because you can assume that the first objects you sample will be corrected later by human labelers, even if you don't know what those labels are.

Regardless of the type of neural architecture you use for object detection, you can use the hidden layer(s) as the features for a binary "Correct"/"Incorrect" model that you train on validation data. As an interesting extension, instead of a binary "Correct"/"Incorrect" task, you could calculate the IoU of the validation data and create a model that predicts the IoU. That is, you can predict a continuous value instead of the binary "Correct"/"Incorrect." This process could be as simple as making the final layer a regression task instead of a classification task and having that regression task model the IoU of each validation item. This extension could involve changing only one or two lines of code from the ATLAS example in chapter 5.

6.1.5 *Setting a low object detection threshold to avoid perpetuating bias*

Set your confidence threshold for object detection low, whatever method you use. You don't want to find only objects that are similar to those that already exist in your data, which would perpetuate bias toward those types of objects.

You may find that a low threshold produces too many candidates. You might get 100 predicted images at 50% or greater confidence but 10,000 at 10% confidence, and most of those 10,000 predictions are the background (false positives that are not objects). So you might be tempted to raise the threshold in this case. Don't.

Unless you are confident that you have set the threshold correctly to get near-perfect recall in your predictions, you're still in danger of perpetuating bias in your models. Instead, stratify by confidence and sample from within each:

- Sample 100 predicted images at 10–20% confidence.
- Sample 100 predicted images at 20–30% confidence.
- Sample 100 predicted images at 30–40% confidence, and so on.

Figure 6.5 shows an example of the general strategy for stratifying by confidence.

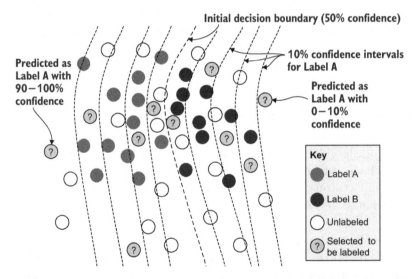

Figure 6.5 Stratifying by confidence: sampling an equal number of items at 0–10% confidence, 10–20% confidence, and so on up to 90–100% confidence. In this example, one item is sampled from each 10% confidence interval for label A. Stratifying by confidence helps most when you have a large number imbalance between labels.

As figure 6.5 shows, you can sample the same number of items at different confidence intervals. This strategy is helpful for a task such as object detection because most of your images will not contain objects that you care about. Using a sample strategy that is stratified by confidence, you'll be spending most of your time sampling high-confidence objects and still have a selection of lower-confidence ones. Note that although it feels like a waste of time to identify non-objects, that's not the case for your machine learning algorithm. Learning what is not an object but is currently predicted as an object with nontrivial confidence can be as important for your model's accuracy as learning new objects.

This kind of stratification is important for avoiding bias in your data. You can also try combinations of methods as alternatives to random sampling within each confidence:

- Take the 10,000 objects with 10–20% confidence, apply clustering, and sample the centroids to get the 100 most diverse objects within that sample.
- Take the 10,000 objects with 10–20% confidence and apply representative sampling to get the 100 objects most like your target domain.
- Take the 10,000 objects with 10–20% confidence and sample for model-based outliers to get the 100 objects most unlike the current training data.

Note that you can apply this method for stratifying by confidence to any type of task, not only object detection.

6.1.6 Creating training data samples for representative sampling that are similar to your predictions

Because you are cropping or masking your unlabeled images, you should do the same thing with training data if you are implementing representative sampling. If you use only the perfect bounding boxes from your training data but then the imperfect predictions from your unlabeled data, the "representative" samples could end up being the result of different box sizes and cropping strategies instead of the actual objects. Here are four options, in order of preference:

- Cross-validate your training data. You might split your training data into 10 equal datasets. Iteratively train on each group of nine, and predict bounding boxes on each held out dataset. Combine all the predictions, and use the combination as the training data portion of your corpus for representative sampling.
- Use a validation dataset from the same distribution as your training data, get bounding-box predictions over the validation set, and use those validation bounding boxes as the training data portion of your corpus for representative sampling.
- Predict on the training data and then randomly expand or contract the boxes so that they have the same average variation in your predictions.
- Use your actual boxes from the training data and then randomly expand or contract the boxes so that they have the same average variation in your predictions.

Options 1 and 2 are statistically equally good. If you've got a held-out validation set, the process is a little easier than retraining your entire model, but it won't be the exact data in your training set even though it is as close as possible.

For options 3 and 4, although you can increase the sizes of the bounding boxes so that the average is the same, you won't be able to match the kind of errors that you get in predictions. The predicted bounding-box errors will not be randomly distributed; they will depend on the image itself in ways that are hard to duplicate when you create artificial noise.

6.1.7   *Sampling for image-level diversity in object detection*

As with any other method, you should always randomly sample some images for review. This sample provides your evaluation data and gives you a baseline for how successful your active learning strategy is.

For a small amount of samples, you can use image-level sampling, which helps diversity in a way that prevents bias more easily than the other methods introduced in this section. If you apply clustering at the whole-image level and find whole clusters with few or no existing training items, you have good evidence that you should get human review for some items in those clusters, because you could be missing something.

If you are introducing new kinds of data to your model (maybe you are using a new camera or collecting from a new location), representative sampling at the image level should help you adapt faster. This strategy also helps you adapt with less bias than trying to implement only object-level active learning when you try to incorporate new data.

If you try object-level methods on different types of data, it will be hard to avoid biasing toward objects you have already seen, as some of those objects might still slip below the threshold you use. Confidence thresholds tend to be least reliable for out-of-domain data.

6.1.8   *Considering tighter masks when using polygons*

If you are using polygons rather than bounding boxes, as shown in figure 6.6, all the methods still apply. You have one additional option: instead of masking outside the bounding box, you can mask at a certain distance from the nearest polygon edge. In our bicycle example, this approach more closely captures the bicycle itself and not so much of the empty space.

For the same reason, error detection can be more accurate, especially for irregularly shaped objects. You can imagine that a bicycle like the one in figure 6.6 could have a handlebar sticking out in many photos. The bounding-box extension to capture only that handlebar could easily be almost half the box's area, creating a lot of room for error over pixels that aren't part of the object. The next level of complexity in image recognition, after bounding boxes and polygons, is semantic segmentation.

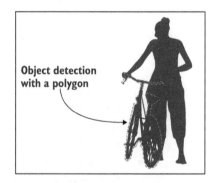

Figure 6.6   An example of object detection using a polygon rather than a bounding box. You can use the same active learning methods for both bounding boxes and polygons, with the extra option to have a closer mask for a polygon.

6.2   *Applying active learning to semantic segmentation*

Semantic segmentation occurs when the entire image receives a label, with accurate polygon boundaries around all objects. Because this technique labels every pixel in the image, it is also referred to as *pixel labeling*. Figure 6.7 shows an example.

Figure 6.7   **An example of semantic segmentation in which every pixel is labeled. This kind of colored photograph is what a lot of semantic segmentation tools look like: a coloring-in exercise. We'll cover those tools later in the book, especially in chapter 10. If you're looking at this image in black and white, the contrasting shades of gray should give you a good idea of what it would look like in color. If the objects receive a label (the four trees are labeled separately, for example), the task is known as *instance segmentation*.**

If you are trying to estimate objects that extend behind some other object (occlusion), it is more common to use the bounding-box-type object detection you learned about in section 6.1. It is also more common to paint all objects as a single type with semantic segmentation rather than identify each object separately. Every tree in figure 6.7 is the same color, for example, but the image is not distinguishing one tree from another. These commonalities are not set in stone, however: there are cases in which bounding boxes that ignore occlusion are used, semantic segmentation tries to capture occlusion, and semantic segmentation distinguishes objects (called *instance segmentation*). If a model combines all these methods, it is sometimes known as *panoptic segmentation*, identifying objects and background pixels. All the methods in this chapter should be generic enough that they can apply to any variation on bounding boxes or semantic segmentation.

The methods can apply to other kinds of sensor data, such as the 2D and 3D images that from lidar, radar, or sonar, which are all common for autonomous vehicles. It is also common to collect data outside the range of human vision in the infrared and ultraviolet bands and then shift those results into visible colors for human annotation, which is common in agriculture. Search for "infrared forest" or "ultraviolet flower" photos, and you'll see why: a lot of useful information falls outside human-viewable range! The principles in this section should still apply if additional dimensions and sensor information are involved.

6.2.1   *Accuracy for semantic segmentation*

Accuracy for semantic segmentation is calculated on a per pixel-level. How many of the pixels are classified correctly, relative to a held-out dataset? You can use all the accuracy metrics that you have learned so far: precision, recall, F-score, AUC, IoU, and micro and macro scores. The right choice for machine learning accuracy depends on your use case.

For determining uncertainty, the macro F-score or macro IoU is often most useful. As with our bounding-box examples, we often have a lot of space in semantic segmentation that we don't care about much, such as the sky and background. You can get into trouble if you have many discontinuous regions. For instance, figure 6.7 probably has more than 100 separate regions of sky between the leaves. By overall size and total number, those sky regions would dominate a micro score on a per-pixel or per-region basis, and tree-leaf confusion would dominate our uncertainty sampling strategies. So assuming that you care about all the labels equally, but not about how much of an image that object happens to take up, use a macro score: the average IoU of each region per label or the average F-score of each pixel per label.

You might also decide to ignore some labels. Perhaps you care only about people and bicycles, so you can choose a macro accuracy value that looks only at those labels. You will still get inputs from errors distinguishing people and bicycles from the background, the ground, and the sky, but not errors between those irrelevant labels. Note that exactly what matters will be specific to your use case. If your task is identifying the amount of forest coverage, the regions between leaves and the sky will matter most!

Use your deployed machine learning model accuracy as your guide for calculating uncertainty. You should make this calculation in either of two ways, depending on whether you weight your labels for your accuracy calculation:

- If you don't weight your labels (you either 100% care or don't care if each label equals absolute weightings), use the same metric that you use for model accuracy to determine where to sample. If you care about confusion for only two labels in your model accuracy, sample only predictions with confusion involving one or both of those labels for active learning.
- If you have an accuracy metric that is weighted, do *not* use the same metric as for model accuracy. Instead, use the stratified sampling methods that you learned in chapter 3. Figure 6.8 shows an example.

As figure 6.8 shows, stratified sampling by label helps focus your active learning strategy on the pixels that matter most. Although you can use stratified sampling for any machine learning problem, semantic segmentation is one of the clearest examples of where it can help.

Note that stratified sampling may diverge from your strategy for evaluating model accuracy. Suppose that you care about Label A nine times as much as you care about Label B. Calculate your model accuracy as 90% × Label A's F-score + 10% × Label B's F-score (a weighted macro F-score). This strategy is fine for model accuracy, but unfortunately, you can't apply weights in a similar way to uncertainty scores, because your weighting will almost certainty rank only Label A items highest, moving them exclusively to the top of your rankings. Instead, use those weights as a ratio of how many to sample. You might sample the 90 most uncertain Label A items and the 10 most uncertain Label B items, for example. This technique is simpler to implement than trying to create a weighted sampling strategy across labels and much more effective. If

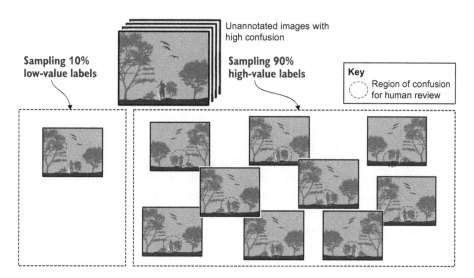

Figure 6.8 An example of stratified sampling by label applied to segmentation. For this example task, assume that we care about errors related to human and bicycle pixels more than we care about errors related to tree and sky pixels. Our active learning sample will consist of a 90:10 split: 90% will be the most confusing samples for the labels that we care about most, and 10% will be about the labels that we don't care about. Note that the pixels bordering the sky and trees vastly outnumber the pixels bordering humans and bicycles, so stratified sampling helps us focus on the errors that we care about most. Therefore, your sampling strategy might diverge from your accuracy evaluation strategy, in which you can simply apply relative weights of 90% and 10% to high- or low-value errors. The uncertainty sampling metrics don't lend themselves as easily to this kind of weighting, so unless you are confident enough in your statistics skills to tune your weighting strategy, use this stratification method.

there are labels that you don't care about, still consider sampling a small number, especially using model-based outliers and representative sampling, because they may be false negatives for the labels you *do* care about.

6.2.2 *Uncertainty sampling for semantic segmentation*

Most semantic segmentation algorithms are built on variations of CNNs, using softmax to generate a probability distribution across the possible labels for every pixel. So you can calculate the uncertainty on a per-pixel basis, using the methods you learned in chapter 3. Your model is unlikely to make a prediction for every pixel, which would be inefficient, but instead predict regions and select only small (maybe pixel-sized) regions when forced. Know exactly where your predicted confidences are coming from.

As with bounding boxes, the confidence you get from your models probably reflects your label confidence, not the confidence on the borders of your objects. If so, you can derive the localization confidence from the pixel confidences: you know which pixels are next to pixels from a different label, so the aggregate confidence from all boundary pixels is the localization confidence. You may be OK with errors of a few pixels; if so, use this margin of error to determine where you calculate confidence. If you are measuring the accuracy of your machine learning model by forgiving all errors of less than 3 pixels, for example, do the same for uncertainty, measuring the average uncertainty of the pixels that are 3 pixels away from a border.

For some reason, you may be using a model that does not give a probability distribution for a given label. In that case, you can use ensemble methods and/or dropouts to create multiple predictions and calculate uncertainty as the amount of label agreement across your predictions.

Now that you are sampling only the pixels that you care about and have an uncertainty score for each pixel, you can apply any of the uncertainty sampling algorithms. The simplest way to calculate uncertainty for the entire image is to take the average uncertainty from each of the pixels you care about. If you care mainly about the borders, you can sample the items only within a few pixels of another label.

Depending on your task, you can try metrics other than average if (for example) you want to give the image an uncertainty score that is the maximum uncertainty for any one region. Your ability to focus only on regions within the images will partially depend on your annotation setup. Will someone need to annotate the entire image, or can they annotate only the labels you care about? These considerations are addressed from the annotation point of view in chapter 9.

6.2.3   *Diversity sampling for semantic segmentation*

You cannot sample for model-based outliers straight from your model for diversity sampling, as you can for object recognition. This approach works with object recognition because you are already forcing the model to focus on the areas that you care about, but a semantic segmentation algorithm is forced to classify every pixel. So you should mask or crop the images to contain only the predicted labels you care about, as outlined in section 6.1, and then apply model-based outliers.

The same is true for clustering and representative sampling: crop or mask the image to the areas you care about and then apply clustering and/or representative sampling. For real-world diversity, the strategy is the same as for bounding boxes: use all the techniques that you know in active learning to sample for diversity across and within the demographics that you care about. See section 6.1 on object detection for more about these methods.

6.2.4   *Active transfer learning for semantic segmentation*

You can apply active transfer learning to semantic segmentation in the same way that you applied it to image-level labels, but you should use the adaptive method: ATLAS. If you don't use the adaptive version of this algorithm, you could sample confusion exclusively in the areas that you don't care about, such as the division between leaves and the sky when you care mainly about objects on the ground. Note that ATLAS won't completely solve this problem; it might initially sample types of confusion that you don't care about. But it will adapt quickly to assume that those types of confusion are solved and therefore also cover the areas that you care about. If you think about how many pairwise sets of labels exist in your data and what percentage of those pairs you actually care about, you will have some idea of how successful ATLAS will be out-of-the-box.

To get the most out of ATLAS for semantic segmentation, you can be strategic about how you set up your validation data for transfer learning. If you don't care about errors between leaves and the sky, for example, you can ignore those errors when you run the validation data through the original model to generate your "Correct"/ "Incorrect" labels. That way, your model is now predicting errors for only the types of labels you care about.

6.2.5 Sampling for image-level diversity in semantic segmentation

As with object detection, you may want to sample a small number of items from the whole image (especially if you are introducing data from new locations, camera types, and so on) so that you can adapt quickly and find false negatives for the labels that you care about. You could also experiment with loosening the restriction to crop or mask if you are combining methods. You could use representative sampling on the entire image to find images most representative of a new domain or type of image and then sample for the most representative images, apply the mask/crop to those samples, and cluster those samples for diversity. This technique gives you the most diverse selection of items you care about from whole images that are representative of the domain you care about.

6.3 Applying active learning to sequence labeling

Sequence labeling is machine learning applied to labeling spans within a sequence and is one of the most common tasks in NLP. Suppose that you have this sentence (sequence):

> *"The E-Coli outbreak was first seen in a San Francisco supermarket"*

If you are implementing a model to track outbreaks from text reports, you may want to extract information from the sentence, such as the name of the disease, any locations in the data, and the important keywords, as shown in table 6.1.

Table 6.1 An example sequence labels: keyword detection and two types of named entities, diseases, and locations. Label B (beginning) is applied to the beginning of the span, and Label I (inside) is applied to the other words within the span, allowing us to unambiguously distinguish spans that are next to each other, such as "San Francisco" and "supermarket". This process is called *IOB tagging*, in which O (outside) is the nonlabel. (O is omitted from this table for readability.)

	The	E-Coli	outbreak	was	first	seen	in	a	San	Francisco	supermarket
Keywords		B	I						B	I	B
Diseases		B									
Locations									B	I	

In the literature, you most commonly see IOB tagging for spans, as in table 6.1. Notice that you might define spans in different ways for different types of labels. The named entity "E-Coli" is one word, but when we extract the keywords, it's the phrase "E-Coli outbreak." And although "San Francisco" is both an entity (location) and a keyword, the common noun "supermarket" is a keyword but not an entity. Strictly, this process is called *IOB2 tagging*, and IOB uses the B only when there are multiple tokens in a single span. IOB2 is the most common approach that you'll encounter in the literature, sometimes called IOB for short.

Other encodings mark the end of the span rather than the start. This type of encoding is common for whole-sentence segmentation tasks, such as tagging the end of every word and subword span and tagging the end of every sentence. For sentences, the end is tagged because it's a little easier to identify the end of a sentence (typically with punctuation) than the start. The methods in this chapter work for any type of sequence encoding, so the chapter will stick with the IOB2 examples and assume that it is easily adapted if your encoding system is different.

You might also treat some labels as being naturally part of the same task. I have worked a lot in named entity recognition (NER), which considers identifying "Location" and "Disease" as part of the same task, but treats keyword identification as a different task. Even within one task, there can be a lot of variation in how labels are defined. Some popular NER datasets have only four types of entities: "People," "Locations," "Organizations," and "Miscellaneous." By contrast, I once helped build an entity recognition system for a car company that had thousands of entity types; every kind of engine, door, and even headrest had multiple types and names.

Although you might perform a large variety of sequence labeling tasks in NLP, all of them come down to identifying spans of text in a sequence. These kinds of sequence labeling tasks are called *information extraction* in the literature and are often the building blocks for more complicated multifield information extraction tasks. If you have a sentence with one disease and multiple locations, you would also determine the locations at which the disease was detected, if any. In this chapter, we will stick to the example of identifying individual spans and assume that you can extend them to more complicated information extraction tasks.

6.3.1 *Accuracy for sequence labeling*

The accuracy metric for sequence labeling depends on the task. For named entities, it is typically F-score on the entire span. So predicting "San Francisco" as a location would count 100% toward accuracy, but predicting "Francisco" or "San Francisco supermarket" would count 0% toward accuracy.

In some cases, this strict form of accuracy may be relaxed or reported along with more forgiving metrics, such as per-word accuracy (called *per-token* because not all tokens are exact words). In other cases, the accuracy might be reported for entity versus nonentity, with the type of entity (such as Disease or Location) reported separately.

You will most likely not care about the "O" label for your sequence tasks. F-score will capture the confusion between other labels and "O," which might be enough. As in object detection and semantic segmentation, you care about some parts of each data item more than others. Focusing on these parts of the data for active learning will lead to better samples.

As with the computer vision examples, you should use a metric for active learning sampling that is consistent with how you are measuring accuracy for your NLP model. For many NLP tasks, the context is more important than for object detection. You know that "San Francisco" is a location and not an organization with "San Francisco" in the name because of the context of the full sentence. So it is safer to have a broader context around the predicted sequences and often desirable, as the context can be an important predictor.

6.3.2 Uncertainty sampling for sequence labeling

Almost all sequence-labeling algorithms give you a probability distribution for your labels, most often using softmax, so that you can calculate the per-token uncertainty directly. In place of (or in addition to) the softmax confidences, you can use ensemble models and/or dropouts to produce multiple predictions and calculate the uncertainty as the level of agreement or entropy across those predictions. This approach is like the computer vision example for object detection.

Also as in the computer vision example, your confidences will be about the label confidence for each token, not the span as a whole or the boundary of the spans. But if you are using IOB2 tagging, your "B" tag will jointly predict the label and start boundary.

You can decide the best way to calculate the uncertainty for the entire span. The product of all the confidences is the (mathematically) most correct joint probability. You will also have to normalize for the number of tokens, however, which can be complicated. So the average or minimum confidence over all the tokens in a span might be easier to work with than the product.

Uncertainty can be important for tokens immediately outside the span. If we wrongly predicted that "Francisco" was not a location, we would want to take into account the fact that it might have been. Table 6.2 shows an example.

Table 6.2 An example of location identification and confidence associated with each label. The table shows an error in that only "San" from "San Francisco" is a location, but "Francisco" was reasonably high confidence. So we want to make sure that we take into account information outside the predicted spans when calculating confidence.

	The	E-Coli	outbreak	was	first	seen	in	a	San	Francisco	supermarket
Locations									B		
Confidence	0.01	0.32	0.02	0	0.01	0.03	0	0	0.81	0.46	0.12

Table 6.2 shows an error, in which only "San" from "San Francisco" is predicted to be a location. Even though "Francisco" was a false negative, however, it had reasonably high confidence (0.46). For this reason, we want to calculate uncertainty from more than the predicted span; we want to make sure the boundary is correct too.

In Table 6.2, we can treat "Francisco" as $1 - 0.46 = 0.54$, which will lower our confidence for the span boundary. By contrast, at the start of the prediction, the "a" has zero confidence. So $1 - 0 = 1$, which will increase our confidence. The "B" tag also helps with the confidence of the initial boundary.

6.3.3   *Diversity sampling for sequence labeling*

For your machine learning models, you are almost certainly using an architecture and/or feature representation that captures a wide window of context. In some models, you are encoding this representation directly. If you're using transformer-based methods, that context (attention) is discovered as part of the model itself, and you are probably providing only a maximum size. To help determine the context to use in active learning, choose a window for sampling that is consistent with the context your predictive model is using. Chapter 4 covered four types of diversity sampling:

- Model-based outlier sampling
- Cluster-based sampling
- Representative sampling
- Sampling for real-world diversity

We'll start with the first and last approaches, which are easiest, as we did for object detection:

- You can apply model-based outlier detection to a sequence labeling problem in the same way that you apply it to a document labeling problem.
- You can sample for real-world diversity in a sequence labeling problem in the same way that you sample for a document labeling problem.

For model-based outliers, the hidden layers focus on the spans you care about. That is, your neurons will be capturing information primarily to distinguish your spans from the nonspans ("B" and "I" from "O") and from the different labels of your spans. So you can apply model-based outliers directly without truncating the sentences to the immediate context of every predicted span.

You can see different feature representations in figure 6.9: one-hot, noncontextual embeddings (such as word2vec) and contextual embeddings (such as BERT). If you have worked in NLP, you probably used these common feature representations. In all three cases, we want to extract the predicted span of text and create a single feature vector to represent that span. The main differences are that we sum the one-hot encodings instead of using max (although max would probably work) and that there is no need to sample beyond the predicted span when using contextual embeddings because the context is already captured in the vectors. Calculate the contextual embeddings before you extract the phrase. For the other methods, it doesn't matter

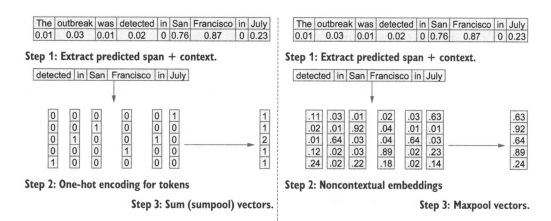

The	outbreak	was	detected	in	San	Francisco	in	July
0.01	0.03	0.01	0.02	0	0.76	0.87	0	0.23

Step 1: Extract predicted span + context.

detected | in | San | Francisco | in | July

Step 2: One-hot encoding for tokens

Step 3: Sum (sumpool) vectors.

The	outbreak	was	detected	in	San	Francisco	in	July
0.01	0.03	0.01	0.02	0	0.76	0.87	0	0.23

Step 1: Extract predicted span + context.

detected | in | San | Francisco | in | July

Step 2: Noncontextual embeddings

Step 3: Maxpool vectors.

The	outbreak	was	detected	in	San	Francisco	in	July
0.01	0.03	0.01	0.02	0	0.76	0.87	0	0.23

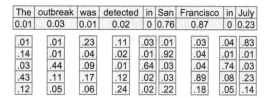

Step 1: Contextual embeddings for entire sentence

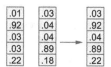

Step 2: Extract predicted span *without* context.

Step 3: Maxpool vectors.

Figure 6.9 Three ways to encode predicted spans for active learning: using one-hot encoding to encode each token as its own feature (top left); using a noncontextual vector (embedding) such as word2vec (top right); and using a contextual embedding such as **BERT** (bottom). You can also experiment with average pooling (avepool) in place of or in addition to maximum pooling (maxpool).

whether you extract the phrase before or after you calculate the vector. For diversity sampling, the principles from chapter 4 also apply: you need to combine all the active learning methods to ensure fairer data across real-world demographics.

So far, you can see that diversity sampling for sequence labeling has many similarities to diversity sampling for object detection. You care about context of the objects/spans, but you don't necessarily need to worry about them for model-based outliers, as your model will already be focusing most of the neurons on the parts of the image/text you care about most.

For cluster-based sampling and representative sampling, we want to focus our models on the spans themselves, not too far into the context on either side. If you are using contextual vector-representations of the tokens, you may not need extra context; that context is already captured in your vectors.

The preceding and following text should be cropped at meaningful distances and at word or sentence boundaries (or at phrasal boundaries, if you have this information). Because your model isn't 100% accurate, you need to ensure that you are capturing the full span:

- Crop at a given threshold. If the span is a Location, expand the selection to words before or after the prediction where Location is predicted with at least some low (say, 10%) confidence.
- Crop a wide threshold, maybe the whole sentence, and weight each word or subword sequence by the probability of each word's being part of the span.

Not all algorithms allow you to weight your features in a meaningful way. If you can't do this, use the same strategy as in object detection: generate multiple spans from an ensemble or dropout. Then try representative sampling for each of those predictions, weighted by their average overlap with the other predicted spans. You can use the words and subwords in each span directly for clustering and representative sampling, as you did in chapter 5.

If you are cropping the text and using the hidden layers of the model for cluster-based sampling, model-based outliers, or representative sampling, get those hidden layers before you crop the text. The full sentence context will be necessary for getting accurate contextual representations for each word in the span. When you have a vector of neuron activations for every word or subword in the sentence, you can crop the selection to the span.

The final problem that you'll need to solve is how to combine the vectors for each word or subword. If all your spans are the same length, you can concatenate them. If not, you'll need to combine them—a process known as *pooling* for neural vectors. The vectors tend to be sparse, so maxpooling is probably best (taking the maximum value in each vector index for each word or subword), but you could try averaging or some other pooling method to see the difference.

Whether you are using the words or subwords or a vector representation, you can apply cluster-based sampling and representative sampling as you learned in chapter 4. You can sample centroids, outliers, and random cluster members, and you can sample the most representative items from your target domain.

6.3.4   *Active transfer learning for sequence labeling*

You can apply active transfer learning to sequence labeling in the same way that you applied it to document-level labels. You can also apply ATLAS, adapting within one active learning cycle because you can assume that the first sequences you sample will be corrected later by human labelers, even if you don't know what those labels are.

Regardless of the type of neural architecture you use for sequence labeling, you can use the hidden layer(s) as the features for a binary "Correct"/"Incorrect" model that you train on validation data. You will need to decide what counts as "Correct" and "Incorrect" in your validation data. If you care about some sequences more than others, you may want to count only errors with those sequences as "Incorrect" in your new model, focusing on the types of errors you care most about. You also need to decide whether to calculate errors in terms of the per-token error or for the sequence as a whole. As a starting point, it makes sense to calculate errors by using the same method that you use for calculating accuracy in your machine learning model, but you may want to experiment with other methods.

6.3.5 *Stratified sampling by confidence and tokens*

Set your threshold for predicting spans low, whatever method you use. You don't want to find only spans that are similar to those that already exist in your data, which will perpetuate the bias. You can use the same stratified sampling by confidence method (section 6.1.5) for object detection, perhaps sampling an equal number of spans at 0%–10% confidence, 10%–20% confidence, and so on.

Also, you can stratify the sample according to the tokens themselves. You might cap the sample of spans that are "San Francisco" (or any other sequence) to sample a maximum of 5 or 10 instances, thereby sampling a greater diversity of tokens overall.

6.3.6 *Create training data samples for representative sampling that are similar to your predictions*

If you are cropping your unlabeled text for representative sampling, you should do the same with the training data. If you use only the perfect span annotations from your training data, but then the imperfect predictions from your unlabeled data, the "representative" samples could end up being the result of different cropping strategies instead of the actual span differences.

Section 6.1.6 covered some strategies for cropping the training data and unlabeled data to reduce bias. These strategies apply to spans too, so look at those methods if you are applying representative sampling to your spans.

As with object detection, you should consider using some sampling methods on uncropped text. You might do more of this here, because the context for a span typically is contextually relevant pieces of that language optimized to encode information; while the backgrounds for object detection are more likely to be random junk in the world.

Some simple approaches to representative sampling can be effective, and you may not need to build a model. You might even choose to focus only on predicted spans that don't yet occur in your training data.

6.3.7 *Full-sequence labeling*

For a handful of tasks in NLP, you want to label every item in the text. An example is part-of-speech (POS) tagging, as shown in table 6.3.

Table 6.3   An example of a full-sequence parse, showing POS tags (labels) such as nouns, verbs, adverbs (Adv), proper nouns (PRP), and so on

	The	E-Coli	outbreak	was	first	seen	in	a	San	Francisco	supermarket
POS	Dt	PRP	Noun	Aux	Adv	Verb	PR	Dt	PRP	PRP	Noun
Confidence	0.01	0.32	0.02	0	0.01	0.03	0	0	0.81	0.46	0.12

You can treat this task the same as tagging sequences within the text, but it is simplified in that you have to worry less about cropping the text or ignoring "O" labels. Stratification by labels is likely to help for cases such as those in table 6.3, taking the 100 most uncertain nouns, the 100 most uncertain verbs, the 100 most uncertain adverbs, and so on. You can use this sampling method along with macro F-score to evaluate the model accuracy.

6.3.8   *Sampling for document-level diversity in sequence labeling*

As with any other method, you should always randomly sample text for review. This practice provides your evaluation data and gives you a baseline for how successful your active learning is. If you apply clustering at the whole-document level and find whole clusters with little or no existing training items, you have good evidence that you should get human review for some items in those clusters because you could be missing something.

There is a good chance that there are real-world diversity considerations at the document level, too: the genre of the text, the fluency of the person who created it, the language(s), and so on. Stratified sampling for real-world diversity may be more effective at document level than at sequence level for these cases.

6.4   *Applying active learning to language generation*

For some NLP tasks, the machine learning algorithm is producing sequences like natural language. The most common use case is text generation, which are the example use cases in this section. Most language generation for signed and spoken languages starts with text generation and then generates the signs or speech as a separate task. The machine learning models are typically general sequence generation architectures that can be applied to other types of sequences, like genes and music, but these are also less common than text.

Even then, it is only on the back of recent advances in transfer learning that full text generation systems are at a level of accuracy that enables us to start using them in real-world applications.

The most obvious exception is machine translation, which has been popular in academic and industry settings for some time. Machine translation is a well-defined problem, taking a sentence in one language and producing one in a new language. Historically, machine translation has a lot of existing training data to draw from in the form of books, articles, and web pages that have been translated between languages manually.

Question-answering, in which a full sentence is given in response to a question, is growing in popularity as an example of text generation. Another example is a dialogue system such as a chatbot, producing sentences in response to interactions. Summarization is yet another example, producing a smaller number of sentences from a larger text. Not all of these use cases necessarily use full text generation, however. Many question-answering systems, chatbots, and summarization algorithms use templated outputs to create what seem like real communications after extracting the important sequences from the inputs. In these cases, they are using document-level labels and sequence labels, so the active learning strategies that you have already learned for document-labeling and sequence labeling will be sufficient.

6.4.1   Calculating accuracy for language generation systems

One complicating factor for language generation is that there is rarely one correct answer. This situation is often addressed by having multiple correct responses in the evaluation data and allowing the best match to be the score that is used. In translation tasks, the evaluation data often contains several correct translations, and accuracy is calculated by the best match of a translation against any of them.

In the past few years, major advances in neural machine translation have been full sentence-to-sentence generation; the machine learning takes in examples of the same sentences in two languages and then trains a model that can translate directly from one sentence to another. This feature is incredibly powerful. Previously, machine translation system had multiple steps to parse in and out of different languages and align the two sentences. Each step used a machine learning system of its own, and the steps were often put together with a meta- machine learning system to combine them. The newer neural machine translation systems that need only parallel text and can take care of the entire pipeline use only about 1% of the code of the earlier cobbled-together systems and are much more accurate. The only step back is that neural machine translation systems are less interpretable today than their non-neural predecessors, so it is harder to identify confusion in the models.

6.4.2   Uncertainty sampling for language generation

For uncertainty sampling, you can look at the variation across multiple predictions, as you did for sequence labeling and the computer vision tasks, but this area is much less studied. If you are building models for text generation, you are probably using an algorithm that generates multiple candidates. It may be possible to look at the variation in these candidates to measure uncertainty. But the neural machine translation models typically generate a small number of candidates by using a method called beam search (around 5), which isn't enough to measure the variation accurately. Recent research shows that widening the search can reduce overall model accuracy, which you obviously want to avoid.[1]

---

[1] "Analyzing Uncertainty in Neural Machine Translation," by Myle Ott, Michael Auli, David Grangier, and Marc'Aurelio Ranzato (https://arxiv.org/abs/1803.00047).

You could try to model uncertainty with ensemble models or dropouts from a single model. Measuring the level of agreement across ensemble models is a long-standing practice in machine translation for determining uncertainty, but the models are expensive to train (often taking days or weeks), so training multiple models simply to sample for uncertainty could be prohibitively expensive.

Using dropouts during sentence generation can help generate uncertainty scores by getting multiple sentences from a single model. I experimented with this approach for the first time in a paper presented during the writing of this book.[2] Initially, I was going to include this study, which focused on bias detection in language models, as an example in the final chapter in this book. Given that the content is already in that paper and that the disaster-response examples in this book became even more relevant with the COVID-19 pandemic that began while I was writing it, however, I replaced that example in chapter 12 with the example task tracking potential foodborne outbreaks.

6.4.3   *Diversity sampling for language generation*

Diversity sampling for language generation is more straightforward than uncertainty sampling. If your input is text, you can implement diversity sampling exactly as you did in chapter 4 for document-level labeling. You can use clustering to ensure that you have a diverse set of inputs, representative sampling to adapt to new domains, and model-based outliers to sample what is confusing to your current model. You can also stratify your samples by any real-world demographics.

Diversity sampling has typically been a major focus of machine translation. Most machine translation systems are general-purpose, so the training data needs to cover as many words as possible in your language pairs, with each word in as many contexts as possible, especially if that word has multiple translations depending on context.

For domain-specific machine translation systems, representative sampling is often used to ensure that any new words or phrases that are important to a domain have translations. When you are adapting a machine translation system to a new technical domain, for example, it is good strategy to oversample the technical terms for that domain, as they are important to get correct and are unlikely to be known by a more general machine translation system.

One of the most exciting applications for diversity sampling for text generation is creating new data for other tasks. One long-standing method is *back translation*. If you have a segment of English text labeled as negative sentiment, you could use machine translation to translate that sentence into many other languages and then back into English. The text itself might change, but the label of negative sentiment is probably still correct. This kind of generative approach to training data, known as *data augmentation*, includes some exciting recent advances in human-in-the-loop machine learning that we will cover in chapter 9.

---

[2] "Detecting Independent Pronoun Bias with Partially-Synthetic Data Generation," by Robert (Munro) Monarch and Alex (Carmen) Morrison (https://www.aclweb.org/anthology/2020.emnlp-main.157.pdf).

6.4.4   *Active transfer learning for language generation*

You can apply active transfer learning to language generation in a similar way to the other use cases in this chapter. You can also apply ATLAS, adapting within one active learning cycle because you can assume that the first sequences you sample will be corrected by human labelers later, even if you don't know what those labels are.

You need to carefully define what counts as a "Correct" or "Incorrect" prediction in your validation data, however. Typically, this task involves setting some threshold of accuracy at which a sentence is considered to be correct or incorrect. If you can calculate accuracy on a per-token basis, you have the option of aggregating the accuracy across all tokens to create a numerical accuracy value. You can predict a continuous value instead of the binary "Correct"/"Incorrect," as in the IoU example for object detection in section 6.1.1.

6.5   *Applying active learning to other machine learning tasks*

The active learning principles in chapters 3, 4, and 5 can be applied to almost any machine learning task. This section covers a few more at a high level. This section doesn't go into the level of implementation detail that you learned for the computer vision and NLP examples, but it will give you an idea about how the same principles apply to different data types.

For some use cases, it isn't possible to collect new unlabeled data at all and you will need to find ways to measure your accuracy by other means. See the following sidebar for more about one such method: synthetic controls.

> **Synthetic controls: Evaluating your model without evaluation data**
> *Expert anecdote by Dr. Elena Grewal*
>
> How can you measure your model's success if you are deploying an application where you can't run A/B tests? Synthetic control methods are a technique that you can use in this case: you find existing data that is closest in features to where you are deploying the model and use that data as your control group.
>
> I first learned about synthetic controls when studying education policy analysis. When a school tries some new method to improve their students' learning environment, they can't be expected to improve only half the students' lives so that the other half can be a statistical control group. Instead, education researchers might create a synthetic control group of schools that are most similar in terms of the student demographics and performance. I took this strategy, and we applied it at Airbnb when I was leading data science there. When Airbnb was rolling out a product or policy change in a new city/market and could not run an experiment, we would create a synthetic control group of the most similar cities/markets. We could then measure the impact of our models compared with the synthetic controls for metrics such as engagement, revenue, user ratings, and search relevance. Synthetic controls allowed us to take a data-driven approach to measuring the impact of our models, even where we didn't have evaluation data.

6.5.1   *Active learning for information retrieval*

Information retrieval is the set of algorithms that drives search engines and recommendation systems. Multiple metrics can be used for calculating the accuracy of retrieval systems that return multiple results from a query. The most common of those metrics today is discounted cumulative gain (DCG), in which rel_i is the graded relevance of the result at a ranked position p:

$$DCG_p = \sum_{i=1}^{p} \frac{2^{rel_i} - 1}{\log_2(i+1)}$$

The `log()` is used to deweight the lower entries. Perhaps you want the first search result to be the most accurate; you care slightly less about the second search result; slightly less again about the third search result; and so on. The use of a log was a fairly arbitrary weighting when first introduced, but some relatively recent theory suggests that it has mathematical validity.[3]

Real-world search systems are some of the most sophisticated uses cases for human-in-the-loop machine learning today. Think about a simple search in an online store. The store is using one form of machine learning to retrieve the search results. It uses a second form of machine learning to identify keywords and entities in your search string. It uses a third form of machine learning to extract the relevant summary text from each product in the results. The products are categorized into the type of product (electronics, books, and so on) to help with search relevance in a fourth kind of machine learning. The store might also be using a fifth form of machine learning to decide what is an ideal display image (plain background or in context). Many modern search engines also try to maximize diversity, returning different product types rather than 10 versions of the same product. So six or more different machine learning systems may be contributing to your search results, even before any models try to personalize the results for your experience. Each of these machine learning systems needs its own training data. Some of that data can be derived from what people click, but much of it is from offline annotators who provide that feedback.

You may not realize that you're using cutting-edge machine learning when you shop online, but a lot is going on behind the scenes. In fact, this use case is why the best-known crowdsourcing platform, Amazon's Mechanical Turk, was invented: to clean up catalog information for products in the online store.

---

[3] "A Theoretical Analysis of NDCG Type Ranking Measures," by Yining Wang, Liwei Wang, Yuanzhi Li, Di He, Wei Chen, and Tie-Yan Liu (https://arxiv.org/abs/1304.6480).

Information retrieval also tends to use more real-world accuracy metrics than other machine learning applications. Although DCG is popular for offline evaluation of search relevance, the results for people using the system are often optimized for business-oriented metrics: the number of purchases a person makes, the number of clicks/seconds between a search and a purchase is made, the value of the customer over the next six months, and so on. Because these metrics are about use of the model, they are sometimes called *online metrics*, as opposed to F-score and IoU, which are offline metrics. These metrics are different from F-score and IoU, and much more human-centric, so other use cases can learn a lot from the information retrieval community.

6.5.2 *Active learning for video*

Most of the solutions for still images also apply to object detection and/or semantic segmentation in videos. Focus on the regions you care about the most in the video, and use them for your samples. If your model focuses only on objects or labels you care about, you can implement uncertainty sampling and model-based outliers without necessarily cropping or masking your videos to the objects you care about. If you are applying diversity sampling, you almost certainly want to crop or mask to those objects first.

The biggest difference between videos and still images is that you have many frames of data from the same video with almost identical images. The obvious solution is the best one: if you have multiple frames from what your model thinks is the same object, sample the frame with the highest uncertainty. The iterative process of retraining on that new object is likely to give you some or all the other frames with high confidence afterward.

Diversity sampling should already reduce the number of times the same object is selected in different frames because the object will look the same across frames. If the object changes form, you probably want to sample it in different forms, so this situation works out. An example is sign language. You are not tracking an object so much as trying to interpret a stream of information, so your active learning strategy might look more like text and speech than object detection.

Note that if you don't use diversity sampling for object detection in videos, you might find that your most uncertain samples are the same object in successive frames. Most companies I've seen sample every Nth frame and/or sample an exact number of frames per video, typically the first, last, and some number of intermediary ones. There is nothing wrong with this approach to stratified sampling, but sampling diversity through clustering and adaptive representative sampling in addition generally leads to much richer samples. You might also need to oversample some videos to get more frames containing certain rarer labels to improve real-world diversity. You have a lot of individual images if you take every frame of every video, so you can also try large-scale clustering on the whole images first and use the total number of videos as a guide:

- If you have fewer clusters than the total number videos, combine similar videos into one cluster to have targeted diversity.
- If you have more clusters than the total number of videos, you should end up with some videos split into multiple clusters, ideally the videos that have more diverse content.

This approach gives you a lot of scope to combine the active learning methods covered in this book to annotate a video as quickly as possible.

6.5.3 Active learning for speech

Like text or signed language, speech can be a labeling task, a sequence task, or a language generation task. You approach each use case differently, as you do for text or images.

If you are labeling speech at the level of entire speech acts (called *intent* if you are labeling commands spoken to a smart device or similar object), your model is already focused on the phenomena you care about, as with object detection and sequence labeling. So the uncertainty sampling and model-based outliers should work on your speech data without cropping.

If you are transcribing speech into text, or performing some other task that looks at error across the whole recording, this process is more similar to text generation, in which you want to focus on diversity to sample as many speech acts as possible. In pretty much every language of the world, the writing system is more standardized than the spoken language. So diversity becomes more important when you're trying to capture every possible accent and language variation compared with working with text.

Speech falls between text and images in terms of how much data collection technology matters. The quality of the microphone, ambient noise, recording device, file format, and compression techniques can all produce artifacts that your model could learn erroneously instead of the actual information.

More than any other data type covered here, speech differs most between its perceived structure and actual physical structure. You perceive gaps between words, for example, but that perception is an illusion, because real speech almost always runs words together. Almost every sound changes in immediate context, too. The English plural is *s* or *z* depending on the previous phoneme (*cats* and *dogz*), but you might have assumed that the plural suffix was only one sound. When you sample speech data, be careful not to rely only on text transcriptions of that speech.

6.6 Choosing the right number of items for human review

For advanced active learning techniques, the principles that you have already learned apply. You can make some of the active learning strategies, such as representative sampling, adaptive within an active learning iteration, but most combinations of techniques still produce the most benefit when you retrain the model with the newly annotated data.

You probably need to sample a minimum number of items as a result of drawing from a certain number of clusters or stratification to real-world demographics. Your maximum number of items per iteration will vary depending on data type. You might be able to annotate locations in 1,000 short text messages per hour, but only complete semantic segmentation on 1 image over the same time period. So a big factor in your decision will be your data types and the annotation strategies that you are deploying—something that we'll cover in chapters 7–12.

6.6.1 Active labeling for fully or partially annotated data

If your machine learning models can learn from partially annotated data, you are going to make your systems a lot more efficient. To continue the example we've used throughout this book, imagine that you are implementing an object detection model for city streets. Your model might be accurate enough to identify cars and pedestrians, but not accurate enough to identify bicycles and animals.

You might have thousands of images of bicycles and animals, but each image has dozens of cars and pedestrians on average too. Ideally, you'd like to be able to annotate only the bicycles and animals in those images and not spend more than 10 times the resources to make sure that all the cars and pedestrians are also labeled in those same images. A lot of machine learning architectures don't allow you to partially annotate data, however; they need to have every object annotated, because otherwise, those objects will erroneously count toward the background.

You might sample the 100 bicycles and animals that maximize confusion and diversity, but then spend most of your resources annotating 1,000 cars and pedestrians around them for relatively little extra gain. There is no shortcut: if you sample only images without many cars or pedestrians, you are biasing your data toward certain environments that are not representative of your entire dataset. If you are stuck with systems that need full annotation for every image or document, you want to be extra-careful to ensure that you are sampling the highest-value items every time.

Increasingly, it is easier to combine different models or have heterogeneous training data. You might be able to train separate models for pedestrians and cars, and then have a model that combines them via transfer learning.

6.6.2 Combining machine learning with annotation

You should take these options into account when designing your annotation and model strategies, because you might find that a slightly less accurate machine learning architecture will end up producing much more accurate models when you are not constrained to annotating images entirely or not at all.

The best solution to the problem of needing to annotate only a few objects/spans in a large image/document is to incorporate machine learning into the annotation process. It might take an hour to annotate an entire image for semantic segmentation, but only 30 seconds to accept/reject every annotation. The danger when combining predictions and human annotation is that the people might be primed to trust a prediction that was not correct, therefore perpetuating an existing bias. This situation is a complicated human–computer interaction problem. Chapters 9, 10, and 11 cover the problem of combining model predictions and human annotations in the most effective ways possible.

6.7 *Further reading*

For more information about calculating confidence for sequence labeling and sequence generation, see "Modeling Confidence in Sequence-to-Sequence Models," by Jan Niehues and Ngoc-Quan Pham (http://mng.bz/9Mqo). The authors look at speech recognition and also extend the machine translation problem in an interesting way by calculating confidence (uncertainty) on the source text tokens, not only the predicted tokens.

For an overview of active learning techniques for machine translation, see "Empirical Evaluation of Active Learning Techniques for Neural MT," by Xiangkai Zeng, Sarthak Garg, Rajen Chatterjee, Udhyakumar Nallasamy, and Matthias Paulik (http://mng.bz/j4Np). Many of the techniques in this paper can be applied to other sequence generation tasks.

Summary

- In many use cases, you want to identify or extract information within an image or document rather than label the entire image or document. The same active learning strategies can be applied to these use cases. Understanding the right strategy helps you understand the kinds of problems to which you can apply active learning and how to build the right strategy for your use case.
- You need to crop or mask your images and documents to get the most out of some active learning strategies. The right cropping or masking strategy produces better samples for human review, and understanding when you need to crop or mask your items helps you select the right method for your use cases.
- Active learning can be applied to many tasks beyond computer vision and NLP, including information retrieval, speech recognition, and videos. Understanding the broader landscape of active learning application areas will help you adapt any machine learning problem.
- The number of items to select for human review in each iteration of advanced active learning is highly specific to your data. Understanding the right strategy for your data is important for deploying the most efficient human-in-the-loop machine learning systems for your problems.

Part 3

Annotation

Annotation puts the human in human-in-the-loop machine learning. Creating datasets with accurate and representative labels for machine learning is often the most underestimated component of a machine learning application.

Chapter 7 covers how to find and manage the right people to annotate data. Chapter 8 covers the basics of quality control for annotation, introducing the most common ways to calculate the overall accuracy and agreement for an entire dataset and between annotators, labels, and on a per-task basis. Unlike with machine learning accuracy, we typically need to adjust for random chance accuracy and agreement for human annotators, which means that the evaluation metrics are more complicated when evaluating human performance.

Chapter 9 covers advanced strategies for annotation quality control, starting with techniques to elicit subjective annotations and then expanding to machine learning models for quality control. The chapter also covers a wide range of methods to semi-automate annotation with rule-based systems, search-based systems, transfer learning, semi-supervised learning, self-supervised learning, and synthetic data creation. These methods are among the most exciting research areas on the machine learning side of human–computer interaction today.

Chapter 10 starts by examining how often wisdom of the crowds applies to data annotation with an example of continuous value annotation (hint: less often than many people realize). The chapter covers how annotation quality control techniques can be applied to different kinds of machine learning tasks, including object detection, semantic segmentation, sequence labeling, and language generation. This information will allow you to develop annotation quality control strategies for any machine learning problem and think about how to break a complicated annotation task into simpler subtasks.

Working with the people annotating your data

7

This chapter covers

- Understanding in-house, contracted, and pay-per-task annotation workforces
- Motivating different workforces using three key principles
- Evaluating workforces when compensation is nonmonetary
- Evaluating your annotation volume requirements
- Understanding the training and/or expertise that annotators need for a given task

In the first two parts of this book, you learned how to select the right data for human review. The chapters in this part cover how to optimize that human interaction, starting with how to find and manage the right people to provide human feedback. Machine learning models often require thousands (and sometimes millions) of instances of human feedback to get the training data necessary to be accurate.

191

The type of workforce you need will depend on your task, scale, and urgency. If you have a simple task, such as identifying whether a social media posting is positive or negative sentiment, and you need millions of human annotations as soon as possible, your ideal workforce doesn't need specialized skills. But ideally, that workforce can scale to thousands of people in parallel, and each person can be employed for short amounts of time.

If, however, you have a complicated task, such as identifying evidence of fraud in financial documents that are dense with financial terms, you probably want annotators who are experienced in the financial domain or who can be trained to understand it. If the documents are in a language that you don't speak yourself, finding and evaluating the right people to annotate the data is going to be even more complicated.

Often, you want a data annotation strategy that combines different kinds of workforces. Imagine that you work at a large financial company, and you are building a system to monitor financial news articles that might indicate a change in the value of the companies. This system will be part of a widely used application that people use to make decisions about buying and selling shares of companies listed on the stock market. You need to annotate the data with two types of labels: which company each article is about and whether the information in each article implies a change in share price.

For the first type of label—company identification—you can easily employ non-expert annotators. You don't need to understand financial news to identify company names. However, it is complicated to understand which factors can change the share price. In some cases, general fluency in the language is enough if the content is explicit (such as "Shares are expected to tumble"). In other cases, the context is not so obvious. Is the sentence "Acme Corporation meets adjusted Q3 projections," for example, positive or negative for a company's chances of meeting an adjusted quarterly projection? You need to understand the context of the adjustment. For more complicated language with financial acronyms, it is impossible for a person without training in the financial domain to understand.

Therefore, you may decide that you need three kinds of workforces:

- *Crowdsourced workers*, who can scale up and down fastest when news articles are published to identify what companies are being spoken about
- *Contract workers*, who can learn financial terminology to understand changes in share prices
- *In-house experts*, who can label the most difficult edge cases, adjudicate conflicting labels, and provide instructions for other workers

No matter who the right people are, they will do the best work when they are paid fairly, are secure in their jobs, and have transparency about the work that they are completing. In other words, the most ethical way to manage a workforce is also the best for your organization. This chapter covers how to select and manage the right workforces for any annotation task.

7.1 Introduction to annotation

Annotation is the process of creating training data for your models. For almost all machine learning applications that are expected to operate autonomously, you will need more data labels than it is practical for one person to annotate, so you will need to choose the right workforce(s) to annotate your data and the best ways to manage them. The human-in-the-loop diagram in figure 7.1 shows the annotation process, taking unlabeled data and outputting labeled training data.

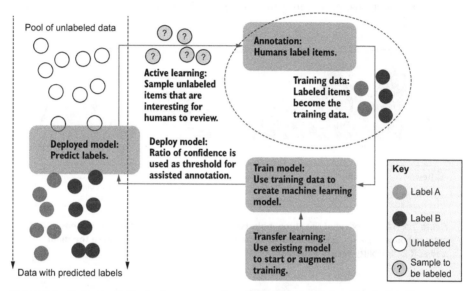

Figure 7.1 *Data annotation* is the process of creating unlabeled data, either by labeling unlabeled data or reviewing labels generated from a model.

In this chapter and the following ones, we will dive into the annotation component of figure 7.1, showing the subprocesses and algorithms needed to run annotation projects correctly. One piece of advice: start your data strategy with your algorithm strategy. It takes as long to refine your annotation strategy and guidelines as it does to create your algorithm architecture and tune your hyperparameters, and your choice of algorithm and architecture should be informed by the type and volume of annotations that you expect.

7.1.1 Three principles of good data annotation

The more respect you show the people who label your data, the better your data becomes. Whether the person is an in-house subject-matter expert (SME) or an outsourced worker who will contribute only a few minutes to your annotations, these basic principles will ensure that you get the best possible annotations:

- *Salary*—Pay fairly.
- *Security*—Pay regularly.
- *Ownership*—Provide transparency.

The three main types of workforces are summarized in figure 7.2, which shows an uneven amount of work needed over time. The crowdsourced workers are easiest to scale up and down, but the quality of their work is typically lowest. In-house workers are hardest to scale, but they are often SMEs, who provide the highest-quality data. Outsourced workers fall in between: they have some of the flexibility of crowdsourced workers and can be trained to high levels of expertise. These differences should influence your choice of workforce(s). We will cover each workforce in more detail in the following sections, expanding on the principles of salary, security, and ownership for each one.

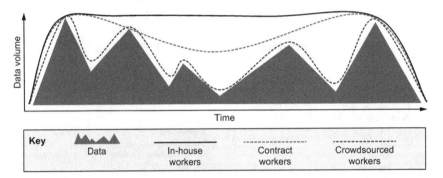

Figure 7.2   An overview of the three main types of workforces you can use to annotate data, in-house workers, contract workers, and crowdsourced workers, where the main trade-off is flexibility versus expertise.

Work in supervised machine learning is people management

If you work with human-annotated data, you work in people management. Most real-world machine learning applications use supervised learning with data that has been annotated for that purpose. There is no way to avoid the responsibility you have for the people who are annotating the data for you: if their work is used in the models you are creating, you have a duty of care for them.

Many data scientists see their work being as pure research. Many senior data scientists in companies do not have to manage other researchers, precisely because people management is seen as getting in the way of doing "real" work in research. Unfortunately for those people, you have no way to outsource your responsibility for the people who annotate the data, even if your organization has a separate data annotation team or has outsourced annotation.

This chapter may seem to be more like management advice than technical advice, but this focus is deliberate, because knowing how to manage distributed teams of people is an important skill for any data scientist. For the reasons outlined in this chapter, good management is also necessary to ensure fair working conditions for every person who contributes to your models.

Your responsibilities include talking to the people who annotate your data. I doubt that you've met a good manager who gave their staff guidelines only at the start of a project and didn't invite feedback. Eliciting feedback can be complicated when there is a power imbalance, so you need to implement communication channels mindfully and with empathy.

7.1.2 Annotating data and reviewing model predictions

In this book, the term *annotation* is used broadly. In some cases, it means annotating raw data; in other cases, it means humans assisted by or interacting with machine learning models.

We will return to user-interfaces and quality control in chapter 11. For now, understand that when you calculate the volume of work required for annotation, you need to take into account the different ways that you might present your data for annotation and the different amounts of work required.

7.1.3 Annotations from machine learning-assisted humans

For many tasks, the goal is to assist human processes. In fact, many models could be used for automation or to assist humans, depending on the application. You could train a collision-detection algorithm to power a fully autonomous vehicle or to alert the driver, for example. Similarly, you could train a medical imaging algorithm to make diagnoses or to inform a medical practitioner's decision-making.

This chapter applies to both types of applications. We will cover the concept of end users as annotators in section 7.5.1. As that section discusses, you may still want to employ annotators other than your end users, even if your application gets many annotations for free as it assists with human tasks.

For machine-learning-assisted humans, one extra point is related to the job security and transparency principles: be clear that your goal is to assist the work of end users, not to train their automated replacements. But if you know that you are getting end user feedback to automate people out of a given task, you must be transparent about that fact so that expectations are realistic, and you should compensate those people accordingly.

7.2 In-house experts

The largest workforce for most machine learning projects is in-house workers—people who work in the same organization as the people who build the algorithms. Despite this fact, quality control and worker management are the least well-studied for in-house annotators compared with outsourced and crowdsourced workers. Most of the academic papers on annotation focus on outsourced and (in particular) crowdsourced pay-per-task workers. You obviously gain a lot by having model builders and annotators within the same organization because they are able to communicate directly.

The advantages of in-house works are domain expertise and protection for sensitive data. If you work on complicated problems, such as analyzing financial reports or diagnosing medical images, the members of your in-house team may be some of the few people in the world who have the skills needed to annotate your data. If your data contains sensitive information, in-house workers also provide the most privacy and security for your data.

For some use cases, you may be restricted to keeping data in-house for regulatory reasons. The data-generation tools that we will cover in chapter 10 can help you in these cases. Even if your synthetic data is not 100% accurate, there's a good chance that your synthetic data will not be as sensitive as your real data. So, you have an opportunity to employ outsourced workforces to filter or edit the synthetic data to your desired level of accuracy when the actual data is too sensitive to share with outsourced workers.

Although in-house workers often have more subject-matter expertise than other workers do, it can be a mistake to think that means that they represent the full range of people who will be using your applications. See the following sidebar for more information about who the best SMEs can be.

Parents are the perfect SMEs

Expert anecdote by Ayanna Howard

Models about people are rarely accurate for people who are not represented in the data. Many demographic biases can lead to people being underrepresented, such as ability, age, ethnicity, and gender. There are often intersectional biases too: if people are underrepresented across multiple demographics, sometimes the intersection of those demographics is more than the sum of the parts. Even if you do have the data, it may be difficult to find annotators with the right experience to annotate it correctly.

When building robots for kids with special needs, I found that there was not sufficient data for detecting emotion in children, detecting emotion in people from underrepresented ethnicities, and detecting emotion in people on the autism spectrum. People without immersive experience tend to be poor at recognizing emotions in these children, which limits who can provide the training data that says when a child is happy or upset. Even some trained child physicians have difficulties accurately annotating data when addressing the intersectionality of ability, age, and/or ethnicity. Fortunately, we found that a child's own parents were the best judges of their emotions, so we created interfaces for parents to quickly accept or reject a model's prediction of the child's mood. This interface allowed us to get as much training data as possible while minimizing the time and technical expertise that parents needed to provide that feedback. Those children's parents turned out to be the perfect SMEs to tune our systems to their child's needs.

Ayanna Howard is dean of the College of Engineering at Ohio State University in Columbus. She was previously chair of the School of Interactive Computing at Georgia Tech University and co-founder of Zyrobotics, which makes therapy and educational products for children with special needs. She formerly worked at NASA and has a PhD from the University of Southern California.

7.2.1 Salary for in-house workers

You probably don't set the salary for the annotators within your company, so this principle comes for free: they are already getting a salary that they have agreed to. If you do set the salary for your in-house annotators, make sure that they are treated with the same respect and fairness as other employees.

7.2.2 Security for in-house workers

An in-house worker already has a job (by definition), so security comes from their ability to keep that job while you have work for them—that is, while you ensure that they can keep that job. If your in-house workers' employment and organizational positions provide less job security because they are temporary or contract workers, use some of the principles for outsourced workers. For contract workers, for example, try to structure the amount of work available to be as consistent as possible and with clear expectations of how long their employment will last. Be transparent about job mobility. Can a person become permanent and/or move into other roles?

7.2.3 Ownership for in-house workers

Transparency is often the most important principle for in-house workers. If workers are already getting paid regardless of whether they are creating annotations, you need to make the task inherently interesting.

The best way to make any repetitive task interesting is to make it clear how important that work is. If your in-house annotators have transparency into how their work is improving your company, this information can be good motivation. In fact, annotation can be one of the most transparent ways to contribute to an organization. If you have daily targets for the number of annotations or can share how the accuracy goes up in your trained models, it is easy to tie the annotation work to company goals. An annotator is much more likely to contribute to an increase in accuracy than a scientist experimenting with new algorithms, so you should share this fact with your annotators.

Beyond having the daily motivation of seeing how annotations help the company quantitatively, in-house annotators should be clear about how their work is contributing to overall company goals. An annotator who spends 400 hours annotating data that powers a new application should feel as much ownership as an engineer who spends 400 hours coding it.

I see companies get this concept wrong all the time, leaving their in-house annotation teams in the dark about the impact that their work has on daily or long-term goals. That failure is disrespectful to the people who do the work and leads to poor motivation, high churn, and low-quality annotations, which doesn't help anyone.

In addition, you have a responsibility to ensure that work is consistently available for in-house workers. Your data might come in bursts for reasons that you can't control. If you are classifying news articles, for example, you will have more data at the times of day and week when news articles are published in certain time zones. This situation lends itself to a crowdsourced annotation workforce, but you may be able to

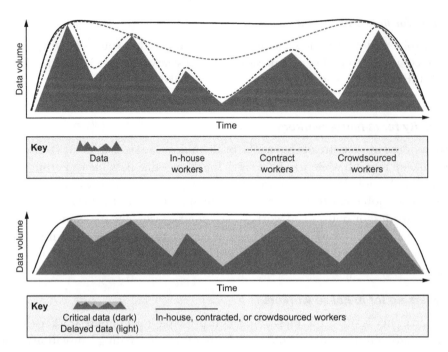

Figure 7.3 Smoothing your work for in-house workers. When data comes in bursts for reasons that you can't control, it can be smoothed out, with the most critical data annotated first and the other data annotated later. The bottom graph shows the annotation workload smoothed out.

decide that some data labeling can be delayed. Figure 7.3 shows an example in which the most critical data is annotated as it comes in and the other data is annotated later.

The more consistently the data needs to be labeled, the easier it will be to manage the annotation processes. When trying to smooth out the workload, you can randomize which data comes first, but you have other options to experiment with. You might cluster all the data first and ensure that the centroids are all annotated first to ensure diversity, for example. Alternatively, or in addition, you may want to apply representative sampling to annotate the newest-looking items first. All these approaches are good ways to smooth out the volume of annotations needed while getting the most out of the data as soon as it arrives.

7.2.4 *Tip: Always run in-house annotation sessions*

No matter what combination of workforces you use, I recommend running annotation sessions among the most diverse group of internal staff members possible. This approach has several benefits:

- The high-quality annotations that are created by people in-house can become your (human) training examples that form part of your quality control data (see chapter 8).

- Your in-house annotation sessions help surface edge cases early, such as data items that are hard to label because they are not covered by the current annotation guidelines. Understanding these edge cases will help you refine your task definition and your instructions to the people annotate your data.
- This process is a great team-building exercise. If you get people from every department of your organization in one room (with food and drinks if they'll be working for an extended period), the process is a lot of fun, and it allows everybody in your company to contribute to your machine learning applications. Have everyone annotate data for at least one hour while discussing their edge cases as they come across them. For many companies I have worked in, "annotation hour" is many people's favorite time of the week.

This exercise can also be a good way to establish an in-house team of experts to create and update guidelines for your bigger annotation team. Especially if you have data that is changing over time, you will want to update your annotation guidelines regularly and provide current example annotations.

You can also use some outsourced annotators as experts, and occasionally, a great crowdsourced worker may be able to help with this process. A lot of organizations that focus on annotation have internal expertise about the best way to create guidelines and training material. Trust their expertise, and consider inviting people from outsourced organizations to your in-house annotation sessions.

Figure 7.4 shows some examples of integrating expert annotators, from models that ignore expert annotators altogether (recommended only for pilots) to more sophisticated workflows that optimize how experts can help ensure quality control when data is changing over time.

If you implement the first method in figure 7.4 in a pilot, exclude the items that are confusing rather than include them with potentially incorrect labels. If 5% of your items could not be labeled, exclude those 5% of items from your training and evaluation data, and assume that you have 5% additional error.

If you include noisy data resulting from incorrect labels in your training and evaluation data, it will be difficult to measure your accuracy. Do not believe that including noisy training data from hard-to-label items is OK. Many algorithms can remain accurate over noisy training data, but they assume predictable noise (random, uniform, Gaussian, and so on). If items were hard to label, those items are probably not randomly distributed.

The second example in figure 7.4 is the most common in industry, with hard examples being redirected to experts for human review. This method works fine if you have data that is fairly consistent over time.

If your data is changing quickly, the third method in figure 7.4 is recommended. In the third method, the expert annotators are looking at new data before the main annotation team, using active learning strategies to surface as many edge cases as

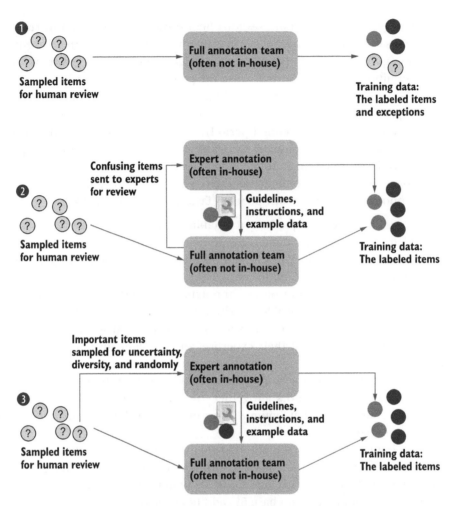

Figure 7.4   Three workflows for in-house annotation. The top workflow is recommended only for pilots; it doesn't use in-house annotators and ignores items that are hard to annotate. The second example is the most common in industry: hard examples are redirected to experts for human review. This approach works fine if you have data that is fairly consistent over time. If your data is changing quickly, the third method is recommended. In this method, the expert annotators are looking for potential new edge cases with diversity sampling and uncertainty sampling before the main annotation process happens; then these examples and updated guidelines are passed to the main annotation team. This method is the only one that ensures that the guidelines are not trailing the actual data. The expert annotators also annotate some randomly selected items for quality-control reasons that we will cover in chapter 8.

possible, to ensure that the guidelines are not trailing the actual data. If you have data coming in regularly, this method allows you to schedule your in-house workers more predictably than asking them to respond to ad-hoc hard examples, as in the second example.

You can combine the second and third methods, trying to get ahead of the new use cases as much as possible but still allowing the hard examples to be redirected for expert human review. You probably need to do this only if your data is particularly difficult to annotate or in the early iterations of annotations, before you have discovered all the major edge cases.

7.3 Outsourced workers

Outsourced workers are the fastest-growing workforce for data annotation. In the past five years, I have seen the amount of work going to outsourcing companies (sometimes called business-process outsourcers) grow at a greater rate than the other types of annotation workforces.

Outsourcing itself is nothing new. There have always been outsourcing companies in the technical industries, with large numbers of employees who can be contracted for different kinds of tasks. The best-known example is call centers. You are probably reaching a call center when you call your bank or a utility company, speaking to someone who is employed by an outsourcing company that is contracted by the company you are calling.

Increasingly, outsourcing companies focus on machine learning. Some focus only on providing a workforce; others also offer some machine learning technology as part of their broader offerings. Most of the time, workers in outsourcing companies are located in parts of the world where the cost of living is relatively low, meaning that salaries are lower too. Cost is often cited as the main reason to outsource; outsourcing is cheaper than hiring people to do the work in-house.

Scalability is another reason to use outsourced workers. It is often easier to scale outsourced workers up and down than it is to scale internal workforces. For machine learning, this flexibility can be especially useful when you don't know whether your application will be successful until you have a large amount of training data. If you are setting the expectations correctly with the outsourcing firm, this approach works better for everyone: you don't have to scale up in-house workers who expect their jobs to last longer, and the outsourcing firm can plan for its staff to switch tasks, which they do regularly and which should be factored into their compensation packages.

Finally, not all outsourced workers should be considered to be low-skilled. If an annotator has been working on annotation for autonomous vehicles for several years, they are a highly skilled individual. If a company is new to autonomous vehicles, outsourced workers can be a valuable source of expertise; they have intuition about what to label and what is important for models from their years of experience.

If you can't smooth out your annotation volume requirements for in-house workers, you might find a middle ground where you can smooth the annotation enough to use outsourced workers, who can cycle on and off faster than in-house workers (but not as fast as crowdsourced workers). Figure 7.5 shows an example.

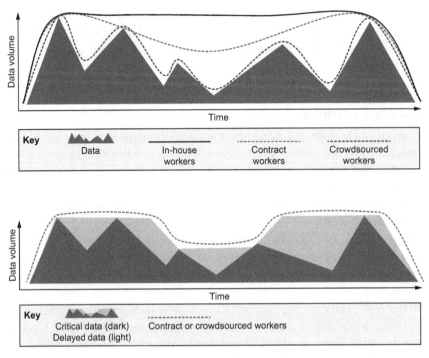

Figure 7.5 Smoothing your work for outsourced workers. If you can't fully smooth out the data volume, you might be able to smooth it out enough to fit the scale at which outsourced workers can scale up and down.

7.3.1 *Salary for outsourced workers*

Outsourced workers should be offered fair salaries by their employers, but you still have a responsibility to check that the compensation is fair. You have a duty of care for any person who works for you, even if they are contractors provided by another company. This duty of care comes from a power dynamic in which you are in the most powerful position. You don't want an outsourcing firm trying to win your business with lower prices by underpaying its workers. Especially if you are using an outsourcing firm that you are not familiar with, you should ask these questions:

- How much is each worker compensated per hour/day, and how does this pay compare to published numbers for the minimum wage and minimum cost of living at their location?
- Will workers get paid for the time that they are being trained on the task or only when they are annotating?
- Are workers compensated between projects or when your project has less work, or only when they're working directly on projects?

You can drill down into any of these questions. With regard to compensation, for example, you can ask about benefits such as health care, retirement, and paid leave.

Calculate whether compensation is fair for the cost of living where the workers are working, taking into account any reduced or absent pay between projects. Note that you are part of this equation; if you can provide a consistent stream of work for your projects, there will be less downtime for individual workers as they wait for your data to come in or as they switch between projects.

If an outsourcing organization can't give specific answers, it probably isn't a good option. At best, the company might be operating as a layer of management on top of other outsourcing firms or crowdsourced workers, and you don't want to be so many steps removed from your annotators because you are unlikely to get high-quality annotations. At worst, the organization might be covering up the fact that it pays exploitative wages.

Be mindful of cultural and national differences in compensation. Workers based in most countries in Europe have good national health care and may not think about the importance of employer-based health care, for example, and workers based in the United States may not expect a parental-leave benefit. The opposite can also be true: if you're in the United States, you don't need to insist that workers in countries with good national health care options also have employer-based health care.

My advice is to err on the side of asking more questions and apologize afterward if your questions came across as culturally insensitive. It is better to offend someone you pay fairly and then grow from that experience than to contribute to any person being compensated unfairly because you were afraid to ask.

7.3.2 *Security for outsourced workers*

Job security for outsourced workers comes from their direct employers. In addition to asking about their compensation, you should ask about job security and opportunities for advancement.

Many outsourcing firms have clear paths for promotion within their organizations. The annotators can become line managers, then site managers, and so on. They might also have specializations, such as being trusted with particular difficult annotation tasks and sensitive data, which are compensated at a higher rate.

If there is no opportunity for advancement within an organization for your workers, consider whether they should be compensated more for performing your tasks, knowing that they might need to pay for training and education out of pocket to advance their careers. It is also fine if someone is happy as a professional annotator and does not want to move into management or specialized roles. If the person is working in a positive environment, is paid fairly, and feels ownership of the work they are performing, then it is dignified work.

7.3.3 *Ownership for outsourced workers*

Outsourced workers are the group most likely to be working as annotators full-time. Therefore, transparency is important so that these workers know they are contributing to your organization. Like in-house workers, outsourced workers will be more motivated if they have transparency into why they are annotating data. If they are annotating scenes in city parks, for example, they should know whether the use case focuses on pedestrians or plants. Knowing the goals greatly improves the accuracy of the data and gives workers a sense of how they are contributing to an important task.

If possible, let your outsourced workers feel that they are contributing directly to your company. Some companies actively avoid naming their outsourced workers as part of their organizations. This approach might be understandable from a brand perspective (concern that an employee of another company could misrepresent your company), but may be not fair if the goal is to hide the fact that a business process is being outsourced.

Regardless of your organization's policies, someone who works full-time as a contractor is contributing as much on a given day as someone who is employed full-time in-house, and they deserve to feel that way. To the extent possible, let these workers know how they are contributing to your organization, but also let them know if they can't talk about it publicly. There is often a middle ground where you can be transparent with outsourced workers about the value that they are creating, but make it clear that they can talk about it only privately. You probably have in-house people who can't talk about what they work on publicly either.

Outsourced workers are going to have less intuition about your company's goals than your in-house workers do. Your company might be a large multinational or a hot neighborhood startup, but there is no guarantee that an outsourced worker knows this fact, so don't assume too much. It is a win-win situation when an outsourced worker knows more about the context of the work they are completing: they will do higher-quality work that deserves higher pay at a faster rate and feel better about the process. Try to maintain a communication channel with your annotators while you are working with them.

7.3.4 *Tip: Talk to your outsourced workers*

If you are running a machine learning project, you should have direct communication with the line managers who are managing the annotation day to day. This communication can be emails, forums, or (ideally) something like online chat. Direct communication with the annotators themselves can be even richer, but depending on scale and privacy concerns, that interaction may not be permitted.

As a middle ground, you might have an open channel with the line manager and regular all-hands meetings with the annotators. If you have regular meetings, make it clear to the outsourcing company that this time is billable time for which the annotators should be paid. Questions always come up during annotation work, such as edge cases that you didn't think about and assumptions you made that weren't explicit in your guidelines. Also, it is respectful to give annotators direct communication with the people they are creating data for.

I've commonly seen outsourced workers four or five people removed from the people who build the machine learning models. Data scientists might engage someone else internally to manage the data; that data manager works with an account manager at the outsourcing company; that account manager works with annotation leadership at the company; the annotation leadership work with the line managers; and finally, the line managers work with the individual annotators. That's five steps to communicate any guidelines or feedback!

Remember that in addition to paying the annotators, you are effectively paying for all the intermediate people. In some industries, 50% of the spend goes to this management overhead. If you're forced to use inefficient management structures, your communication doesn't have to follow that path. Establish direct relationships with the annotators or their immediate managers.

7.4 Crowdsourced workers

Crowdsourced workers who are paid on a per-task basis are the most-talked-about workforce for data annotation, but they are also the smallest group. I worked at the companies that have the two largest marketplaces for crowdsourced annotation work, and even then, I used outsourced workers (who were paid fair hourly wages) more than I used crowdsourced workers.

Online marketplaces for crowdsourced work typically allow you to post your annotation jobs; then people choose to complete that work for a posted price per task. If bonuses or pro-rata hourly wages are offered, these amounts are supplemental to the per-task price. The workers are typically anonymous, and this anonymity is often enforced by the platforms both technically and by their terms and conditions.

Because *crowdsourcing* is a general term that also includes data collection, annotation is also referred to as *microtasking*. Because the work is paid on a per-data-item basis, the process is also called *pay-per-task* or, more generally, considered to be part of the *gig economy*. In all cases, it refers to the greatest flexibility in work but also the greatest vulnerability to exploitation.

The biggest advantage of using crowdsourced workers is how quickly they can scale up and down. If you need only a few minutes of work, but you need it from thousands of people, pay-per-task crowdsourced workers are ideal.

In most companies, it is rare for any large, sustained machine learning project to rely on crowdsourced workers, who are more typically used for quick experiments to validate whether some level of accuracy on a new task is possible. Crowdsourced workers are also used when quick turnaround on annotations is needed on short notice, although some outsourcing companies offer 24/7 workforces that can agree to shorter turnaround times.

Because academic research is more often about quick experiments for different use cases than about sustained increases in accuracy for one use case, crowdsourced workers have been the annotation workforce of choice for many academic departments. The prominence of this work is why crowdsourced work is sometimes wrongly viewed as being a widespread method for annotation in industry. See "Don't apply graduate-student economics to your data labeling strategy" in section 7.4.3 for more perspective on the relationship between academia and crowdsourcing in terms of how it influences real-world machine learning.

On the worker side, there are valid reasons why a person will choose to be a crowd-sourced worker rather than work for an outsourcing company. The biggest reason is that there might not be an outsourcing company that can employ them at their location. You can be a crowdsourced worker from almost anywhere with an internet connection.

For someone who might otherwise face discrimination, crowdsourced work can be an equalizer. The anonymity makes it much less likely that workers are going to be discriminated against based on ethnicity, gender, criminal record, nationality, disability, or any other reason that often limits people's employment. Their work will be evaluated for its inherent merit.

Some people prefer crowdsourced work because they are limited to or prefer pay-per-task work. Perhaps they can contribute only a few minutes at a time due to other commitments, such as caring for their family or working at a full-time job that allows them time to do additional crowdsourced work. This area is the most difficult one in which to ensure fairness. If one worker takes 60 minutes to complete a task that takes most people 15 minutes, it is not fair to pay them for only 15 minutes; they should be paid for 60 minutes. If that pay is not within your budget, exclude those workers from accepting future tasks of yours in a way that doesn't negatively reflect on them in any online reputation system.

Crowdsourced workers are the most easily exploited workforce. It is difficult to predict how long some tasks will take in advance, so pay-per-task compensation can easily underpay someone even if the tasks are set up with good intentions. Also, it is easy for someone to set up tasks *without* good intentions, either misrepresenting the time it will take to complete a task or offering exploitative wages.

I have seen people make the argument that low-paid work (say, around $1 per hour) is better than nothing to someone who has free time and no other source of income. But this argument isn't true. It is ethically wrong to pay someone less than they need to live on. Beyond that, it contributes to that same inequality. If you have a business model that is viable only via exploitative wages, you are driving down the entire industry, and the rest of your industry can remain competitive only by doing the same. Therefore, you are helping create an entire industry that can survive only if it perpetuates an exploitative wage model, which helps no one.

7.4.1   *Salary for crowdsourced workers*

You should always pay crowdsourced workers fairly. All the major crowdsourcing platforms will tell you how long someone worked on your task, but this figure can be inaccurate because it relies on a browser to track time and may not include the time the worker spent studying the task before they started working on it.

I recommended paying people a fair hourly wage for the work they complete, based on their location in the world and published data on fair pay at that location. Every crowdsourcing marketplace allows you to pay effectively an hourly rate with bonus structures, even if it is not possible to put hourly pay directly into the payment process. If you can't work out the exact amount of time that someone has spent, you should ask the workers directly rather than risk underpaying them. Software is available to help too.[1]

If you don't think that someone has completed crowdsourced work for you within your budget, every crowdsourcing platform will allow you to exclude them from future work. You should still pay them for the work that they completed. Even if you are 99% sure that they were not genuine in their work, you should pay them so that the 1% doesn't unfairly miss out.

Every major crowdsourcing platform allows you to restrict work to certain workers. This restriction might be implemented as qualifications that you can award or lists of worker IDs, but the result is the same: only those people will be allowed to work on your task. After you find people who can complete your tasks well, you can limit your most important work to them.

Every major crowdsourcing platform also implements some "trusted worker" category that automates how well someone has done in the past, typically based on the amount of work they have completed that was validated. These systems get scammed pretty easily with bots controlled by bad actors, however, so you will likely need to curate your own trusted-worker pool.

Producing good instructions is trickier than for other workforces, because you often can't interact directly. Also, the worker may not speak your language and is using machine translation in their browser to follow your instructions. If people are not being paid to read instructions, they are more likely to skim them and to be annoyed if they have to continually scroll past them, so it is important to have accurate, succinct instructions that make sense when translated into other languages with machine translation. That's not easy, but it is also the respectful thing to do; if you are paying people per task instead of per hour, you should make your interfaces as efficient as possible. I recommend breaking your task into simpler subtasks, not just for your benefit in quality, but so that workers who are being paid per task can be as efficient as possible and therefore earn more per hour.

7.4.2 *Security for crowdsourced workers*

Job security for crowdsourced workers comes primarily from the marketplace itself. The people who complete the tasks know that other work will be available when yours is complete.

For short-term security, it helps workers if you indicate how much work is available. If a worker knows that they can work on your tasks for many hours, days, or months, they are more likely to start your tasks, but job security may not be obvious to a worker if you break your tasks into smaller jobs. If you have only 100 items that need annotation in a given task, but you will be repeating that same task with millions of items in

---

[1] One recent example is in the paper "Fair Work: Crowd Work Minimum Wage with One Line of Code," by Mark Whiting, Grant Hugh, and Michael Bernstein (http://mng.bz/WdQw).

total, include that fact in your task description. Your task is more appealing for work-ers when they know that more work that they are familiar with is coming.

In general, you should factor in the fact that workers receive no benefits for pay-per-task jobs and may spend a lot of their time (often 50% or more) not getting paid while they are looking for projects to work on and reading instructions. Pay people accordingly, and pay extra for short, one-off tasks.

7.4.3   *Ownership for crowdsourced workers*

Like outsourced workers, crowdsourced workers typically feel more ownership and produce better results when they have as much transparency as possible. Transparency goes both ways: you should always elicit feedback about your task from crowdsourced workers. A simple comments field can be enough.

Even if you can't identify your company for sensitivity reasons, you should share the motivation for your annotation project and the benefits that it can have. Everyone feels better when they know they are creating value.

> #### Don't apply graduate-student economics to your data labeling strategy
> Too many data scientists take their data annotation experience from university to industry. In most computer science programs, data annotation is not valued as a sci-ence, or at least not as highly valued as algorithm development. At the same time, students are taught not to value their own time; it is fine for students to spend weeks working on a problem that could be outsourced for a few hundred dollars.
>
> A compounding factor is that graduate students typically have little or no budget for human annotation. They might have access to a computer cluster or free credits from a cloud provider, but they might have no easy way to access funds to pay people to annotate new data.
>
> As a result, pay-per-task crowdsourcing platforms are popular with graduate students who are trying to get the most out of their data budgets. They are also willing to spend a lot of time on quality control rather than pay people who have more expertise to ensure data quality, due to the same budget constraints. Because their tasks are often low-volume, they are rarely targeted by spammers, so quality seems to be arti-ficially high.
>
> Because the annotation itself is not part of the science that students are hoping to advance, annotation is often treated as a means to an end. Early in their careers, data scientists too often approach annotation with this same mindset. They want to ignore data as something that is not their problem and spend their own resources curating the right low-paid workers instead of paying better workers a fair salary to annotate the data more accurately.
>
> Be careful that you don't have graduate-student economics wrongly influencing your data annotation strategy. Many of the suggestions in this chapter, such as holding internal data labeling sessions and establishing direct communication with out-sourced annotators, will help your company culture and ensure that you are approach-ing data labeling in a way that benefits everyone.

7.4.4 *Tip: Create a path to secure work and career advancement*

There's a good chance that you will eventually want some annotators to be available full-time, even if you need only part-time workers to begin with. If there is a path to becoming a full-time worker, you should include this fact in your task description to attract the best workers.

You need to structure the possibility of full-time work based on individual merit, however, not make the situation competitive. If people know that they might miss out in a competitive environment, there is too great a power imbalance for the work to be fair, which could result in people compromising too much for the promise of future work. In plain terms, don't say something like "The 10 best people will get a 3-month contract." Say something like "Anyone who reaches volume X at accuracy Y will get a 3-month contract." Promise nothing if you can't make that commitment so that you don't inadvertently set up an exploitative environment.

If the marketplace offers feedback and review, use it! Anyone who has worked well deserves that recognition, which can help with their future work and career advancement.

7.5 *Other workforces*

The three workforces that you have seen so far—in-house workers, outsourced workers, and crowdsourced workers—probably cover most machine learning projects that you work on, but other types of workforces may fall between those categories. An outsourcing company might employ subcontractors in structures similar to crowdsourcing, or you might have in-house annotators who are employed as contractors at remote locations. You can apply the right combination of the principles of salary, security, and ownership for any of these configurations to be most respectful to these workforces and ensure that you get the best-quality work.

When running smaller companies, I have found a lot of success when contracting people directly rather than using outsourcing companies. Some online marketplaces for contract annotators allow you transparency into someone's past work, and it is easier to ensure that you are paying someone fairly and communicating openly when you are working with them directly. This approach doesn't always scale, but it can be successful for smaller one-off annotation projects.

You might also engage a handful of other workforces: end users, volunteers, people playing games, and computer-generated annotations. We'll cover them briefly in the following sections.

7.5.1 *End users*

If you can get your data labels for free from your end users, you have a powerful business model! The ability to get labels from end users might even be an important factor in deciding what products you need to build. If you can get your first working application from data labels that don't cost you anything, you can worry about running annotation projects later. By that point, you'll also have good user data to sample via active learning to focus your annotation efforts.

For many applications, users provide feedback that can power your machine learning models. Many applications that seem to rely on end users for training data, however, still use large numbers of annotators. The most obvious, widespread example is search engines. Whether you are searching for a website, a product, or a location on a map, your choice from the search results helps that search engine become smarter about matching similar queries in the future.

It would be easy to assume that search systems rely only on user feedback, but that isn't the case. Search relevance is the single largest use case for employing annotators. Paid annotators often work on the components. A product page might be indexed for the type of product (electronics, food, and so on), have the keywords extracted from the page, and have the best display images selected automatically, with each task being a separate annotation task. Most systems that can get data from end users spend a lot of time annotating the same data offline.

The biggest shortcoming of training data provided by users is that the users essentially drive your sampling strategy. You learned in chapters 3 and 4 how easy it is to bias your model by annotating the wrong sample of data. If you are sampling only data that seems to be the most interesting to your users on a given day, you run the risk of data that lacks diversity. Chances are that the most popular interactions from your users are not the same as those from a random distribution, or are the most important for your model to learn about, so you could end up with data that is worse than random sampling. Your model might end up accurate for only the most common use cases and be bad for everything else, which can have real-world diversity implications.

If you have a large pool of raw data, the best way to combat bias from end users is to use representative sampling to discover what you are missing from user-provided annotations and then get additional annotations for the items sampled via representative sampling. This approach will mitigate the bias in your training data if it has oversampled what is important to users instead of what was best for the model.

Some of the smartest ways to get user-generated annotations are indirect. CAPTCHAs are examples that you may encounter daily. A *CAPTCHA* (completely automated public Turing test to tell computers and humans apart) is the test that you complete to tell a website or application that you are not a robot. If you completed a CAPTCHA that asked you to transcribe scanned text or identify objects in photographs, there is a good chance that you were creating training data for some company. This use case is a clever one because if machine learning was already good enough to complete the task, that training data wouldn't be needed in the first place. A limited workforce exists for this kind of task, so unless you're in an organization that offers this kind of workforce, it's probably not worth pursuing.

Even if you can't rely on your users for annotations, you should use them for uncertainty sampling. If no data-sensitivity concerns apply, regularly look at examples in which your model was uncertain in its predictions while deployed. This information will enhance your intuition about where your model is falling short, and the sampled items will help your model when they are annotated.

7.5.2 *Volunteers*

For tasks that have an inherent benefit, you may be able to get people to contribute as volunteer crowdsourced workers. In 2010, I ran the largest use of crowdsourcing for disaster response. An earthquake struck Haiti and killed more than 100,000 people immediately, leaving more than a million homeless. I was responsible for the first step in a disaster-response and reporting system. We set up a free phone number, 4636, that anyone in Haiti could send a text message to, requesting help or reporting on local conditions. Most people in Haiti speak only Haitian Kreyol, and most people from the international disaster response community coming into Haiti only spoke English. So I recruited and managed 2,000 members of the Haitian diaspora from 49 countries to volunteer to help. When a text message was sent to 4636 in Haiti, a volunteer would translate it, categorize the request (food, medicine, etc.), and plot the location on a map. Over the first month following the earthquake, more than 45,000 structured reports were streamed to the English-speaking disaster responders, with a median turnaround of less than 5 minutes.

At the same time, we shared the translations with machine translation teams at Microsoft and Google so that they could use the data to launch machine translation services for Haitian Kreyol that were accurate for disaster-response related data. It was the first time that human-in-the-loop machine learning had been deployed for disaster response. This approach has become more common since, but rarely successfully when volunteers are engaged instead of paid workers.

Other high-profile, volunteer-driven projects that I have seen are in science, such as the gene-folding project Fold It,[2] but these projects tend to be the exception rather than the rule. In general, it is hard to get crowdsourced volunteer projects off the ground. Haiti was a special circumstance, with a large, well-educated group of people who wanted to contribute anything they could from far away.

If you are looking for volunteers, I recommend that you find and manage them via strong social ties. Many people try to launch volunteer crowdsourcing efforts with general callouts on social media, and 99% of them do not get the volume of people required. Worse, volunteers come and leave quickly, so they may not be ramped up to the right level of accuracy by the time they leave and have taken up a lot of resources for training. It is also demoralizing for volunteers who *are* providing substantial volumes of work to see so many people come and go.

When you reach out to people directly and build a community around a smaller number of volunteers, you are more likely to be successful. You will see this same pattern in open-source coding projects and projects like Wikipedia; the majority of work is done by a small number of people.

---

[2] "Building de novo cryo-electron microscopy structures collaboratively with citizen scientists," by Firas Khatib, Ambroise Desfosses, Foldit Players, Brian Koepnick, Jeff Flatten, Zoran Popović, David Baker, Seth Cooper, Irina Gutsche, and Scott Horowitz (http://mng.bz/8NqB).

7.5.3   *People playing games*

Gamifying work falls somewhere between paid workers and volunteers. Most attempts to get training data from games have failed miserably. You can use this strategy, but I don't recommend it as a way to get annotations.

The greatest success that I have had with games came when I worked in epidemic tracking. During an E-Coli outbreak in Europe, we needed people to annotate German news reports about the number of people affected. We couldn't find enough German speakers on crowdsourcing platforms, and this event predated outsourcing companies that specialized in annotation for machine learning. We ultimately found German speakers in an online game, Farmville, and paid them in virtual currency within the game to annotate the news articles. So people indoors in Germany were being paid in virtual agriculture to help track the real agricultural outbreak happening outside in German fields.

This case was a one-off use case, and it is difficult to see how it might have been exploitative. We paid small amounts of money per task, but the people playing the game were compensated for work that would have taken them 10 times longer within the game.

I have yet to see a game that generates interesting training data except for AI within the game itself or in focused academic studies. People spend an incredible amount of time playing online games, but this potential workforce is largely untapped right now.

Note that I do not recommended that you gamify *paid* work. If you force someone to do paid work within a gamelike environment, that person will get annoyed quickly if the work does not feel like the most efficient way to annotate data. Think about your own work. Would it be more fun if it had the kinds of artificial hurdles that you encounter in games?

There is also a lot of evidence that strategies such as providing a leaderboard are net-negative, motivating only a small number of leaders while demotivating the majority who are not near the top of the leaderboard. If you want to take any one thing from the gaming industry into paid work, use the principle of transparency: let people know their individual progress, but do it in terms of what they are contributing to your organization, not how they compare with their peers.

7.5.4   *Model predictions as annotations*

If you can get annotations from another machine learning application, you can get a lot of annotations cheaply. This strategy will rarely be your only strategy for getting annotations. If a machine learning algorithm can already produce accurate data, why do you need annotations for a new model? Using high-confidence predictions from your existing model as annotations is a strategy known as semi-supervised machine learning.

Chapter 9 covers using model predictions as annotations in more detail. All automated labeling strategies can perpetuate the existing biases of your model, so they should be used in combination with human-annotated labels. All the academic papers showing domain-adaptation without additional human labels are in narrow domains.

Figure 7.6 shows an example of how to get started with computer-generated annotations when you want to avoid perpetuating bias and limitations in the past model as much as possible. First, you can autogenerate annotations with an existing model and select only those annotations that have high confidence. As you learned in chapter 3, you can't always trust the confidence alone, especially if you know that you are applying the model to a new domain of data. If the existing model is a neural network, and you can access its logits or hidden layers, also exclude predictions that have low overall activation in the model (model-based outliers), which indicate that they are not similar to the data on which the model was trained. Then use representative sampling to identify the items that you couldn't label automatically and sample those items for human review.

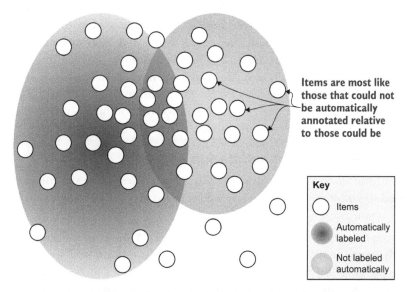

Figure 7.6 Using computer-generated annotations and then augmenting them with representative sampling. If you have a separate model for your task, you can autogenerate labels with that model. It is best to focus on highly confident predictions and (if you can access them) predictions with high activation in your network: model-based outliers. Then use representative sampling to identify the items that you couldn't label automatically and sample those items for human review.

For a slightly more sophisticated approach, you could use adaptive representative sampling to reduce the number of sampled items you need. With a little more sophistication, you could use a combination of clustering and representative sampling, as you learned in chapter 5. Combining clustering and representative sampling is ideal if the problem you are addressing is inherently heterogeneous in the feature space of your dataset.

Using computer-generated annotations can be the biggest kick-start to your model or the biggest rabbit hole, depending on your data and the quality of existing available models. To determine whether this approach is right for you, factor in the whole cost of the human annotation component. If you already need to spend a lot of time refining the right instructions and integrating and training a human workforce, you may not be saving much money by cutting down on how much the workers need to annotate. That is, the advantage might be less than you think.

In some cases, such as machine translation, using an existing model is the best starting point. It is expensive to get human translations for large amounts of data, so it will almost always be more cost-effective to bootstrap a model that starts with a dataset that was machine-translated in the first place.

Another case in which to use computer-generated annotations as a starting point is when you are adapting legacy systems to newer machine learning models. Suppose that you have a legacy system with a lot of hand-coded rules or hand-tuned systems for extracting the right features, and you want to adapt that system to a newer neural machine learning system that doesn't require handcrafted rules or features. You can apply the legacy system to a large amount of raw data and use the resulting predictions as your annotations. It is unlikely that this model will immediately achieve the accuracy you want, but it can be a good starting point, and additional active learning and annotation can build on it. Chapter 9 covers many methods of combining model predictions with human annotations—an exciting and rapidly growing area of research.

7.6   *Estimating the volume of annotation needed*

Regardless of the workforce you use, you often need to estimate the total amount of time needed to annotate your data. It is useful to break your annotation strategy into four stages as you annotate more data:

- *Meaningful signal*—Better-than-chance accuracy. Your model's accuracy is statistically better than chance, but small changes in parameters or starting conditions produce different models in the accuracy and in which items are classified correctly. At this point, you have enough signal to indicate that more annotations should increase accuracy and that this strategy is worth pursuing.
- *Stable accuracy*—Consistent but low accuracy. Your model's accuracy is still low, but it is stable because small changes in parameters or starting conditions produce models that are similar in terms of accuracy and in which items are classified correctly. You can start to trust the model's confidence and activation at this stage, getting the most out of active learning.
- *Deployed model*—High-enough accuracy for your use case. You have a model that is accurate enough for your use case, and you can start deploying it to your applications. You can start identifying items in your deployed models that are uncertain or that represent new, unseen examples, adapting your model to the changing data it encounters.

- *State-of-the-art model*—Industry-leading accuracy. Your model is the most accurate in your industry. You continue to identify items in your deployed models that are uncertain or that represent new, unseen examples so that you can maintain accuracy in a changing environment.

In every industry I have seen, the state-of-the-art model that won long-term was the winner because of better training data, not because of new algorithms. For this reason, better data is often referred to as a *data moat*: the data is the barrier that prevents your competitors from reaching the same levels of accuracy.

7.6.1 *The orders-of-magnitude equation for number of annotations needed*

The best way to start thinking about the amount of data needed for your project is in terms of orders of magnitude. In other words, the number of annotations needed to grow exponentially to hit certain milestones in model accuracy.

Suppose that you have a relatively straightforward binary prediction task, such as the example in chapter 2 of this book of predicting disaster-related and non-disaster-related messages. You might get a progression that looks something like this, assuming that N=2 (figure 7.7):

- 100 (10^N) annotations—Meaningful signal
- 1,000 (10^{N+1}) annotations—Stable accuracy
- 10,000 (10^{N+2}) annotations—Deployed model
- 100,000 (10^{N+3}) annotations—State-of-the-art model

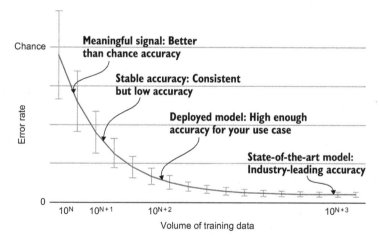

Figure 7.7 The orders-of-magnitude principle for training data. Estimate an order of magnitude more data to move from meaningful signal to stable accuracy to deployed model and to state-of-the-art model. Use this principle as a benchmark to estimate the amount of data you need before you start seeing what your actual increase in accuracy looks like as you start annotating data.

You will be able to reduce the number of items you need to annotate with active learning and transfer learning, but the step function is still approximately exponential with a lower N (say, N=1.2). Similarly, it may take more annotations for tasks that a large number of labels or complicated tasks such as full-text generation (say, N=3), in which case you should assume that the step function is still approximately exponential but with a higher N.

When actual annotations start coming in, you can start plotting your true increase in accuracy and making better estimates of how much data you need. The plotted increase in accuracy (or decrease in error, as in figure 7.7) is called the *learning curve* of your model, but this name doubles up: people often refer to the increase in accuracy as a single model converges as the learning curve too. If your machine learning framework of choice shows you a learning curve, check whether that name refers to an increase in accuracy with more data or an increase in accuracy as the model converges on a constant amount of data. The two cases are not the same.

Even when you have your own data coming in, it is a good idea to keep the diminishing returns of figure 7.7 in mind. It can be exciting when your accuracy moves up quickly with the first 100 or 1,000 annotations but less so when your accuracy improves much more slowly thereafter. This experience is typical. Don't jump too quickly into playing with algorithm architectures and parameters because that is what you are most familiar with. If you can see that the accuracy is improving with more data but the rate is slowing exponentially, this model may be behaving as expected.

7.6.2 *Anticipate one to four weeks of annotation training and task refinement*

You've got your machine model ready to go, and you've proved that it works with a popular open-source dataset. Now you're ready to turn on the firehose of real annotated data for your application!

If you haven't set up your annotation strategy in parallel, you're in for a surprise: you probably need to wait a few weeks. Waiting is frustrating, but as I recommend at the start of this chapter, you should start your data and algorithm strategies at the same time. If you find that data is too different from the open-source dataset that you first piloted on (maybe some labels are much rarer or the diversity of data is much higher), you will be back to the drawing board for your machine learning architecture in any case. Don't rush your annotation, but if you have to rush for quick results, be prepared to drop those annotations later because they will have too many errors because of the lack of quality control.

It will likely take several iterations with your data labeling leaders to get the instructions correct, to investigate any systematic errors, and to refine your guidelines appropriately before you can confidently turn on the firehose to annotate large amounts of data.

Expect it to take a few weeks to get the annotation process working smoothly, not a few days (although it shouldn't take you many months to get an annotation process working smoothly). If the task is a simple one, such as labeling photographs with a relatively small number of labels, it will take closer to one week; you will need crisp definitions of what counts for each label, but that should not take too long to refine. If you have a more complicated task with unusual data and labeling requirements, it will take closer to a month to refine your task and for the annotators to ramp up in training, and you will be continually refining your task as more edge cases are discovered.

If you need data right away while you wait for your annotation workforce to get trained, start annotating data yourself. You will learn a lot about your data, which will help with both your models and your annotation guidelines.

7.6.3   Use your pilot annotations and accuracy goal to estimate cost

When you have refined your annotation process to the point where you are confident that your guidelines are comprehensive and your annotators are trained on your task, you can estimate the cost. Take into account your accuracy requirement, using the guideline for orders of magnitude in section 7.6.1 to estimate the total number of annotations required. Do you need state-of-the-art? If so, you can multiply the orders of magnitude required for state-of-the-art results by your per-annotation cost and estimate the total cost. The result might help determine your product strategy. If you don't have the budget to get to state-of-the-art accuracy, as you originally planned, you may still be able to get high-enough accuracy for your use case, which could change your product development strategy. It is important to be honest with yourself and your stakeholders about the accuracy you can achieve. If your model was state-of-the-art on an open-source dataset, but it will not reach that accuracy on your own data due to budget constraints, then you need to set expectations for all the stakeholders in your project.

One variable that we have not covered yet is the number of annotators per item. You will often give the same task to multiple people to find agreement among them and produce training data that is more accurate than any single annotator can create. We will cover that method of quality control in chapter 8. For now, it is enough to understand that you may end up with multiple annotations per item, and that result needs to be part of your budget.

Your budget for labeling might be fixed from the start, of course. In that case, make sure that you carefully implement good active learning strategies so that you get the most out of each annotation.

7.6.4   Combining types of workforces

One common reason that you might want to combine workforces is quality control. Workflows and choice of labeling workforce are common ways to ensure that you get accurate labels for your data (chapter 8). Other common reasons include data sensitivity and complexity, meaning that some data is too sensitive or complex to be outsourced and some is not, resulting in multiple workforces.

When working at larger companies, I typically engaged multiple data labeling companies at the same time to derisk my pipelines, not relying on any vendor to be the only source of data labels. If you end up with multiple workforces, you obviously need to work out the budget for each workforce and combine the budgets to get your total project spend.

Summary

- There are three main types of workforces for annotation: in-house, outsourced, and crowdsourced. Understanding these workforces will help you choose which workforce or combination is best for your tasks.
- The three key principles of motivating annotators are salary, security, and transparency. Understanding how to apply these principles to different workforces will ensure that you get the best possible work by having the happiest possible workforce.
- You can consider some nonmonetary compensation systems, including application end users, volunteers, and computer-generated data/annotations. You may want to consider these alternative workforces when you are constrained by budget or need special qualifications.
- Don't apply graduate-student economics to your data labeling strategy.
- The orders-of-magnitude principle lets you estimate your total annotation volume requirements. This principle helps you plan your annotation strategy with meaningful early estimates that you can refine as you continue.

Quality control
for data annotation

8

This chapter covers

- Calculating the accuracy of an annotator compared with ground truth data
- Calculating the overall agreement and reliability of a dataset
- Generating a confidence score for each training data label
- Incorporating subject-matter experts into annotation workflow
- Breaking a task into simpler subtasks to improve annotation

You have your machine learning model ready to go, and you have people lined up to annotate your data, so you are almost ready to deploy! But you know that your model is going to be only as accurate as the data that it is trained on, so if you can't get high-quality annotations, you won't have an accurate model. You need to give the same task to multiple people and take the majority vote, right?

Unfortunately, your annotation task is probably much harder. I've seen annotation underestimated more often than any other part of the human-in-the-loop machine learning cycle. Even if you have a simple labeling task—such as deciding whether an image contains a pedestrian, an animal, a cyclist, or a sign—how do you decide on the right threshold for majority agreement among annotators when all those annotators have seen different combinations of tasks? How do you know when your overall agreement is so low that you need to change your guidelines or the way you define your task? The statistics to calculate agreement in even the simpler labeling tasks are more advanced than the statistics underlying most neural models, so understanding them takes time and practice.

This chapter and the next two chapters use the concepts of *expected* and *actual* annotation accuracy. If, for example, someone guessed randomly for each annotation, we would expect them to get some percentage correct, so we adjust the actual accuracy to account for a baseline of random chance. The concepts of *expected* and *actual* behavior apply to many types of tasks and annotation scenarios.

8.1   Comparing annotations with ground truth answers

The simplest method for measuring annotation quality is also one of the most powerful: compare the responses from each annotator with a set of known answers, called *ground truth answers*. An annotator might annotate 1,000 items, of which 100 have known answers. If the annotator gets 80 of those known answers correct, you can estimate that they are 80% accurate over the 1,000 items.

You can implement the creation of ground truth data incorrectly in many ways, however, and unfortunately almost all errors make your dataset appear to be more accurate than it is. If you are creating your evaluation data and training data at the same time and don't have good quality controls, you will end up with the same kinds of errors in both your training data and evaluation data. The resulting model may predict the wrong label in some contexts, but the ground truth evaluation data will have the same type of errors, so you may not realize that you have the errors until you deploy your application and it fails.

The most common cause of errors is wrong items sampled for ground truth. Three general sampling strategies identify the items that should become ground truth data:

- *A random sample of data*—You should evaluate the accuracy of your individual annotators on random data. If a random selection isn't possible, or if you know that a random sample is not representative of the population that your application is serving, you should try to get a sample that is as close to representative as possible.
- *A sample of data with the same distribution of features and labels as the batch of data that is being annotated*—If you are using active learning, this sample should be a random sample from your current iteration of active learning, which allows you to calculate the (human) accuracy of each sample of data and, by extension, the accuracy of the dataset as a whole.

- *A sample of data found during the annotation process that is most useful for annotation guidelines*—These guidelines often exemplify important edge cases that are useful for teaching the annotators to be as accurate as possible.

Within our diagram for human-in-the-loop architectures, if we zoom in on the annotation component, we see that the workflow is a little more complicated than the high-level diagram shown in figure 8.1.

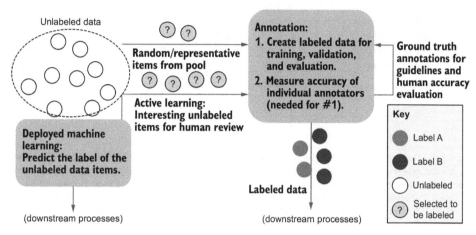

Figure 8.1 **The flow of information for annotation. In addition to taking data sampled according to our current active learning strategies, we sample a random or representative set of data and data that some annotators have already seen. Sampling random/representative data lets us calculate the accuracy of annotators in a way that makes it easier to determine their reliability across datasets and whether they are candidates for promotion to experts. Sampling within the current active learning batch allows us to calculate the accuracy for this particular dataset. Sampling during the annotation process finds items that are most useful for annotation guidelines and for adjudication by experts.**

To be confident that your ground truth items are as accurate as possible, you need to draw on many of the methods in this chapter and possibly the next two chapters. You must be confident that your ground truth items have few errors; otherwise, you will create misleading guidelines and won't have reliable accuracy metrics, resulting in bad training data. You can't cut corners. If your ground truth items are only items that had the highest agreement, you are likely to have oversampled the easiest items to annotate, which will make your accuracy look better than it is.

When you have a ground truth dataset that you can use to evaluate each annotator, you can calibrate your annotation projects to be higher-quality and more efficient. Using interannotator agreement for quality control also becomes much more effectively with a small but reliable ground truth dataset to support it. As chapter 9 shows, you can still get reliable signals from the least accurate annotator when you know their pattern of errors.

In this chapter and chapter 9, we will use the example data shown in figure 8.2. Although your datasets will have many more items than the 11 rows in figure 8.2, these 11 rows are enough for learning the kinds of quality controls that you might implement.

Annotator/ annotations	Alex	Blake	Cameron	Dancer	Evan
Task 1	Pedestrian	Pedestrian	Pedestrian		
Task 2		Sign	Sign	Sign	
Task 3	Pedestrian	Pedestrian	Cyclist	Cyclist	Pedestrian
Task 4		Cyclist	Cyclist	Cyclist	
Task 5	Pedestrian	Pedestrian	Pedestrian	Pedestrian	
Task 6	Cyclist	Cyclist			Cyclist
Task 7	Pedestrian	Pedestrian		Pedestrian	
Task 8	Animal	Animal		Animal	
Task 9	Sign		Animal	Animal	Animal
Task 10		Sign	Sign		Sign
Task 11		Animal			
...					

What type of object is in this image?

- ⦿ Pedestrian
- ◯ Cylist
- ◯ Animal
- ◯ Sign

Figure 8.2 Throughout the remainder of this chapter and in chapters 9 and 10, we will use this example data. Five annotators—named Alex, Blake, Cameron, Dancer, and Evan—have annotated an image according to the object in that image. We will assume that the image is the same type that was used in previous chapters, with four labels, "Animal," "Cyclist," "Pedestrian," and "Sign." In this example, Alex has seen seven images (tasks 1, 3, 5, 6, 7, 8, and 9); annotated the first three as "Pedestrian"; and annotated each of the rest as "Cyclist," "Pedestrian," "Animal," or "Sign." The image on the right shows what the annotation interface might look like.

We will use different variations of the correct answer for the data in figure 8.2 throughout this chapter but keep the annotations the same as in the figure. For this section, let's assume that we had ground truth labels for each of these examples.

What should you call an annotator?

Many terms are used for a person who creates training and evaluation data, including *rater, coder, adjudicator, agent, assessor, editor, judge, labeler, oracle, worker,* and *turker* (from the Mechanical Turk platform, sometimes used for other software). In industry, the annotator might go by their job title, such as *analyst,* by the skill they are using, such as *linguist,* or by their employment status, such as *contractor* or *gig-economy worker.* In other cases, an annotator is referred to as a *subject-matter expert,* sometimes truncated to *expert* or to the acronym *SME* (pronounced "smee").

If you are searching for additional reading, make sure to try the different names as search terms. You might find similar papers on *interannotator agreement, inter-rater agreement,* and *intercoder agreement,* for example.

This book uses the term *annotator* because it is the least likely to be confused with any other role. If you're working with people who annotate data, use the correct title for that person in your organization. This book also avoids saying *training* annotators (to eliminate confusion with training a model) and uses terms such as *guidelines* and *instructions* instead of *training materials.* Again, use the preferred description in your organization for the process of teaching annotators the instructions for a given task.

8.1.1 Annotator agreement with ground truth data

The basic math for agreement with ground truth data in labeling tasks is simple: the percentage of known answers that an annotator scored correctly. Figure 8.3 gives hypothetical accuracy for each annotator on our example data.

Annotator/annotations	Alex	Blake	Cameron	Dancer	Evan	Ground truth		Correct? Alex	Blake	Cameron	Drew	Evan
Accuracy								0.714	0.900	1.000	1.000 (Ave)	0.750
Task 1	Pedestrian	Pedestrian	Pedestrian			Pedestrian		1	1	1		
Task 2		Sign	Sign	Sign		Sign			1	1	1	
Task 3	Pedestrian	Pedestrian	Cyclist	Cyclist	Pedestrian	Cyclist		0	0	1	1	0
Task 4		Cyclist	Cyclist	Cyclist		Cyclist			1	1	1	
Task 5	Pedestrian	Pedestrian	Pedestrian	Pedestrian		Pedestrian		1	1	1	1	
Task 6	Cyclist	Cyclist			Cyclist	Cyclist		1	1			1
Task 7	Pedestrian	Pedestrian		Pedestrian		Pedestrian		1	1		1	
Task 8	Animal	Animal		Animal		Animal		1	1		1	
Task 9	Sign		Animal	Animal	Animal	Animal		0		1	1	1
Task 10		Sign	Sign		Sign	Sign			1	1		1
Task 11		Animal				Animal			1			
...							Correct?					

Figure 8.3 An example of annotator accuracy compared with ground truth data. Assume that the Ground Truth column has the known answers for each task (image labels). We calculate each annotator's accuracy as the fraction that they got correct.

You typically want to adjust results like those in figure 8.3 according to a baseline of random chance guessing. We can calculate three baselines for our random-chance labeling. Let's assume that 75% of the images are "Pedestrian," 10% are "Sign," 10% are "Cyclist," and 5% are "Animal." The three baselines are

- *Random*—The annotator guesses one of the four labels. This baseline is 25% in our example data because we have four labels.
- *Most frequent label (mode label)*—The annotator knows that "Pedestrian" is the most frequent label, so they always guess that label. This baseline is 75%.
- *Data frequency*—The annotator guesses according to the frequency of each label. They guess "Pedestrian" 75% of the time, "Sign" 10% of the time, and so on. This baseline can be calculated as the sum of the squares of each probability.

Figure 8.4 shows the calculations.

The adjusted accuracy normalizes the annotator's score so that the baseline from random guessing becomes 0. Let's assume that someone had 90% accuracy overall. Their actual accuracy, adjusted for chance, is shown in figure 8.5.

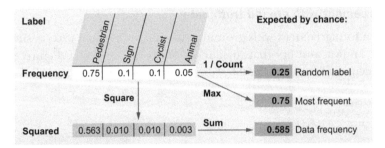

Figure 8.4   The three calculations for different accuracies that would be expected through random chance, showing a wide range of expected accuracy depending on what baseline we use

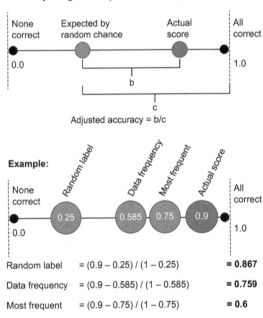

Figure 8.5   Different ways of establishing a baseline expected from random guessing or chance-adjusted accuracy when testing annotators against ground truth data. *Top:* How we normalize the result. If someone was randomly choosing a label, they would sometimes pick the correct one, so we measure accuracy in terms of distance between the random accuracy and 1. *Bottom:* How the different adjusted accuracies look with our example data. Note that the normalized score of 60% accuracy for always guessing "Pedestrian" is different from the 90% raw accuracy score or 86.7% when normalized according to the number of labels. This example highlights why the correct baseline for expected accuracy is so important. There are cases in which each of the three baselines is the better choice, so it is important to know all three.

As figure 8.5 shows, we have different ways to normalize the annotation counts. The most common one used in the statistics community is *data frequency*—a datacentric way to think of expected behavior. It always falls between the random selection and the most frequent, so it has the nice property of being the safe middle option.

Because the expected baseline becomes zero, any result less than zero means that the person guessed worse than random chance. Typically, this result means that the annotator understood the instructions incorrectly or was scamming the system in a simple way, such as always guessing a response that isn't the most frequent. In any of these cases, normalizing the baseline to zero gives us an easy way to set up alerts for any task. No matter what the task is, a negative score after adjusting for random chance should cause an alert in your annotation process!

If you are familiar with the literature on quality control for annotation, you know that a metric that is normalized according to the expected behavior is often called *chance-corrected* or *chance-adjusted*. In many cases throughout this book, the expected behavior is not random chance, such as when we ask annotators what they expect other annotators to choose (chapter 9). The more general term *expected* is used for those cases, but for objective labeling tasks, *expected* and *chance* mean the same thing.

8.1.2 Which baseline should you use for expected accuracy?

For the three baselines for expected accuracy—random, data frequency, and most frequent—calculating all three metrics will help with your intuition about the data. The right metric to normalize your accuracy will be specific to your task and the experience of the people labeling the data.

When a person is first working on a task, they will not have intuition about which label is more frequent, so they are more likely to be closer to random labeling. But after some time, they realize that one label is much more frequent than the others and may feel safe guessing that label when they are uncertain. For that reason, chapter 11 is devoted entirely to user interfaces for annotation.

My practical recommendation is to wait until an after annotator becomes familiar with a task and then apply the strictest baseline: the most frequent label. You can consider the first few minutes, hours, or days of your task to be a ramp-up period for the annotator to become familiar. When an annotator has a strong intuition about the data, they will be taking the relative frequency of the labels into account. As you will see in section 8.2.3, however, data frequency is more relevant for calculating agreement at the level of the entire dataset. So it's important to understand all the baselines and apply them at the right time.

Good quality control for data annotation can take a lot of resources and should be factored into your budget. See the following sidebar for an example of how quality control led to the engagement of a different set of annotators for a project.

> ### Consider the total cost of annotation projects
> *Expert anecdote by Matthew Honnibal*
>
> It helps to communicate directly with the people who are annotating your data, like anyone else in your organization. Inevitably, some of your instructions won't work in practice, and you will need to work closely with your annotators to refine them. You're also likely to keep refining the instructions and adding annotations long after you go into production. If you don't take the time to factor in refining the instructions and discarding wrongly labeled items, it is easy to end up with an outsourced solution that looked cheap on paper but was expensive in practice.

(continued)
In 2009, I was part of a joint project between the University of Sydney and a major Australian news publisher that required named entity recognition, named entity linking, and event linking. Although academics were increasingly using crowdsourced workers at that time, we instead built a small team of annotators that we contracted directly. This ended up being much cheaper in the long run, especially for the more complicated "entity linking" and "event linking" tasks where crowdsourced workers struggled and our annotators were helped by working and communicating with us directly.

Matthew Honnibal is creator of the spaCy NLP library and co-founder of Explosion. He has been working on NLP research since 2005.

8.2   Interannotator agreement

When data scientists talk about their machine learning models being more accurate than people, they often mean that the models are more accurate than the average person. Speech recognition technologies, for example, are now more accurate than the average English speaker for nontechnical transcription in common accents. How can we evaluate the quality of these speech recognition technologies if humans can't create evaluation data with that level of accuracy?

The "wisdom of the crowd" produces data that is more accurate than any one human. For more than a century, people have studied how to aggregate the judgments of multiple people into a single, more accurate result. In the earliest examples, it was famously shown that when multiple people guess the weight of a cow, the average of all the guesses was close to correct. That result doesn't mean that everyone was less accurate than average: individuals will guess the weight of a cow more accurately than the average, but the average guess was closer to the real weight than *most* people.

So when data scientists brag that their model is more accurate than humans, they often mean that their model is more accurate than the agreement among the annotators, which is called *interannotator agreement*. Model accuracy and annotator agreement are two different numbers that shouldn't be compared directly, so try to avoid making this common mistake.

It is possible, however, to create training data that is more accurate than every individual person who contributed to annotations, and this chapter returns to this topic in section 8.3 after introducing the basics.

8.2.1   Introduction to interannotator agreement

Interannotator agreement is typically calculated on a –1 to 1 scale, where 1 is perfect agreement, –1 is perfect disagreement, and 0 is random-chance labeling. We calculate the agreement by asking how much better our agreement is than expected, similar to our earlier individual annotator accuracy score, but in this case for agreement. Figure 8.6 shows an example.

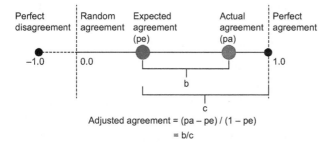

Figure 8.6 How agreement metrics are calculated. Agreement is typically on a –1 to 1 scale, where 1 is perfect agreement, –1 is perfect disagreement, and 0 is random distribution. The resulting agreement is variously known as *actual agreement*, *adjusted agreement*, or *agreement adjusted for random chance*.

Figure 8.6 shows how we calculate agreement that takes random chance agreement into account. This adjustment is similar to adjusting accuracy according to ground truth answers, but in this case, it compares annotators.

We cover different types of interannotator agreement in this book, including overall agreement at the level of the entire dataset, individual agreement between annotators, agreement between labels, and agreement on a per-task basis. The concepts are fairly simple, and we will start with the simple naive agreement algorithm in figure 8.7. This algorithm is so simple that you shouldn't use it, but it is a useful starting point for understanding the equations in this chapter and the next two chapters.

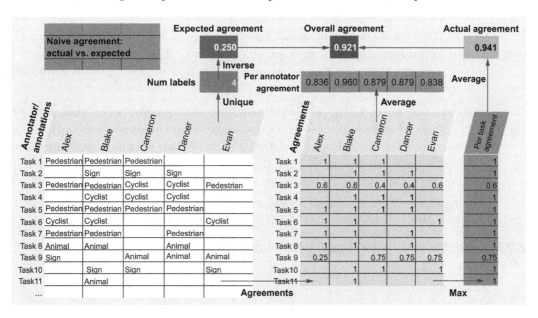

Figure 8.7 A naive way to find agreement per annotator, agreement per task, and overall agreement for the entire set of annotations. We calculate the expected agreement in terms of randomly selecting one of four labels. We calculate the agreements for each task in the large middle table. We derive the per-person and per-task agreements from the Agreements table. We derive the overall agreement by using the combination of the expected and the average task-level agreement. Although you shouldn't use this method for your actual data, because it is too simple, the diagram is useful for highlighting the concepts.

Figure 8.7 shows the basic idea behind three types of agreements. Although all of these calculations are sensible, they fall short a little. Here are some shortcomings of figure 8.7, highlighting the complications in calculating agreement:

- The overall expected agreement is based on the number of labels, but some labels are more frequent than others. If a fifth label was never chosen, it would seem strange to reduce the overall expected agreement as a result.
- The person agreement seems to unfairly penalize people for errors that other people make on the same task. Evan, for example, always agrees with the majority vote for the label but has the second-lowest agreement score.
- The task agreement scores seem to be overly optimistic because they do not take into account the accuracy of individual annotators.
- The actual agreement averages the task agreement, but it would be much lower if we decided to calculate it by averaging the person agreement. What is the right way to aggregate the individual agreements to produce a more correct overall observed actual agreement?
- Task 11 has only one response, so it seems wrong to calculate the response as being 100% in agreement; there is nothing for that one response to agree with.
- We are not tracking agreement for labels. Is "Pedestrian" more likely to be confused than "Sign," for example?
- We are not taking the overall number of annotations into account. Especially with a relatively small number of annotations, there might be artifacts of the data size (although this is less relevant for typical training datasets with thousands of items).

You can play around with this implementation as a spreadsheet at http://mng.bz/ E2qj. This spreadsheet also contains some of the other equations in this chapter.

Sections 8.2.2 through 8.2.7 are dedicated to the best ways to address these issues. Although the math gets more complicated than anything you've seen so far in this book, keep in mind that it is solving one simple question:

How can we fairly calculate the agreement between annotators to evaluate the accuracy of our dataset, individual tasks, individual labels, or individual annotators?

8.2.2 Benefits from calculating interannotator agreement

You can use interannotator agreement as part of your human-in-the-loop machine learning strategy in multiple ways:

- *The reliability of your dataset*—Do the annotators agree with one another often enough that you can rely on the labels that have been created? If not, you may need to redesign your instructions or the task as a whole.
- *The least reliable annotators*—Do any individual annotators disagree with the others too often? They may have misunderstood the task or may not be qualified to keep taking part. Either way, you may want to ignore their past annotations and potentially get new judgments. Alternatively, an unreliable annotator may in

fact have valid but underrepresented annotations, especially for subjective tasks (see "Measuring natural variation" later in this list).

- *The most reliable annotators*—The annotators with high agreement are likely to be the most accurate for your task, so identifying these people for potential reward and promotion is helpful.

- *Collaboration between annotators*—Do any annotators agree nearly perfectly? They might be sharing notes innocently because they sit near one another, in which case you need to remove those responses from any calculations of agreement that assumes independence. On the other hand, this result may be evidence that a bot is duplicating one person's work so that the person wrongly gets paid twice. Regardless of the underlying cause, it is helpful to know when two sets of answers are only one set that has been repeated.

- *An annotator's consistency over time*—If you give the same task to the same person at different times, do they give the same result? This metric, known as *intra-annotator agreement*, can be evidence that an annotator is not paying attention, that your task has ordering effects, and/or that the task is inherently subjective. Also, the annotator may be genuinely changing their mind as they see more data, which is known as *concept evolution*.

- *Creating examples for the instructions*—You can assume that items with high agreement among a large number of annotators are correct and let these items become examples in the guidelines for new annotators. Because you run two risks with this strategy—some errors will still get through and propagate, and only easier tasks will get through with higher agreement—you should not use it as your only strategy for creating ground truth data.

- *Evaluating the inherent difficulty of a machine learning problem*—In general, if the task is hard for humans, it will be hard for your model. This information is especially helpful for adapting to new domains. If your data historically has 90% agreement, but data from a new source has only 70% agreement, this result tells you to expect your model to be less accurate on data from that new source.

- *Measuring the accuracy of your dataset*—If you know the individual reliability of each annotator and how many people have annotated each item, you can calculate the probability that any given label will be annotated incorrectly. From this result, you can calculate the overall accuracy of your data. Taking individual annotator accuracy into account gives you a better upper boundary for the accuracy of a model that is trained on the data, compared with simple interannotator agreement. Models can be more or less sensitive to noise in the training data, so the limit is not a hard one. The limit *is* a hard limit on how precisely you can measure your model's accuracy, because you can't calculate your model's accuracy to be higher than your dataset's accuracy.

- *Measuring natural variation*—For some datasets, lack of agreement is a good thing because it can indicate that multiple annotation interpretations are valid. If you have a task that is subjective, you may want to ensure that you have a diverse selection of annotators so that no one set of social, cultural, or linguistic backgrounds is inadvertently resulting in biased data.

- *Escalating difficult tasks to experts*—This example was covered in chapter 7, and we return to it again in section 8.5. Low agreement between less-qualified workers might mean that the task should be routed to an expert automatically for review.

The remainder of section 8.2 contains some of the best current methods for calculating agreement in your data.

Don't use agreement as the only measure of accuracy

You should not rely on interannotator agreement alone to find the correct label for your data; always use interannotator agreement in combination with ground truth data. Many data scientists resist this practice, because it means losing training data. If 5% of the labeled data is set aside for quality control, for example, they have 5% less data for their model to train on. Although no one likes having less training data, in the real world you can have the opposite effect: if you are relying on interannotator agreement alone for your labels, you will use more than 5% more human judgments because you can use ground truth data to calibrate your agreement better.

Looking at agreement alone can also hide cases in which the wrong annotations agree. Without ground truth data, you won't be able to calibrate for these errors.

On the other hand, agreement allows you to extend your accuracy analysis beyond what is practical with ground truth data alone, so you get the biggest benefits when you combine agreement with ground truth data. For example, you can calculate the accuray of each annotator with ground truth data and then use that accuracy as your confidence when aggregating multiple annotations for a task. This chapter and chapter 9 show many examples of combining agreement and ground truth data, depending on the problem you are solving, but they are introduced independently to explain the concepts in isolation.

8.2.3   *Dataset-level agreement with Krippendorff's alpha*

Krippendorff's alpha is a method that aims to answer a simple question: what is the overall agreement in my dataset? To account for the fact that not every item will be annotated by every annotator, Krippendorff's alpha made considerable advances on existing agreement algorithms that were popular in social sciences when used for tasks such as measuring the level of agreement in surveys and census data.

The simple interpretation of Krippendorff's alpha is that it is a [–1,1] range, which can be read as follows:

- *>0.8*—This range is reliable. If you apply Krippendorff's alpha to your data, and you get a result of 0.8 or higher, you have high agreement and a dataset that you can use to train your model.
- *0.67–0.8*—This range has low reliability. It is likely that some of the labels are highly consistent and others are not.

- *0–0.67*—At less than 0.67, your dataset is considered to have low reliability. Something is probably wrong with your task design or with the annotators.
- *0*—Random distribution.
- *–1*—Perfect disagreement.

Krippendorff's alpha also has the nice property that it can be used for categorical, ordinal, hierarchical, and continuous data. Most of the time in practice, you can use Krippendorff's alpha without knowing how the algorithm works and interpret the output according to the 0.8 and 0.67 thresholds. But in order to understand what is happening under the hood and when it might not be appropriate, it is a good idea to get an intuition for the mathematics. Don't worry if you don't get all the steps on the first go. When I re-derived all the equations in this book, it took me longer to derive Krippendorff's alpha than any of the active learning or machine learning algorithms.

Krippendorff's alpha aims to calculate the same metric as the simple example in figure 8.7 earlier in this chapter: what is our actual agreement relative to our expected agreement? We'll start with a partial implementation of Krippendorff's alpha that works for mutually exclusive labels and then move to a more general version.

The expected agreement for Krippendorff's alpha is the data frequency: the sum of the squares of the frequency of each label for a labeling task. The actual agreement for Krippendorff's alpha comes from the average amount that each annotation agrees with the other annotations for the same task. Krippendorff's alpha makes a slight adjustment to the average, epsilon, to account for the loss of precision given the finite number of annotations.

Krippendorff's alpha is the adjusted agreement of the expected and actual agreement from figure 8.6. We can see Krippendorff's alpha from our example data using a simplified representation in figure 8.8.

The agreement in figure 8.8 is much lower than our "naive agreement" in figure 8.7 (0.803 compared with 0.921), so it shows that we need to be careful in how we calculate agreement and that small changes in our assumptions can result in large differences in our quality control metrics.

Figure 8.8 is a partial implementation of Krippendorff's alpha. The full equation takes into account the fact that you might weight some types of disagreements more severely than others. The full implementation of Krippendorff's alpha is shown in figure 8.9.

Although figure 8.9 shows some complicated processes, the main difference between it and figure 8.8 come from how Krippendorff's alpha incorporates the label weights. The label-weights component allows Krippendorff's alpha to be adapted to different types of problems, such as continuous, ordinal, or other tasks in which multiple labels can be applied to one item.

For more details, look at the implementations in the spreadsheet introduced in section 8.2.1. You can see that the expected agreement and actual agreement need to take in some matrix operations to incorporate the weights in the full Krippendorff's alpha implementation, compared with the partial implementation. Also, the epsilon

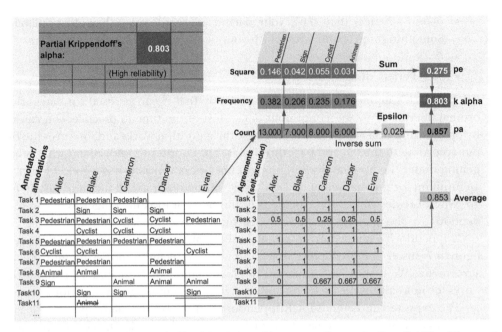

Figure 8.8   A simplified Krippendorff's alpha that provides an overall score for the reliability of the annotators for our example data. The expected agreement is the sum of squares of the frequency of each label. The actual agreement is the average amount by which each annotation agreed with the other annotations for that task, with a small adjustment (epsilon) made to account for precision in our calculations.

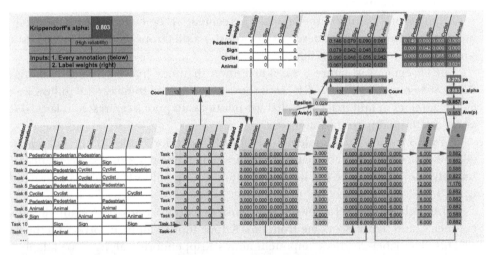

Figure 8.9   Krippendorff's alpha, calculating the overall level of agreement in a dataset to determine whether it is reliable enough to use for training data. The inputs are the white areas: the annotations (bottom left) and the label weights (top middle). Because we have mutually exclusive labels, this example has each label weighted only with itself. If we had hierarchical, ordinal, or other types of data, we would enter different values as label weights. The top row of calculations contains the expected agreement by random chance, and the bottom row of calculations calculates the actual agreement in the data. The two rows are used to calculate the expected agreement (pe) and actual agreement (pa) for the dataset, from which the adjusted overall agreement alpha is calculated.

adjustment takes the weights into account and is not simply the inverse of the total count. The general idea behind the simple and full implementations is the same, however: we are calculating an adjusted agreement according to the actual and expected agreements. If you keep that concept in mind and appreciate the fact that all the extra steps in the full implementation of Krippendorff's alpha come from the flexibility needed for different types of annotations, you have the right idea about how to apply it.

When do I need to calculate confidence intervals for Krippendorff's alpha?

This book omits the extensions to Krippendorff's alpha for calculating the confidence intervals because the confidence intervals anticipate the kind of smaller surveys that Krippendorff's alpha was designed for. Most of the time, you won't need confidence intervals for training data because the biggest factor for confidence intervals will be the total number of judgments. Because your training data will likely contain thousands or even millions of examples, the confidence intervals will be tiny.

You need to worry about confidence intervals only if you are going to use Krippendorff's alpha on a small dataset or a small subset of your dataset. Note that if you are using a small amount of data because of a cutting-edge, lightly supervised, few-shot, or data-augmentation technique, you'll need better statistical knowledge to help ensure significance for your smaller datasets. You may have assumed that less data makes the required supporting infrastructure easier to build, but the opposite is true.

Even in these edge cases, I don't recommend relying on confidence intervals alone. If you have a small number of training examples, you should include other types of quality control, including review tasks for experts and incorporating known ground truth examples. Otherwise, your confidence intervals will be so wide that it will be difficult to trust a model built on the data.

Alternatives to Krippendorff's alpha

You may encounter alternatives to Krippendorff's alpha in the literature, such as Cohen's kappa and Fleiss's kappa. Krippendorff's alpha is generally seen as being a refinement of those earlier metrics. The differences are details such as whether all errors should be punished equally, the correct way to calculate the expected prior, the treatment of missing values, and how to aggregate the overall agreement (aggregating per annotation, like Krippendorff's alpha, or per task/annotator, like Cohen's kappa). The additional reading in section 8.6 has some examples.

You may also encounter Krippendorff's alpha expressed in terms of disagreement, instead of agreement, including in Krippendorff's own publications. The techniques are mathematically equivalent and produce the same alpha value. Agreement is more widely used than disagreement in other metrics and is arguably more intuitive, which is why agreement is used here. Assume that disagreement is the complement of agreement: $D = (1 - P)$. Keep this assumption in mind when you look at the literature and libraries, which may have versions of Krippendorff's alpha that are calculated by using disagreement.

8.2.4   *Calculating Krippendorff's alpha beyond labeling*

Here are some examples of how Krippendorff's alpha can be used for tasks that are more complicated than mutually exclusive labeling tasks. Figure 8.10 shows how we can change the label weights in the Krippendorff's alpha equation to capture ordinal and rotational data.

Labeling (mutually exclusive)				
Label Weights	Pedestrian	Sign	Cyclist	Animal
Pedestrian	1	0	0	0
Sign	0	1	0	0
Cyclist	0	0	1	0
Animal	0	0	0	1

Ordinal categories				
Label Weights	Excellent	Good	Neutral	Bad
Excellent	1	0.5	0.25	0
Good	0.5	1	0.5	0.25
Neutral	0.25	0.5	1	0.5
Bad	0	0.25	0.5	1

Rotational categories				
Label Weights	North	East	South	West
North	1	0.5	0	0.5
East	0.5	1	0.5	0
South	0	0.5	1	0.5
West	0.5	0	0.5	1

Figure 8.10   An example of three types of classification tasks and how the label weights from Krippendorff's alpha can be used for those tasks. The first example repeats the label weights from figure 8.9, showing the mutually exclusive labeling tasks that have been used as an example throughout this chapter. The second example shows an ordinal scale from "Bad" to "Excellent," where we want to give partial credit to adjacent annotations such as "Good" and "Excellent." The third example shows rotational categories—in this case, the compass points. In this case, we give a partial score to anything that is off by 90 degrees, such as "North" and "West," but a zero score to anything that is off by 180 degrees, such as "North" and "South."

The rest of this chapter sticks to mutually exclusive labeling. We'll cover to other types of machine learning problems in chapter 9.

Krippendorff's alpha has some shortcomings when it's used for training data, because it was originally derived for use cases such as when a school is randomly distributing exam papers across multiple graders (annotators). It doesn't capture the fact that some annotators will have a different expected agreement based on what they have seen. When creating training data, we have many good reasons to distribute annotations nonrandomly, such as giving a hard example to additional people to adjudicate. Sections 8.2.5 through 8.2.7 differ from Krippendorff's alpha in key ways for calculating agreement at annotator, label, and task levels.

8.2.5   *Individual annotator agreement*

Agreement at individual annotator level can be useful in multiple ways. For one thing, it can tell you how reliable each annotator is. You can calculate agreement at the macro level, calculating an annotator's reliability across every response they made, or you may want to see whether they have higher or lower agreement for certain labels or segments of the data. This result might tell you that the annotator is more or less accurate or may highlight a diverse set of valid annotations.

The simplest metric for agreement between annotators is to calculate how often each annotator agrees with the majority of people for a given task. Figure 8.11 shows an example.

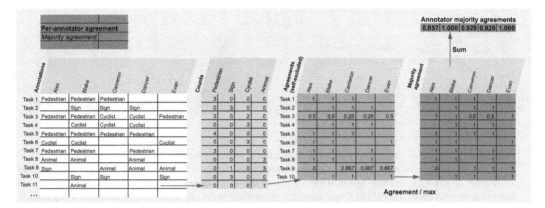

Figure 8.11 The per-annotator agreement with the most common annotation for each task (majority agreement). This example shows that two annotators, Blake and Evan, always agreed with the majority. This method is the simplest way to calculate agreement between annotators; it can be effective when you have a large number of annotators per task but is rarely used for creating training data due to budget constraints. This method can provide insight into your data but should not be your sole means of determining data quality.

Majority agreement, as shown in figure 8.11, looks at the number of times a person agrees with the most commonly annotated label for each task. This result can also be calculated as a count of the fraction of times that a person agrees with the majority, but it is a little more accurate when normalized for agreement on a per-annotation basis. In figure 8.11 and other example data in this chapter, Cameron and Dancer agree that task 3 is "Cyclist," even though most people think task 3 is "Pedestrian." By contrast, Alex is the only one who thinks that task 9 is "Sign." So in our Majority Agreement table in figure 8.11, Cameron and Dancer get 0.5 for task 3, and Alex gets 0 for task 9.

Majority agreement can provide a good quick check on whether your annotators have seen easier or harder examples. In the naive agreement example in figure 8.6 earlier in this chapter, Evan has the next-to-lowest agreement (0.836), but they have the equal highest agreement in figure 8.11 (1.0). In other words, Evan had low agreement on average with other people but always agreed with the majority. This result tells you that Evan saw tasks with lower overall agreement than other people. A good agreement metric, therefore, should take into account the fact that Evan saw harder tasks.

Expected agreement is the biggest piece missing from figure 8.11. Figure 8.12 shows one way to calculate expected agreement, which shows that Evan has the lowest expected agreement if they always chose "Pedestrian."

The first thing to notice in figure 8.12 is that we are using the most frequent label (mode label) to calculate our baseline. Recall that Krippendorff's alpha uses the same number of labels in the data, as though they were assigned randomly. In our example,

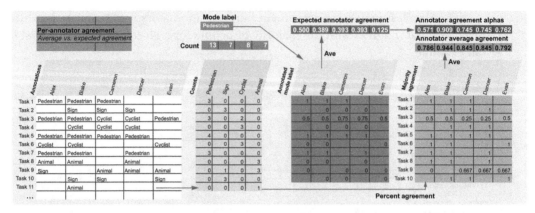

Figure 8.12   The per-annotator agreement is calculated in terms of the actual agreements (bottom right), with the expected agreement calculated on a per-annotator basis (top middle). Note that Evan has an expected agreement of only 0.15. In other words, if Evan guessed the most common label, "Pedestrian," every time, they would agree with about 15% of the other annotations on their tasks. By contrast, Alex could have guessed "Pedestrian" every time and got about 51% agreement. This method takes into account the fact that Evan saw tasks with lower agreement that were presumably more difficult.

someone might randomly assign 13 "Pedestrian" labels, 7 "Sign" labels, and so on. While this example is the (statistical) definition of an expected distribution, it is unlikely that a human annotator will have that probability for each label in mind when annotating. The more likely scenario is that an annotator will have an intuition about the most frequent label (mode label). This result is common in data labeling. Often, one label is obviously more frequent than all the others and feels like a safe default option. There are ways to mitigate the problem of bad labels because a person feels pressured to label a default option when they are uncertain, which we'll cover in chapter 9. Here, we'll treat this most common label as our expected baseline.

The second difference between figure 8.12 and standard Krippendorff's alpha calculation is that figure 8.12 calculates agreement per task, whereas Krippendorff's alpha calculates agreement per annotation. If you have the same number of annotations per task, the numbers would be identical. In our example data, task 3 has five annotations, so it effectively has a larger weight than the other tasks in Krippendorff's alpha. Krippendorff's alpha, however, gives task 3 the same weight as every other task when calculating individual agreement.

You don't want to give different weights to different tasks for data annotation for many reasons. You might deliberately give the same task to more annotators to resolve disagreements, for example, or you might give easier tasks to fewer people based on the label or external information. In both cases, Krippendorff's alpha would be biased toward the more difficult tasks, giving you an artificially low score. If you truly have a random distribution of annotators across tasks, and it is arbitrary that some tasks end up with more annotations, the standard Krippendorff's alpha approach is fine.

Don't p-hack Krippendorff's alpha by iteratively removing annotators with the lowest agreement

Often, you want to ignore the annotations made by your least-accurate annotators. You can improve the overall agreement and accuracy of your training data by removing the worst performers and giving their tasks to other annotators.

You would make a mistake, however, if you iteratively removed the worst performers until your dataset reaches the magic k-alpha=0.8 number, which indicates high agreement. Using the threshold of significance itself as a threshold for removing people is what Regina Nuzzo called *p-hacking* in *Nature* in 2014 (http://mng.bz/8NZP).

Instead of relying on Krippendorff's alpha, you should remove people by one of the following criteria, in order of preference:

- *Use a different criterion from Krippendorff's alpha to decide who is a good or bad performer.* Ideally, you should use the annotator's agreement with known ground truth answers. Then you can use that criterion to remove the worst performers. You can set a threshold level of accuracy on the known answers or decide that you will remove some percentage of annotators (such as the worst 5%). You should make the decision about a threshold or percentage without taking Krippendorff's alpha into account.
- *Remove low performers who are statistical outliers in terms of how badly they performed.* Use this technique if you are confident about your mathematical skills. If you can calculate that all the agreement scores fall in a normal distribution, for example, you can remove any annotator with agreement that is three standard deviations below the average agreement. If you are not confident in your ability to identify the type of distribution and the appropriate outlier metric, stick to the first option and create additional questions with known answers if necessary.
- *Decide in advance what your expected percent of low-performing annotators will be, and remove only those annotators.* If you typically find that 5% perform poorly, remove the bottom 5%, but do not keep going if you are not yet at your target agreement. This approach could contain a little bias, because you are still using Krippendorff's alpha to calculate the lowest 5%. The bias is probably minor, however, and in any case, you shouldn't use this approach if you can use the first two options.

What happens if you p-hack Krippendorff's alpha? You may get bad instructions or an impossible task, but you will never learn that result. You may end up removing everyone except annotators who happened to be sitting next to one another and sharing notes.

If you have established that an annotator is not reliable enough to trust, you should remove that annotator's judgments from your calculation of agreement. Figure 8.13 shows this result with our example data, assuming that we removed the first person.

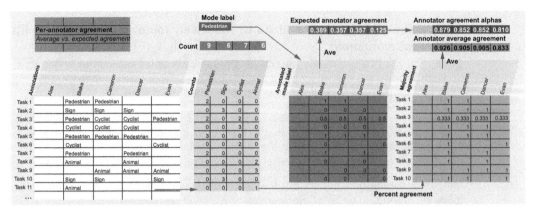

Figure 8.13   Recalculating agreement for our annotators after the first annotator has been removed. Note that three of the four scores went up compared with figure 8.12, but Blake's agreement dropped slightly, and Evan went from second-highest to lowest agreement.

As figure 8.13 shows when compared with figure 8.12, you generally expect overall agreement to go up when the least-accurate person is removed, but some individual agreement scores may still go down (as in the case of Blake), and the rankings may change considerably, as is the case with Evan. Evan has the highest agreement when we

calculate agreement with the majority in figure 8.11 but has the lowest agreement when we calculate for chance-adjusted agreement after Alex is removed in figure 8.13. This figure is a good example of why you need to be careful about using agreement as the only way to calculate accuracy: your choices can produce different results for individuals.

8.2.6   Per-label and per-demographic agreement

Ideally, you have some ground truth labels for your dataset, so you can use these labels to plot the errors in a confusion matrix. This confusion matrix is identical to the kind that you use for machine learning models, except that it is the pattern of human errors in place of model errors.

You can also use a confusion matrix for agreement, plotting which annotations occur with others. Figure 8.14 shows the matrices for our example data.

Predicted / Actual	Pedestrian	Sign	Cyclist	Animal
Pedestrian	10	0	0	0
Sign	0	6	0	0
Cyclist	3	0	8	0
Animal	0	1	0	7

Counts	Pedestrian	Sign	Cyclist	Animal
Pedestrian	30	0	6	0
Sign	0	12	0	3
Cyclist	6	0	14	0
Animal	0	3	0	12

Figure 8.14   Annotation confusion matrices: compared with ground truth data in our example data (top) and compared with every pairwise agreement or disagreement (bottom)

This second type of confusion matrix doesn't tell you what the errors are—only where the agreement or disagreement occurs. With either type of matrix, you can see where the greatest pairwise confusion occurs in your annotations, and this information should help you refine your instructions for annotators, as well as indicate which labels may be hardest for your model to predict.

8.2.7 *Extending accuracy with agreement for real-world diversity*

It can be especially useful to use agreement as an extension of accuracy when you want to track a large number of fine-grained demographics. If you want to track the intersection of demographics, you may have too many combinations of demographic categories for which you are able to collect enough ground truth data.

Consider the example where we suspected that images taken at night are more difficult to annotate than images taken during the day. Now suppose that you also want to track the accuracy of annotation across 1,000 locations. You are unlikely to have a large volume of ground truth labels for every one of these 24,000 time/place combinations, because it would be expensive to create so much ground truth data.

Therefore, looking at agreement for each of the 24,000 time/place combinations is your best window into the difficulty of each demographic intersection. There won't always be a perfect correlation between agreement and accuracy, but this approach can reveal some areas of high agreement that you can review and potentially target for more ground truth data.

8.3 *Aggregating multiple annotations to create training data*

Task-level confidence is the most important quality control metric for many annotation projects, because it allows us to aggregate the (potentially conflicting) annotations of each annotator and create the label that will become the training and evaluation data.

Therefore, it is important to understand how to combine multiple annotations to create the single label that will become the actual label. Aggregating multiple annotations in a task builds on the other types of quality control metrics that you have seen in this chapter: we want to take our confidence in each annotator into account when calculating the overall agreement for a given task, and ideally, we want to know whether this particular task is inherently easier or more difficult.

8.3.1 *Aggregating annotations when everyone agrees*

It can be easiest to think about agreement in terms of the chance of error instead of the chance of being correct. Suppose that we have three annotators and they are each 90% accurate. The chance that any one annotator makes an error is 10%. The chance that a second annotator made an error on the same task is 10%, so combined, there is a 1% ($0.1 \times 0.1 = 0.01$) chance that two people made an error on the same item. With three annotators, that chance becomes a 0.1% chance ($0.1 \times 0.1 \times 0.1$). In other words, there is a 1-in-1,000 chance of being incorrect and a 0.999 chance of being correct. If three annotators are 90% accurate, and all three agree, we can assume with

99.9% confidence that the label is correct. Letting the accuracy of the ith annotator be a_i, the overall confidence that the label is correct is

$$1 - \prod_{i=1} (1 - a_i)$$

Unfortunately, this method has limitations because it assumes that the errors are independent. If the first annotator makes an error, does the second annotator still have only a 10% chance of error, or do the errors tend to cluster or diverge?

It is easy to imagine scenarios in which the patterns of errors are nonrandom. Most obviously, some tasks tend to be harder than others. If 10% of all tasks lead to people choosing the wrong label, perhaps that task is where all three annotators made mistakes. If you have a task with a large number of labels, this problem is less common, because people are less likely to choose the same wrong label. You often want to reduce your tasks to as few annotations as possible to make them more efficient, so there is a trade-off between accuracy and cost.

The ground truth data allows you to calculate the following: for each incorrect annotation, what % of annotations for the task are also incorrect? Let's work through an example. Assume that in our example data, every item's actual label is the one shown in figure 8.3 earlier in the chapter. The following table shows two tasks, 3 and 9, with the errors in bold:

Task 3	**Pedestrian**	**Pedestrian**	Cyclist	Cyclist	**Pedestrian**

Task 9	**Sign**		Animal	Animal	Animal

In task 3, each of the three wrong "Pedestrian" annotations agrees with the two other "Pedestrian" annotations, giving us six total agreements for the incorrect label. Note this number is in the column sum(AW) from Krippendorff's alpha. In task 9, the "Sign" error was alone, so there are no agreeing errors. For the correct answers, we have two agreements in task 3 (the two "Cyclists" annotations agreeing with each other) and each of three "Animals" annotations agreeing with each other. So in total, there are eight cases of annotators agreeing with one another when they are correct and six cases of annotators agreeing with one another when they are incorrect. To calculate how often incorrect annotations agree, we calculate

Correlation of errors = 6 / (8 + 6) = 0.429

Therefore, although our overall error rate is 10%, the likelihood that errors in annotation will co-occur is 42.9%—more than four times higher! After the first error, we should assume that errors co-occur at this rate. With agreement from three annotators, the overall confidence in our label would be

$1 - (0.1 \times 0.429 \times 0.429) = 0.982$

So instead of having 99.9% confidence, we are have 98.2% confidence in our label when all three annotators agree, going from an error in every 1,000 items to an error in about every 55 items.

The opposite pattern can also occur, in which the pattern of errors diverges. Let's assume that the three annotators are still 90% accurate individually, but they make different errors. One annotator makes most of their errors identifying "Sign," whereas another annotator might make most of their errors identifying "Animal." They might make errors on different images, so the chance that the errors will co-occur is 2%:

$$1 - (0.1 \times 0.02 \times 0.02) = 0.99996$$

In this case, where your annotators have complementary skills, you can be 99.996% confident that agreement between annotators means that your annotation is correct, and so an error occurs once in every 25,000 items.

8.3.2 The mathematical case for diverse annotators and low agreement

There is a big difference in how errors pattern across annotators, as the example in section 8.3.1 showed. We can expand on this example as the mathematical proof that having a diverse set of annotators will result in more accurate data.

Given the same overall error rate on a per-annotation basis, the data with the highest accuracy will have the lowest agreement, because the errors are spread out and create more opportunities for disagreement. Therefore, this condition has the lowest Krippendorff's alpha score, showing why we don't want to rely on Krippendorff's alpha score alone because it can penalize diversity unfairly. You can see this result in our example data with a Krippendorff's alpha score of 0.803. If we spread out the disagreements so that there is no more than one disagreement per task, however, we get a Krippendorff's alpha score of 0.685. So even though our data has the same frequency for each label and the majority is much more reliable, our dataset looks less reliable.

It is easy to imagine scenarios in which the agreement is clustered: some examples are harder than others or annotators have subjective but similar judgments. It is also easy to imagine scenarios in which agreement is divergent: annotators are diverse and bring different but legitimate perspectives to the data.

It is difficult, however, to imagine real-world scenarios in which annotators are making errors completely independently (except perhaps because of fatigue). Yet almost all agreement metrics make the assumption of independence, which is why they should be used with caution. As this section and section 8.3.1 show, our ground truth data allows us to calibrate to the correct numbers for a given dataset. The advanced methods in chapter 9 go into more detail on data-driven agreement metrics.

8.3.3 Aggregating annotations when annotators disagree

When annotators disagree, you are essentially converging a probability distribution across all the potential labels. Let's expand our example from task 3 and assume that everyone is 90% accurate on average (figure 8.15).

Annotations	Alex	Blake	Cameron	Dancer	Evan
Task 3	Pedestrian	Pedestrian	Cyclist	Cyclist	Pedestrian
Confidence	0.9	0.9	0.9	0.9	0.9

Probability	Alex	Blake	Cameron	Dancer	Evan	Sum	Confidence
Pedestrian	0.9	0.9			0.9	2.700	0.600
Sign							0.000
Cyclist			0.9	0.9		1.800	0.400
Animal							0.000

Figure 8.15   Using per-annotator accuracy as probabilities for per-task agreement

In figure 8.15, we have three annotators who labeled the image in this task as "Pedestrian" and two who labeled it "Cyclist." The simplest way to calculate confidence when not all annotators agree is to treat the confidences as a weighted vote. Let's assume that we're calculating confidence for task 3 and that we have 90% confidence in every annotator:

Pedestrian = 3 * 0.9 = 2.7
Cyclist = 2 * 0.9 = 1.8
Confidence in Pedestrian = 2.7 / (2.7 + 1.8) = 0.6
Confidence in Cyclist = 1.8 / (2.7 + 1.8) = 0.4

Another way to think of this calculation is that because we're equally confident in everyone in this example, three-fifths of the annotators agree, so we are 3/5 = 60% confident.

One problem with this method is that it does not leave any confidence for other labels. Recall that when we had perfect agreement, there was still a small chance that it was wrong and that therefore, the correct label was one not annotated by anyone. We can incorporate the possibility that a non-annotated label might be correct by treating the confidence as a probability distribution and assume that all other labels get the weight divided among them, as shown in figure 8.16.

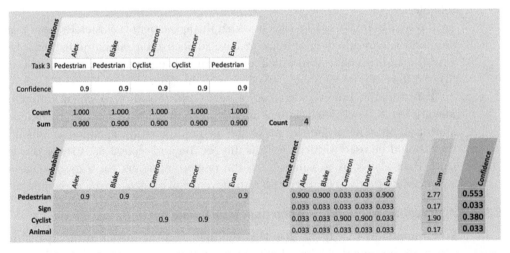

Figure 8.16   Expanding all the confidences in annotators to give some weight to all labels. We have 0.9 confidence for each annotator, so we distribute the remaining 0.1 across the other labels.

This example gives a conservative estimate to confidence, with a large amount of weight going to unseen answers. Note also this method is not the one we used when there was perfect agreement. There are several ways to get a more accurate probability distribution for the annotations, most of which involve a regression or machine learning model because they can't be computed with simple heuristics like those used here. Chapter 9 covers these advanced approaches. This example is enough to build on for the remainder of this chapter.

8.3.4 Annotator-reported confidences

Annotators often have good intuitions about their own errors and which tasks are inherently harder than others. As part of the annotation process, you can ask when annotators are less than 100% confident on a certain task. An example with our data might look like figure 8.17.

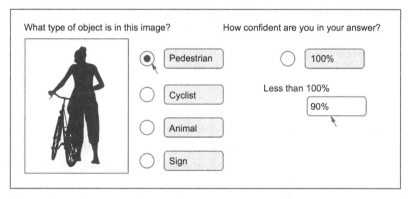

Figure 8.17 Requesting confidence explicitly from the annotator is an alternative (or addition) to calculating the confidence in their response from their accuracy and/or agreement.

You could also request the entire probability distribution, as shown in figure 8.18.

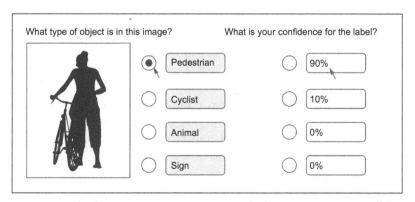

Figure 8.18 Requesting the annotator confidence for every label as an alternative to dividing their remaining confidence across the other labels programmatically

With the approach shown in figure 8.18, you can treat the entered amount as the probability for this label for this annotator, or you might choose to ignore all annotations when the annotator is less than 100% confident. This kind of interface can be extended to ask annotators how other annotators might respond to the question, which has some nice statistical outcomes that help with accuracy and diversity, especially for subjective tasks. These extensions are covered in chapter 9.

Entering this information can greatly increase the annotation time for a simple labeling task like our example, so you will have to weigh the cost of capturing this information against the value that it adds.

8.3.5　*Deciding which labels to trust: Annotation uncertainty*

When you have the probability distribution for your labels for a given task, you need to set a threshold for when not to trust a label and decide what to do if you don't trust the label. You have three options when you don't trust the label:

- Assign the task to an additional annotator, and recalculate the confidence to see whether the confidence is high enough.
- Assign the task to an expert annotator to adjudicate on the correct label (more on this topic in section 8.4).
- Exclude this item from the dataset so that a potential error won't produce errors in the model.

Generally, you want to avoid the third scenario because you are wasting the effort put into that task. You are also risking introducing bias into your data because the harder tasks are unlikely to be random. Budget or staffing constraints might prevent you from giving the same task to many people, however.

Before you can make a decision about whether you trust your label, you need to work out how to calculate overall confidence in your label. Let's assume that our probability distribution is taken from the example we have been using in this chapter:

Pedestrian = 0.553
Sign = 0.033
Cyclist = 0.380
Animal = 0.033

We have different ways to calculate our overall confidence uncertainty: look only at the 0.553 confidence for "Pedestrian," take into account the next-most-confident label ("Cyclist"), or take all the potential labels into account.

If you recall from chapter 3, this scenario is the same one that we had with uncertainty sampling for active learning. You have different ways to measure your uncertainty for annotation agreement, and each method makes a different assumption about what you care about. Using PyTorch, the example can be expressed as a tensor:

prob = torch.tensor([0.533, 0.033, 0.380, 0.033])

Reproducing the equations from chapter 3, we can calculate different uncertainty scores, as shown in figure 8.19.

Least confidence: Difference between the most confident prediction and 100% confidence

$$\frac{n\,(1 - P_\theta(y^*_1 \mid x))}{n - 1}$$

```
most_conf = torch.max(prob)
num_labels = prob.numel ()
numerator = (num_labels * (1 - most_conf))
denominator = (num_labels - 1)

least_conf = numerator/denominator
```

Margin of confidence: Difference between the two most confident predictions

$$1 - (P_\theta(y^*_1 \mid x) - P_\theta(y^*_2 \mid x))$$

```
prob, _ = torch.sort (prob, descending=True)
difference = (prob.data [0] - prob.data[1])

margin_conf = 1 - difference
```

Ratio of confidence: Ratio between the two most confident predictions

$$\frac{P_\theta(y^*_2 \mid x)}{P_\theta(y^*_1 \mid x)}$$

```
prob, _ = torch.sort (prob, descending=True)

ratio_conf = (prob.data [1] / prob.data [0])
```

Entropy: Difference between all predictions, as defined by information theory

$$\frac{-\sum_y P_\theta(y \mid x)\, log_2\, P_\theta(y \mid x)}{log_2(n)}$$

```
prbslogs  = prob * torch.log2 (prob)
numerator = 0 - torch.sum(prbslogs)
denominator = torch.log2(prob.numel ())

entropy = numerator / denominator
```

Figure 8.19   Different methods of calculating an uncertainty score for a probability distribution. These methods are the same one that are used in active learning to calculate uncertainty (or confidence) from a model's prediction, used here to calculate uncertainty for agreement among annotators.

For our example, we get these uncertainty scores (remember that 1.0 is the most uncertain):

- Least confidence = 0.6227
- Margin of confidence = 0.8470
- Ratio of confidence = 0.7129
- Entropy = 0.6696

To get our overall confidence, instead of uncertainty, we subtract one of these metrics from 1.

After you have your uncertainty scores, you can plot your overall annotation accuracy at different scores on your ground truth data. Then you can use this plot to calculate the accuracy threshold that will give you the desired accuracy for your data (figure 8.20).

You plot a curve like the one shown in figure 8.20 for each of the uncertainty metrics as one way to decide which is the best for your data: which uncertainty sampling method selects the most items at the right threshold?

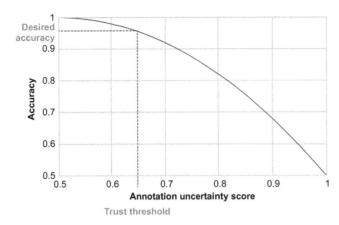

Figure 8.20 Calculating the threshold at which you can trust your annotations. In this example, the desired annotation accuracy of ~0.96, calculated on ground truth data, will be achieved if items with agreement uncertainty below ~0.65 are trusted.

The rank order of the different uncertainty scores is identical for binary data, so if you have broken your task into binary problems, you can choose any one of these metrics and not worry about deciding which is best for your data.

As an alternative to calculating the threshold on your ground truth data, as in figure 8.20, you can find the best threshold for your machine learning model's accuracy when trained on data at different thresholds. Try different thresholds for which items to ignore and then observe the downstream accuracy of your model with each threshold. Your model's sensitivity to errors in the training data will probably change with the total number of training items, so you may want to keep revisiting past training data and reevaluate the threshold with each new addition to the training data.

8.4 *Quality control by expert review*

One of the most common methods of quality control is to engage SMEs to label the most important data points. Generally, experts are rarer and/or more expensive than other workers, so you typically give some tasks only to experts, often for one of these reasons:

- To annotate a subset of items to become ground truth examples for guidelines and quality control
- To adjudicate examples that have low agreement among nonexpert annotators
- To annotate a subset of items to become machine learning evaluation items, for which human label accuracy is more important
- To annotate items that are known to be important for external reasons. If you are annotating data from your customers, for example, you may want expert annotators to focus on examples from the customers who generate the most revenue for you

Figure 8.21 copies a figure from chapter 7 about using experts for review. It illustrates the first two examples in the preceding list: creating ground truth examples for guidelines and quality control, and adjudicating examples that have low agreement (confusing items).

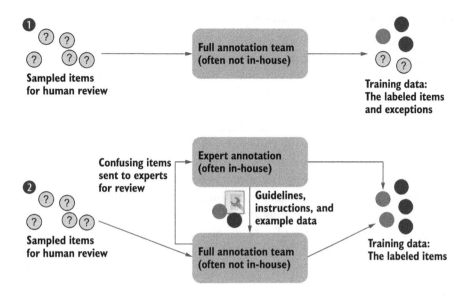

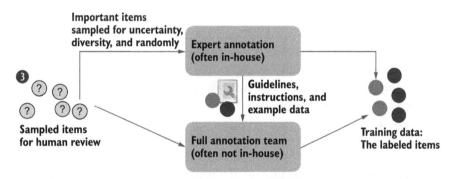

Figure 8.21 Three workflows for expert in-house annotation, repeated from chapter 7. The bottom two workflows show different ways that experts might be incorporated: adjudicating items that were difficult for annotators and creating guidelines for annotators. Both workflows might exist in the same task, and there might be many more steps for more complicated workflows.

To aggregate annotations after expert review, you can treat that expert as being one additional annotator, or you can ignore the previous annotations and calculate confidence in terms of the confidence in the expert(s). Choose the latter option if you know that your experts are much more reliable than most of your workforce.

8.4.1 *Recruiting and training qualified people*

As we discussed in chapter 7, it is common to have SMEs in-house, but you can often outsource this expertise. An annotator who has been working on annotation for autonomous vehicles for several years, for example, is highly skilled. See chapter 7 for more information about choosing the right workforce for your tasks, including experts.

8.4.2   *Training people to become experts*

You can take a data-driven approach to identifying experts within your nonexpert annotator pool. Keeping track of individual annotator accuracy, not overall dataset accuracy alone, will allow you to discover experts and promote them to that role.

As a stepping stone to making some annotators expert adjudicators, you might allow those annotators to review but not adjudicate the work of others. This approach will let those people get intuition about the common errors that people are making.

You should track the demographics of your experts, as you track the demographics of your annotators, to ensure diversity (except when tracking violates their privacy). An annotator's age, country of residence, education level, gender, language fluency, and many other factors may be important for a task. If you don't track the demographics of your annotators and use agreement as one metric for determining the best annotators, you run the risk of taking biases from your annotator pool into your expert annotator pool. For this reason, you should ideally identify experts from representative data, not a random sample.

8.4.3   *Machine-learning-assisted experts*

A common use case for SMEs is for their daily tasks to be augmented by machine learning. If you recall from chapter 1, human-in-the-loop machine learning can have two distinct goals: making a machine learning application more accurate with human input, and improving a human task with the aid of machine learning.

Search engines are a great example. You may be a domain expert in some scientific field searching for a particular research paper. The search engine helps you find this paper after you type the right search terms and learns from what you clicked to become more accurate.

Another common use case is e-discovery. Like search, but often with a more sophisticated interface, e-discovery is used in contexts such as audits where expert analysts are trying to find certain information in a large amount of text. Suppose the audit was for a legal case to detect fraud. An expert analyst in fraud detection might use a tool to find relevant documents and communications for that legal case, and that tool might adapt to what the analyst has found, surfacing all the similar documents and communications that have been tagged as relevant in the case so far. E-discovery was a $10 billion industry in 2020. Although you may not have heard about it in machine learning circles, it is one of the single largest use cases for machine learning.

You can deploy the same quality control measures in these cases: look for agreement between experts, employ adjudication by higher-level experts, evaluate against known answers, and so on. The expert, however, will likely be using an interface that supports their day-to-day tasks, not the annotation process itself. The interface may not be optimized for collecting training data, and their work process might introduce ordering effects that you can't control. So the user interface implications for quality control in chapter 11 will be important in these contexts.

8.5 *Multistep workflows and review tasks*

One of the most effective ways to get higher-quality labels is to break a complicated task into smaller subtasks. You can get several benefits from breaking your task into simpler subtasks:

- People generally work faster and more accurately on simpler tasks.
- It is easier to perform quality control on simpler tasks.
- You can engage different workforces for different subtasks.

The main downside is the overhead of managing the more complicated workflows. You will end up with a lot of custom code to route data based on certain conditions, and that code may not be reusable for other work. I have never seen an annotation platform that solved these problems with plug-and-play or drop-down options: there are almost always complicated combinations of conditions that require coding or a coding-like environment to be implemented fully.

Figure 8.22 shows how we might break an object labeling task into multiple steps, the last one being a review task for the preceding step.

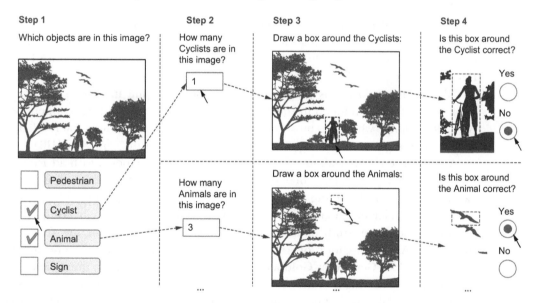

Figure 8.22 An example of a multistep workflow. If we divide steps 2–4 among the four object types, we have 13 total tasks. The individual responses in step 1 and the evaluation in step 4 are binary tasks. Therefore, although our goal is to create a bounding box that requires the advanced quality control metrics from chapter 9, we can use the simpler label-based quality control metrics for this chapter. Compared with a single task that captures every bounding box in one go, we can expect higher throughput and accuracy because annotators are concentrating on one task at a time; easier budgeting if we're paying per task, because there will be less variability in the time needed per task; and easier division of tasks among workforces if only some annotators are trusted for the most complicated tasks.

The most complicated workflow I have seen had about 40 tasks. This workflow, for a computer vision task for autonomous vehicles, had several steps for each type of object that was being tracked in addition to semantic segmentation.

Simpler tasks have some user experience trade-offs. Generally, people appreciate the efficiency, but the tasks feel more repetitive, which can lead to fatigue. Also, some people, especially in-house SMEs, might be offended that a complicated task that they performed in the past has been broken down into simpler tasks; they may interpret this situation as implying that they are not sophisticated enough to solve all the steps in one interface. We will return to the topic of user experience in chapter 11. In these cases, you can clarify that the workflow choice was made due to limitations related to getting good training data for machine learning, not because of annotator expertise.

8.6   *Further reading*

Quality control for annotation is a fast-changing field, and many of the problems we face are unsolved. A good high-level overview is "Truth Is a Lie: Crowd Truth and the Seven Myths of Human Annotation," by Lora Aroyo and Chris Welty (http://mng .bz/NYq7).

For a recent overview specific to the problems related to agreement, I recommend "Let's Agree to Disagree: Fixing Agreement Measures for Crowdsourcing," by Alessandro Checco, Kevin Roitero, Eddy Maddalena, Stefano Mizzaro, and Gianluca Demartini (http://mng.bz/DRqa).

Klaus Krippendorff has published Krippendorff's alpha in several papers and books since it was developed in the 1970s. I recommend "Computing Krippendorff's Alpha-Reliability," which was most recently updated in 2011, but note that it calculates in terms of disagreement, not agreement, as in this book (http://mng.bz/l1lB).

A good recent paper about workflows that back off to experts, with advice about how annotators can explain their decision process effectively to experts, is "Revolt: Collaborative Crowdsourcing for Labeling Machine Learning Datasets," by Joseph Chee Chang, Saleema Amershi, and Ece Semiha Kamar (http://mng.bz/BRqr).

For a good recent study of annotator bias, see "Are We Modeling the Task or the Annotator? An Investigation of Annotator Bias in Natural Language Understanding Datasets," by Mor Geva, Yoav Goldberg, and Jonathan Berant (http://mng.bz/d4Kv).

For a paper showing how diversity among annotators improves accuracy but lowers agreement, see "Broad Twitter Corpus: A Diverse Named Entity Recognition Resource," by Leon Derczynski, Kalina Bontcheva, and Ian Roberts (http://mng.bz/ry4e).

Although not free, *Handbook of Linguistic Annotation*, edited by Nancy Ide and James Pustejovsky, is a comprehensive book that covers a lot of NLP tasks and has a good diversity of use cases. If you don't want to purchase the book, consider emailing the authors of the chapters that are interesting to you; they might share their contributions.

Summary

- Ground truth examples are tasks that have known answers. By creating ground truth examples for the dataset, you can evaluate the accuracy of annotators, create guidelines for those annotators, and better calibrate other quality control techniques.

- You have many ways to calculate agreement in a dataset, including overall agreement, agreement between annotators, agreement between labels, and agreement at task level. Understanding each type of agreement will help you calculate the accuracy of your training and evaluation data and better manage your annotators.

- For any evaluation metric, you should calculate an expected result that would occur by random chance as a baseline. This approach allows you to normalize your accuracy/agreement metric to a score adjusted for random chance, which makes the score more easily comparable across different tasks.

- You will get the best results when using both ground truth data and interannotator agreement, because ground truth agreement allows you to better calibrate your agreement metrics, and agreement metrics can be applied to more annotations than is practical with ground truth alone.

- You can aggregate multiple annotations to create a single label for each task. This approach allows you to create the training data for your machine learning models and calculate the likelihood that each label is correct.

- Quality control by expert review is one common method of resolving disagreements between annotators. Because experts tend to be rare and/or expensive, they can focus mostly on the tough edge cases and the cases that will become part of the guidelines for other annotators.

- Multistep workflows allow you to break an annotation task into simpler tasks that flow into one another. This approach can create annotations faster and more accurately and allow easier-to-implement quality control strategies.

Advanced data annotation and augmentation

For many tasks, simple quality control metrics aren't enough. Imagine that you need to annotate images for labels like "Cyclist" and "Pedestrian." Some images, such as a person pushing a bicycle, are inherently subjective, and an annotator should not be punished for having a valid but minority interpretation. Some annotators will be more or less familiar with different data items, depending on their familiarity with the locations in the images and whether they themselves are cyclists. Machine learning can help estimate which annotator is expected to be more or less accurate on a given data point. Machine learning can also automate some of the annotation processes by presenting candidate annotations for faster human review. If there are some contexts with few or no cyclists, you might create new data items synthetically to fill the gaps. Knowing that perfect annotation is rare across an entire dataset, you may want to remove some items from the data before building a model on that data or incorporate the uncertainty into the downstream models. You may also want to perform exploratory data analysis on the dataset without necessarily wanting to build a downstream model. This chapter covers methods for addressing all these advanced problems.

9.1 Annotation quality for subjective tasks

There is not always one single, correct annotation for a given task. You may have a task that is inherently subjective; therefore, you expect different responses. We can use our example data from chapter 8, reproduced here in figure 9.1, showing an item that may have multiple correct annotations.

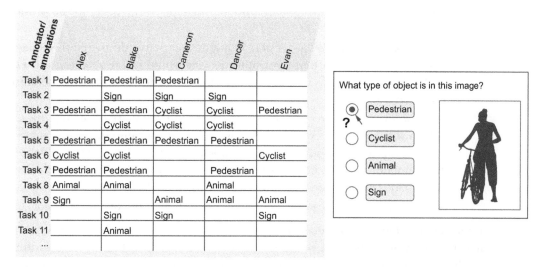

Annotator/ annotations	Alex	Blake	Cameron	Dancer	Evan
Task 1	Pedestrian	Pedestrian	Pedestrian		
Task 2		Sign	Sign	Sign	
Task 3	Pedestrian	Pedestrian	Cyclist	Cyclist	Pedestrian
Task 4		Cyclist	Cyclist	Cyclist	
Task 5	Pedestrian	Pedestrian	Pedestrian	Pedestrian	
Task 6	Cyclist	Cyclist			Cyclist
Task 7	Pedestrian	Pedestrian		Pedestrian	
Task 8	Animal	Animal		Animal	
Task 9	Sign		Animal	Animal	Animal
Task 10		Sign	Sign		Sign
Task 11		Animal			
...					

What type of object is in this image?

⦿ Pedestrian
?
○ Cyclist
○ Animal
○ Sign

Figure 9.1 A copy of an image from chapter 8, showing how task 3 might have multiple valid interpretations because of the ambiguity between "Pedestrian" and "Cyclist."

There could be multiple reasons why "Pedestrian" or "Cyclist" is favored by one annotator over another, including

- *Actual context*—The person is currently on the road or this image is part of a video in which the person gets on or off the bike.
- *Implied context*—The person looks as though they are getting on or off the bike.

- *Socially influenced variation*—It is likely that local laws treat a person on or off a bicycle differently in different parts of the world. Different laws specify whether bicycles are allowed on a footpath, a road, or a dedicated bike path, and whether people can push a bicycle in any of those places instead of riding it. The laws or common practices with which each annotator is familiar could influence their interpretation.

- *Personal experience*—We might expect people who are themselves cyclists to give different answers from people who are not.

- *Personal variation*—Irrespective of social influences and personal experience, two people may have different opinions about the difference between a pedestrian and a cyclist.

- *Linguistic variation*—A cyclist could be strictly interpreted as "anyone who cycles" instead of "someone who is currently cycling," especially if the annotators don't speak English as a first language (common among crowdsourced and outsourced annotators) and the translation of *cyclist* into their first language(s) is not the same definition as in English.

- *Ordering effects*—A person might be primed to interpret this image as a cyclist or pedestrian based on having seen more of one type or the other in the previous annotations.

- *Desire to conform to normality*—A person might themselves think that this image is a cyclist but also think that most other people would call it a pedestrian. They might choose the answer that they don't believe in for fear of being penalized afterward.

- *Perceived power imbalances*—A person who thinks that you are collecting this data to help with safety for cyclists might favor "Cyclist" because they think that you prefer this answer. This kind of accommodation and power imbalance between the annotator and the person who created the task can be important for tasks with obvious negative answers, such as sentiment analysis.

- *Genuine ambiguity*—The photo may be low-resolution or out of focus and not clear.

It may be possible to have detailed guidelines for how our example image should be interpreted, which will mean that there is one objective correct answer. This will not be the case with all datasets, however, and it is often hard to anticipate all the edge cases in advance. So we often want to capture subjective judgments in the best way possible to ensure that we collect the full diversity of possible responses.

In our example in this chapter, we will assume that there is a set of correct answers. For open-ended tasks, this assumption is much harder, and expert review is much more important in these cases. See the following expert anecdote for an example of what can go wrong when you don't take subjectivity into account for open-ended tasks.

In our example dataset, one thing we know from our example image is that "Animal" and "Sign" are not correct answers, so we want an approach to subjective quality control that identifies "Pedestrian" and "Cyclist" as valid answers, but not "Animal" and "Sign."

Annotation bias is no joke

Expert anecdote by Lisa Braden-Harder

Data scientists usually underestimate the effort needed to collect high-quality, highly subjective data. Human agreement for relevance tasks is not easy when you are trying to annotate data without solid ground truth data, and engaging human annotators is successful only with strongly communicated goals, guidelines, and quality control measures, especially important when working across languages and cultures.

I once had a request for Korean knock-knock jokes from a US personal-assistant company expanding into South Korea. The conversation wasn't to explain to the product manager why that wouldn't work and to find culturally appropriate content for their application; it unraveled a lot of assumed knowledge. Even among Korean speakers, the annotators creating and evaluating the jokes needed to be from the same demographics as the intended customers. This case is one example of why the strategies to mitigate bias will touch every part of your data pipeline, from guidelines to compensation strategies that target the most appropriate annotation workforce. Annotation bias is no joke!

Lisa Braden-Harder is a mentor at the Global Social Benefit Institute at Santa Clara University. She was founder and CEO of the Butler Hill Group, one of the largest and most successful annotation companies; and prior to that, she worked as a programmer for IBM and completed computer science degrees at Purdue and NYU.

9.1.1 Requesting annotator expectations

When multiple correct answers exist, the easiest way to understand the possible answers is to ask the annotators directly, and the best way to frame the task is to ask the annotators how they think other annotators might respond. Figure 9.2 shows an example.

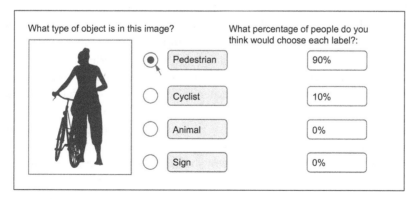

Figure 9.2 **Asking people what they expect other annotators to choose for answers. Here, the annotator has indicated that they think that the image is a pedestrian and that 90% of annotators will agree with them, but 10% will think that it is a cyclist. This approach motivates people to give honest responses and provides data to help you decide when multiple responses are valid. In turn, we can capture more diversity in correct answers than the ones offered by any one annotator.**

The interface is similar to the example in chapter 8 in which we asked annotators to give their own confidence for each label, but here, we are asking them about other annotators. This relatively simple change has several desirable properties:

- The task design explicitly gives people permission to give an answer that they don't think is the majority answer, which encourages diverse responses and reduces the pressure to conform.
- You can overcome some limitations in annotator diversity. It may not be possible to have an annotator from every demographic that you care about to look at every single item. With this method, you need only annotators who have the right intuition about the full diversity of responses, even if they do not share every interpretation.
- Problems with perceived power dynamics are reduced because you are asking what other annotators think, which makes it easier to report negative responses. This strategy can be a good one when you think that power dynamics or personal biases are influencing responses. Ask what most people would respond instead of what that annotator thinks.
- You can create data that separates valid from nonvalid answers. If we score every person's actual answer as 100% for observed and know that they will divide their expected numbers across multiple labels, they will give less than a 100% score for their expected response for their actual response. So if the actual scores for a label exceed the expected scores, we can trust that label, even if it has low overall percentages of actual and expected.

The last is a lesser-known principle of Bayesian reasoning: people tend to undervalue the probability of their own response. For this reason, we'll look at a popular method called Bayesian Truth Serum in section 9.4.1.

9.1.2   *Assessing viable labels for subjective tasks*

To start our analysis of viable labels, we can calculate the likelihood that we would have seen each of the labels among the actual annotations, given the number of annotators who have worked on the task. This information will help us decide which labels are valid. If a valid label is expected to occur in only 10% of annotations for a task, but we have only one or two annotators, we wouldn't expect to see an actual annotation for that label.

We calculate the probability that we should have seen each label by using the product of the expected probabilities. Just like when we calculate agreement, we use the complement of the expected annotation percentages. The complement of the expected percentage is calculating the probability that no one annotated a given label, and the probability that at least one person chose that annotation is the complement. Figure 9.3 shows the calculations for our example data.

Figure 9.3 shows that for this task, annotators have selected two labels as being the most likely: "Pedestrian" and "Cyclist" (the same as for our example data) and that people variously believe that "Sign" and "Animal" will be selected by 0% or 5% of people.

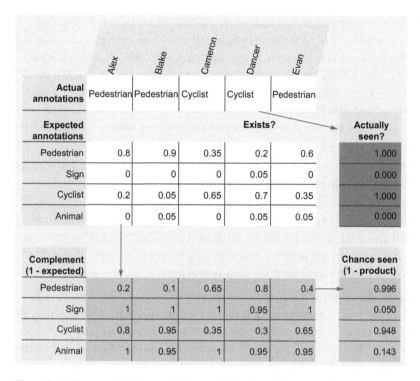

Actual annotations	Alex Pedestrian	Blake Pedestrian	Cameron Cyclist	Dancer Cyclist	Evan Pedestrian	
Expected annotations			Exists?			Actually seen?
Pedestrian	0.8	0.9	0.35	0.2	0.6	1.000
Sign	0	0	0	0.05	0	0.000
Cyclist	0.2	0.05	0.65	0.7	0.35	1.000
Animal	0	0.05	0	0.05	0.05	0.000
Complement (1 - expected)						**Chance seen (1 - product)**
Pedestrian	0.2	0.1	0.65	0.8	0.4	0.996
Sign	1	1	1	0.95	1	0.050
Cyclist	0.8	0.95	0.35	0.3	0.65	0.948
Animal	1	0.95	1	0.95	0.95	0.143

Figure 9.3 Testing whether a subjective label is viable. Here, the five annotators reported their annotation for the label and what percentage of people they think would choose each label. Blake thinks that the label is "Pedestrian", that 90% of people would choose "Pedestrian," and that 5% each would choose "Cyclist" and "Animal." Taking the product of the complement gives us the probability that we should have encountered this label with this number of annotations, which we can compare with whether we have seen the label.

You can find a copy of the spreadsheet in figure 9.3 and all the other examples in this chapter at http://mng.bz/Vd4W.

First, let's imagine that no one chose "Pedestrian" as the actual annotation, but people still gave some weight to "Pedestrian" in their expected score. Here are the calculations from figure 9.3:

Expected: [0.8, 0.9, 0.35, 0.2, 0.6]
Not Expected: [0.2, 0.1, 0.65, 0.8, 0.4]
Product of Not Expected = 0.004
Probability Seen = 1 − 0.004 = 0.996

With those expected scores, we are 99.6% certain that we should have seen at least one actual "Pedestrian." So we could be fairly certain that this result was an error in the annotators' perception. When there is a high probability that a label will be seen, according to the expected annotations, but has not been seen, we can more confidently rule it out as a viable label.

Now let's look at one of the less expected labels in figure 9.3: "Animal." Although three annotators believe that some people will annotate the image as "Animal," there is a 14.3% chance that one of the five annotators will have chosen "Animal." The fact that no one has chosen "Animal" yet doesn't necessarily rule it out. We wouldn't have expected to see someone choose "Animal" with only five annotators, if we trust these numbers, and wouldn't expect to see one until about 20 annotators have seen this item. We can take several approaches can to discover whether "Animal" is a viable label, each with increasing complexity:

- Add more annotators until "Animal" is seen or the probability seen is so high that we can rule out "Animal" as a viable label.
- Trust an expert annotator to decide whether "Animal" is a viable label when that expert annotator is experienced at putting personal biases aside.
- Find annotators who correctly annotated items as "Animal" in the ground truth data when that annotation was rare but correct and give this task to them (a programmatic way to find the best nonexpert).

Although the first option is easiest to implement, it works only if you are confident in the diversity of your annotators. There may be people who would correctly choose "Animal," but they are not among your annotators, so that situation never arises. On the other hand, it might be objectively incorrect to choose "Animal," but this example is a tough one, and 5% of people would be expected to get it wrong. You probably don't want to select "Animal" in this case.

Therefore, when there is ambiguity about whether a label is valid for a subjective task, you will want to find another annotator (possibly an expert) who can be trusted to understand the diversity of possible responses.

9.1.3 *Trusting an annotator to understand diverse responses*

We can calculate our trust in an individual annotator's expected annotations by looking at the difference between their expected annotations and the actual annotations calculated across all annotators. The basic concept is simple. If an annotator expected a 50:50 split of annotations between two labels and was correct that there was a 50:50 split, that annotator should get a score of 100% for that task.

If there were an odd number of annotators, a 50:50 split wouldn't be possible, so we need to take into account the possible precision given the finite number of annotators. Figure 9.4 illustrates a slightly more complicated example.

In figure 9.4, the annotator overestimated the number of annotators by 0.25. Every value between 0.15 and 0.65 is closer to the actual number of 0.4, and $0.65 - 0.15 = 0.5$. So 50% of the possible expected values are closer to 0.4. Given enough annotators, however, the true actual value would be higher than 0.4, so we adjust by the minimum precision of 0.2, which gives us $0.5 * (1 - 0.2) + 0.2 = 0.6$. The annotator's accuracy score is 60%.

Expected annotation accuracy example

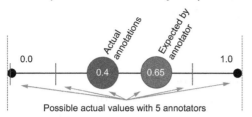

Possible actual values with 5 annotators

Annotator accuracy: The fraction of values that are further from 0.4 than 0.65, taking into account the annotator didn't know that only 0.2 increments were possible because there were 5 annotators

Figure 9.4 The accuracy of one annotator to estimate the range of responses across all annotators by comparing the actual fraction of annotations for a given label with the number of annotations expected by an annotator. For our example data, this would correspond to Cameron's expectation that 65% of people would choose "Cyclist" for this task, compared with the 40% of people who actually chose it.

Figure 9.5 gives the calculation for every estimate by every annotator in our example data. To get the overall accuracy for an annotator, you average their accuracy across every subjective task in the dataset.

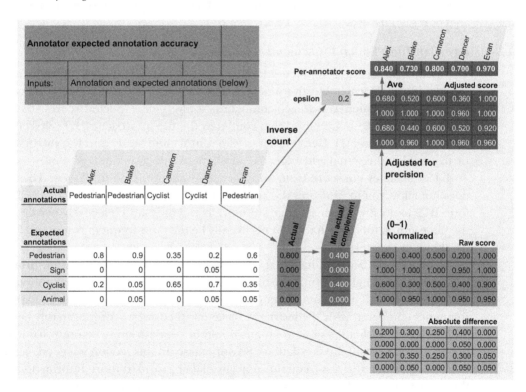

Figure 9.5 Calculating the accuracy of each annotator's estimate as the adjusted score and then averaging those scores to get a per-annotator score for this task. Cameron is 80% accurate in estimating how close the expected distribution was to the actual distribution. Evan is the most accurate, with a score of 97%, and Blake is the least accurate, with a score of 73%.

In figure 9.5, epsilon is the same epsilon used in Krippendorff's alpha in chapter 8. It wasn't important then, because Krippendorff's alpha calculated epsilon over the total number of annotations in the dataset. Here, we are calculating epsilon over the annotations within a single task. You can see by comparing the raw score and adjusted score that epsilon makes a big difference, adjusting the results by 20%.

You can use several variations and extensions if it is especially important to know how accurately your annotators can estimate the actual distributions. A 0 score won't be possible for some tasks because the distribution of each annotator's expected annotations has to add up to 1; therefore, they can't always provide the worst estimate for every label. (In figure 9.5, the worst possible score is 0.44 if an annotator expected that only "Animal" or "Sign" would be chosen.) You could normalize for this baseline, as for ground truth accuracy and agreement in chapter 8.

Cross-entropy is another way to calculate the difference between the expected and the actual distributions. Although cross-entropy is a common way to compare probability distributions in machine learning, I have never seen it used to compare actual and expected annotations for training data. This technique would be an interesting area of research.

9.1.4   *Bayesian Truth Serum for subjective judgments*

The method in section 9.1.3 focused on how accurately each annotator predicted the frequency of different subjective judgments, but the scores did not take into account the actual annotation from each annotator—only their expected scores. Bayesian Truth Serum (BTS) is a method that combines the two approaches. BTS was created by Dražen Prelec at MIT (see the *Science* paper in section 9.9.1) and was the first metric to combine the actual and expected annotations into a single score.

BTS calculates the score from an information-theoretic point of view. This score does not allow you to interpret the accuracy of an annotator or label directly. Therefore, BTS looks for responses that are more common than collectively predicted by the same annotators, which will not necessarily be the most frequent responses. Figure 9.6 shows an example.

In figure 9.6, Cameron has the highest score from a BTS point of view, primarily because there is high information from choosing "Cyclist" as the actual annotation. That is, the actual annotation frequency for "Cyclist" was higher than the expected frequency compared with "Pedestrian." Blake has the lowest score, primarily because of the prediction that 0.9 of annotations would be "Pedestrian" when only 0.6 were—the largest error of all the predictions. So our dataset in this section is a good example of a case in which the less-frequent subjective label provided more information than the more-frequent label. In some cases, however, the highest-frequency actual label can provide the most information.

Figure 9.6 is also a good example of how information differs from accuracy. Recall that in figure 9.5, Evan had the highest score because Evan's expected annotation frequencies were closest to the actual annotation frequencies. For BTS, Cameron ended

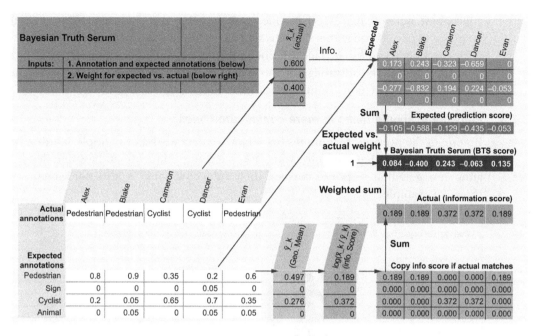

Figure 9.6 BTS combines the person's actual annotation with the predictions for expected annotations into a single score. Info is the information theoretic score (Expected × log(Actual / Expected)). The scores for each annotator show Cameron with the highest score. For both the expected and the actual annotations, the scores are based on information theory. The score is not only about the accuracy of each annotator; it is also about how much information each annotator is providing.

up with the highest score because even though Cameron was less accurate than Evan, there was more value in Cameron's predictions about "Cyclist," the less-frequent label that might have been overlooked.

If you consistently find that an annotator with the highest information score via BTS is not the annotator with the highest accuracy in predicting expected annotation frequencies, this finding can be evidence of a lack of diversity in your annotators. Check whether the annotator with the highest BTS score is typically selecting the less-frequent label; if so, you have evidence that your annotator pool is choosing the most-frequent label more often than a random or representative population would.

In an interesting extension to BTS, the inventors observed that when the actual percentage of annotations exceeds the average expected percentage for a label, this finding is good evidence that the surprisingly popular label is the correct one, even if it is not the majority. But this result relies on having enough annotators that at least one annotator gets chooses that label, which is unlikely for rare but valid labels when you have only a few annotators per task.

Note that we are not adjusting the BTS score in figure 9.6 for the fact that there are only five annotators, so only multiples of 0.2 were possible (epsilon in figure 9.5). The example in this section is the original calculation for BTS, so for educational purposes, it is taught here as it appears in the literature. It would be fine to add this adjustment, but note that BTS has a nice symmetry that you will lose in that case; if the weight of expected and actual scores is set to 1, as in our example (equal weights), the BTS scores always add to 0. This will not be the case if you adjust for precision, so you won't be able to take advantage of this symmetry with this modification. See section 9.9 for more information about extensions to BTS.

9.1.5   *Embedding simple tasks in more complicated ones*

If none of the previous techniques for subjective data works, one simple solution is to create an additional question for your task that is not subjective and assume that if an annotator gets that response correct, their subjective label is also valid. Figure 9.7 shows an example.

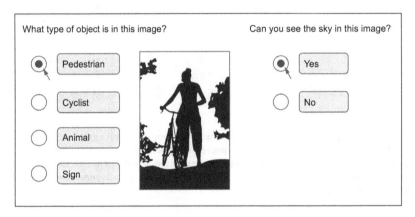

Figure 9.7   A subjective task with an additional question that is objective. This example allows easier quality control by assuming that if a person gets the objective question correct, their subjective judgment is also correct and not an error.

In figure 9.7, we are asking an additional question about whether the sky can be seen in the message. Unlike the object type, this question should be unambiguous and objective: the sky is either visible or not. Therefore, we can easily test whether people are getting the product question correct by embedding known answers for some questions and/or by looking for agreement between annotators, using the techniques discussed in this chapter. Then we assume that the people are equally accurate for the subjective task.

When using this method, we rely on the assumption that accuracy for the simpler objective task will strongly correlate with accuracy for the subjective task, which will be more or less true depending on your data. As a general principle, the closer the question is to the relevant content, the closer this correlation should be. In our example, we are asking about the context of the object, so the accuracy should be highly correlated.

This approach is most effective when the actual task is time-consuming. If you were asking someone to type a summary of a large passage, which typically would take many minutes, there is little additional annotation cost to ask an additional objective question about the passage.

9.2 *Machine learning for annotation quality control*

Because most quality control strategies for data annotations are statistically driven decision processes, machine learning can be used for the quality control process itself. In fact, most of the heuristics in this chapter and chapter 8 can be modeled as machine learning problems that are trained on held-out data. Four types of machine learning-driven quality controls are introduced here, all of which use the annotator's performance on ground truth data and/or agreement as training data:

- Treating the model predictions as an optimization task. Using the annotator's performance on the ground truth data, find a probability distribution for the actual label that optimizes a loss function.
- Creating a model that predicts whether a single annotation by an annotator is correct or incorrect.
- Creating a model that predicts whether a single annotation by an annotator is likely to be in agreement with other annotators.
- Predicting whether an annotator is actually a bot.

Some methods can be used independently or in combination. The following sections cover these methods in turn.

9.2.1 *Calculating annotation confidence as an optimization task*

In chapter 8, you learned that you can take the average confidence across all labels. If the confidence in one annotator's annotation was less than 100%, the remaining confidence was spread across the labels that the annotator didn't choose. We can build on this approach by looking at all the annotators' annotation patterns on the ground truth data and then treat our confidence as an optimization problem. Figure 9.8 shows an example.

Converge label confidence

| Inputs: | 1. Actual Annotation | | | | |
| | 2. Fraction in Ground-Truth for Annotation | | | | |

	Alex	Blake	Cameron	Dancer	Evan
Actual Annotations	Pedestrian	Pedestrian	Cyclist	Cyclist	Pedestrian
Ground-Truth Fraction					
Pedestrian	0.91	0.93	0.28	0.72	0.58
Sign	0.01	0	0.04	0.07	0.01
Cyclist	0.04	0.05	0.67	0.21	0.39
Animal	0.04	0.02	0.01	0	0.02

Figure 9.8 Using performance on the ground truth data to calculate model confidence as an optimization task. On the ground truth data, when Alex annotated items as "Pedestrian," they were actually "Pedestrians" 91% of the time, "Signs" 1% of the time, "Cyclists" 4% of the time, and "Animals" 4% of the time. When we see that Alex has annotated some new item as "Pedestrian," we can assume the same probability distribution. When Dancer annotates an item as "Cyclist," we know that it is actually a "Pedestrian" 72% of the time, showing confusion about these categories.

Figure 9.8 shows the actual distribution of the annotations in the ground truth data. If you have a small amount of ground truth data, you might consider smoothing this number with a simple smoothing method such as adding a constant (Laplace smoothing).

A nice property of this approach, compared with the methods in chapter 8, is that you might not have to discard all annotations from a low accuracy annotator. Dancer is wrong most of the time in figure 9.8 because they are only correct 21% of the time when they annotate an item as "Cyclist." There is useful information, however, in the fact that "Pedestrian" was the correct answer 72% of the time. So instead of removing Dancer from our annotations because of poor accuracy, we can keep their annotations and let them contribute to our overall confidence by modeling their accuracy.

To calculate the overall confidence, you can take the average of these numbers, which would give 68.4% confidence in "Pedestrian," 2.6% confidence in "Sign," 27.2% confidence in "Cyclist," and 1.8% confidence in "Animal." The average is only one way to calculate the overall confidence, however. You can also treat this task as an optimization task and find the probability distribution that minimizes a distance function, such as mean absolute error, mean squared error, or cross-entropy. If you come from a machine learning background, you will recognize these methods as loss functions, and you can think of this problem as a machine learning problem: you are optimizing for the least loss by finding a probability distribution that best matches the data.

If you try different loss functions on our example data, you will find that they don't differ much from the average. The biggest benefits from making this problem a machine learning problem is that you can incorporate information other than the annotations themselves into your confidence prediction.

9.2.2   *Converging on label confidence when annotators disagree*

Building on the treatment of aggregation as a machine learning problem, we can use the ground truth data as training data. That is, instead of optimizing the probability distributions that are taken from the ground truth data, we can build a model that uses the ground truth data as labels. Figure 9.9 shows how the ground truth data example from chapter 8 can be expanded to show the feature representation for each ground truth item.

If we build a model with the data in figure 9.9, our model will learn to trust our annotators relative to their overall accuracy on the ground truth data. We don't explicitly tell the model that the annotations have the same values as the labels; the model discovers the correlations itself.

The biggest shortcoming of this method is that people who have annotated more ground truth data will be weighted higher because their features (annotations) have appeared in more training data. You can avoid this result by having most of the ground truth data annotated early in the annotation process (a good idea in any case to determine accuracy and to fine-tune other processes) and by sampling an equal number of annotations per annotator in each training epoch when you build your

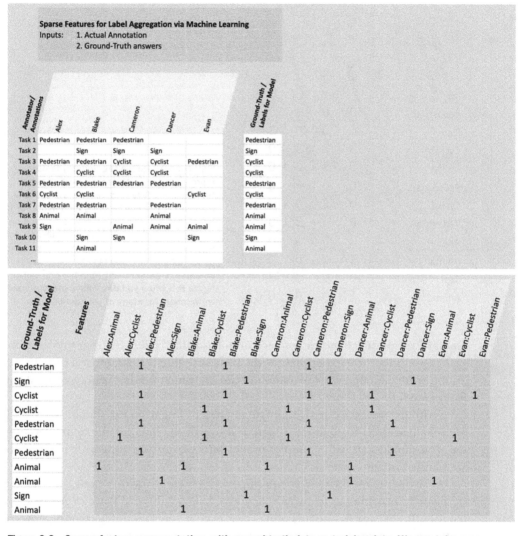

Figure 9.9 Sparse feature representation, with ground truth data as training data. We can take every annotation on the ground truth dataset, and use the actual annotations as features and the ground truth labels as the labels for a machine learning model. Then we have a model that can predict the correct label and give a confidence associated with that prediction.

model. You can also overcome this shortcoming by aggregating the number of labels but ignoring who did the annotations, as shown in figure 9.10.

You may need to normalize the entries in figure 9.10 if your model expects a [0–1] range in feature values. For both the sparse representation in figure 9.9 and the aggregated information in figure 9.10, you can experiment with using your confidence in each prediction instead of counting each annotation as 1. This confidence score could be the self-reported confidence of the annotator, as demonstrated in chapter 8, or an expected distribution, as in the subjective judgments in section 9.1. You might

Ground-Truth / Labels for Model	Features			
	Animal	Cyclist	Pedestrian	Sign
Pedestrian	0	0	3	0
Sign	0	0	0	3
Cyclist	0	2	3	0
Cyclist	0	3	0	0
Pedestrian	0	0	4	0
Cyclist	0	3	0	0
Pedestrian	0	0	3	0
Animal	3	0	0	0
Animal	3	0	0	1
Sign	0	0	0	3
Animal	1	0	0	0

Figure 9.10 Dense (aggregate) feature representation, with ground truth data as training data. The features are the count of each label, thereby ignoring the identity of the annotator. We can take every annotation on the ground truth dataset, count each annotation as the features, and use the ground truth labels as the labels for a machine learning model. This example is more robust than the one shown in figure 9.9 when you don't have many ground truth labels for many of your annotators.

also have a confidence metric for each annotator that is derived from their past work. Whatever number you experiment with, make sure that it's not derived from the same ground truth data that you are about to train on, which would overfit your quality prediction model.

As with the sparse example, a single neuron or linear model should be enough to give reliable results for figure 9.10 and not overfit the data for the dense representation. You should start with a simpler model before experimenting with anything more complicated in any case.

At this point, you may be wondering why you can't include both the sparse and aggregate information as features in a model. You can do this! You can create a model that uses these features plus any others that may be relevant for calculating how confidently we can aggregate multiple annotations. But even if you decide to take the "throw everything into a model" kitchen-sink approach to aggregation, you should use the feature representations in figures 9.9 and 9.10 as a baseline before you start experimenting with more complicated models and hyperparameter tuning.

To evaluate how accurate this model is, you need to split your ground truth data into training and evaluation data so that you can evaluate the confidence on held-out data. If you are using anything more complicated than a linear model or single neuron, such that you are doing hyperparameter tuning, you also need a further split to create a validation set that you can use for tuning. Both the sparse and aggregate representations are compatible with using a model's predictions as though it were an annotator. For the aggregate representation, you might think about whether you want to aggregate model predictions separately from human annotations.

9.2.3 *Predicting whether a single annotation is correct*

The most flexible way to use machine learning for quality control in annotation is as a binary classifier to predict whether an individual annotation was correct. The advantage of a simple classification binary task is that you can train a model on relatively little data. If you are training on ground truth data, you are unlikely to have much data to train on, so this approach allows you to get the most out of the limited data you have.

This method is especially useful if you have a small number of annotators per item. You may have the budget for only a single annotator to look at most of your items, especially if annotator is a subject-matter expert (SME) who is reliable most of the time. In this context, you want to identify the small number of cases in which the SME might be wrong, but you don't have agreement information to help with this identification because you have only one annotation most of the time.

The simplest implementation to start with would include the annotator's identity and their annotation as the features, like in figure 9.9. Therefore, this model will tell you which annotators are the strongest or weakest on particular labels in the ground truth data.

You can think about the additional features that might provide additional context as to whether an annotator might make an error. The features that you might try in the model, in addition to annotator identity and annotation, could include

- The number or percentage of annotators who agree with that annotation (where they exist)
- Metadata about the item being annotated (time, place, and other categories) and the annotator (relevant demographics, qualifications, experience on this task, and so on)
- Embeddings from the predictive model or other models

The metadata features can help your model identify areas where there might be biases or meaningful trends in annotation quality. If a metadata feature captured the time of day when a photo was taken, your model might be able to learn that photos taken at night are generally harder to annotate accurately. The same is true for your annotators. If your annotators are themselves cyclists, they might have biases about images that contain cyclists, and the model can learn about this bias.

This approach works with subjective data too. If you have subjective data with multiple correct answers, each of those correct ones could be correct for the binary model. This technique is fairly flexible; it also works for many types of machine learning problems, as covered in chapter 10.

> **Showing the correct ground truth answers to annotators**
> You have the option of showing the correct answer to an annotator when they get it wrong. This review should improve that annotator's performance, but it will also make it harder to evaluate that annotator's accuracy. There is a trade-off in design: do you tell the annotator every time they make an error, making that annotator more accurate, or do you keep some or all ground truth items anonymous so that you can perform better quality control on that annotator's performance? You may need to strike a balance.

(continued)
For models built on ground truth data, be careful using items for which the annotator has learned the correct answer. For example, an annotator might have made errors with ground truth data items that had a person pushing a bike. If the annotator was told about that error and given the correct answer, however, that annotator is less likely to make that same error later. Therefore, your quality control model might erroneously predict errors for that annotator on types of items for which they are now highly accurate.

9.2.4   *Predicting whether a single annotation is in agreement*

As an alternative to predicting whether the annotator is correct, you could predict whether the annotator agrees with other annotators. This approach can increase the number of training items, because you can train a model to predict agreement on all the items that have been annotated by multiple people, not only the ones in the ground truth data. This model is likely to be more powerful.

Predicting agreement can be useful to surface items for which disagreement was expected but didn't occur. Perhaps it was by random chance that a small number of annotators agreed with one another. If you can predict confidently that disagreement should have occurred, even by annotators who didn't work on that task, that finding can be evidence that additional annotation may be needed for that item.

You can try both approaches: build one model that predicts when an annotator is correct, and build a separate model that predicts when an annotator will agree with other annotators. Then you can review the task or elicit additional annotations when an annotation is predicted to be an error or predicted to disagree with other annotations.

9.2.5   *Predicting whether an annotator is a bot*

If you are working with anonymous annotators and discover that one annotator was really a bot that was scamming your work, you can make a binary classification task to identify other bots. If we discovered that Dancer in our annotation data is a bot, we might suspect that the same bot is posing as other human annotators.

If you are certain that some subset of annotators are human, their annotations can become human training data for your model. This approach effectively allows you to train a model to ask an annotator, "Are we human, or are we Dancer?"

Sometimes, a bot is a good addition to the annotation team. Machine learning models can annotate the data or create data autonomously or in combination with humans. The rest of this chapter is devoted to methods that automate or semi-automate data annotation.

9.3   *Model predictions as annotations*

The simplest approach to semi-automating annotation is to treat the model's predictions as though the model was an annotator. This process is often called *semi-supervised learning*, although that term has been applied to pretty much any combination of supervised and unsupervised learning.

You can trust a model's predictions or incorporate the model's predictions as one annotator among many. The two approaches have different implications for how you should treat model confidence and the workflows that you might implement to review the model's output, so they are explored separately. You can also use your model predictions to look for potential errors in noisy data, which is covered in section 9.3.3.

Will we replace human annotators?

Every few years since the 1990s, someone has claimed to have solved automated labeling. Thirty years later, however, we still need to label data for more than 99% of supervised machine learning problems.

There are two common problems with many academic papers about automated labeling, whether it is using model confidence, a rule-based system, or some other method. First, they almost always compare the auto-labeling methods with random sampling. As you saw in chapter 2, even a simple active learning system can quickly improve the accuracy of your model, so it can be difficult to evaluate the benefit compared with active learning from these papers. Second, the papers typically assume that the evaluation data already exists, which is true for academic datasets. In the real world, however, you still need to set up annotation processes to create your evaluation data, manage the annotators, create the annotation guidelines, and implement quality control on the annotations. If you are doing all this for your evaluation data, why not put in the extra effort in the annotation component to create training data too?

The reality is rarely an all-or-nothing solution. Although we can't remove human annotators from the majority of supervised machine learning systems, we have some exciting ways to improve our models and annotation strategies, such as using model predictions as labels, embeddings and contextual representations, rule-based systems, semi-supervised machine learning, lightly supervised machine learning, and synthetic data. All these techniques have interesting human-in-the-loop implications and are introduced in this chapter.

9.3.1 *Trusting annotations from confident model predictions*

The simplest way to use a model as an annotator is to trust the model predictions as labels, trusting predictions beyond a certain confidence threshold as labels. Figure 9.11 shows an example.

Figure 9.11 shows how items are labeled automatically by a predictive model. We can bootstrap our model from that starting point. This approach is suitable if you have an existing model but don't have access to the data that the model is trained on. This situation is common in machine translation. Google released the first major machine translation system, and every major machine translation system since then has used translated data from Google's engine. Although this approach is less accurate than annotating data directly, it can be effective for getting a quick start cheaply.

This kind of semi-supervised learning, sometimes known as *bootstrapped semi-supervised learning*, rarely works in isolation when adapting an existing model to new types of data. If you can confidently classify something correctly, your model gains little extra information with the additional items that it is already confident about, and you run the risk of amplifying bias. If something is truly novel, the model is probably

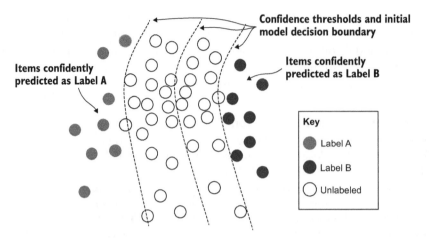

Figure 9.11 Treating the most confident predictions as labels. A model predicts the items as being Label A or Label B, and the most confidently predicted items are treated as the correct label. This example allows us to build a model quickly but has a shortcoming: the model is built from items *away* from the decision boundary, which leaves a large amount of error for where that boundary might be.

not classifying it confidently or (worse) could be misclassifying it. This approach, however, can be effective when used in combination with active learning techniques to ensure that there is enough representative data. Figure 9.12 shows a typical workflow for trusting model predictions as annotations.

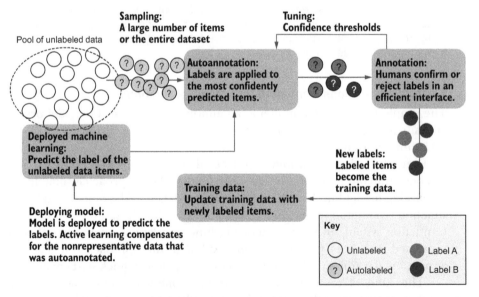

Figure 9.12 A workflow for using confident predictions as annotations. The model is used to predict the labels of a large number of unlabeled items (potentially all of them). Human annotators review some of the labels, and the accepted labels become annotations for the training data. The human annotators also use this process to tune the threshold at which the labels can be confidently turned into annotations.

Here are some tips for using confident model predictions to create annotations:

- Margin-of-Confidence and Ratio-of-Confidence are likely to be the best measure of confidence because you want the highest confidence relative to the other labels. So these metrics are good starting points, but you can test the other uncertainty sampling metrics to see what is best for your data.
- Set a confidence threshold on a per-label basis, or sample the top N predictions for each label, rather than try to set one confidence threshold for all labels. Otherwise, your most confident predictions are likely to be from a small number of easy-to-predict labels.
- Keep two models trained in each iteration: one trained on all annotations and one trained only on the annotations that a human has seen. Do not trust the predictions when confidence is high for the first model but low for the second.
- Keep track of human-labeled and auto-labeled items, and ensure that a certain number of training epochs use only the human-labeled items, to keep your model from straying too far. (This strategy is often called *pseudo-labeling.*)
- Use uncertainty sampling in your next iteration of active learning to focus on your new decision boundary.
- Use representative sampling to find data that was different from what the prior model was trained on (See section 7.5.4 for more about using representative sampling when combining human and machine labels.)

Using model predictions to generate candidates for human review, instead of trusting them fully, can be effective if the annotation task is time-consuming. If we had a classification task with hundreds of labels, it would be much faster for an annotator to accept or reject the predicted label as a binary classification task than to choose among the hundreds of labels manually. This scenario tends to be more true of other types of machine learning, such as sequence labeling and semantic segmentation, than of labeling. Chapter 10 goes into more detail on using model predictions for these use cases.

Review workflows like in figure 9.12 can lead to bias where humans trust the model too much, perpetuating and sometimes amplifying the errors. We will cover ways to mitigate these errors in chapter 11 when we discuss user experience and annotation interfaces.

9.3.2 *Treating model predictions as a single annotator*

A second way to incorporate machine learning into the annotation process is to include the predictions from your downstream model as though they were annotations by one annotator. Suppose that the annotator Evan in our examples is not human; it's our downstream machine learning model. Looking at figure 9.13, we can see that Evan is reasonably accurate, getting every label correct except for task 3, where Evan incorrectly predicted "Cyclist" to be "Pedestrian." Therefore, if we add Evan's predictions as though Evan were a human annotator, we can apply the exact same methods to converge on the right agreement.

Ground-Truth Fraction	Alex	Blake	Cameron	Dancer	Model Predictions (Evan)
Actual Annotations	Pedestrian	Pedestrian	Cyclist	Cyclist	Pedestrian
Pedestrian	0.91	0.93	0.28	0.72	0.58
Sign	0.01	0	0.04	0.07	0.01
Cyclist	0.04	0.05	0.67	0.21	0.39
Animal	0.04	0.02	0.01	0	0.02

Figure 9.13 Incorporating predictions from a model as though they were annotations. From our example data, we can assume that Evan was in fact a predictive model, not a human annotator. For any of our methods that take into account the accuracy of each annotator, it is generally fine to incorporate model predictions as human annotations in this part of the workflow.

You can incorporate a model's prediction as you would the annotations of any other annotator. By applying the techniques from section 9.2.1, where we took the annotator's accuracy into account when calculating our final probability distribution, we are using the accuracy of the model on the ground truth data.

You might consider different workflows, depending on how an item was sampled to be annotated. If you consider that Evan was trained by past human interactions and acted on that knowledge, Evan will be shaped by the past interactions and training data and will mirror those human behaviors unless Evan becomes adversarial to humans.

Therefore, if an item was sampled that is similar to past training data and was confidently classified by Evan, you might ask one more annotator to confirm that annotation instead of the minimum number of annotators that you would otherwise use. This approach falls between our strategies of trusting confident predictions and treating the model as an annotator.

9.3.3   *Cross-validating to find mislabeled data*

If you have an existing annotated dataset and are not certain that all the labels are correct, you can use the model to find candidates for human review. When your model predicts a different label from the ones that have been annotated, you have good evidence that the label might be wrong and that a human annotator should review that label.

If you are looking at your existing dataset, however, your model should not be trained on the same data that it is evaluating, because your model will overfit that data and likely miss many cases. If you cross-validate, such as splitting your data into 10 partitions with 90% of the data as training data and 10% as evaluation data, you can train and predict on different data.

Although there is a large body of literature on training models on noisy data, most of it assumes that it is not possible for humans to review or correct the wrongly labeled data. At the same time, the literature assumes that it is possible to spend a lot of time tuning models to automatically identify and account for noisy data (see graduate-student economics from chapter 7). In almost all real-world use cases, you should be able to annotate more data. If you know that your data is noisy, you should at least set up an annotation process for your evaluation data so that you know your actual accuracy.

There are some legitimate reasons why you might have noisy data that you can't avoid. The data might be inherently ambiguous, you might get a large amount of free but noisy labels, or you might have an annotation interface that sacrifices a little accuracy for much greater throughput. We'll return to ways to account for noisy data later, with the caveat that it is better to have accurate training data in almost all use cases.

9.4 *Embeddings and contextual representations*

Much current machine learning research focuses on transfer learning: adapting a model from one task to another. This technique opens some interesting possibilities for annotation strategies. If your annotation task is especially time-consuming, such as semantic segmentation, you may be able to annotate orders of magnitude more data in some other way and then use that data in a model that is adapted to the semantic segmentation task. We'll return to this specific example later in this section.

Because transfer learning is a popular research area right now, there is a lot of changing terminology. If a model is specifically built to be adapted to new tasks, it is often called a *pretrained* model, and the information in that model is referred to as an *embedding* or *contextual representation*. Figure 9.14 shows a general architecture for using contextual embeddings.

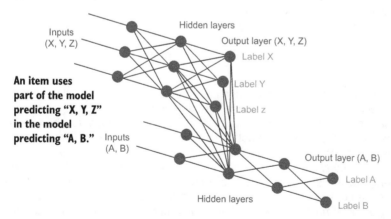

Figure 9.14   **An example of transfer learning. We have the task of predicting whether an item is "A" or "B," and we think that our existing model that predicts "X," "Y," or "Z" will have useful information because of similarities between the two tasks. So we can use the neurons from the "X," "Y," or "Z" model as features (a** *representation***) in our model predicting "A" or "B." This example is similar to the examples earlier in the book that use the hidden layers as features for clustering and use transfer learning to adapt an existing model to a new task. In some cases, we might ignore the inputs "A" and "B," using only the pretrained model as a representation for our new model.**

You may want to experiment with variations of the architecture in figure 9.1. You could choose to use only some layers in the representation, especially if you are worried about having too many dimensions. Alternatively, you might want only the predicted labels and not any model-internal representation, which will be the only choice if you only have access to model predictions. This approach might called something like "using another model's predictions as features" in the literature rather than a representation.

You can also decide whether you want to adapt or tune an existing model or to use the existing model as features in a new model. We did the latter for adaptive transfer learning in chapter 5, and as that chapter pointed out, having one model feed into another (as in figure 9.14) is the equivalent of adapting a model with frozen weights. If you are training all the models and not using existing ones, yet another option is to have a multitask model; you have one model with shared layers but with different output layers or transformer heads for different tasks. If you start with a pretrained model and adapt it with an adjacent task before adapting it again to your actual task, the process is known as *intermediate task training*.

You might also decide to use multiple model representations in your final model, which one of the practical examples in chapter 12 implements.

Transfer learning, pretrained models, representations, or embeddings?

The machine learning community has not yet settled on the names for different transfer learning methods and where they fall on the unsupervised-to-supervised spectrum of models. Embeddings were historically the result of unsupervised learning, but supervised variations of all variants quickly arose. Most recently, NLP researchers have started using supervised models with clever ways to get "free" labels, such as predicting a missing word in a sentence and predicting whether two sentences followed each other in the source documents. Because these models are predicting the words or sentences in context, they are often called *contextual representations* or *contextual embeddings*, and the models are known as *contextual models*. Because the models are specifically trained with transfer learning in mind, they are also called *pretrained models*.

The most recent supervised approaches are sometimes referred to as unsupervised, either as a continuation of the historical tradition of embeddings being unsupervised or because the researchers didn't have to pay to create training data when predicting a word that is removed from an existing sentence. In the literature, you might come across any combination of *transfer learning, pretrained models, contextual representations*, and *embeddings* alongside learning described as *supervised, unsupervised, semi-supervised*, or *self-supervised*. The reduction in annotation effort that results from these methods is often referred to as *one-shot, few-shot*, or *zero-shot* learning, depending on how many iterations of additional annotations are required and how long it takes the model to adapt to the new use case.

The terms will no doubt evolve and be added to after this book is published, so look closely at what the researchers are talking about in any paper.

Here are some ways that you can use embeddings and contextual representations in your annotation process:

- Use existing embeddings or adapt a pretrained model for your deployed model.
- Use inherent labels in your data to train a custom set of embeddings on your data.
- Get human annotations much more efficiently on a task that is adjacent to your actual task and then build a contextual model from those annotations.

We'll cover each of these examples in turn in sections 9.4.1 through 9.4.3.

9.4.1 *Transfer learning from an existing model*

To the extent that there is any traditional approach to transfer learning with neural models, it is the process of taking a model designed for one task and adapting it to another. The best-known task in computer vision adapts an ImageNet model to other tasks. You may have experimented with this kind of transfer learning, which is the kind of transfer learning used in active transfer learning in chapter 5, so we won't go into detail about it again here.

One variation that you may not have seen uses a dataset like ImageNet for a machine learning task that is more complicated than image-level labeling, such as semantic segmentation. Suppose that we are doing semantic segmentation on images to identify "Animal," "Cyclist," "Pedestrian," and "Sign" in our example use case. Also suppose that we have 2 million images, that it takes about an hour to annotate each image for semantic segmentation (typical time for some tasks), and that there is a budget for the equivalent of six years of full-time annotation.

Completing semantic segmentation would take 40 hours * 50 weeks * 6 people = 12,000 images. That is, the training data would contain about 12,000 images (or slightly less, because some would be held out as evaluation data). Although 12,000 is an acceptable number of items to train on, it's not a large amount and less than 1% of the available data. Even with good active learning, there may be only 1,000 examples of some of the rarest labels.

You know, however, that ImageNet has millions of examples of people, bicycles, and types of animals. So you use an existing ImageNet database, knowing that neurons in that model will contain representations of each of those object types. Therefore, you know that the semantic segmentation model, which is trained only on 12,000 examples, can take advantage of representations in ImageNet that are trained on millions of examples. This representation might help your model, and this principle can be applied to other types of representations. We will build on this observation in section 9.4.2.

9.4.2   *Representations from adjacent easy-to-annotate tasks*

The shortcoming of using an existing model like ImageNet is that it is trained on different labels and most likely trained on different kinds of images. You can dedicate some of your annotation budget to image-level labeling of your data according to the same labels that you used in your semantic segmentation task. Although semantic segmentation is time-consuming, you can create a simple annotation task for questions such as "Is there an animal in this image?", which takes only 20 seconds per image and is therefore faster than full segmentation.

If you take the budget of six person-years and move one person-year to annotation at image level, you get 3 per minute * 60 minutes * 40 hours * 50 weeks = 360,000 image-level labels for the different object types. Then you can train a model on those labels, knowing that the model will contain representations of each of those object types and that it covers much more variety than the semantic segmentation annotations (now 10,000 from 5 people).

If you have 360,000 relevant labels on your images for a reduction of only 2,000 fewer semantic segmentations, you can provide much richer information in your model. If your model architecture allows efficient embeddings, this strategy is one to consider.

This strategy also has additional advantages: it is easier to implement quality control on the labeling task, and you will be able to draw on a broader workforce that can't necessarily work on semantic segmentation but can do labeling.

The hard thing to predict is whether you will get a net positive from taking away 2,000 semantic segmentation training data items to add the 360,000 image-level labels for your pretrained model. You may want to start experimenting with a smaller number. Recall the workflow example in chapter 8 that used a image-level labeling task first, asking "Are there any bicycles in this image?" If you have a similar workflow, you are already generating data that can be used in a model to create embeddings. This example would be a good place to start experimenting before you need to divert any resources.

9.4.3   *Self-supervision: Using inherent labels in the data*

The data might have inherent labels that you can use for free to create other contextual models. Any metadata associated with the data is a potential source of labels on which you can build a model, and that model can be used as a representation for your actual task.

In our example data, suppose that we have a problem with accuracy in certain lighting conditions, but it is too expensive to annotate each image manually according to lighting conditions, and some lighting conditions are rare. You have timestamps on most of your images, so you can use those timestamps to confidently filter a million images into buckets for different times of day (perhaps by hour or by daytime and nighttime buckets). Then you can train a model to classify images according to time of day, knowing that the model will contain representations of the lighting. Without getting humans to analyze the data, you have a model that approximates a prediction for lighting conditions that you can use as a representation for other tasks. These three examples of how you can incorporate embeddings are shown in figure 9.15.

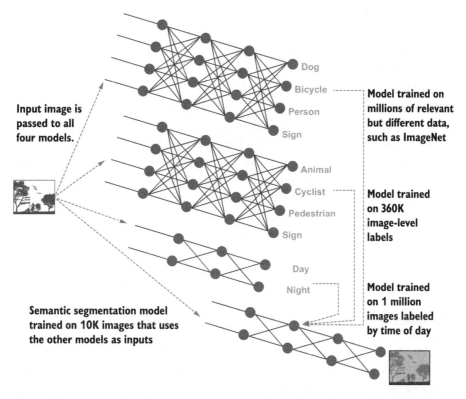

Figure 9.15 An example of how transfer learning can be used to make a model more accurate and how it might influence the annotation strategy. Here, three other models are feeding into a semantic segmentation model. The top example is adapting a model trained on ImageNet, which is the most common type of transfer learning. The second model is trained on 300,000 image-level labels for the objects we care about. The third model uses the timestamps of the images to train a model to predict the time of day. Because the top three models have been trained on much more data than the semantic segmentation model, with only 10,000 training items, they should have richer representations of the image that can help with the semantic segmentation task.

Free labels are appealing, and there are likely to be some options for your data. Even noisy labels can help. Every social media company uses models built from hashtags for computer vision and natural language processing (NLP) tasks. Even though hashtags are used differently by different people, there is enough signal in predicting those hashtags that it helps with downstream computer vision and NLP tasks. Your final model treats the contextual model as input embeddings and weights them accordingly, so errors don't necessarily propagate. Here are some examples that you might find in your data:

- User-generated tags, such as hashtags and user-defined topics
- Meaningful time periods, such as day/night and weekday/weekend
- Geographic information about the data or the person who created it
- (Especially for computer vision) The type of device that created the data
- (Especially for web text) The domain or URL of linked text
- (Especially for NLP) The word or token in context, as used in many pretrained models
- (Especially for NLP) Whether two sentences or paragraphs follow each other
- (Especially for computer vision) The pixel values of a video frame in context

In brief, if any metadata or linked data can become a label, or if you can meaningfully remove part of the data and predict it in context, that data might be a candidate for inherent labels that you can use to build a representation. These methods of incorporating free adjacent labels into models have been popular since search engines first used them in the early 2000s and are enjoying a recent surge of popularity with neural models.

Note that although the labels are free, dimensionality is a problem, especially early in the annotation process, when you don't have many annotations for your actual task. Some of this problem is outside the scope of this book; dimensionality is a broad problem in machine learning, and many papers have been written about how to solve it when building models on limited data. But some of the problem can be mitigated by the design of your contextual models. If you have a near-final layer in your model that you will use as your representation, you may want to set that layer to be an order of magnitude smaller than the number of training data items you have. Your accuracy for that contextual model may go down, but the information is now distilled into fewer dimensions (fewer neurons), so it might improve the accuracy of your downstream model. Look at the literature on *model distillation* for additional ways to reduce the dimensionality of your models without losing too much accuracy. You can also use classic statistical methods such as PCA (chapter 4).

9.5 *Search-based and rule-based systems*

Rule-based systems predate statistical machine learning, especially in NLP, and are still an active area of research. Among the biggest advantages of rule-based systems are the senses of ownership and agency that they give annotators, especially ones who are SMEs, making them feel as though they are in the driver's seat. I have built rule-based systems on top of machine learning systems specifically because the analysts using the system wanted a way to input their expert knowledge directly into the system. It isn't as easy to provide that level of user experience in an annotation interface, and we will return to the human–computer interaction side of this problem in chapter 11.

9.5.1 Data filtering with rules

Manually crafted rule-based systems are widely used for data filtering. For stratified sampling, this approach can make a lot of sense. To continue an example in this chapter, if you are classifying images outdoors and care about lighting conditions, you could create a rule-based system to sample an even number of images from different times of day to make the data more balanced.

On the other hand, if rules are being used to filter data based on untested intuitions, you may end up with biased data and a system that won't perform well when applied to real-world data. This situation is especially likely in language tasks; any keyword-based rules are biased against rarer spellings, people with less literacy in a language might make more errors, or synonyms may not be known by the person who created the rule.

Even if you can use a rule-based system for a labeling task and don't need annotations (except for your evaluation data), you still might be better off using the rule-based system to autoannotate the data annotation and then build a machine learning model on those annotations, rather than use a rule-based system in production. It is difficult to add contextual models to rule-based systems, so creating a machine learning version of your rule-based system will make it easier to integrate with pretrained models.

> ### Beware of scope creep with rule-based systems
>
> I have seen many people get locked into rule-based systems through incremental scope creep that they had trouble escaping. A popular smart-device company used machine learning for converting speech to text but then used a rule-based system to classify that text into different commands or questions (intents). A rule-based approach made sense while the company was first testing the system on a limited set of problems, but this approach became increasingly difficult as the product took off, requiring new functionality and support for more languages. The company ended up employing hundreds of people in parallel to write new rules for how certain combinations of keywords mapped to different commands. The company barely kept the system running while it spent more than a year building out the machine learning capabilities in parallel and had trouble scaling the management of all the rules and how they interacted. The company concluded that the quick start that rules provided was not ultimately worthwhile; even a simple machine learning model with good training data would have been a better start.

9.5.2 Training data search

Search engine interfaces provide a nice middle ground between rule-based systems and machine learning systems. An SME can search for items that they think belong to a certain category (label) and quickly accept or reject the items returned by that search. If the SME knows that some items are going to be tricky for the model or are inherently important for their application, they have a way to dive into the relevant data quickly. This example is similar to our workflow in which an expert reviews earlier annotations, but in this case, the expert is driving the entire process.

Training data search can be thought of as a type of annotator-driven diversity sampling, in which the person responsible for finding all the relevant data to sample is also creating the annotations. If that person is routing the data to other people to annotate, the process is almost like the reverse of the workflow for expert review. The process starts with the SME, who finds the most important data points manually; then nonexpert annotators complete the more time-consuming annotation tasks.

There are advantages to allowing search functionality for stakeholders other than domain exports. An annotator can get a good idea of the type of data they are annotating by being permitted to search that data. A machine learning scientist can quickly test their assumptions about which features will be important in their models. This form of exploratory data analysis is also valuable in lightly supervised systems.

9.5.3   *Masked feature filtering*

If you are quickly building a model with training data by rules or by search, you should consider masking the features that you used to generate that training data when you are training your model. If you are quickly building a sentiment analysis classifier, and you create your initial training data by searching or filtering for text that says "happy" and text that says "angry," consider masking the terms "happy" and "angry" in your feature space. Otherwise, your model can easily overfit the terms "happy" and "angry" and not learn the surrounding words that should contribute to the sentiment of the text.

You can consider different masking strategies. You might mask these words in 50% of your training epochs, for example, so that your model needs to spend 50% of the time learning about words that weren't part of the search or rule strategy. This approach can be thought of as a targeted variation of dropouts to mitigate biased propagating from your data collection methods. If you will have later iterations of active learning, you could remove these words from the early iterations, minimizing their bias early in the process while knowing that models in later iterations will include them to maximize their accuracy for the model that will be deployed for your application.

9.6   *Light supervision on unsupervised models*

One of the most widely used methods for exploratory data analysis is allowing annotators, typically SMEs, to interact with unsupervised models. One of the examples in chapter 12 is an implementation of exploratory data analysis. Figure 9.16 shows a simple extension to the clustering method for diversity sampling (chapter 4).

There are many variations in figure 9.16 that you may want to experiment with. In addition to clustering, you could use the related topic modeling techniques, especially for text data. In addition to distance-based clustering, you could use cosine distance (chapter 4), proximity-based clustering such as K-Nearest Neighbors (KNN), or graph-based clustering.

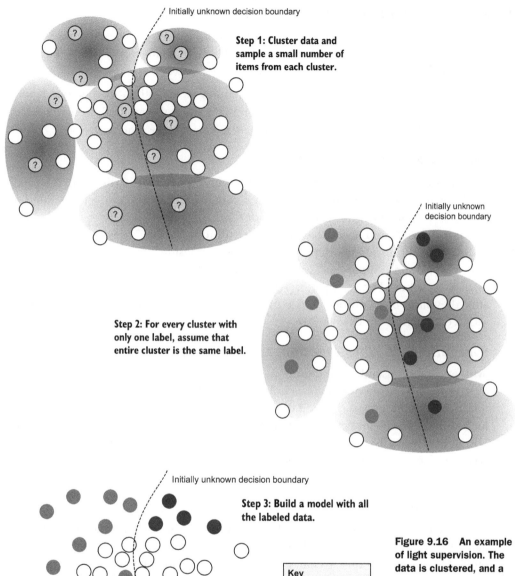

Initially unknown decision boundary

Step 1: Cluster data and sample a small number of items from each cluster.

Initially unknown decision boundary

Step 2: For every cluster with only one label, assume that entire cluster is the same label.

Initially unknown decision boundary

Step 3: Build a model with all the labeled data.

Key

- Label A
- Label B
- Unlabeled
- ? Selected to be labeled
- Cluster

Figure 9.16 An example of light supervision. The data is clustered, and a small number of items are sampled from each cluster. For every cluster in which all the labels are the same, the entire cluster is given that label. A supervised model can be built on all the items, ignoring the items that did not get a label in clusters where there was disagreement.

9.6.1 *Adapting an unsupervised model to a supervised model*

The clustering algorithm in figure 9.16 extends the clustering examples in chapter 4 by assuming that all clusters with only one label have that label for all items. There are other ways to convert this type of model to a fully supervised one:

- Recursively cluster for the clusters containing items with more than one label.
- Switch to uncertainty sampling after initially using the methods in figure 9.16.
- De-weighting or removing the auto-labeled items over time.

9.6.2 *Human-guided exploratory data analysis*

Sometimes, a data scientist's goal is pure exploration, not necessarily to build a supervised classification model. In this case, the annotator might not have a predefined set of labels. A scientist might use clustering or other unsupervised techniques to look for trends in the data and decide based on those trends what labels might apply.

Search and rule-based systems might be used alongside unsupervised methods and time-based trends. Supervised systems can be used for tagging the data and to segment the analysis. For example, a person may want to cluster social media messages after they have been divided into positive and negative sentiment to see the trends within each sentiment extreme.

9.7   Synthetic data, data creation, and data augmentation

Synthetic data is useful when the raw data is not available and when creating the data from scratch is cheaper than annotating the data. For use cases such as speech recognition, it is common to use created data. If you are creating a speech recognition system for hospitals, you might get people to read a list of medical-related words or sentences. It wouldn't be feasible to find audio recordings of every relevant medical word in every accent or language that you care about in a generally available speech data corpus, so data creation is used.

9.7.1 *Synthetic data*

Small, manually created evaluation data is common. You might create an evaluation dataset with known pathological edge cases that you use with each model that you build. Or you might build a small evaluation dataset with some easy-to-classify examples and make 100% accuracy on this dataset a precondition for shipping a new model—the machine learning equivalent of a software developer's unit test. Purely synthetic training data, often created programmatically instead of manually, is most useful in one or more of these situations:

- There is a constrained problem, such as restructuring data that started in a structured format but ended up with predictable types of noise.
- There are barriers to getting enough data (such as cost or rarity).
- There are privacy or security concerns with using real data.
- There are acceptable fallbacks to humans when the model fails.

I am aware of only one widely used case of purely synthetic data for machine learning: scanning credit card numbers. If you have added your credit card number to an application on your phone, you may have noticed the option to take a photograph of your credit card instead of typing the numbers. The model that recognizes your credit card numbers was almost certainly built on purely synthetic data with no human annotation. It qualifies for all four cases above. Your credit card number started as structured data, but it was printed on a physical card and a photo was taken of that printed number, which is a constrained problem restructuring 16 numbers. There are no large open data repositories of scanned credit cards. Privacy and security concerns would arise if data scientists and annotators could see all the scanned images from actual cards to annotate. Finally, the end users are generally OK with typing their card numbers manually if the scan doesn't work.

Most applications using synthetic data still include some data annotation, so the following strategies are typically used to complement human annotation. If you could create all the data you need for the model programmatically, you probably wouldn't need machine learning in the first place.

9.7.2   *Data creation*

One effective method to address the lack of data is to ask the annotators to create it. This approach is a common one for creating speech data (chapter 10). For text data, this approach can be effective for addressing gaps in the data. Although not as realistic as spontaneous text, this approach can be preferable to having no data.

> **Data about disease outbreaks**
>
> When I started writing this book, I included an example of data creation based on the observation that there were few news headlines about disease outbreaks in North America. Sadly, that's no longer true during COVID-19.
>
> For the dataset creation task, I asked annotators to imagine that they were experiencing a disease outbreak and used a rule-based system to generate a different prompt for each annotator. The rules varied the prompts by factors such as whether they were directly experiencing, witnessing, or hearing about the outbreaks secondhand; by how many people were infected or exposed; and so on. This approach was designed to get as much variety as possible to overcome the limitations in artificial text over spontaneous text.
>
> I'm leaving this dataset out of the book and will consider releasing it when the pandemic is over. It may be interesting to see how someone's lived experience changes how realistically they can create example data at that time.

Some interesting recent techniques for automated data creation combine data creation and synthetic data, including generative adversarial networks (GANs) for images and language models for text. If you want pictures of bicycles, you can train GANs on existing pictures of bicycles to create new but realistic pictures of bicycles. Similarly, you can train language models to create novel sentences containing certain phrases or about certain topics. These models are often the same types of pretrained models that are used for contextual embeddings. In both cases, the data is rarely 100% accurate, so human review can help filter which generated data is realistic.

When data is created by humans or automated processes, it can help address the sensitivity of training data. You might have a language model built on data scraped from the web that effectively captures some sensitive data, such as people's addresses, which could leave a model vulnerable to reverse engineering to expose those addresses. If you can rewrite all the sequences with a language model and test that the new sequences do not occur in the original data, however, you can build a second model on that new data. That model should be much harder to reverse-engineer to discover the sensitive information. Data sensitivity is outside the scope of this book, but it is flagged here as an important area in which human-in-the-loop machine learning can help.

9.7.3   Data augmentation

If you work in computer vision, you are familiar with data augmentation techniques such as flipping, cropping, rotating, darkening, and otherwise modifying some of the training data items to create more items or more diversity within those items. A similar technique exists in NLP, replacing words with synonyms from a database of synonyms or programmatically from words with similar embeddings.

In machine translation and other use cases, back translation is a popular data augmentation method, translating a sentence into another language and back again to create potentially new but synonymous sentences. If you translated "This is great" into French and back into English, the sentence might come back as "This is very good." You can treat "This is very good" as another valid translation. This approach works for other use cases too. If you are implementing sentiment analysis and have "This is great" as a data point labeled as positive sentiment, you can use back translation to create "This is very good" as another labeled data item for positive sentiment.

Masked language modeling with pretrained models is a similar technique. Recall that commonly used pretrained models predict missing words in context. This technique can be used to create similar sentences. You could take the sentence "Alex drove to the shop" and ask the system to predict the MASK in the sentence "Alex [MASK] to the shop." This example might produce sentences like "Alex went to the shop," "Alex walked to the shop," and sentences with similar meanings, which can make a much larger dataset quickly and efficiently.

9.8   Incorporating annotation information into machine learning models

You can't always avoid wrongly labeled data. But you can use several strategies to get the most accurate possible model downstream even when you know that not all the labels are correct.

9.8.1   Filtering or weighting items by confidence in their labels

The easiest method is to drop all training data items with low annotation confidence. You can tune the right number to drop using held-out validation data. This approach almost always improves the accuracy of a model but is too often overlooked because people want to use every possible annotation. If you are dropping some items, make sure that you at least spot-check what you are dropping so that you aren't creating biases in your data. Something might be low-confidence because it comes from an underrepresented demographic. Use diversity sampling to help rebalance the data in this case.

Instead of dropping low-confidence items, you can de-weight them in your model. Some models allow you to weight items differently as part of their inputs. If that isn't the case with your model, you can programmatically select items in your training epochs according to your confidence in the labels, selecting the more confident labels more often.

9.8.2   Including the annotator identity in inputs

Including the annotators' identities as a feature in your model can increase your model's predictive abilities, especially for predicting uncertainty. You can include additional binary fields that indicate which annotator contributed to the label. This approach is similar to including annotator identity in models to converge on the right label when annotators disagreed, but here, we are including their identities in the downstream model that we are deploying on new data.

Obviously, your unlabeled data does not have annotators associated with it. You can get predictions from the model without any annotator fields for your actual prediction. Then you can get additional predictions with the different annotator fields set. If the prediction changes based on the different field, your model is telling you that different annotators would have annotated that data point differently. This information is useful for identifying items on which agreement among annotators may have been low.

The accuracy of the overall model might go down if you are introducing a field to capture the annotator identity. In that case, you can set all the annotator fields to 0 for some of the training items, either in the data itself or as a mask for some training epochs. You should be able to tune this process with validation data so that you can get the optimal predictive accuracy but still have a model that incorporates the annotator identities.

9.8.3   *Incorporating uncertainty into the loss function*

The most direct way to use label uncertainty in the downstream model is to incorporate it directly into the loss function. For many machine learning tasks, you will be encoding your labels as all-or-nothing one-hot encodings:

Animal	Cyclist	Pedestrian	Sign
0	1	0	0

Suppose, however, that this was your actual label confidence from your annotations:

Animal	Cyclist	Pedestrian	Sign
0	0.7	0.3	0

Instead of declaring "Cyclist" to be the correct label and encoding it as 1, your model might allow your objective function to take 0.7 as the value that your loss function is trying to minimize. That is, you are asking the model to converge on 0.7 instead of 1.0 for this example. If you have confidence intervals, you have some more options. Suppose that our confidence is 0.7, plus or minus 0.1:

Animal	Cyclist	Pedestrian	Sign
0	0.7 (±0.1)	0.3 (±0.1)	0

In this case, we might be equally happy if the model converges on any value between 0.6 and 0.8 for "Cyclist." So, we can modify our training to account for this result. Depending on your architecture, you may not have to change the output of the loss function itself; you may be able to skip this item in any training epoch when the model is predicting "Cyclist" between 0.6 and 0.8.

If you have a more finely calibrated understanding of your label confidence, you can modify the output of the loss function itself. If you are 0.7 confident in the label, but with a Gaussian degree of certainty on either side of that 0.7 number, you might be able to incorporate the degree of uncertainty into your loss function, forgiving some but not all of the loss, as the prediction is closer to 0.7.

You can experiment with the methods in this section programmatically, so it should be relatively easy to try different ways to incorporate the annotators and annotation uncertainty in your models to see how they work for your tasks.

9.9 Further reading for advanced annotation

This chapter mostly used the relatively simple example of labeling at the image and document level, with some extensions to semantic segmentation and machine translation. Chapter 10 talks about how these methods can be applied to many types of machine learning problems. The same principles apply, but some techniques are better or worse for certain problems.

Some of the further reading in this section assumes more complicated tasks than labeling, so depending on the paper, you may want to read chapter 10 before returning to the literature.

9.9.1 Further reading for subjective data

In 2017, Dražen Prelec, H. Sebastian Seung, and John McCoy published "A solution to the single-question crowd wisdom problem" (http://mng.bz/xmgg), specifically looking at answers for which the actual response rate is more popular than predicted response, even if it is not the most popular response overall. (This paper is not open.) Dražen Prelec's original manuscript for BTS for subjective data is at https://economics .mit.edu/files/1966. A shorter version, later published in *Science*, is at http://mng.bz/ A0qg.

For an interesting extension to BTS that addresses some of the concerns raised in this chapter, see "A Robust Bayesian Truth Serum for Non-Binary Signals," by Goran Radanovic and Boi Faltings (https://www.aaai.org/ocs/index.php/AAAI/AAAI13/ paper/view/6451).

9.9.2 Further reading for machine learning for annotation quality control

For methods to calculate confidence that combines machine and human confidence, see "Beyond Accuracy: The Role of Mental Models in Human-AI Team Performance," by Gagan Bansa, Besmira Nushi, Ece Kamar, Walter Lasecki, Daniel Weld, and Eric Horvitz (http://mng.bz/ZPM5).

For the problems with annotator bias in NLP tasks, see "Are We Modeling the Task or the Annotator? An Investigation of Annotator Bias in Natural Language Understanding Datasets," by Mor Geva, Yoav Goldberg, and Jonathan Berant, who suggest that evaluation data (test sets) should be created by different annotators from those creating the training data (http://mng.bz/RX6D).

"Learning from Noisy Singly-Labeled Data," by Ashish Khetan, Zachary C. Lipton, and Anima Anandkumar, gives a detailed method for estimating confidence in annotations by using both annotator performance and model predictions (http://mng .bz/2ed9).

One of the earliest and most influential papers about using model predictions as labels is "Learning from Labeled and Unlabeled Data with Label Propagation," by Xiaojin Zhu and Zoubin Ghahramani (http://mng.bz/1rdy). Both authors continue to publish papers related to active learning and semi-supervised learning, which are also worth looking into.

9.9.3   *Further reading for embeddings/contextual representations*

More than any other machine learning research featured in this book, the literature for transfer learning looks the least far into the past. Embeddings started with methods such as latent semantic indexing (LSI) in information retrieval to support search engines in the 1990s and the 2000s saw many supervised variations of LSI, often with clever ways of getting free labels, such as looking at links between documents. Supervised embeddings became widely popular in computer vision in the early 2010s, particularly with transfer learning from large computer vision datasets like ImageNet, and in NLP in the late 2010s. NLP and computer vision scientists, however, rarely reference one another or early information retrieval work. If you are interested in this topic, I recommend looking into all three fields.

You can start with the seminal 1990 paper "Indexing by Latent Semantic Analysis," by Scott Deerwester, Susan Dumais, George Furnas, Thomas Landauer, and Richard Harshman (http://mng.bz/PPqg).

For cutting-edge research on how contextual models with more labels on adjacent tasks can help, see "Intermediate-Task Transfer Learning with Pretrained Language Models: When and Why Does It Work?", by Yada Pruksachatkun, Jason Phang, Haokun Liu, Phu Mon Htut, Xiaoyi Zhang, Richard Yuanzhe Pang, Clara Vania, Katharina Kann, and Samuel R. Bowman (http://mng.bz/JDqP). As an extension to this paper in multilingual settings, see this paper by the same authors, with Jason Phang as lead researcher: "English Intermediate-Task Training Improves Zero-Shot Cross-Lingual Transfer Too" (http://mng.bz/w9aW).

9.9.4   *Further reading for rule-based systems*

For current research on rule-based systems, see "Snorkel: Rapid Training Data Creation with Weak Supervision," by Alexander Ratner, Stephen H. Bach, Henry Ehrenberg, Jason Fries, Sen Wu, and Christopher Ré (http://mng.bz/q9vE) and the list of applications and resources on their website: https://www.snorkel.org/resources.

For a nonfree resource that dives deep into these technologies, see Russell Jurney's upcoming (at the time of publication) book *Weakly Supervised Learning: Doing More with Less Data* (O'Reilly).

9.9.5   *Further reading for incorporating uncertainty in annotations into the downstream models*

For recent research on ways to model uncertainty about annotations in downstream models, "Learning from noisy singly-labeled data" (section 9.9.2) is a good starting point, tackling the hard task that arises in the case of little agreement information and many errors by annotators.

Summary

- Subjective tasks have items with multiple correct annotations. You can elicit the set of valid responses that people might give from the annotators and then use methods such as BTS to discover all the valid responses and avoid penalizing correct but rarer annotations.

- Machine learning can be used to calculate the confidence of a single annotation and to resolve disagreements among annotators. For many annotation tasks, simple heuristics are not enough to accurately calculate annotation quality or to aggregate the annotations of different people, so machine learning gives us more powerful ways to create the most accurate labels from human annotations.

- The predictions from a model can be used as the source of annotations. By using the most confident predictions from a model or by treating a model as one annotator among other annotators, you can reduce the overall number of human annotations that are needed. This technique can be especially helpful when you want to take the predictions from an old model and use them in a new model architecture and when annotation is a time-consuming task compared with accepting or rejecting model predictions.

- Embeddings and contextual representations allow you to adapt the knowledge from existing models into your target model as feature embeddings or tuning pretrained models. This approach can inform your annotation strategy. If you can find a related task that is 10 times or 100 times faster to annotate than your target task, for example, you might get a more accurate model if you devote some resources to the simpler task and use the simpler task as an embedding in the actual task.

- Search-based and rule-based systems allow you to quickly filter and possibly label your data. These systems are especially useful for annotating a model quickly with noisy data and finding important low-frequency data to annotate.

- Light supervision on unsupervised models are common ways that annotators, especially SMEs, bootstrap a model from a small number of labels or perform exploratory data analysis when the goal is improved human understanding of the data, not necessarily a supervised model.

- Synthetic data, data creation, and data augmentation are related strategies that create novel data items, especially useful when the available unlabeled data does not contain the required diversity of data, often because data is rare or sensitive.

- There are several ways to incorporate annotation uncertainty into a downstream model: filtering out or de-weighting items with uncertain label accuracy, including the annotator identities in the training data, and incorporating the uncertainty into the loss function while training. These methods can help prevent annotation errors from becoming unwanted biases in your models.

Annotation quality for different machine learning tasks

This chapter covers

- Adapting annotation quality control methods from labeling to continuous tasks
- Managing annotation quality for computer vision tasks
- Managing annotation quality for natural language processing tasks
- Understanding annotation quality for other tasks

Most machine learning tasks are more complicated than labeling an entire image or document. Imagine that you need to generate subtitles for movies in a creative way. Creating transcriptions of spoken and signed language is a language generation task. If you want to emphasize angry language with bold text, that task is an additional sequence labeling task. If you want to display the transcriptions like the speech bubbles of text in comics, you could use object detection to make sure that the speech bubble comes from the right person, and you could also use semantic segmentation to ensure that the speech bubble is placed over background elements in the scene. You might also want to predict what a given person might rate the film as part of a recommendation system or feed the content into a search engine that can find matches for abstract phrases such as *motivational speeches.*

For this one simple application to add subtitles to video, you need many types of annotation to train your models. Chapters 8 and 9 covered introductory and advanced techniques for annotation, using image- or document-level labeling as the example task in most cases. This chapter covers methods of managing annotation quality for additional types of machine learning tasks.

You are most likely to use the methods in isolation and can skip to the section of interest. If you have a more complicated task such as the movie example, however, or if you are interested in adapting different types of annotation techniques, it is valuable to understand all the methods for machine learning problems. Ground truth data, interannotator agreement, machine-learning-driven methods, and synthetic data are all useful, and their effectiveness and actual implementation designs vary among machine learning tasks. Therefore, each section of this chapter highlights the pros and cons of annotation quality control strategies. We will start with the simplest task beyond simple labeling—annotating continuous data—and expand into more complicated machine learning scenarios.

10.1 Annotation quality for continuous tasks

If you are annotating data that is continuous, than many of the quality control strategies are the same the same as for labeling at the image/document level, but there are important differences about what counts as ground truth, agreement, subjectivity, and (especially) aggregating multiple judgments. We will cover each topic in turn in the following sections.

10.1.1 Ground truth for continuous tasks

Ground truth for continuous tasks is most often implemented as an acceptable range of responses. If you have a sentiment analysis task on a 0–100 scale and have a positive item, you might accept any annotation in an 80–100 range as being correct and anything below 80 as incorrect. This approach allows you to treat quality control as though it were labeling, so all the methods in chapter 9 can be applied.

The acceptable range will depend on your exact task. If you are asking people to read a number in an image—such as the time, temperature, or battery charge—you might allow only exact matches.

If you have established a range of acceptable answers, you can calculate the individual annotator accuracy in the same way that you did for labeling tasks: calculate how often they fall within the acceptable range for each ground truth response.

10.1.2 Agreement for continuous tasks

If your data is ordinal—such as a three-point "Bad," "Neutral," "Good" scale—you should also look into the Krippendorff's alpha example for ordinal values in chapter 8. You need to change the label weight inputs only to adapt from a labeling task to a continuous task.

As with ground truth data, you can treat two annotations within an acceptable range of each other as being in agreement and use the methods in chapter 9 to calculate agreement for labeling tasks. For expected agreement, you can calculate how many annotations would randomly be in a given range. If you are accepting an 80–100 range for a sentiment task, you will calculate how many annotations are in the 80–100 across all your annotations (figure 10.1).

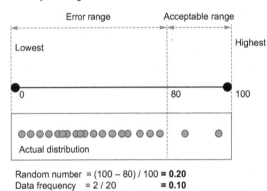

Figure 10.1   Two ways of calculating the expected agreement in a continuous task: the chance that a random number falls in that range, and the percentage of annotations across the entire dataset that fall into the range

The expected agreement might be smaller if your dataset has mostly negative sentiment, like the example in figure 10.1 for the 80–100 range. For a response in the 10–30 range, where there are many more responses, the expected agreement will be much higher.

The distributional properties of the data allow more detailed agreement calculations. If you have a normal distribution, you could use standard deviations instead of the ranges in our example. So if you are confident in your statistical abilities, look at the distributional properties of the data.

10.1.3 Subjectivity in continuous tasks

Continuous datasets can be deterministic or subjective, or a dataset might be deterministic for some items but not for others. Figure 10.2 shows an example.

As figure 10.2 shows, you might have deterministic and nondeterministic data even within one dataset. For this reason, this book can't give you one techniques that will apply to every possible dataset; you will need to estimate how much of your dataset is subjective and factor this estimate into your quality control strategy.

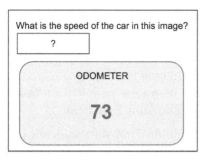 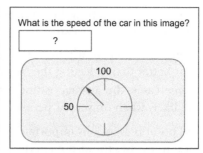

Figure 10.2   An example of deterministic and nondeterministic continuous tasks: estimating the speed of a car from an image of the odometer. Imagine that you had two annotations, 73 and 78. For the left image, the image is digital, so you know that there is a correct answer. Perhaps the image is blurry, which made the 3 look like an 8. So the correct strategy is to pick the better annotation (73 or 78). But for the analog odometer on the right, 73 and 78 are both reasonable estimates, and the average of 75.5 is probably better. So the correct strategy is to aggregate the annotations.

For inherently ambiguous or subjective items, you can ask the annotators for a range instead of a single value. You can reduce accomodation bias by asking what range annotators think other people will annotate, as in chapter 9 for subjectivity for categorical labeling (section 9.1) but in this case for ranges.

10.1.4   *Aggregating continuous judgments to create training data*

Aggregation for continuous variables can use the wisdom of the crowds. The classic examples are guessing the weight of a cow or the number of marbles in a jar; the average guess is typically closer to the correct value than most people's guesses. Figure 10.3 shows an example distribution.

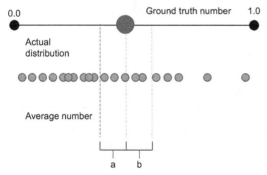

Figure 10.3   An example of wisdom of the crowds. Although the average score of the 20 annotators (the dashed line) is not correct, it is closer to the correct (ground truth) score than 15 of the 20 annotators' individual scores. Therefore, the average number is more accurate than most annotators.

Most people are farther from the real (ground truth) score than the average. Of 20 people, only 5 are closer (a = b).

As figure 10.3 shows, we expect the average annotation to be better than most annotators' annotations, with two caveats:

- Although the average will be better than most people, it is not necessarily optimal or better than selecting the best annotation in all cases.
- In some cases, the average is not better than most people for a task, which is more likely when only a few people are annotating each item.

This second point is especially important for training data. Most academic papers that look at continuous tasks for wisdom of the crowds assume that there is a crowd! It would be too expensive to have hundreds of people annotate every data point; it is more typical to have five or fewer people. So when people talk about wisdom of the crowds in relation to crowdsourcing, it applies least well to typical crowdsourced annotation systems.

As a general guideline, if you have fewer than five annotators, you should consider selecting the best annotator; if you have hundreds of annotators, you should take the average. For anything in between, you'll have to choose the right strategy for your data and problem. Figure 10.4 illustrates when to apply the wisdom-of-the-crowds methodology.

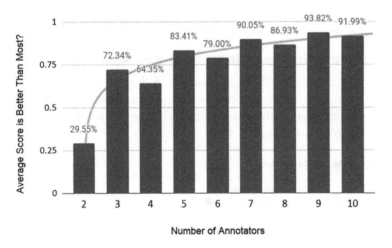

Figure 10.4 For wisdom of the crowds, you need the crowds. This graph shows how often the average score of the annotators is closer to the ground truth score than most annotators. If there are three annotators, about 70% of the time, the average score of those annotators will be closer to the actual score than at least two of those annotators. It is rare to have more than ten annotators for each item when creating training data, and this graph shows that the average annotation is better than most annotators about 90% of the time when there are ten annotators.

Figure 10.4 shows what the wisdom-of-the-crowds distribution looks like on a dataset that assumes a normal distribution. In this example, for three or more annotators, you are still better off taking the average score than picking the score of one of the annotators at random. This example data assumes a normal distribution in which the correct score is the mean, median, and mode of the annotators' individual scores. Your own data's distribution is probably less reliable, with the mean (average) annotation drawn from non-normal distributions that will tend to be higher or lower than the true scores. So you should calculate your own graph as in figure 10.4, using your ground truth data, and see how reliably you can use the average score for continuous data. You may find that selecting one annotator's score is more reliable than taking the average, especially if you have a small number of annotators.

For the normal distribution in figure 10.4 and for most other distributions, at least one annotator will be closer to the ground truth than the average most of the time, which sets up competing observations about your aggregation strategy:

- Most of the time, the average annotation will be better than randomly selecting any single annotation.
- Most of the time, at least one annotation will be better than the average annotation.

You can tune your strategy based on how many annotations you have and how confident you are in individual annotators. If your data looks like figure 10.4, and you have only two annotators, you should randomly choose one of those two rather than taking the average. If you have three annotators and are not certain whether any of those annotators is more accurate than the others, you should use the average. If you have three annotators and are more than 73.34% certain that one of those annotators is more correct than the others, you should choose that annotation instead of the average.

If your data is inherently nondeterministic, you might choose not to aggregate at all; you might include every annotation that you trust as a training item. Having a valid range of responses in your training data will also help stop your model from overfitting.

10.1.5 *Machine learning for aggregating continuous tasks to create training data*

Continuous tasks lend themselves well to machine-learning-driven quality control. You can apply most of the machine learning techniques from quality control for labeling tasks in chapter 9, but instead of predicting the labels, your machine learning model can use regression to predict a continuous value.

To predict the correct annotation using sparse features, you should be able to encode the actual annotations directly. The feature space will look more or less the same as for labeled data, but instead of the 1 or 0 values, you will have the actual number that each annotator annotated. If an annotator regularly annotates too high in the ground truth data, the model will take that fact into account when predicting the correct annotation. You may need to scale the annotations to a 0–1 range, depending on your architecture, but should otherwise be able to include these sparse features without additional processing. If you have a large number of annotators, your data might be too sparse, and as with labeling tasks, you can aggregate some of the annotations for a denser representation.

If you have data that is homogenous across the possible ranges, you might get better results by encoding the annotations relative to the average score. Figure 10.5 shows an example.

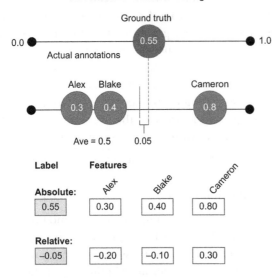

Figure 10.5   **A comparison of absolute and relative encodings when using machine learning to predict the correct number from the annotations. Here, Alex, Blake, and Cameron have annotated 0.3, 0.4, and 0.8 for a ground truth item for which the actual value is 0.55. We can encode the absolute values of the annotations with the ground truth as the label (target value) for this training-data item. Alternatively, we can take the average of the annotators, which is 0.5, and encode the fact that this value should be 0.05 higher. We similarly encode each annotation by how much it differs from the average. Another way to think of the relative encoding is that it is encoding the *error* of our average instead of the values.**

If your data is homogenous—if 0.05 error is equally likely in all parts of your data, for example—the relative encoding in figure 10.5 is likely to be a more accurate representation for machine learning to assist in quality control. You can also combine all these features into one model: absolute features, relative features, aggregate (dense) features, metadata, model predictions, model embeddings, and so on. As with the categorical data examples, you need to be conscious about how many dimensions you end up with, because you are likely to have limited ground truth data for the training data. Start with simpler models and a small number of aggregate features to establish a baseline, and build from there.

10.2   Annotation quality for object detection

Object detection is often divided into object labeling (identifying the label of an object) and object localization (identifying the boundaries of that object). In our examples, such as active learning for object detection in chapter 6, we assume that a bounding box is used for localization, but other types are possible, such as polygons or dots marking the center.

Object labeling follows the same quality control methods as image labeling, the main example in chapters 8 and 9. Quality control for object localization annotation quality control is most often completed via workflows, for practical reasons: it takes only a few seconds to evaluate the quality of a bounding box that may have taken a few minutes to draw. So you are typically adding less than 10% more time and cost to an annotation task by adding a review step to a workflow for bounding-box annotation. This approach is often more efficient than implementing automated quality controls. The example workflow in chapter 8, repeated in figure 10.6, is one such case.

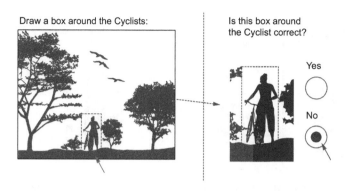

Figure 10.6 A review task in which an annotator is evaluating whether a bounding box (typically created by a different annotator) is correct or incorrect. Review tasks form the backbone of many quality control strategies when programmatic quality control is difficult or will take more resources.

Including a review task like the one shown in figure 10.6 can reduce the overall cost because you won't need to give the bounding-box drawing task to many people. Review tasks with a simple accept/reject distinction will not tell you how big the errors were, however, so it can still be useful to compare the bounding boxes with ground truth data bounding boxes in some cases. It can also be useful to look at agreement between annotators for all the reasons outlined in chapter 8 on the benefits of agreement, especially for identifying potentially ambiguous items. Having some statistical quality control for object detection annotations is typically a good idea in addition to reviewing tasks in workflows.

Next, we'll revisit the metrics of model uncertainty introduced in chapter 6, applying them to human quality and uncertainty. Note that some of this section duplicates the section on active learning for object detection in chapter 6, because the metrics for uncertainty in human quality are the same as for model uncertainty. Because you may be reading the chapters out of order or after a break, some important metrics are repeated here.

10.2.1 *Ground truth for object detection*

Ground truth examples for object detection are most often created by a small number of expert annotators. To align incentives, it is generally better to pay people by the hour when you want the most accurate bounding boxes possible, because it can be a time-consuming process to get a box as accurate as possible, and paying per task does not align effective hourly compensation with the need for good data.

You can create ground truth data as part of a workflow, too. Figure 10.7 shows how figure 10.6 can be extended so that an expert annotator can turn a nonexpert annotation into a ground truth example, editing the actual box only when necessary.

It is common to allow a margin of error when comparing an annotation with a ground truth example because the boundary might be ambiguous at the level of a few pixels. You can use the experts to calibrate the margin of error for your data. If expert annotators disagree by up to 3 pixels relatively often, it may be OK to forgive any errors that are 3 pixels or less. You might also allow for a wider margin of error when

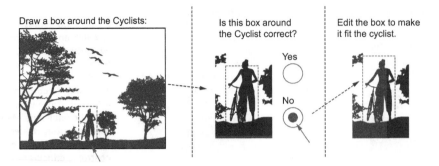

Figure 10.7   **Extending the review task in figure 10.6 so that an expert annotator can edit the bounding box created by nonexpert annotators. This approach is one way to create ground truth data.**

people are estimating the boundaries of objects that are not fully in view (occluded behind another object) or out of frame.

As with labeling tasks, you may want to specifically sample ground truth items for diversity. In addition to labels and real-world diversity, the sample could include diversity in object size, object dimensions, and the location of the object within the image.

Intersection over union (IoU) is the most common metric for calculating annotator accuracy compared with ground truth. Figure 10.8 shows an example of IoU. Accuracy is calculated as the area where the predicted and actual bounding boxes intersect, divided by the total area covered by those two boxes.

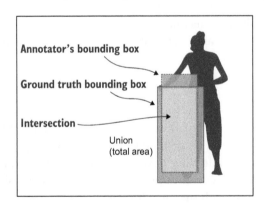

Figure 10.8   **An example of IoU for measuring the accuracy of a bounding box (location accuracy). The accuracy is calculated as the area that intersects the annotator's bounding box with the ground truth bounding box, divided by the area that is the union of the two boxes.**

It is rare for IoU to be corrected for random-chance guessing for object detection. If the objects are small relative to the image size, the difference may not matter because the random chance of guessing a meaningfully overlapping box is so low. You may have cases, however, in which the objects take up a large percentage of the image, especially if you have workflows in which people are asked to add or edit a box on a zoomed-in image.

If you want to adjust for random chance, you can take the percentage of the image that is within the box as the baseline. Suppose that an annotation has an IoU of 0.8, and the object takes up 10% of the image:

Adjusted IoU = 0.8 − (0.1 / (1 − 0.1)) = 0.6889

This adjustment calculation is the same as though the entire image were said to be the object because the IoU of 10% of the image, compared with all of the image, is 10%.

IoU is stricter than precision, recall, and F-score in that it tends to have lower values over the same data. Think of IoU in terms of the amount of area (or pixels) that are correct or incorrectly predicted:

$$\text{precision} = \frac{\text{true positives}}{\text{true positives} + \text{false positives}}$$

$$\text{recall} = \frac{\text{true positives}}{\text{true positives} + \text{false negatives}}$$

$$\text{IoU} = \frac{\text{true positives}}{\text{true positives} + \text{false positives} + \text{false negatives}}$$

IoU is more frequently used in computer vision, which does not allow a direct comparison with accuracy on tasks that use precision, recall, or a combination of the two (such as F-score, the harmonic mean of precision and recall). If you use precision, recall, and F-score instead of IoU, you should still use the whole image object as the basis for adjusting for chance, but note that you will have a different number. Suppose that the annotation has an F-score of 0.9 for the same object that takes up 10% of the image:

Expected precision = 0.1
Expected recall = 1.0
Expected F-score = (2 * 0.1 * 1.0) / (0.1 + 1.0) = 0.1818
Adjusted F-score = 0.9 − (0.1818)/(1 − 0.1818) = 0.6778

You can see that although we started with 10% different accuracies for IoU and F-score (0.8 and 0.9), when we adjusted for chance, they end up much closer to a 1% difference (0.6889 and 0.6778). You can experiment with your dataset to see whether there is a significant difference between the two approaches to accuracy.

10.2.2 *Agreement for object detection*

Label agreement for object detection is the same as for image labeling; you can calculate the level of agreement between each label and adjust it according to the baseline of random-chance guessing one of those labels. As with image labeling, you need to decide which baseline calculation is most appropriate for your data: random label, data frequency, or most frequent. (See section 8.1 for definitions.)

Localization agreement between two annotators is calculated as the IoU of their two boxes. The agreement for the entire object is the average of all pairwise IoUs. Figure 10.9 shows an example of multiple bounding boxes annotated for one image.

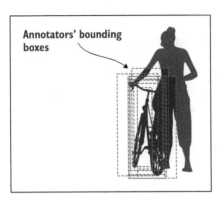

Figure 10.9   **An example of multiple bounding boxes from multiple annotators. Overall agreement is calculated as the average pairwise IoU of all boxes.**

You can use the same adjustment for random chance that you used for ground truth, but note that this practice is rare; most people look at agreement in object detection by using only unadjusted IoU.

10.2.3 *Dimensionality and accuracy in object detection*

Object detection can produce lower scores than other machine learning tasks as a result of the dimensionality of the problem. If an annotator's box is 20% bigger than the ground truth on each side, it is 40% bigger per dimension. For two dimensions, $140\%^2 = 196\%$, making the error almost twice the size, so an annotator's 20% error can become an IoU score of about 51%. This figure goes up with dimensions. A 3D bounding box that is 20% larger in all dimensions produces an IOU of about 36%.

This example highlights one reason why annotation accuracy for object detection can be so difficult: the metrics we use for comparison will compound the errors. This margin of error can be important for some tasks. Suppose that you are trying to predict the volume of cardboard boxes for shipping logistics or stocking supermarket shelves. If you forgave the annotators within a 5% margin of error, which sounds like a reasonable error, and an annotator goes over by 5% on all dimensions, 33% ($110\%^3 = 133.1\%$) is added to the total volume! If your model is trained on data with 33% error, you can't expect it to predict with greater accuracy when deployed. So you should be careful when designing your task and deciding the acceptable level of annotation accuracy. If you are tracking the annotators' accuracy across different types of work, such as image-level labeling, it may be simplest to track their accuracy for object detection separately from other tasks rather than let their low object detection results bring down their general accuracy score.

10.2.4 Subjectivity for object detection

You can treat subjectivity for object detection the same way that you treat subjectivity for continuous tasks: you can ask the annotators whether multiple viable boxes are possible for an object and ask them to annotate those boxes. You can treat each of those boxes as a viable annotation and potentially end up with multiple boxes per object.

You can also ask annotators what they think other people would annotate to elicit a more diverse range of responses and to make annotators more comfortable annotating a valid but minority interpretation.

10.2.5 Aggregating object annotations to create training data

The problem with aggregating multiple annotations into a single bounding box is similar to the problem with continuous values: there is no guarantee that the average bounding box is the correct one or that any single annotator has the correct one. For example, if you are putting a bounding box around a "Pedestrian" wearing a backpack, it may be correct to include or exclude the backpack, but the average of half a backpack won't be correct.

You can use multiple strategies to aggregate bounding boxes. This list is loosely ordered from the most effective to the least effective strategies I have encountered:

- Add a task for experts to review or adjudicate each box.
- Use the average bounding box (but note the limitations).
- Use the most accurate annotator's box.
- Create the minimum box that surrounds the boxes of *N* annotators.
- Use machine learning to predict the best box (section 10.2.6).

The most effective strategy might not be the first one for your particular dataset. You may need a combination of strategies instead of one. For the fourth strategy, you also need to decide what *N* should be. If you have four annotators, should you aggregate by the smallest box that surrounds the annotations of two or three annotators? There might not be a right answer.

Overlapping objects can also present a tough problem for aggregating bounding boxes. Figure 10.10 shows an example of overlapping bounding boxes where two annotators have a different number of boxes.

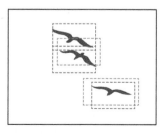

Figure 10.10 An example of overlapping bounding boxes. It is difficult to distinguish which box from different annotators applies to the same object. One annotator (long dashes) has annotated two objects. The other annotator (short dashes) has annotated three objects.

You can use several methods to determine how many objects are within one area of an image, often in combination:

- Create a separate task to ask how many objects appear.
- Add a task for experts to review and adjudicate overlapping boxes.
- Use a greedy search technique to combine boxes from different annotators.

You have different options for aggregation, as in the third strategy. A simple option is to use the maximum IoU as the criteria for which two boxes to combine next. You can assume one box per object per annotator (although there may be errors) and an IoU threshold below which you won't combine.

A greedy search is not necessarily optimal, so in theory, you could extend this strategy to a more exhaustive search of your data. In practice, if you can't resolve overlapping objects with a simple greedy search, you should use a separate review or adjudication task.

10.2.6 *Machine learning for object annotations*

The most powerful way to use machine learning for bounding-box annotation is to predict the IoU of every annotated box. This approach allows us to get a confidence score for each annotation that will be more accurate than taking the average IoU of each annotator.

For every bounding box that annotators created on the ground truth data, the IoU of that bounding box becomes the target for your model to predict. In addition to the image itself, you can encode the features related to each annotation, which can include

- The bounding box from each annotator
- The identity of each annotator
- The label that the annotator provided in their annotation

These features will help the model weight the relative accuracies of the annotators, taking into account the fact that they can be more or less accurate on different types of images. Having encoded the training data, you can train your model with a continuous-output function to predict the IoU. Apply that model to predict the IoU of any new bounding box created by an annotator to get an estimate of the IoU for that annotator for that bounding box.

You can also experiment with ensembles of models and/or Monte Carlo sampling within one model to get multiple predictions per bounding box. This approach will give you a clearer idea of the range of possible IoUs for that annotator for that image. Note that you need to be confident in your sampling strategy for ground truth data because you are using these images as part of your model. Any bias in the ground truth data can lead to bias in this technique for predicting the confidence of each annotator.

By looking at the predicted IoU of your annotators and their agreement, you can tune your overall workflow. You might decide, for example, to trust all annotations with predicted IoU over 95%, get an expert to review all annotations with predicted IoU between 70% and 85%, and ignore all annotations below 70%. The exact numbers can be tuned based on your data.

You can also use machine learning to aggregate bounding boxes from different annotators into a single bounding box. Although this approach is the most accurate way to aggregate bounding boxes, you might still have a workflow that experts review because often, it is too difficult to automate the aggregation process so that no errors get through.

As with continuous data, you can encode bounding-box locations by using absolute or relative encodings. Figure 10.11 shows an example of relative encodings.

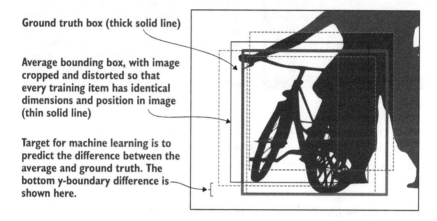

Ground truth box (thick solid line)

Average bounding box, with image cropped and distorted so that every training item has identical dimensions and position in image (thin solid line)

Target for machine learning is to predict the difference between the average and ground truth. The bottom y-boundary difference is shown here.

Figure 10.11 Relative encodings for bounding boxes. The image is cropped and stretched so that every training item has identical dimensions and position. The relative encoding addresses the problem with objects being in different locations within the image and lets the model focus on a smaller number of features to make the predictions.

The relative encodings in figure 10.11 are built on the same principles as the absolute and relative encodings for continuous tasks, covered in section 10.1.5. If your data is homogenous—if a 5-pixel error is equally likely in all parts of your images, for example—the relative encoding is likely to be a more accurate representation for machine learning to assist in quality control.

You can use many augmentation techniques to improve machine learning for aggregating bounding boxes. These techniques include flipping; rotating; resizing; blurring; and adjusting colors, brightness, and contrast. If you have worked in computer vision, you are probably familiar with these techniques for improving your machine learning model. If you have not worked in computer vision, learning about these techniques from an algorithm-focused computer vision book would be the best place to start.

10.3   Annotation quality for semantic segmentation

In *semantic segmentation,* also known as *pixel labeling,* annotators label every pixel in an image. Figure 10.12 shows an example repeated from chapter 6, in the section on active learning for semantic segmentation (section 6.2). Also see chapter 6 for more information about the distinction between object detection and semantic segmentation.

Figure 10.12   An example of semantic segmentation in which every pixel is labeled as "Person," "Plant," "Ground," "Bicycle," "Bird," or "Sky." This kind of colored photograph is what a lot of semantic segmentation tools look like: a coloring-in exercise. We'll cover those tools in chapter 11. If you're looking at this image in black and white, the contrastive shades of gray should give you a good idea of what the image would look like in color. If the different objects of the same class receive a label (the four trees are labeled separately, for example), the task is known as *instance segmentation.*

For most of the quality control that you need for semantic segmentation, you are simply adapting the methods for image-level labeling. But in this case, you are looking at the accuracy of every pixel instead of the label as a whole. You typically average the per-pixel annotation accuracy to get the overall annotation accuracy for the image.

10.3.1   Ground truth for semantic segmentation annotation

Comparing semantic segmentation annotations with ground truth data is like labeling at the pixel level: the percentage of pixels that the person labeled correctly relative to random chance. You might accept a small buffer (such as a few pixels) when an incorrectly labeled pixel is within a certain distance of a pixel with the correct label. You can treat those errors as though they were correct or ignore those pixels in your accuracy calculations.

If you forgive errors that occur within a few pixels of the correct answers, look carefully for errors that all annotators make on the same pixels near boundaries, because these errors can be the result of annotation tools. More than any other machine learning task, semantic segmentation uses smart tools, such a magic wand or lasso tool to select a region, to speed up the process. Those tools are typically based on simple heuristics such as contrast in adjacent pixels. If the annotators don't notice errors from using these tools, you will teach your model the simple heuristics of the tools instead of the correct boundaries between your labels. Errors from tooling can happen in any machine learning task, and chapter 11 goes into these problems more deeply, but this problem is flagged here because of how commonly it occurs in semantic segmentation.

You looked at the pattern of errors between labels for image labeling, and you should also look at the pattern of errors between pixel labels. You can weight some labels more than others if they are more important. If you care about bicycles more than the sky, for example, you can weight bicycles higher. Taking the macro average is the most common way to weight all labels equally. In some cases, you might even ignore some labels in the calculation of the accuracy, especially if you have a generic background label for everything you don't care about except when it is confused with other labels.

10.3.2 Agreement for semantic segmentation

You measure agreement for each pixel exactly the same as for image labeling: measuring the agreement between annotators on the label of that pixel. You can calculate the expected agreement in the same three ways: the frequency of that label across all the data, the frequency of the most common label, or the inverse of the total number of labels. You should choose the most appropriate expected frequency for your dataset. If you have a generic background label, the overall frequency of this label might be a good candidate for the expected agreement.

10.3.3 Subjectivity for semantic segmentation annotations

In practice, the most common way to resolve ambiguity for semantic segmentation is via review or adjudication. If a region is annotated as uncertain, or if annotators disagree, an additional annotator can adjudicate.

It is common for semantic segmentation tasks to require that all pixels receive a label, which can be problematic when annotators are uncertain about some regions or multiple interpretations are valid. The simplest way to elicit subjectivity for semantic segmentation is to have an extra label called "Uncertain" that the annotator can use to indicate that they don't know the correct label for that region. The "Uncertain" region can be a separate region, or you can ask the annotator to layer the "Uncertain" region on top of a completed segmentation so that you know what the most likely label was despite the confusion.

See section 10.7 for examples of how Bayesian Truth Serum (BTS) can be extended beyond labeling tasks. I am not aware of any work extending BTS to subjective semantic segmentation tasks, but the papers listed in section 10.7 would be the best places to start.

10.3.4 Aggregating semantic segmentation to create training data

Aggregating training data from multiple annotations is the same as for labeling tasks, but at per-pixel level. Although all the same strategies are available, however, it is expensive to give an entire image to an additional annotator when only a small amount of disagreement exists. So using workflows to adjudicate certain regions of the image is a better option in cases such as these:

- Give images with low agreement over the entire image to additional annotators.
- Use experts to adjudicate images that have low agreement in localized regions within an image.

Figure 10.13 shows an example of the adjudication process.

Figure 10.13 An example of semantic segmentation aggregation via workflows. Two annotators disagreed about a region, and that region is passed to a third annotator to review and adjudicate. There are two interface options: the adjudicator can select one of the two regions from the first two annotators, or they might annotate directly on the image, where the region with disagreement is presented as unannotated.

As figure 10.13 shows, you can define a region of disagreement as any set of contiguous pixels where there is low agreement among annotators. You can define agreement at the pixel level in the same way as for labels: percentage of agreement among annotators, potentially taking into account your confidence in their accuracy. In practice, you are unlikely to have more than two or three annotators per image because semantic segmentation is a time-consuming task. You might simply treat any disagreement as a region that needs to be adjudicated instead of setting a threshold via performance on ground truth data.

Assuming that you have a limited budget to adjudicate the disagreements, you can rank-order disagreements across the dataset by size and adjudicate from largest to smallest. You can also take the level of disagreement into account.

If you care about some labels more than others, stratify the adjudication according to how much you care about each label. If you care about bicycles ten times more than you care about the sky, adjudicate ten disagreements that might be "Bicycle" for every one disagreement that might be "Sky." Don't try to apply that 10:1 ratio as a weighting to the region size, because it is too difficult to hand-tune these kinds of heuristics.

10.3.5 Machine learning for aggregating semantic segmentation tasks to create training data

You can use the same machine learning methods for semantic segmentation that you did for labeling, but at the individual pixel level. One added complication is that you might need to resolve disagreements within unrealistic patchworks of pixels. If the wing of the birds in figure 10.13 became a checkerboard of "Sky" and "Bird" pixels, that result might be worse than incorrectly calling the entire wing "Sky" because you would be erroneously teaching your downstream model that checkerboard patterns are possible.

To simplify the application of machine learning, you can implement a model to predict the binary "correct"/"incorrect" distinction for each pixel. Using your held-out ground truth data, build a model to predict which pixels were labeled incorrectly by your annotators, apply all your newly labeled data, and generate candidate "incorrect" regions for expert review.

This machine-learning-driven method can be especially effective for discovering errors that come from the tooling, such as a smart selection tool. It is likely that in some cases, two or more annotators will have the same errors due to the tooling, and agreement won't discover these regions as being potential errors. Your ground truth data, however, should tell you what kind of errors to expect from tooling (maybe "Sky" is called "Trees" too often); therefore, your model will predict the errors in similar parts of other images.

10.4 Annotation quality for sequence labeling

In practice, sequence labeling uses human-in-the-loop methods for annotation more often than not. The most common use case is identifying rare sequences of text, such as the names of locations in long documents. Annotation interfaces for sequence labeling, therefore, typically present candidate sequences for review or generate sequences with autocompletes rather than ask annotators to annotate raw text.

You can use different kinds of interfaces for this kind of review task in sequence labeling, and chapter 11 covers them. For review tasks, quality control can be implemented in the same way as labeling tasks, which is an additional advantage of this approach to sequence labeling: it is easier to perform annotation quality control on a binary or categorical labeling task than on a sequence labeling task.

You can't always annotate sequence data as a review task, however, especially at the start of a project, when you don't yet have a model that can be used to predict sequence candidates in unlabeled data. You also run the risk of perpetuating model bias by surfacing only candidates from your existing model. So it is still useful to run some annotations on raw, unlabeled data.

The quality control methods for sequence labeling follow many of the methods in chapter 6 on active learning for sequence labeling. This section will revise them, assuming that you might not have read the section on active learning (or not recently). Let's revisit the example from that section:

> "*The E-Coli outbreak was first seen in a San Francisco supermarket*"

If you are implementing a model to track outbreaks from text reports, you may want to extract information from the sentence, such as the syntactic category (part of speech [POS]) of each word ("Nouns," "Proper Nouns," "Determiners," "Verbs," and "Adverbs"), the name of the disease, any locations in the data, and the important keywords, as shown in table 10.1.

Table 10.1   Types of sequence labels: POS; keyword detection; and two types of named entities, diseases, and locations. The POS labels are one per token and can be treated similarly to labeling tasks for quality control. "B" (Beginning) is applied to the beginning of the span, and "I" (Inside) is applied to the other words within the span. Marking the start explicitly allows us to unambiguously distinguish spans that are next to each other, such as "San Francisco" and "supermarket." This encoding technique is called IOB tagging, in which "O" (Outside) is the nonlabel. ("O" is omitted from this table for readability.) For multispan tasks, such as keywords and entities, quality control is more complicated than for labeling tasks.

	The	E-Coli	outbreak	was	first	seen	in	a	San	Francisco	supermarket
POS	DET	PNOUN	NOUN	VERB	ADV	VERB	PRP	DET	PNOUN	PNOUN	NOUN
Keywords		B	I						B	I	B
Diseases		B									
Locations									B	I	

In the literature, you will most commonly see IOB tagging for spans, as in table 10.1. You might define multitoken spans in different ways for different types of labels. "E-Coli" is the one word as an entity but two words for the keyword phrase "E-Coli outbreak," for example. Strictly, the annotation convention in table 10.1 is called IOB2 tagging, and vanilla IOB uses "B" only when there are multiple tokens in a single span.

For longer sequences, such as splitting a document into sentences or identifying people taking turns in speech, you may want to annotate only the start or end of each sequence rather than the sequence as a whole for annotator efficiency.

10.4.1 *Ground truth for sequence labeling*

For most sequence labeling tasks with multitoken spans, quality control is evaluated over the correctness of the entire span. If an annotator identified "San" as an entity but did not identify "Francisco" as part of that same entity, the annotator is not awarded partial accuracy. Unlike object detection in computer vision, there is no widely used convention like IoU for sequences of text.

If you have a contiguous task such as our named entity example, it can be insightful to look at per-token accuracy in addition to full span accuracy. My recommendation is to separate the label task from the span task when evaluating annotator accuracy:

- Calculate *label* accuracy on a per-token basis. If someone labels only "San" as a location, they get that label correct, but "Francisco" would be a false negative for location and a false positive for whichever other label was chosen.
- Calculate *span* accuracy on the entire span. If someone labels only "San" as a location, they get 0% credit for the span.

This distinction allows you to separate an annotator's pragmatic understanding of what words belong to which labels from their syntactic understanding of what constitutes a multitoken phrase in the instructions.

You can combine per-label accuracies with micro or macro average to calculate the overall accuracy for that annotator. You might drop the "O" (nonspans) from this calculation if you have sparse data, especially if you are calculating the micro average, because otherwise, the "O" tokens will dominate the accuracy. You can make this decision based on how you are evaluating your downstream model: if you are ignoring the "O" tokens when evaluating your model accuracy (except as false positives and false negatives in other labels), you can ignore the "O" label for evaluating annotator quality.

If you want to compare the accuracy of the annotator on this task with their accuracy on other tasks, you need to include the "O" label and adjust for random-chance. Although ignoring the "O" task is similar to adjusting for random chance, it will not produce the same final accuracy score, because ignoring the "O" does not account for its actual frequency.

Get the instructions correct!

I have built named entity datasets for almost every major tech company and for specific use cases including public health, auto, and finance. In all cases, we spent more time on refining the definition of what goes into a span than on any other part of the task, working closely with the annotators to incorporate their expertise into the decision process. An example is when "San Francisco" is written as "San Francisco city," should "city" be part of the location? What if it was "New York city"? We often see "New York City" or the abbreviation "NYC," but not "SFC," so these cases might be different. Also, in the San Francisco Bay area, San Francisco is known as "The City." When should this name be called a location—only when capitalized, and if so, what about in social media, where it may not be capitalized regularly? What about other languages, which use capitals for entities rarely or not at all?

These types of cases are where most errors occur in most sequence tasks, both in annotation and machine learning models. It's important to work closely with annotators to identify tough cases and add them to instruction. You can also include some of these cases in the nonrepresentative portion of your ground truth data.

10.4.2 *Ground truth for sequence labeling in truly continuous data*

Unlike our text examples, which are contiguous sequences, some sequence tasks are truly continuous. Speech and signed languages are two good examples. Unlike text, spoken language doesn't leave gaps between most words, and signers don't pause between words when signing them. In both cases, our brains add most gaps between words later from a continuous input, so there isn't always a single obvious point where one word ends and the next one begins.

This example is similar to the bounding-box examples in computer vision in section 10.2, where IoU is used to measure ground truth accuracy. The convention for quality control in most sequence tasks, however, is to allow a margin of error from a ground truth example and not use IoU.

But there is no reason not to use IoU if it makes sense for your particular sequence task, even though it has not been the convention for language data. In that case, you can use the methods for ground truth accuracy and agreement in section 10.2. You will gain one advantage, too: because sequences are 1D, the effects of the margin of error won't be as bad as the 2D and 3D annotations that are more common in computer vision.

10.4.3 *Agreement for sequence labeling*

For tasks in which every token or pre-segmented sequence receives a label, as in POS tagging, you can treat each token or segment like a single labeling task and apply the labeling methods from chapters 8 and 9.

For text sequence tasks with sparse labels, such as the keyword extraction and named entity recognition examples, agreement can be calculated on a per-token basis or across the span. I recommend separating the prediction of the span itself from the label, along the same division as for ground truth data:

- Calculate label agreement on a per-token basis. If one annotator labels only "San" as a location, and another labels "San Francisco," there is 50% agreement for the label.
- Calculate span agreement on the entire span. If one annotator labels only "San" as a location, and another labels "San Francisco," there is 0% agreement for the span.

Use review and adjudication tasks to resolve disagreements. If annotators disagree on the boundaries of two overlapping spans, have another annotator resolve that disagreement. It is typically prohibitively expensive to have an entire document annotated by a large number of annotators to resolve a single dispute, so a simple adjudication system is typically your best bet.

10.4.4 *Machine learning and transfer learning for sequence labeling*

All state-of-the-art sequence classifiers use pretrained contextual models. You should experiment with these models for your own sequence tasks, keeping in mind that as you get more training data, different pretrained models may be more or less helpful than others. It is easy to understand why pretrained models help. For our location example, a model pretrained on billions of sentences will have learned that "City," "Village," "Town," and other location names are semantically similar and that the words preceding them are more likely to be locations. But it probably takes millions of documents before you see enough examples of "City," "Village," and "Town" in enough similar contexts that a pretrained model can make that generalization, and you are unlikely to be annotating millions of documents annotated for your sequence labeling task.

If you have pretrained models and also have access to those models' training data, you should use representative sampling as one of your active learning strategies to sample items that are most similar to your target domain. If you have a large amount of unlabeled data in your target domain, you can also try tuning the pretrained models to your domain.

As section 10.4 stated, most real-world annotation strategies for sequence labeling use model predictions as candidate sequences for human review. The model is used to predict candidate sequences, and annotators can accept or reject those annotations as a binary task that allows for easy quality control. Make sure that you create some ground truth examples of good and bad examples so that you can evaluate annotators against ground truth on the binary review task, in addition to looking at agreement.

There is a risk of bias by using model predictions to generate candidates. Annotators might be primed to trust the model predictions when the model is incorrect. This type of bias is covered in chapter 11.

Another potential source of bias from using model predictions is that you will miss sequences that the model did not predict with any confidence. This bias can amplify the bias in your model if you are not careful. A good solution that can also help with embeddings is to have a simple task in which all texts are evaluated for whether they contain a sequence. Figure 10.14 shows an example for location entities.

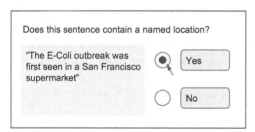

Figure 10.14   An example of a labeling task that asks whether a sequence is present in the text without asking the annotator to label that sequence. This approach is especially useful for quickly ensuring that no text is missed for potential entities, and it can use a broader workforce that might not be as accurate in identifying the entity boundaries.

Using a workflow like the one shown in figure 10.14 and using a separate task to get the actual sequence span reduces the chance that the sequences will be missed because they were not candidates from your model.

One byproduct of using a task to reduce bias and engage a broader workforce is that you can build a model specifically to predict whether a sequence occurs. This model can be used as an embedding for your actual sequence model, as in figure 10.15.

If you have a much larger volume of data that is labeled as containing or not containing the sequence, architectures like the one shown in figure 10.15 can improve the accuracy of your downstream model. See section 9.4 for strategies for annotating data on adjacent tasks to create representations for transfer learning.

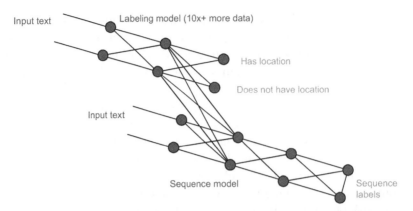

Figure 10.15   **An example of a labeling task that asks whether a sequence is present in the text, which creates a model that can be used as an embedding within the sequence labeling task. This approach is especially useful when there is a much larger volume of data with annotations for the labeling task than for the sequence task (ten times or more) which can be the byproduct of workflows aimed at reducing bias and engaging nonexpert annotators.**

10.4.5 *Rule-based, search-based, and synthetic data for sequence labeling*

Rule-based, search-based, and synthetic data generation methods are especially useful for generating candidates within sparse data. With our location example identifying sequences like "San Francisco," there are several ways to use automated annotation to get a quick start on generating candidates. You might use a list of known place names as a rule-based system or construct synthetic sentences from that same list of place names, for example.

I've used all these methods for sequence annotations, typically taking the ratio of relevant annotations in something like 100:1 when randomly sampled to an initial ratio closer to 2:1. These methods allows the model to be bootstrapped quickly when there is little initial data.

Using synthetic data also improves the coverage. When I have built named entity systems for organizations, for example, I typically made sure that there were at least a few synthetic training-data examples with the names of all the products, people, locations, and other entities that were important to that organization.

10.5 *Annotation quality for language generation*

For most language generation tasks, quality control is done by human experts, not automated. When humans create translations of sentences from one language into another, for example, quality control is typically implemented by an expert translator who reviews the work and evaluates the quality of the translations.

This situation is also true of the models themselves. Most of the literature for language generation quality control is about how to trust the human experts for their subjective judgments. There is a large body of literature about how to judge the quality of machine translation output on a 1–5 scale, knowing that each 1–5 judgment can be a subjective task. Data sampling for evaluation data is important in these cases too, because instead of using held-out data for automated analysis, people need to spend time evaluating the output manually, which is expensive. So it is extra-important to evaluate on a combination of randomly sampled data and/or data that is representative of the diversity of data where your model is deployed.

The right workforce is the most important factor in creating quality training data for language generation tasks. As stated in chapter 7, it can take a lot of careful planning to make sure that you have the required language fluency and diversity among your annotators. See the following sidebar for an interesting story about the lengths you may need to go to find the right people.

Confessions about sourcing languages
Expert anecdote by Daniela Braga

At our company, we pride ourselves on going the extra mile to ensure that we're getting the best data, which sometimes leads to hilarious situations. For text and speech data, the hardest problem is often finding fluent speakers. Finding people with the right qualifications and who speak the right language is one of the most difficult and overlooked problems in machine learning.

Recently, we were doing a major project collection for a client with specific language requirements. After a few missed attempts to source the right people for a rare language, one of our people went to a church where he knew he'd find individuals who would meet the requirements. Although he found the people he needed for our client, he accidentally turned up during confession time. The priest assumed that he was there for this reason, so true to form, he made his full confession, including about sourcing languages.

Daniela Braga is founder and CEO of DefinedCrowd, a company that provides training data for language and vision tasks (including text and speech in more than 50 languages).

10.5.1 Ground truth for language generation

When automated analysis *is* possible with ground truth data, there are often multiple acceptable ground truth answers, and the best match is used. Machine translation datasets often have multiple translations of the same sentence, for example. A machine-translated sentence is compared with each of the ground truth translations, and the best match is considered to be the appropriate one for calculating accuracy.

For machine translation, you have many ways of calculating the match, the simplest and most widespread being bilingual evaluation understudy (BLEU), which calculates the percentage of matching subsequences between the machine translation and the ground truth example. Most automated quality control metrics for sequence tasks use simple methods like BLEU, looking at the percentage of overlap between the output and a set of ground truth examples.

For annotation quality, you often need to create multiple ground truth examples for evaluation data. Depending on that type of task, those examples could be multiple valid translations of one sentence, multiple summaries of a longer text, or multiple replies that a chatbot could make to a prompt

You should ask annotators to come up with multiple solutions each in addition to giving the task to multiple annotators in parallel. For more sophisticated quality control, you could have the experts rank the quality of the ground truth data examples and incorporate that ranking into your evaluation metrics.

10.5.2   *Agreement and aggregation for language generation*

Interannotator agreement is rarely used for language generation tasks itself, although it can be used for people judging the quality of the generated text. In theory, you could track when an annotator is disagreeing with other annotators by looking at the difference between their text and other annotators using BLEU, cosine distance, or other metrics. In practice, it is much easier to have an expert quickly review their output for quality.

It is rarely meaningful to aggregate multiple language generation outputs into a single training data item. If the model requires a single piece of text, that task is most often done by selecting the best candidate from the examples. Although this task could be done programmatically, it is rarely done that way in practice. If you have multiple annotators generating text for the same task, having one expert select the best one takes little additional time.

10.5.3   *Machine learning and transfer learning for language generation*

Because it takes a lot of time to create data for language generation manually, you can get great speed-up from machine learning. In fact, you probably use one example of this kind of technology regularly. If your phone or email client offers predictive next-word or sentence-completion functionality, you are the human in human-in-the-loop sequence generation! Depending on the technology, the application might be using transfer learning by starting with a general sentence-completion algorithm and gradually adapting the model to your text.

You can implement this kind of architecture in many ways; it doesn't need to have real-time interactions like the sentence-completion technologies. If your sequence generation model can produce a large number of potential outputs, you can use an expert-review task to choose the best one, which can speed things greatly.

10.5.4   *Synthetic data for language generation*

Synthetic data is popular for many language generation tasks, especially when there are gaps in the diversity of available raw data. One solution for translation is to give the annotators the word and ask them to create both the original sentence containing that word and the translation. You can use other annotators to evaluate how realistic the examples sentences are. For transcription, you can ask someone to speak a sentence with certain words and transcribe it; for question-answering, you can ask someone to provide both the question and answer. Quality control in all cases becomes a labeling task for evaluating the quality of the generated examples and can follow the quality control methods in chapters 8 and 9.

Figure 10.16 shows a workflow for language generation. The annotators are given two types of data that they need to create and use that data to create synthetic examples. For the machine translation example, the two types might be two words that don't currently occur in the training data, and the annotators are asked to create multiple sentences using those words and the translations of those words.

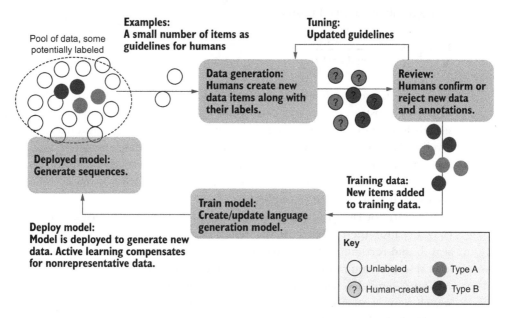

Figure 10.16 A workflow for generating data in contexts where no unlabeled data exists. This workflow looks similar to the other human-in-the-loop workflows, but there is no automation on the data-creation side. Humans look at existing examples and are given instructions about the types of examples that they need to create (Type A and Type B here). Those examples are added to the training data.

The hardest part of synthetic data generation is diversity. It is relatively easy to prompt people to use certain words or to talk about certain events. When they're put on the spot, however, people tend to use more formal language and much shorter sentences compared with natural language, in which people are not self-conscious. Chapter 11 covers some techniques to get data that is as natural as possible.

10.6 *Annotation quality for other machine learning tasks*

The same quality control techniques using ground truth data, interannotator agreement, and machine-learning-driven annotation apply to many other machine learning tasks. This section covers a few more at a high level to highlight important similarities and differences.

10.6.1 Annotation for information retrieval

Information retrieval is machine learning field that covers systems that drive search engines and recommendation systems. Many annotators are employed to tune the results of search engines. These systems are some of the oldest and most sophisticated human-in-the-loop machine learning systems.

In the case of search engines, model accuracy is typically evaluated in terms of whether the relevant results are returned for a given query. To weight the first results more highly than the later results, information retrieval is typically evaluated with methods such as discounted cumulative gain (DCG), where rel_i is the graded relevance of the result at a ranked position p:

$$DCG_p = \sum_{i=1}^{p} \frac{2^{rel_i} - 1}{\log_2(i+1)}$$

The log() is used to de-weight the lower entries. You may want the first search result to be the most accurate; you care slightly less about the second search result and slightly less again for the third search result, and so on. For ground truth data, annotators can be evaluated by producing a ranking of candidate responses that maximizes DCG. In other words, the optimal ranking is one that puts the most-relevant first, the second-most-relevant second, and so on. A good annotator is someone whose ranking is closest to ground truth examples.

It is rare for DCG to be adjusted for random chance in information retrieval, typically because there are so many potential responses for "needle-in-the-haystack" search and recommendation systems that random chance is low. In other words, the data is sparse, and random chance is often close to zero.

The sparseness can prevent effective random sampling, too. If an annotator searches for "basketballs" on a web search engine and has to choose results on a randomly selected page, chances are that all the results will be irrelevant. Similarly, if an annotator searches for "basketballs" on a shopping site, and random products are returned, all the results are probably irrelevant. The annotation interface will use existing models to return relevant results instead of random samples.

To get a 0–1 score for the annotator, normalized discounted cumulative gain (NDCG) can be calculated. NDCG is the annotator's actual score divided by the highest possible score (a perfect ranking from the ground truth data that was presented to the annotator). This score, which normalizes based on what an annotator saw (maybe 10 to 15 candidates) rather than across all possible candidates, is the most popular alternative to random-chance-adjusted accuracy for information retrieval.

Because they oversample higher-likelihood candidates, information systems have the potential to amplify bias, because only high-probability items are returned as candidates. This bias can potentially be balanced by adding a small number of low-probability results to increase the diversity of potential choices. NDCG should be used in these cases; otherwise, the score from the annotator will be artificially low.

Information retrieval systems can also be biased if they are tuned by end users' selections, because most queries tend to be about a small number of high-frequency phrases. Annotators who are employed to tune the models can also be used to balance the training data by being given disproportionately more diverse phrases to evaluate. Knowing how much of your training data comes from annotators or end users informs your active learning strategies too.

Sometimes, you can't simulate someone using an information retrieval by asking annotators to judge relevance, because you are not optimizing for relevance. In these cases, the machine learning model is often optimized for business-oriented metrics: the number of purchases a person makes, the number of clicks or seconds between a search and when a purchase is made, the value of the customer over the next six months, and so on. Because they are about the actual use of the model, these metrics are sometimes called *online metrics*, as opposed to F-score and IoU, which are *offline metrics*.

Information retrieval systems often use other types of machine learning to provide additional features/metadata that will help the information retrieval system. A movie will likely be tagged with the genre of film, for example, and a recommendation system will suggest movies in a genre that it thinks you will like. Examples of tasks that feed into information systems include:

- Labeling query phrases by topic, such as classifying "basketball" searches as types of "sports equipment" to narrow the search results
- Performing object detection to allow search, such as allowing someone to search for products by uploading a photograph of that product
- Labeling genres of content, such as classifying music into categories such as "uplifting" and "dark" to make music recommendations suited to the user's taste
- Labeling the types of locations on a map, such as classifying whether a shop is a grocery or a retail store to improve geographic searches
- Extracting sequences within the content, such as extracting the name, size, color, brand, and similar qualities of a product to support advanced search systems

In all cases, the tasks are simpler than information retrieval itself: labeling, object detection, and sequence labeling. But the components were used by information retrieval systems optimized for user behavior, such as how often the user returned to that company's website. In these cases, the people who build the actual information systems track the importance of these components.

Another useful technique in information retrieval is query reformation, an augmentation technique strategy used by most search engines. If someone searches for "BBall" and doesn't click any results but immediately searches for "Basketball," that fact tells you that "BBall" and "Basketball" are closely related terms, and results for "Basketball" should be similar to those for "BBall." This simple but smart technique produces free additional training data that also adapts your model closer to your end users' preferred interactions.

10.6.2 *Annotation for multifield tasks*

If your annotation task has multiple fields, you should consider breaking the task into subtasks and connecting the subtasks via workflows. Either way, evaluate quality on the individual fields in addition to the task as a whole. Consider the example of tracking outbreaks from text like this:

"The E-Coli outbreak was first seen in a San Francisco supermarket"

If you explicitly wanted to capture the information about this event, the annotation might look something like this:

Disease: E-Coli; Location: San Francisco

So you could evaluate accuracy on "Disease" and "Location" separately, and also evaluate accuracy on the entire event. Note that our example is a simple one, but not all text will be so obvious. Consider these two examples:

"The E-Coli outbreak was first seen in a supermarket far from San Francisco"

"E-Coli and Listeria were detected in San Francisco and Oakland respectively"

In the first example, we don't want to include the location. The second example has two events that we want to capture separately. The task isn't simply a matter of matching every location in a sentence with every disease; it's a more complicated problem of annotation and machine learning. You could break this task its subtasks and semi-automate it with machine learning so that it becomes three labeling tasks:

- Label sentences yes/no as to whether they talk about disease outbreaks.
- Label candidate locations and candidate diseases.
- Label candidate combinations of locations and diseases as the same event.

With the right workflows, interfaces, and reviews and adjudications, the system for annotating complicated events can become a series of labeling tasks for which quality control is much easier than for quality control over the entire event.

Most more complicated annotation tasks like this example can be broken into simpler tasks. The exact interface, quality controls, and machine learning components depend on how you break up the task, the workforce(s) you are using, and the nature of the task itself. But most people can follow the pattern of breaking a complicated task into simpler review tasks on machine learning predictions.

10.6.3 *Annotation for video*

Most quality control methods for images also apply to object detection and/or semantic segmentation in videos. If you need to identify points in time or segments in the videos, the methods from continuous data and sequence labeling also apply.

For object tracking, you are combining the methods for localization (the bounding box), sequence labeling (the frames in which the object is visible), and labeling (the label applied to the object). As in those examples, it is easier to track those metrics separately than try to combine them into a single annotator accuracy score.

Some common video annotation tasks can be treated purely as sequence labeling tasks. A camera recording a person driving a car, for example, can be annotated for the sequences when they don't appear to be looking at the road. The methods for sequence labeling can be applied to these tasks.

Ground truth for object detection and/or semantic segmentation in videos is typically calculated on individual frames. If your videos vary greatly in length, you may want to sample an equal number of frames from each video data instead of randomly sampling frames across all your videos, which would bias toward the longer videos.

Interannotator agreement for video tasks is calculated according to whichever subtask is being evaluated: labeling, object detection, sequence identification, and so on. Those methods should apply to video annotation. As with ground truth data, I recommend that you track agreement separately rather than try to combine them into a single agreement calculation.

Video annotation lends itself well to machine learning automation. A machine learning model can track the movement of objects, for example, and an annotator needs to correct the frames only when the prediction is wrong. This practice can provide substantial speed-up but also perpetuate bias in the model.

Synthetic data can also be effective for video annotation but has limited diversity. If you are creating the objects yourself in a simulated 3D environment, you already have perfect annotations for where those objects move, and you can create many orders of magnitude more data than by human annotation for the same budget. The synthetic data is likely to lack diversity, however, and may introduce pathological errors into the data, making models worse on real-world data. You typically have to be careful with this method and use it in combination with real-world data, using representative sampling to make sure that your annotators work on real-world data that is the most different from your synthetic data.

10.6.4 *Annotation for audio data*

Speech annotation professionals often have highly specialized annotation tools. Professional transcribers use foot pedals that allow them to move a recording backward and forward quickly, for example. Speech segmentation and transcription interfaces predate computers, with many of the specialized technologies having been developed for tape recorders almost a century ago. We'll cover the intersection of quality control and interfaces for audio in chapter 11.

Audio can be annotated as a labeling task, a sequence task, or a generation task, depending on the annotation requirements. Identifying whether human speech occurs is a labeling task, annotating when a certain person is speaking is a sequence task, and transcribing speech is a generation task. You can apply those techniques to these tasks.

Synthetic data is common in speech, especially when humans are asked to speak certain phrases. There aren't many recordings of people speaking different languages that are available as open data. Where those recordings do exist, speech is often sensitive, so even a company that could capture a lot of speech data, such as a mobile-phone company, generally shouldn't capture that data and should be careful about who can hear that data to annotate it. Therefore, asking someone to read text out loud is often the main way that many speech recognition datasets are created.

Synthetic data is also used to ensure diversity of speech. Some combinations of phonemes (individual spoken sounds) are rare in most languages, for example. To make sure that the rarer combinations exist in the training data, people are often be given scripts of nonsensical text to read aloud; the words are carefully chosen to cover the rarer phoneme combinations. This approach might be repeated for people who speak with different accents.

Because of the sensitivity, companies that make smart devices have entire fake living rooms, bedrooms, and kitchens constructed to collect data. Actors are paid to interact with the devices, saying many commands while following instructions such as "Sit on the sofa facing away from the device." If you already work in this area, I recommend inviting your friends and family members to visit one of these studios without giving them any context. It is truly bizarre to walk into a large, dark warehouse with a fake living room set up in the center, populated by people speaking nonsensical words: the experience feels like shape-shifting aliens are preparing to infiltrate the Earth.

10.7   *Further reading for annotation quality for different machine learning tasks*

The literature for quality control for different tasks is sparser than for the other topics in this book, but some relevant papers discuss almost everything covered in the chapter.

10.7.1   *Further reading for computer vision*

A good recent paper on agreement is "Assessing Data Quality of Annotations with Krippendorff Alpha for Applications in Computer Vision," by Joseph Nassar, Viveca Pavon-Harr, Marc Bosch, and Ian McCulloh (http://mng.bz/7Vqg.)

One of the most in-depth studies showing that there is no one right interface for all computer vision tasks is "Two Tools Are Better Than One: Tool Diversity As a means of Improving Aggregate Crowd Performance," by Jean Y. Song, Raymond Fok, Alan Lundgard, Fan Yang, Juho Kim, and Walter S. Lasecki (http://mng.bz/mg5M). This paper is also a good source of references to other recent work in annotation for computer vision.

For data augmentation techniques in computer visions that are used for models but can be applied to annotation, I highly recommend *Computer Vision: Algorithms and Applications*, 2nd ed., by Richard Szeliski (http://szeliski.org/Book).

For an interesting example of automating whether drawing a bounding box or having a review task is optimal for a certain image, see "Learning Intelligent Dialogs for Bounding Box Annotation," by Ksenia Konyushkova, Jasper Uijlings, Christoph H. Lampert, and Vittorio Ferrari (http://mng.bz/5jqD).

10.7.2 *Further reading for annotation for natural language processing*

Specific to natural language processing, "Inter-Coder Agreement for Computational Linguistics," by Ron Artstein and Massimo Poesio, is a good foundational work that is especially strong for its discussion of agreement in sequence labeling and the complications with overlapping spans and identifying tokens or segments (http://mng .bz/6gq6).

For language generation, a good recent paper is "Agreement is overrated: A plea for correlation to assess human evaluation reliability," by Jacopo Amidei, Paul Piwek, and Alistair Willis (http://mng.bz/opov). Note that they are talking about evaluating machine output, so the paper focuses on evaluation data, but this method can be applied to training data.

A recent paper that looks at automated ways to evaluate text generation using machine learning methods that take advantage of pretrained models is "BLEURT: Learning Robust Metrics for Text Generation," by Thibault Sellam, Dipanjan Das, and Ankur P. Parikh (http://mng.bz/nM64). See the references within the paper for other recent work on automated approaches to evaluating the quality of text generation systems.

10.7.3 *Further reading for annotation for information retrieval*

See "How Many Workers to Ask?: Adaptive Exploration for Collecting High Quality Labels," by Ittai Abraham, Omar Alonso, Vasileios Kandylas, Rajesh Patel, Steven Shelford, and Aleksandrs Slivkins (http://mng.bz/vzQr).

Summary

- All machine learning tasks can take advantage of annotation strategies such as ground truth data, interannotator agreement, breaking tasks into subtasks, expert review and adjudication tasks, synthetic data, and (semi)automation via machine learning. Each approach has strengths and weaknesses, depending on the task, the data, and the problem that you are addressing.
- Continuous tasks can accept a range of acceptable answers and in some cases can use wisdom of the crowds to determine whether it is better to accept the annotation of the best annotator instead of the average annotation value for an item.
- Object detection tasks should track localization accuracy and label accuracy separately. Be cautious that IoU will produce lower scores in higher dimensions for the same general level of annotator performance.
- Semantic segmentation can take advantage of review tasks in which expert annotators can adjudicate regions of disagreement instead of reannotating the entire image.
- Sequence labeling tasks typically use human-in-the-loop systems to generate candidates, especially when the important sequences are relatively rare.

- Language generation tasks typically have multiple acceptable answers. These answers can be evaluated against multiple ground truth examples per item or evaluated by humans who rate the output and are in turn evaluated on the accuracy and agreement of their ratings.
- Other machine learning tasks, such as information retrieval, often use human-in-the-loop annotation systems, especially when a random sample of data would rarely surface relevant items.

Part 4

Human–computer interaction for machine learning

The final two chapters complete the loop with a deep dive on interfaces for effective annotation and three examples of human-in-the-loop machine learning applications. The chapters bring together everything you have learned in the book so far, showing how the interface design strategies are influenced by your data sampling and annotation strategies. The most optimal systems are designed holistically with all components in mind.

Chapter 11 shows how human–computer interaction principles can be applied to annotation interfaces and how different types of interfaces can automate some of the annotation process. The chapter covers the nontrivial trade-offs in interface design among annotation efficiency, annotation quality, agency of the annotators, and the engineering effort required to implement each type of interface.

Chapter 12 briefly discusses how to define products for human-in-the-loop machine learning applications and then walks through three example implementations: a system for exploratory data analysis for short text, a system to extract information from text, and a system to maximize the accuracy for an image labeling task. For each example, some potential extensions from other strategies in this book are listed, which will help you critically evaluate how to extend human-in-the-loop machine learning systems after you deploy your first applications.

Interfaces
for data annotation

In the past 10 chapters, we have covered everything about human-in-the-loop machine learning except the vital component of the human-machine interface. This chapter covers how to build interfaces that maximize the efficiency and accuracy of the annotations. This chapter also covers the trade-offs: there is no one set of interface conventions that can be applied to every task, so you must make an informed decision about what is the best user experience for your task and your annotators.

Suppose that you need to extract information about disease outbreaks from text. If you have subject-matter experts (SMEs) who are already completing this task manually, you may want to make some simple machine-learning-powered extensions to the application the experts are using without interrupting their existing work practices. If you are working with nonexpert annotators, you might create a new interface in which most annotators simply accept or reject the predictions from a model, because that interface will maximize efficiency while making quality control easier. If you have both workforces, you might choose both interfaces, using the appropriate one for each workforce.

For any interface, the wrong design can affect the quality and efficiency of the annotation process as a whole. Therefore, building the right interfaces for the right people is a complicated problem even before you add machine learning to the mix. This chapter provides the basic tools to design the right interface(s) for your annotation tasks.

11.1 Basic principles of human–computer interaction

First, let's look at some of the interface conventions for building annotation tools. These conventions and libraries for application development have been optimized by people who specialize in user experience and human–computer interaction, and they can be hard to improve. In some cases, you need to choose among multiple conventions. This section helps you understand the trade-offs.

11.1.1 Introducing affordance, feedback, and agency

Affordance is a design concept that holds that objects should function the way we perceive them to function. In the physical world, for example, a door handle should look like something you turn, and a door should look like something that swings open. In the online world, a button in an application should look like something that you can click. Other examples in online systems include menu systems at the top of a page that display navigation options when hovered over, clicking + to expand hidden content, and clicking ? to access help.

Feedback is the complement to affordance in user experience. If someone clicks a button, some animation, message, or other event should let the annotator know that their action has been recorded. Feedback validates affordance, telling the user that the affordance they perceived was real or that their perception was incorrect (in case there is no action or indication that the action was not legitimate).

An interface built with good affordance and feedback intuitively feels easy to use, so you most often notice it when the conventions are broken. Buttons that don't do anything when you click them feel broken, and you might miss the existence of a button if it looks like a static box. You have probably come across these types of buttons on badly made websites—mistakes that you don't want in your annotation interfaces.

(Hidden bookcase doorways are fun because they break these conventions, but breaking these conventions is rarely fun for annotation.)

Using existing elements within a UI framework generally helps with good design, affordance included. If you are using a web-based interface, you should use existing HTML form elements in their recommended contexts: radio buttons for single selections, check boxes for multiple selections, and so on.

Using existing UI components also improves accessibility. If you use the default HTML elements for buttons instead of creating your own, you better support people who translate those elements or create speech from the text.

Agency is the sense of power and ownership perceived by users. Good affordance and feedback in the design give annotators agency in their individual actions. Agency also refers to the annotator experience more holistically. Following are some of the questions that you need to ask to ensure that annotators feel agency in their work:

- Do annotators feel that the interface allows them to annotate or express all the information that they think is important?
- Do they sense how their work is helping the project on which they are working?
- If they are using interfaces in which machine learning is assisting their annotation, do they perceive the machine learning as improving their work?

This chapter offers examples of different kinds of affordances and feedback, and discusses how each kind relates to the agency of the annotator.

One of the biggest mistakes that people make in annotation interfaces is borrowing conventions from games. As mentioned in chapter 7, I do not recommend that you gamify paid work. If you force someone to do paid work within a gamelike environment, the work will get annoying quickly if it does not feel like the most efficient way to annotate data. See the following sidebar for more on why you don't want to gamify annotation tasks.

Good interfaces give you quality, not just quantity

Expert anecdote by Ines Montani

When I talk to people about usable interfaces for annotation, the reaction is too often "Why bother? Annotations aren't very expensive to collect, so even if your tool is twice as fast, that's still not that valuable." This viewpoint is problematic. First, many projects need buy-in from SMEs such as lawyers, doctors, and engineers who will be doing much of the annotation. More fundamentally, even if you're not paying people much, you still care about their work, and people can't give you good work if you set them up to fail. Bad annotation processes often force workers to switch focus between the example, the annotation scheme, and the interface, which requires active concentration and quickly becomes exhausting.

(continued)

I worked in web programming before I started working in AI, so annotation and visualization tools were the first pieces of AI software I started thinking about. I have been especially inspired by the invisible interfaces in games that make you think about what to do, not how to do it. But it is not gamification to make a task fun like a game; it is making the interface as seamless and immersive as possible to give annotators the best chance to do their task well. That approach results in better data and is more respectful of the people who create that data.

Ines Montani is co-founder of Explosion, a core developer of spaCy, and lead developer of Prodigy.

11.1.2 Designing interfaces for annotation

For simple labeling tasks, good affordance and feedback require using existing components according to their recommended purposes. Any framework you are using should have elements for single or multiple selections, text inputs, drop-down menus, and so on.

You might find some more sophisticated form elements in some frameworks. The React Native JavaScript framework, for example, has an autocomplete component in addition to more general form inputs. You and your annotators have probably used this autocomplete functionality in other web applications and have become familiar with the design conventions of React Native interfaces, so you gain usability by choosing an existing framework instead of creating your own autocomplete functionality.

Conventions evolve, so keep track of current ones when you are implementing your interface. Autocomplete, for example, has gained popularity only recently. Many websites that used large menu systems or radio buttons five years ago now use autocomplete. Your annotation interfaces should build on current conventions, whatever those conventions are when you are building the interface.

For sequence labeling tasks, you will most likely choose keyboard or mouse annotations, or both. In the case of keyboard annotations, the arrow keys should allow the annotator to navigate forward and backward on segments. In the case of mouse-based annotations, the annotator should be able to hover over and/or click the segments. In both cases, the affordance should ensure that the segment that is in focus is highlighted in some way so that the scope of the annotation is clear.

For object detection and semantic segmentation tasks, most widely used UI frameworks aren't enough. No standard UI library for HTML allows you to implement pixel labeling for semantic segmentation tasks, for example. For these tasks, you will use the conventions from image-editing software. The affordances will come from expectations such as the ability to select regions via boxes, polygons, and smart tools that capture regions of similar pixels.

If people are annotating on tablets or phones, affordances include the ability to pinch to zoom in images and to swipe the screen to navigate. Some web frameworks work well on tablets and phones, and some do not. You might consider building interfaces that are native to the Android and iOS operating systems for phones and tablets, but these kinds of annotation interfaces are rare; most people prefer to work on a computer if they will be working for an extended period.

11.1.3 Minimizing eye movement and scrolling

Try to keep all the components of an annotation task on the screen so that annotators don't have to scroll. Also, try to keep all the elements (instructions, input fields, item being annotated, and so on) in the same place for each annotation. If your items come in different sizes, use tables, columns, and other layout choices to make sure that the input fields and the item don't move around or become lost when different sizes are present.

You've probably experienced scrolling fatigue when reading online content. People become less attentive and frustrated when they have to scroll to find content that could have fit on the screen when it first loaded (known as *above the fold* because newspapers prioritized important content at the top of the paper so that it could be seen when folded). The same applies to annotation. If all the content can fit on the screen, scrolling will be a slower and more frustrating experience for annotators.

The instructions and guidelines for annotation can create a problem with fitting all information on the screen. You want detailed instructions for the annotators, but the instructions will take up a lot of the screen. Also, the instructions become redundant after an annotator has completed enough tasks to remember them, so it can be frustrating for annotators to keep scrolling past instructions that they no longer need. The simplest solution is to make the instructions collapsible so that they can be expanded when needed. Another option is to move some or all of the instructions to the relevant fields, showing them only when those fields are in focus. A third option is to have the instructions on a separate page and allow annotators to adjust their browser windows to show the separate annotation and instruction windows. Note that you'll need to take the smaller annotation window into account in your design if you choose the third option.

When considering effective design, it can be easiest to start with an example of what not to do. Figure 11.1 shows an example interface that breaks most of the rules of good UI design.

Now compare figure 11.1 with figure 11.2, which has a more annotator-friendly layout. Although the interface in figure 11.2 is only moderately more difficult to implement than the one in figure 11.1, some of the simpler changes, such as putting the source text next to the input fields, solve many of the problems with figure 11.1.

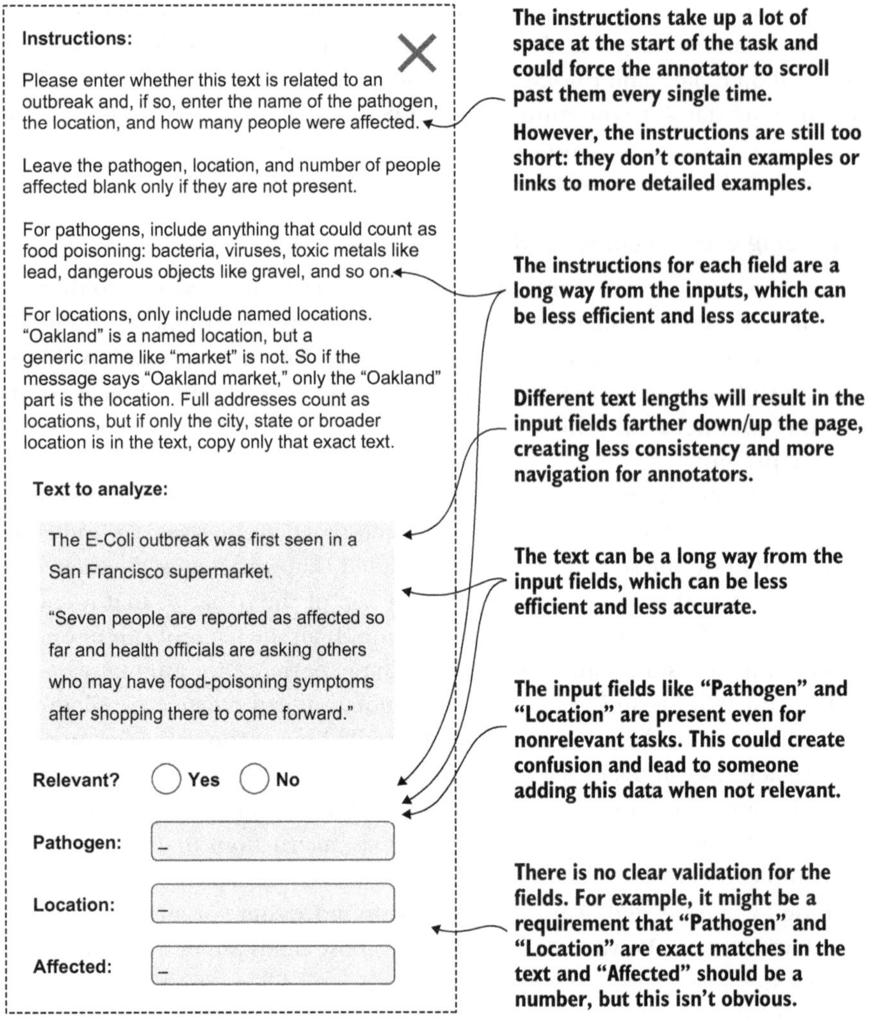

Figure 11.1 An example of a bad interface for annotation. This interface requires an annotator to continually move their attention around the screen, and the length of the input data can change the layout of the objects on the screen, which reduces consistency. This interface is likely to reduce the efficiency and accuracy of the annotations.

In addition to the other benefits in figure 11.2, the two-column layout is more likely to be suited to a horizontal monitor than the one-column layout in figure 11.1. You will need to make assumptions about the screen size and resolution of your annotators' machines, however, and about which browsers they are using.

Consider purchasing machines and/or screens for your annotators, depending on the type of workforce you are using and how long the engagement is. These purchases might pay for themselves via increased throughput and accuracy; they may also let

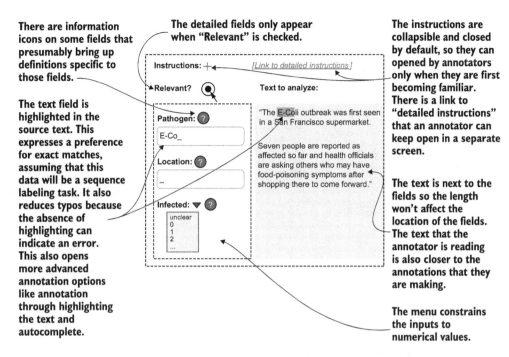

There are information icons on some fields that presumably bring up definitions specific to those fields.

The text field is highlighted in the source text. This expresses a preference for exact matches, assuming that this data will be a sequence labeling task. It also reduces typos because the absence of highlighting can indicate an error. This also opens more advanced annotation options like annotation through highlighting the text and autocomplete.

The detailed fields only appear when "Relevant" is checked.

The instructions are collapsible and closed by default, so they can opened by annotators only when they are first becoming familiar. There is a link to "detailed instructions" that an annotator can keep open in a separate screen.

The text is next to the fields so the length won't affect the location of the fields. The text that the annotator is reading is also closer to the annotations that they are making.

The menu constrains the inputs to numerical values.

Figure 11.2 An example of a good interface for annotation. This interface puts the source text closer to the fields where the annotations are being entered. It also provides multiple options for the annotator to access instructions, which don't interrupt the design or layout of the task. You can expect that this layout will be more efficient and more pleasant to use, and will result in more accurate data than the interface in figure 11.1. (Your interface should also have an obvious Submit button and fields for annotator feedback; these buttons are omitted here to keep the example less cluttered.)

your engineers spend less time ensuring compatibility for every possible browser and screen configuration.

Some assumptions about the layouts of pages have not been covered in this section. Figure 11.1 and to a lesser extent figure 11.2 are biased toward a left-to-right layout, for example. For writers of right-to-left languages, these layouts will not necessarily be intuitive. I recommend reading books dedicated to good web design (and in particular, good design for HTML forms) for deeper study of this topic.

11.1.4 Keyboard shortcuts and input devices

Keyboard shortcuts are central to almost all annotation projects but are easy to overlook. Keyboard shortcuts help with navigation and inputs.

Using a mouse to navigate is much slower than using a keyboard, so pay attention to the tab order (or tab index) of the inputs. Pressing Tab in most applications moves the focus from one element to the next. In the case of forms, this move is typically one form input to the next. The Tab key is the most important keyboard shortcut for efficient annotation, so the order in which an input comes into focus on the screen when

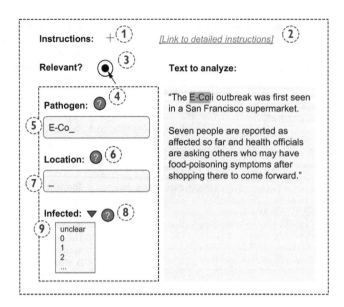

Figure 11.3   An example of tab order, showing the order in which pressing Tab will change the focus from one element to the next. This interface has nine clickable elements that would be part of the default order of focus for web-based interfaces, but only four of these elements are input fields for the annotation task, so the task could be improved by defining a different tab order.

the user presses Tab should be intuitive. Figure 11.3 shows the default tab order for the example interface in figure 11.2.

You may need to define the tab order explicitly to make this interface work. In figure 11.3, for example, the expected tab order after the Pathogen input is the Location input, but the default HTML tab order might put the information link for Location as the next focus. You can define tab order within HTML natively in ascending numerical order by using tabindex= or explicitly define the result of the keystrokes on some element by using JavaScript.

The same is true for navigation via arrow keys. There will be default orders for what comes into focus when a user presses the keys to navigate (the right-arrow key is typically the same as the Tab key), but you may need to explicitly change that order to one that is most intuitive for your interface.

You may need to make decisions about whether to suppress certain default keyboard options. If you are using a web form, pressing the Enter key submits that form. If you have text inputs that include newlines or allow Enter to autocomplete, you may want to suppress Enter from submitting the task unless a Submit button is in focus. Similarly, if your form consists primarily of autocomplete fields, and people expect to use Tab to complete the fields, you may want to allow tab-based navigation only via arrow keys or when Ctrl-Tab is pressed. You may need to do a few iterations of testing to get the focus navigation right.

If you can't reduce all annotation to keyboard shortcuts, you should consider giving your annotators the mouse or trackpad input that will be most suitable for their tasks. The same is true for other inputs, such as microphones, cameras, and specialized tools like the pedals that professional transcribers use to move audio and video records back and forward in time while leaving their hands free to type. You should try using anything you build yourself for a decent amount of time—at least 15 minutes for fast tasks and longer if the average per-task annotation time is more than a few minutes.

11.2 Breaking the rules effectively

You can break the rules of design when you are comfortable with implementing interfaces that adhere to conventions. This section provides three examples of less-conventional interfaces that have worked well for annotation: batch annotation with scrolling, foot pedals as inputs, and audio inputs. Note that you are likely to need to program the interaction scenarios yourself, including any accessibility considerations, so you will have to weigh the cost of implementation against the benefits.

11.2.1 Scrolling for batch annotation

Scrolling can improve annotation for labeling tasks when imbalance data exists. Suppose that you want to find pictures of bicycles from among thousands of images, most of which aren't bicycles. Scrolling through a large selection of images is more efficient than looking at them one by one and reduces some of the repetition priming problems introduced in section 11.3.1. There are good reasons why data is sometimes imbalanced, including random sampling, creating evaluation data on representative data that is inherently imbalanced, and spot-checking the predictions of a model that you know is applied to imbalanced data. When you can't avoid imbalanced data and can reduce the task to a binary decision, scrolling becomes a good convention to use.

11.2.2 Foot pedals

Foot pedals are not widely used with computers, which is a missed opportunity for improving annotation, considering how ubiquitous pedals are for operating vehicles and musical equipment. Pedals were first used in audio to allow people to move forward and backward in reel-to-reel audio recordings (as mentioned in chapter 10), and have remained popular to this day among people working in transcription. Outside transcription, they are not widely used in annotation. For any video or audio task, it should be possible to use pedals to allow annotators to scan backward and forward quickly. Consider purchasing pedals for your annotators if they are annotating audio, video, or any other streaming data and need to navigate back and forth. USB pedals are widely available and relatively cheap. The learning curve is short—on the order of hours, not days or weeks.

In addition to providing forward and backward navigation, pedals can be programmed to specific keys. A pedal-down operation can simulate a press of the Ctrl key, for example, or iterate through menu items. Changing a function is similar to how pressing a piano pedal changes the tone of a note, and iterating menu items is similar to how guitar players use a selector pedal to iterate through sound effects. These kinds of pedals are also widely available and optimized for user experience factors such as button spacing and (physical) affordance, so you can adapt these tried and tested conventions from the music industry to create some new and interesting annotation interfaces. If you annotate any kind of data, you may want to consider a pedal to help speed the process and reduce strain from repetitive hand and wrist movements by making them foot movements instead.

11.2.3 Audio inputs

If you are using your hands for a keyboard and mouse, and your feet have pedals, you have only your mouth left. Audio inputs are common for creating speech recognition data (obviously) but are not widely used elsewhere.

Audio can augment the labeling component of many annotation tasks. Suppose that you have are putting bounding boxes around 100 categories of objects. There is no menu system that an annotator can navigate easily to select 1 of 100 categories, and autocomplete takes their attention away from the item itself. If the annotator can speak the label, they don't need to take their attention away from the annotation process. In addition to labeling, audio can be used to navigate, via commands such as Next, Previous, Zoom, or Enhance.

> **TIP** If you allow speech-based annotation, consider using longer label names, because speech recognition is less accurate on short words. It is probably not worth the resources to create a customized speech recognition model only for annotation, which is why a lot of voice interfaces for voice interface systems fall back on numeric menu systems.

11.3 Priming in annotation interfaces

In addition to deciding on the right interface, you need to consider how order effects and other contextual factors might influence the annotations. Chapters 7, 8, and 9 covered methods for identifying the right workforce and evaluating quality. To summarize the main takeaways: you should ensure that your workforce has the correct training; track the demographic information of annotators that is relevant to the task and not a privacy violation; and employ quality control methods like ground truth data and interannotator agreement to ensure that bias is minimized.

As discussed in chapter 1, *priming* occurs when the annotation can be influenced by context, including task design and order of tasks. Priming is generally seen as being a bad thing, because you don't want the annotations to be influenced by the task itself. You want each annotation to be as objective as possible, although there are some exceptions that we will discuss in section 11.3.2. Priming might operate independently of each annotator's individual background or have a stronger effect on some annotators more than others, so it is important to think carefully about how priming and annotator backgrounds can combine to add bias to annotations.

11.3.1 Repetition priming

The most significant priming problem for annotation is repetition. Annotators might change their interpretation of an item based on the items that they have seen previously. Repetition priming is common in subjective tasks such as sentiment analysis; most annotators change their opinions about the border between adjacent categories such as negative and very negative over time as they recalibrate their interpretation based on the items they saw most recently.

With a large amount of repetition, attention and fatigue also become issues. Lack of diversity in data can lead to mindlessly clicking the same annotation even when it might be the wrong one. In many ordered datasets, the items nearest one another come from the same source and/or time, so randomizing the order of items is a simple way to minimize this effect.

Ensuring long-enough practice and training periods for annotators also helps them become familiar with the data so that they have configured their understanding of the data across more of it before their annotations start contributing to the training and evaluation data. For a task such as sentiment analysis, you might ask annotators to look at thousands of examples before beginning to annotate so that they have calibrated their ratings decisions first.

When you have imbalanced data, randomization and an extended practice period may not be enough. In these cases, you can implement some diversity sampling methods to ensure that each item is as different as possible from the previous one. For a labeling task, you can use the predicted labels to perform stratified sampling. Cluster-based sampling can also help, such as separating the data into 10 clusters and sampling from different clusters in sequence.

You can monitor repetition priming after the annotations, too. If you end up with high disagreement in your annotations, you should look at the sequence of previous annotations to see whether annotator agreement might come from ordering effects. The order of items should not be a predictor for annotations.

11.3.2 *Where priming hurts*

Priming hurts most when annotation requires subjective or continuous judgments. If there is an inherent ranking, such as rating the sentiment on a negative-to-positive scale, a person's interpretation might be influenced by repetition priming. In section 11.4.3, we'll talk about how framing this task as a ranking problem instead of a rating problem can minimize this type of priming. Although people may change the sentiment score over time, their judgment about the rank order of positive-to-negative sentiment is likely to be more stable.

Priming can also hurt categorical tasks in which two categories are close. Our example throughout the book of a person pushing a bicycle is one in which repetition could prime someone to label the image "Pedestrian" or "Cyclist" depending on what they annotated most recently. Chapter 1 offers a good example of associative priming: people were more likely to interpret an accent as being from Australia or New Zealand when a stuffed toy kangaroo or kiwi bird was in the room, even when no mention was made of the toys in the task itself.

11.3.3 *Where priming helps*

Priming is a good thing in some contexts. When annotators get faster over time because of their increased familiarity with the data, this effect is known as *positive priming*, which is almost always beneficial.

Being primed by context (context or associative priming) is also beneficial in some cases. If annotators are transcribing health-related audio and hear a word that might be *patients* or *patience*, they should know from the immediate context and from the task theme that *patients* is more likely. In this context, priming helps the task.

When priming changes someone's emotional state, this effect is known as *affective priming*. If annotators feel more positive about their work, they are more likely to work faster and be more accurate, so everyone wins. Although affective priming is not always desirable for subjective tasks that can have an emotional component, such as sentiment analysis, it can be valuable for motivation. Do you put music on to help your own work? If so, you can tell people that you are positive self-affect priming for productivity. Instead of treating priming as something that is always negative, think of it as a set of non-objective behaviors that you need to be mindful of and manage in your annotation and interface design.

11.4 *Combining human and machine intelligence*

Humans and machines have different strengths and weaknesses. By building to the strengths of each, you should be able to maximize the performance of both. Some of the differences are obvious. A human, for example, can give a short plain-text response about their confusion in a task in a much more sophisticated way than any of the methods for uncertainty and diversity that we covered in chapters 3, 4, 5, and 6. Other differences are more subtle and require a deeper understanding of human–computer interaction. As discussed, machines are consistent when predicting values in continuous tasks, but humans are inconsistent due to priming and will change their scores even when repeating a task.

Annotators quickly become experts on the data that they work on. Researchers are divided as to whether long-term priming exists; some claim that it does not. If long-term priming does exist, it is minimal. The low long-term impact of priming is good for annotation because it means that annotators are building their expertise over time while maintaining a high level of objectivity regardless of the particular data items they have seen, so long as they have seen a comprehensive variety of items. Because annotators are becoming immersive in the problems they are facing, giving and eliciting annotator feedback will improve your tasks.

11.4.1 *Annotator feedback*

You should always provide a mechanism for annotators to give you feedback about the specific tasks on which they are working. Annotators can give feedback on many aspects of the task, such as the intuitiveness of the interface, the clarity and completeness of the instructions, the ambiguity of some data items, the limitations of their knowledge of certain items, and other patterns and trends in the data that you may not have noticed.

Ideally, you should include the option for annotators to give feedback about a task within that task, perhaps via a simple free-text field. You can also invite feedback via email, forums, or real-time chat. Including feedback within the task is typically the easiest way to ensure that the feedback remains linked to the item being annotated, but other feedback mechanisms may be more suitable in some contexts. Forums, for example, can allow annotators who have similar questions to see the response. A real-time chat allows annotators to collaborate on hard-to-annotate items, the only downside being that quality control becomes harder when annotators aren't independent. (See chapters 8–10 on quality control for more about this topic.)

Feedback goes both ways: you should give feedback to annotators about how the annotations are being used. Everyone enjoys their job more when they know it is having an effect. Giving feedback can be difficult, however, if the downstream model isn't retrained for some time after annotations are made or if the use case or accuracy of the model is sensitive. That said, you should still be able to talk about the general value that the annotations are providing.

In some cases, the effect may be obvious, especially for a human task that machine learning is assisting. In our example of extracting information about outbreaks from text, if that extracted data was itself useful and not used only to train a machine learning model, that usefulness can be communicated to annotators.

Annotators' accuracy will improve if they have a better idea of the task that the machine learning model will be performing downstream. For a semantic segmentation task on photos taken outside, it will help annotators to know whether the goal is to count the leaves on trees or whether the trees are only the background in an application that focuses on objects in the foreground. Everyone wins when there is more transparency.

You can also incorporate feedback into the annotation task. If you are annotating sentiment, you can ask the annotator to highlight which words contribute to their interpretation of positive or negative sentiment. An interesting extension to highlighting is to ask the annotator to edit those words to express the opposite sentiment. This process—changing the label with the fewest possible edits—is known as *adversarial annotations*. The items with the edits can become additional training data items, which helps your model learn the words that count most for the labels instead of putting too much weight on the labels that happened to occur with the most important words.

11.4.2 *Maximizing objectivity by asking what other people would annotate*

In chapter 9, we introduced methods to elicit what annotators thought that other people would annotate. This method, popularized in metrics such as Bayesian Truth Serum (BTS), helps us identify annotations that may not be majority judgments but nonetheless are correct.

One benefit is that this method reduces problems with perceived power dynamics because you are asking what *other* annotators think, which makes it easier for an annotator to report negative responses. This can be a good strategy when you think that power dynamics or personal biases are influencing responses: ask what most people would respond instead of what that annotator thinks.

For tasks such as sentiment analysis, an annotator might be reluctant to annotate negative sentiment about the company for which they are working. When this reluctance results from a perceived power imbalance, such as when an annotator is being compensated to create training data, the effect is known as *accommodation* or *deference*. Asking what other people would interpret the sentiment to be gives the annotators permission to distance themselves from their own interpretation of the data and therefore give a more accurate response of their own judgment.

Note that this example is a limitation on the strategies for subjective data in chapter 9. There, we expected the actual annotations to score higher than the predicted annotations to identify viable labels that were not necessarily the majority. If there is a perceived power imbalance on the part of the annotators, a valid label might have a higher predicted score than actual score. Therefore, all labels with high predicted scores should be considered to be potentially viable in these contexts, whether or not they are higher than the actual scores.

11.4.3 *Recasting continuous problems as ranking problems*

People are unreliable when giving judgments on a continuous scale. One person's 70% might be another person's 90%. People are even unreliable with their own judgments. For sentiment analysis, people might rate something as "Very Positive" when they first encounter it, but after seeing many more examples that are even more positive, they might change that rating to "Positive" due to priming or other changes in their personal disposition.

Yet people are often consistent with one another and with themselves when asked to rank two items, even if they're not consistent in their absolute scores. Two annotators might give different scores for the sentiment of two messages but consistently rank one message as being more positive than the other. Figure 11.4 shows an example.

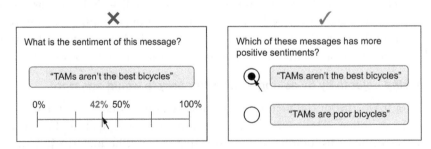

Figure 11.4 An example of using ranking as an alternative to absolute values for a task that requires annotation of continuous values. People are generally much more consistent with one another, and with themselves at different times, when they are asked to rank items instead of give an absolute score.

As figure 11.4 shows, a simple interface can turn a continuous task into a ranking task, which generally results in more consistent annotations. There are pros and cons attached to using ranking rather than absolute values. The benefits include:

- More consistent results. Results will vary depending on your data and task but are fairly easy to test; you can implement both techniques and compare them.
- Per-task time is faster. Checking a box is quicker than typing, sliding, or selecting on a continuous scale.
- Performing quality control is easier for a binary classification task than a continuous task, for both objective tasks and subjective tasks with BTS.

But there are also drawbacks:

- You get only rankings, not the actual scores, so you need some items with absolute scores. You probably created examples in your guidelines of items that are 90%, 50%, 75%, and so on. You can ask annotators where each item ranks relative to these examples and use that information to interpolate the scores for the rest of the items.
- You need to resolve circular rankings, such as when item A is ranked higher than item B, item B is ranked higher than item C, and item C is ranked higher than item A. You can use review and adjudication tasks, ask for a force ranking for all items, or automate this process with simple methods such as iteratively removing the least trusted rankings until the cycles disappear.
- Ranking every items takes more tasks. You need $N \, log(N)$ judgments to rank every item in a dataset with N items. This algorithm is essentially a sorting algorithm in which each judgment is a comparison, and you need only N annotations to give each one a score.

The last point, the $N \, log(N)$ judgments, may seem like a deal-breaker because of the implied scale, because you need $N \, log(N)$ tasks instead of N tasks when providing only a rating. A binary classification task, however, is faster and more consistent. Also, as you learned in chapter 10, it is easier to implement quality control on binary tasks than continuous tasks because you need fewer annotators on average to calculate inter-annotator agreement, so the total cost might even out.

For a worked example, imagine that we are annotating 100,000 items. For a numerical score interface, assume that we want an average of four annotators per task and that it takes 15 seconds each on average for each task:

100,000 tasks × 4 annotators × 15 seconds = 1,667 hours

For pairwise rankings, let's assume that on average, each task needs only two annotators and takes 5 seconds:

100,000 × log(100,000) tasks × 2 annotators × 5 seconds = 1,389 hours

So for around the same budget, you are likely to have a much more accurate dataset if you use a ranking approach, even though there are many more annotations in total.

Many academic papers look at the total number of operations, not the total time, and the same is true if you studied "Big O" approaches to algorithms as a computer scientist. So don't discount different types of interfaces until you have calculated the cost across all the factors, including time per task and ease of quality control.

You can use machine learning to semi-automate both annotation interfaces, but the ranking interface also has an advantage by being less prone to bias. If you have a machine learning prediction that the score is 0.40, you can prepopulate the annotation interface with 0.40 to speed annotation. Prepopulating that 0.40 answer, however, can prime the annotator to think that a score at or near 0.40 is the correct one (known as *anchoring*). By contrast, if you use a ranking interface, you can start comparing the item with ones near 0.40 to reduce the total number of annotations, but you won't bias the annotator toward any pairwise decision; they won't know that they are close to 0.40 in the rankings, and the actual task doesn't indicate which rank order should be preferred. Therefore, the interface decision also has implications for how machine learning can be effectively integrated with the annotation task—for any type of machine learning problem, not only labeling and continuous tasks. The next section goes into more detail about integrating machine learning in different types of annotation tasks.

11.5 Smart interfaces for maximizing human intelligence

With more or less machine learning aiding the annotation, you generally trade efficiency for accuracy, but there are exceptions. Machine learning can spot errors that a person might miss, for example, which can benefit both efficiency and accuracy.

In addition to efficiency and accuracy, the choice of interface changes the amount of power that an annotator perceives that they have (agency), and some types of interfaces will take more engineering resources to implement than others. So you need to understand the pros and cons of different interfaces to choose the right one(s) for your task.

Table 11.1 describes increasing levels of machine learning participation in human tasks, starting with raw annotation (no machine learning input) and ending with adjudication (review tasks in which the human annotator is accepting or rejecting a model prediction).

Table 11.1 also shows four factors that can determine the right kind of interface for your task. Note that none of the factors line up with efficiency in forward or reverse, so the trade-offs are nonlinear. Quality generally goes down with more automation, for example, but adjudication is not the worst because quality control for a binary adjudication task is much easier than for any other annotation task. Assisted annotation interfaces give the most agency because they remove only the most redundant tasks, but they require the most engineering to build and often require models that are adapted or retrained specifically for the purpose of annotation. Predictive annotation interfaces predate modern machine learning approaches and were widely used in rule-based natural language processing (NLP) systems, often called *predictive coding*. A use case that is still a big industry is e-discovery, in which analysts perform

Table 11.1 A scale with increasing levels of machine learning participation in the annotation. Efficiency is the speed at which the annotator works. Quality is the accuracy of the annotations (high quality equals fewer errors). Agency is the sense of power and ownership perceived by the annotator. Implementation effort is the amount of engineering needed to implement the interface. Efficiency increases with more automation through machine learning, but the other columns do not follow the same order, and each approach has trade-offs. The right interface depends on the factor(s) you want to optimize.

Type	Definition	Efficiency	Quality	Agency	Implementation effort
Unassisted annotation	Interaction with raw data, with no assistance by machine learning	Worst	Best	Good	Best
Assisted annotation	Interaction with raw data, with machine learning assisting	Neutral	Good	Best	Worst
Predictive annotation	Machine learning generates candidates that can be edited	Good	Worst	Neutral	Neutral
Adjudication	The annotator can only accept or reject candidates.	Best	Neutral	Worst	Good

tasks such as auditing an organization's digital communications for potential fraud by looking at candidates produced by rule-based models.

To get a better idea of the different types of interfaces, the remainder of this section looks at examples of machine learning tasks. We'll start with semantic segmentation, which has the best-known examples of each interface. I recommend reading all the subsections in this section, even if you are interested in only one type of problem, because insights from one machine learning annotation task may help with a different task.

11.5.1 *Smart interfaces for semantic segmentation*

If you have used image editing tools such as Adobe Photoshop, you are familiar with the user experience of most semantic segmentation annotation tools. Regions of the image can be annotated directly by using paintbrushes or outlining those regions (with polygons or freehand).

Most image-editing software also have smart tools, which can select entire regions via similar colors or edge-detection techniques. In the context of machine learning, some models try to predict exact regions, so these models can be used as smart tools that are adapted to the specific tasks.

Figure 11.5 shows examples of interfaces for semantic segmentation. These examples use entire images, but (as covered in chapters 6 and 10) we might focus on only part of an image, especially when adjudicating confusion. The full range of annotation interface options still applies in both cases.

The annotator experience for the four examples in figure 11.5 will differ greatly. For unassisted annotation, the annotator will feel completely in control. But it will feel tedious to slowly annotate a large region when it is obviously part of the same object. Because an annotator is probably familiar with image-editing software, they will know

Interfaces for semantic segmentation

Unassisted annotation

Color the bicycle.

(manually painted)

Assisted annotation

Click the bicycle.

(boundary predicted after clicking)

Predictive annotation

Is this segmentation correct?

(Predicted with optional edits)

Adjudication

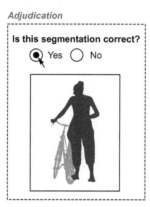

Is this segmentation correct?

◉ Yes   ○ No

Figure 11.5 Semantic segmentation interfaces. An unassisted annotation interface for semantic segmentation looks like simple image-editing software: annotators use brushes, pencils, and other freehand tools to color certain areas, which are given a label (in this case, a bicycle). Most image-editing software (and most semantic segmentation annotation tools) also have assisted annotation.

that better annotation tools exist, but they do not have access to those tools. Therefore, the annotator will not feel optimal agency, even though they have full control, because the expected tools are not available to them.

By contrast, with assisted annotation, the annotator has access to smart selection tools in addition to the ability to annotate the image manually. Therefore, the annotator's agency is higher than for unassisted annotation. Bias is fairly minimal too because the annotator decides on the regions before smart tools predict the boundaries of those regions.

Smart tooling takes more effort to implement, however, especially if we want to use the existing model to predict regions in real time in response to a click. We might have to train a model specifically to predict a region that takes into account where the annotator clicks. (For more about training a model for the interface, see section 11.5.2.)

For predictive annotation, which is the third option in figure 11.6, the implementation will be easier. We can predict all the regions (potentially in advance offline) and allow the annotator to edit any that are incorrect. This approach can introduce bias, however, because the annotator might trust machine learning predictions that were incorrect, perpetuating those errors and making the model worse in the areas in which it was already performing badly. For these reasons, quality is worse for this interface than for all others.

Correcting the outputs from a machine learning model is typically the least interesting task for an annotator. The experience of predictive annotations is that machine learning is getting most of the credit for getting the easy parts correct, and the annotator is left to clean up the errors. Correcting an incorrect boundary is often more time-consuming than creating one from scratch, which can add to an annotator's frustration.

Some tools fall between assisted and predictive annotation in semantic segmentation. An example is *superpixels*, which are groupings of pixels that can make annotation faster (figure 11.6).

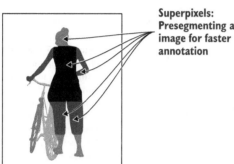

Superpixels: Presegmenting an image for faster annotation

Figure 11.6 Superpixels example. The image is segmented, but not labeled, into regions that are larger than pixels (hence the name *superpixels*) but small enough that they don't overlap with many significant boundaries between the regions that need to be annotated. In most annotation tools, the annotator can control the granularity of the superpixels to optimize annotation efficiency.

With superpixels, the annotator can quickly select which pixels belong to a given object and apply the label. Because superpixels oversegment, this technique minimizes the time-consuming process of editing incorrect boundaries, which provides more agency to the annotator and is a better user experience.

Superpixels, however, are more prone to perpetuating errors at the boundaries than the machine-learning-assisted methods in which the annotator evaluates the image before any suggested boundaries are shown, so the increase in efficiency can come at the expense of accuracy.

11.5.2 Smart interfaces for object detection

Many of the methods that apply to semantic segmentation also apply to object detection. A popular machine-learning-assisted interface generates bounding boxes from a single click. The second interface in figure 11.7 is assisted annotation.

In the assisted annotation example in figure 11.7, the annotator clicks the center of the image, and the bounding box is generated automatically from that click. This type of selection tool is similar to the smart selection used for semantic segmentation and identical to identifying objects as polygons.

The assisted experience can be simulated by precomputing the bounding boxes and making them appear only when an annotator clicks within them. This approach gives more agency to the annotator than predictive bounding boxes do but is less accurate than true assisted bounding-box detection because it does not truly take the

Interfaces for bounding boxes

Unassisted annotation

Draw a box around the bicycle.

(manually drawn)

Assisted annotation

Click the center of the bicycle.

(box predicted from click)

Predictive annotation

Is this box correct?

(Optional edits)

Adjudication

Is this box correct?

⦿ Yes   ○ No

Figure 11.7   Different types of bounding-box annotation interfaces. In an unassisted annotation interface, the annotator manually draws the box (or polygon). In many cases, the box can be guessed for predictive annotation interfaces that a person can edit or adjudicate (bottom row). For assisted interfaces, the annotator can click the middle of the object, and the interface predicts the most likely bounding box for that click.

annotators' clicks into account. The result is that the annotators will not feel that their clicks are being taken into account when good boxes are not displayed after they click. You are also wasting a valuable source of information: the annotator's intuition about the center of the objects. Therefore, it is advisable to build a model that specifically takes an annotator's center click into account when predicting the bounding box. You can get the training data as you go: record where annotators click, and trust any object that was edited after that initial click.

You can also synthetically generate clicks near the middle of the boxes if you have existing bounding-box annotations. The only downside of the synthetic approach is that the perceived middle may be different from the actual middle of the box. In our bicycle example, the middle of the bounding box is often a gap in the frame, not part of the bicycle. You can decide based on the regularity of the objects in your data whether synthetic clicks are enough to begin with before you start getting actual clicks from annotators.

Clicking the middle of the object doesn't give you the dimensions that can lead to errors when the click could reference multiple candidate objects, so a variation on this method asks annotators to click two or more edges of the object. More edges are most helpful for bounding polygons. If an annotator needs to click three or four edges to create a box, that process is not much faster than creating a box unassisted.

Falling between these two options are click-and-drag interfaces, in which the annotator clicks the middle of the box, and as they hold the mouse down and drag out, the box snaps to successfully larger potential boxes. You can generate the data for this interface as you go and/or seed the model for the interface with synthetic examples created from existing data that has only the boxes themselves. One option to minimize bias is to have an unassisted bounding tool with a hot key to enable smart snapping. Dragging a box might follow the cursor to the specific pixel unless the Shift key is held down, in which case the tool snaps to the most likely box with a boundary near the cursor.

11.5.3 Smart interfaces for language generation

Language generation technologies have one well-known assisted interface: autocomplete. If your phone or email client suggests the remainder of a word or sentence when you start typing, you have used this type of assisted annotation technology for language generation. This kind of autocomplete functionality has been used for many years but is still advancing rapidly (see the nearby sidebar).

Four decades of predictive text

If you write in Chinese characters, all your writing probably uses predictive text. It is common for people to know up to 10,000 characters in Chinese and to use 2,000 to 3,000 of them regularly—too many to fit on a keyboard.

Predictive text technology for Chinese, therefore, has been around since the start of personal computing in the 1980s. At that time, scientists in China developed ways to allow people using Latin-script QWERTY keyboards to type combinations of Latin characters that mapped to Chinese characters. The earliest method, called the Wubizixing input method (五笔字型输入法), is still one of the fastest typing methods for any language today.

Japanese cell phone manufacturers in the 1990s introduced inputs and displays that combined four scripts with predictive text: hiragana, katakana, kanji, and Latin characters. The Japanese predictive methods influenced the T9 input system for Latin scripts where each number (0–9) is mapped to multiple Latin characters, and the phone converts the number sequence to the most likely word from among all the possible character sequences. T9 and related systems also helped Latin-script languages use characters and accent marks that are not common on keyboards.

In the early 2000s, more than 100 languages and a dozen scripts were supported by predictive text and were deployed in systems that adapt to individual users, typically with simple dictionary-based lookups. Next-word prediction also became widely available on cell phones and in some word processing applications.

(continued)

In the early 2010s, full-sentence prediction became widely used in applications such as customer service where a small number of responses make up most of what a customer service representative needs to type and can be stored in a knowledge base. At the end of the 2010s, full-sentence prediction became common in consumer email clients.

At the start of the 2020s, advances in neural language generation technologies turned language generation, a largely overlooked field in machine learning for many decades, into one of the most popular topics at every NLP conference. Language generation is a longstanding human-in-the-loop technology but still advancing rapidly.

Predictive text interfaces are now widely used to create training data for language generation in use cases such as summarization and translation. Figure 11.8 shows an example of translation.

Interfaces for language generation
Unassisted annotation

Translate this text:

"The E-Coli outbreak was first seen in a San Francisco supermarket."

—

(Typed)

Assisted annotation

Translate this text:

"The E-Coli outbreak was first seen in a San Francisco supermarket."

El brote_de E. coli fue descubierto en un supermercado de San Francisco originalmente.

(Autocomplete)

Predictive annotation

Is this translation correct?

"The E-Coli outbreak was first seen in a San Francisco supermarket."

El brote de E. coli fue descubierto en un supermercado de San Francisco originalmente.

(Optional edits)

Adjudication

Is this translation correct?

◉ Yes   ○ No

"The E-Coli outbreak was first seen in a San Francisco supermarket."

El brote de E. coli fue descubierto en un supermercado de San Francisco originalmente.

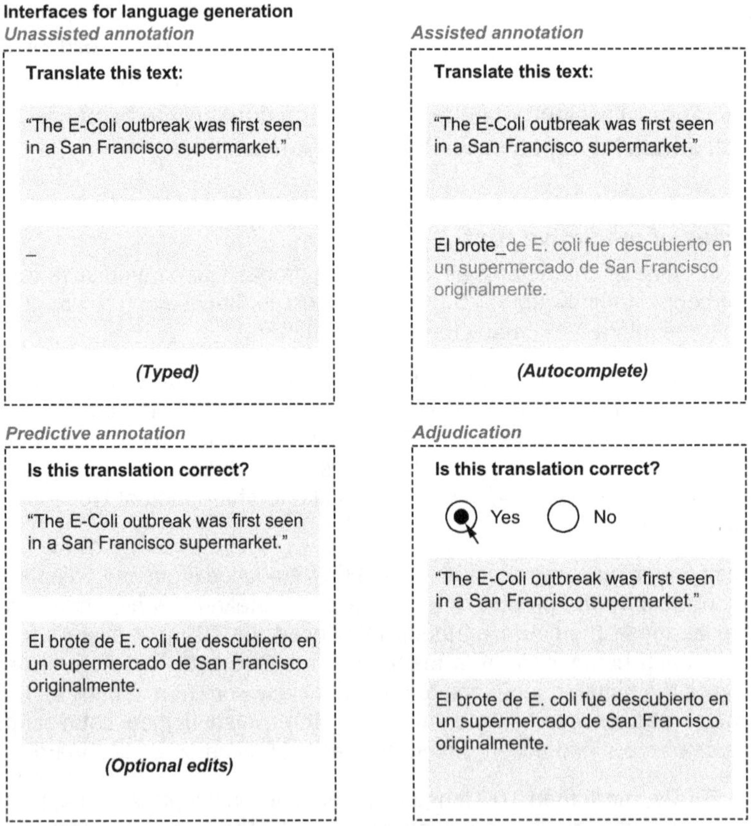

Figure 11.8 Language generation interfaces, using the example of translation between languages. In addition to unassisted typing, assisted interfaces can use autocomplete functionality, and predictive interfaces can present predicted text that can be edited. Adjudication interfaces allow an annotator to accept or reject an annotation.

There is more potential for bias in the machine-learning-assisted annotation example for language generation than in other examples of assisted annotation because the annotator may not have decided what the complete text passage was before seeing the autocomplete suggestion. This feature can be tuned so that autocomplete displays the sequence of following words only when it is confident that only one response is likely or that only so many words can be autocompleted at one time. The trade-off is reduction in efficiency, which can be tested by displaying no predictions for sentence competition and seeing whether the annotator produces the same text.

The predictive annotation interfaces are more or less effective depending on the use case. In the case of customer service response, a message that has the correct information may be sufficient, and there will be many viable options, so a good-enough response can be efficiently selected. For translation, however, as in figure 11.8, only one precise translation may be correct. The effort to make one or two edits in a predicted sentence often takes longer than typing a sentence in an unassisted interface. Editing machine translation output is known as *postediting* in the translation community, and as far as I know, it is the only human-in-the-loop annotation interface to have its own ISO standard (ISO 18587:2017, in case you are interested). If you look at any of the online forum discussions of professional translators, you see how bad the user experience is. Most professional translators prefer unassisted or assisted annotation interfaces.

To reduce the implementation effort, you can create an interface that feels like an assisted interface in which the text sequences are precomputed but displayed only when someone starts to type them. If no autocompletes are possible, the user experience is not negative because the person can keep typing unassisted without breaking their flow of work.

The adjudication interface in figure 11.8 is commonly used to evaluate the quality of other annotators. As discussed in chapter 10, automated quality control is difficult for language generation tasks, so review tasks to adjudicate the work are more common than using ground-truth examples or interannotator agreement. It is common to use human review or adjudication to evaluating model accuracy for language generation tasks, so you should be able to put both human annotations and model predictions through the same workflow to evaluate human and machine outputs.

11.5.4 Smart interfaces for sequence labeling

For sequence labeling, the interface options are similar to those for bounding boxes. An annotator can highlight the sequences in unassisted interfaces at one end of the integration scale and adjudicate a predicted sequence at the other end of the scale. In between, an assisted interface allows the annotator to select the middle of one sequence, and the model will predict the boundaries, whereas a predictive interface will predict the sequences and allow the annotator to accept or edit them. Figure 11.9 shows examples.

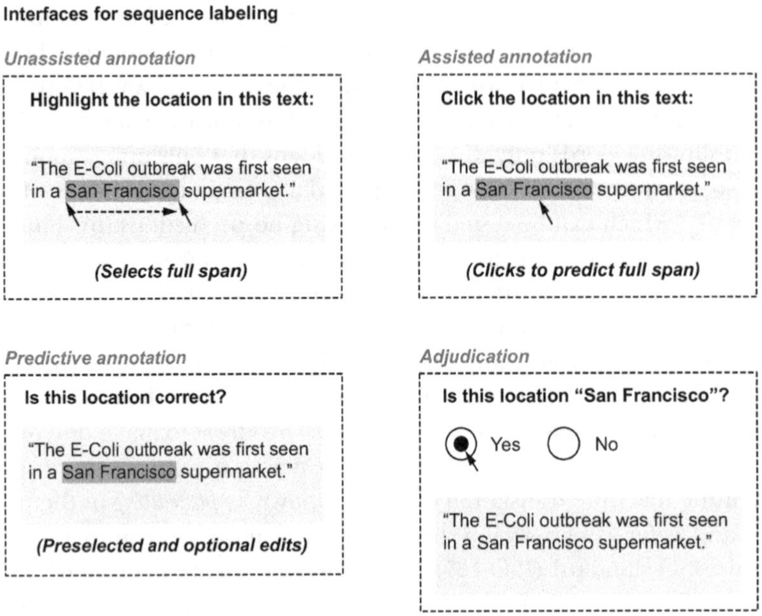

Interfaces for sequence labeling

Unassisted annotation

> **Highlight the location in this text:**
>
> "The E-Coli outbreak was first seen in a San Francisco supermarket."
>
> ***(Selects full span)***

Assisted annotation

> **Click the location in this text:**
>
> "The E-Coli outbreak was first seen in a San Francisco supermarket."
>
> ***(Clicks to predict full span)***

Predictive annotation

> **Is this location correct?**
>
> "The E-Coli outbreak was first seen in a San Francisco supermarket."
>
> ***(Preselected and optional edits)***

Adjudication

> **Is this location "San Francisco"?**
>
> ⦿ Yes　　○ No
>
> "The E-Coli outbreak was first seen in a San Francisco supermarket."

Figure 11.9 Different types of sequence labeling interfaces. For the unassisted interface, the annotator highlights the text starting at one boundary and ending at the other. For the assisted interface, the annotator clicks the middle of the span, and the model predicts the boundaries. For predictive annotation, the annotator is presented with a model's predictions of the spans and can accept or edit them. For adjudication, the annotator is confirming or rejecting the proposed span.

Many sequence labeling tasks are needle-in-the-haystack problems in which the number of sequences are greatly outnumbered by the irrelevant sequences. Even if you have filtered for outbreak-related news articles, as in figure 11.9, fewer than 1% of words are likely to be the locations of an outbreak, so you can increase efficiency significantly by incorporating machine learning.

One approach to predictive annotations is highlighting or underlining the candidate sequences but not pre-annotating them. For our example, an annotator might see that a potential location is underlined, but they still have to click or highlight that sequence to annotate it. This approach to interface design will reduce bias because an annotator can no longer passively accept a machine learning prediction as a label and is forced to interact with the data. An additional benefit is that annotators will be more forgiving of errors in the machine learning model if they are suggestions and not preselected annotations (figure 11.10).

By underlining low-confidence annotations, as in figure 11.10, you can reduce annotator bias by calibrating how often underlines are shown. If the underlined text is correct only 50% of the time, the annotator will not become primed to trust or reject any one prediction and will evaluate predictions on their merits—a big advantage over the predictive interface, in which editing 50% of the annotations would be time-consuming and would negatively impact the user experience.

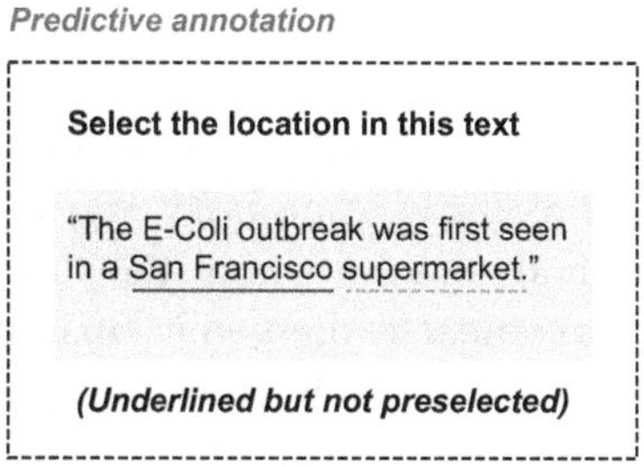

Predictive annotation

```
┌ ─ ─ ─ ─ ─ ─ ─ ─ ─ ─ ─ ─ ─ ─ ─ ─ ─ ┐
  Select the location in this text

  "The E-Coli outbreak was first seen
  in a San Francisco supermarket."

  (Underlined but not preselected)
└ ─ ─ ─ ─ ─ ─ ─ ─ ─ ─ ─ ─ ─ ─ ─ ─ ─ ┘
```

Figure 11.10   A predictive annotation interface that is an alternative to the one in figure 11.9. In this interface, the location is predicted by the model but underlined instead of preselected. Therefore, the annotator needs to highlight or click the location to make the annotation. This interface slows the annotation process compared with having the span selected, but it reduces bias because the annotator cannot passively accept predictions. This interface also allows for a richer annotator experience, with information such as the dotted line indicating a low-confidence prediction.

If the annotator looks only at the underlined candidates in an interface like figure 11.10, they may be more likely to miss sequences that weren't underlined. So this strategy is best when your candidates are near 100% recall but with low enough precision that the predictions aren't trusted without consideration.

Variations on the interface in figure 11.10 combine all the types of interfaces. You could have a system that jumps from one candidate sequence to the next as an adjudication interface, underlining candidates with low certainty, and falling back to assisted and unassisted interactions when the adjudication indicates an error.

11.6 *Machine learning to assist human processes*

We introduced the distinction between machine learning assisting human tasks and humans assisting machine learning tasks in chapter 1. Almost everything in this book applies equally to both use cases, such as sampling through active learning and methods for quality control. The biggest difference is in human–computer interaction. For machine-learning-assisted humans, one principle applies:

> *The person being assisted by machine learning must perceive that their tasks are being improved by machine learning.*

We'll explore this principle in more detail in the remainder of this section and cover some solutions that optimize annotation while maintaining this principle.

11.6.1 *The perception of increased efficiency*

The perception of tasks being improved is important in a couple of ways. You can get away with *less* efficiency from machine learning, so long as less efficiency is not the perception. Conversely, if a person's efficiency is improved, but that improvement isn't being perceived, that person is less likely to have a positive experience with machine learning integrated into their existing day-to-day tasks.

I've seen this effect firsthand many times. I've shipped systems that helped health care workers manage messages more effectively, but that efficiency was not perceived by the health care workers, so the application was not adopted. On the other hand, when I've shipped systems with assistive interfaces for object tracking, the annotators reported a more positive user experience even when they were slower than the control group because the interface was clearly trying to help them even when it was wrong. These experiences were important lessons about the difference between measured and perceived performance for systems that combine human and machine intelligence.

In general, changing a person's day-to-day tasks is tough even before you add machine learning. If you've built new applications for existing tasks, you know that change management is difficult: most people tend stick with what they are already using. You've probably experienced this situation yourself when your email client or favorite social media platform updates its interface. Presumably, those companies had good evidence that the new interface was a better experience, but that fact doesn't help your discomfort with the sudden change. Suppose that an interface is changing, and part of the process is being automated by machine learning in such a way that the user might fear that their job is in danger of being taken over by machines. You can see why this change might not be welcome.

Assisted interfaces, therefore, are a good starting point for adding machine learning to existing work. The initial interface is unchanged, and the annotator maintains agency because they initiate every action, with machine learning accelerating those actions. Consider the assisted interfaces discussed earlier in this chapter to be starting points for integrating machine learning predictions into existing applications.

11.6.2 *Active learning for increased efficiency*

Active learning can increase the efficiency of work without interface changes. If you are sampling items that are more likely to improve your machine learning models, you may not change the annotator experience in any way. If you are using diversity sampling, you might even improve the annotator experience because the items will seem to be less repetitive, which in turn will lead to increased accuracy by reducing repetition priming. The annotator's perception of the change will be minor, however. The model may be getting smarter behind the scenes because of active learning, but the annotator will not necessarily perceive that their work is faster based on sampling strategies alone. Furthermore, if the annotator previously had the ability to determine the order of work, and now active learning determines the order for them, they are likely to feel a loss of agency. So be mindful about taking any functionality away when you introduce active learning.

11.6.3 *Errors can be better than absence to maximize completeness*

Completeness can be an issue when fields are optional. An annotator might leave some fields blank where there are valid responses for the sake of expediency. This situation might not matter for a business process that is not trying to create data for machine learning. But if that same business process also needs to create training data, it can become a problem because empty fields can become erroneous negative cases if you are not careful about how you build your models.

This problem is common when you are relying on end users as annotations. If people are selling clothes on an e-commerce site, that site may want as many details as possible: type of clothing, color, size, style, brand, and so on. You want to motivate users to add these fields, but you have limited options for motivating them. To help with this problem, you can take advantage of the fact that people are more averse to wrong data than to missing data and use a predictive interface to prepopulate fields. Figure 11.11 shows an example in which we assume that a person has the job of extracting information about outbreaks from text.

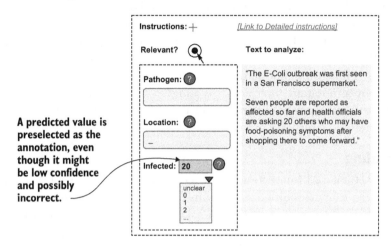

Figure 11.11   A predictive annotation interface encourages completeness of data. People are more likely to correct an error than to add a missing value, so prepopulating an incorrect answer can lead to more complete annotations than leaving values unannotated by default.

You may have heard of Cunningham's Law, which states that the best way to get the right answer to a question is to post the wrong answer online. Cunningham's Law applies to annotation too. If you want to make sure that an annotator gives a correct answer to an optional field, prepopulating with the wrong answer can be more successful than leaving a field blank. This process is a balancing act. If people lose trust in the model predictions or feel that they are being slowed by correcting too many errors, you will be creating a negative user experience for the sake of extra data. For this reason, this approach is most effective when end users are adding data intermittently, not working as annotators full-time.

11.6.4 Keep annotation interfaces separate from daily work interfaces

If it is not possible to get the right volume or balance of data from people in their daily work, you may need to introduce new interfaces for the work. Don't try to change too much in the existing workflow; introduce new interfaces as additions to existing ones, and make sure that they can be used in ways that fit into work schedules.

You may find that you need adjudication interfaces to resolve disagreements between annotators or to annotate large volumes of machine learning predictions efficiently. If you replace a person's powerful unassisted interaction capabilities and limit them to reviewing other tasks, you reduce their agency. Instead of replacing the other interface, make it additive. The person can use their powerful interface and have full agency to complete that work, but now they have an additional interface option that lets them annotate quickly.

Positioned the right way, an adjudication interface can increase the agency of the people who use it, because you are calling on them as SMEs to resolve areas on which other people or machines are confused without taking away their ability to use their full annotation capabilities. How this interface fits into the workflow will be specific to your organization. The annotators may be given the option to switch to an adjudication interface at a time they choose, or there might be dedicated times or workforces for the different annotation interfaces. As long as there is transparency and the agency of the annotators is maintained, you should be able to start incorporating machine learning into daily tasks in a way that feels empowering.

11.7   *Further reading*

"Guidelines for Human-AI Interaction," by Saleema Amershi, Dan Weld, Mihaela Vorvoreanu, Adam Fourney, Besmira Nushi, Penny Collisson, Jina Suh, Shamsi Iqbal, Paul Bennett, Kori Inkpen, Jaime Teevan, Ruth Kikin-Gil, and Eric Horvitz, proposes 18 generally applicable design guidelines for human-AI interaction, all applicable to data annotation and/or machine-learning-assisted human tasks (http://mng.bz/4ZVv). The paper is also a great resource for other recent papers. Most of the authors are in the Adaptive Systems and Interaction Group at Microsoft, which is the world's foremost group for this kind of research.

"Priming for Better Performance in Microtask Crowdsourcing Environments," by Robert R. Morris, Mira Dontcheva, and Elizabeth Gerber (http://mng.bz/QmlQ), talks about how positive affective priming, such as playing music, improves the performance of crowdsourced workers on creative tasks.

"Extreme clicking for efficient object annotation," by Dim Papadopoulos, Jasper Uijlings, Frank Keller, and Vittorio Ferrari (http://mng.bz/w9w5), talks about an efficient interface for creating bounding boxes to create one of the datasets used in chapter 12 of this book. Other work by the same authors experiments with other annotation strategies.

Summary

- The basic principles of human–computer interaction, such as affordance and minimizing scrolling, apply to annotation interfaces. Understanding these principles can help you improve the efficiency of annotation tasks.
- Good affordance means that elements should function as they appear to function, which for annotation typically means using the existing HTML form elements for their intended data types.

- Keyboards are the fastest annotation devices for most tasks, so annotation tools should use keyboard shortcuts and support key-based navigation as much as possible.

- Priming refers to how the context of the task can change the annotators' interpretation of the item. The most common problem from priming in annotation occurs when the order of items changes the perception, especially for subjective tasks such as sentiment analysis.

- Know when to break the rules. High-volume batch labeling breaks the conventions of avoiding scrolling and balanced data. When you can't display balanced data, however, scrolling can reduce the priming bias and speed up annotation.

- In addition to manual unassisted interfaces, three types of interfaces can use machine learning: assisted, predictive, and adjudication. Each type has strengths and weaknesses in efficiency of annotation, annotator agency, annotation quality, and each requires different effort to implement.

- Assisted interfaces present items to annotators without displaying machine learning predictions, using machine learning only to speed up annotator-initiated actions.

- Predictive interfaces present items that are pre-annotated by a machine learning model and allow the annotators to edit them.

- Adjudication interfaces present items to annotators that are pre-annotated by a machine learning model and allow the annotators to accept or reject the annotations.

- For tasks in which machine learning helps people in their daily roles, assisted annotation interfaces are often the most successful because they give the annotator the most agency.

- When integrating machine learning into existing applications, make the fewest changes possible in the current interfaces and workflows.

Human-in-the-loop machine learning products

This chapter covers

- Defining products for human-in-the-loop machine learning applications
- Creating a system for exploratory data analysis for short text
- Creating an information extraction system to support a human process
- Creating an image labeling system to maximize model accuracy
- Evaluating options for extending simple systems

This final chapter contains three worked examples of human-in-the-loop machine learning products. Using everything that you have learned in the first 11 chapters, you will implement three examples. You can think of these examples—one for exploratory data analysis of news headlines, one for extracting information about food safety from text, and one for labeling images containing bicycles—as being first-pass systems that you can create in a few days. The examples are similar to the human-in-the-loop machine learning system in chapter 2 but slightly more sophisticated, building on what you have learned in the chapters since.

Like the example in chapter 2, these examples can be starting points for fully working systems that you are prototyping. In all cases, you could build out many components as the next potential step.

12.1 Defining products for human-in-the-loop machine learning applications

Good product management for human-in-the-loop machine learning applications starts with the problem that you are solving for someone: the actual daily task you are supporting. Understanding the human task that you are solving will help every aspect of your product design: interface, annotations, and machine learning architecture. This section gives you a quick introduction to some good product management techniques that we'll use in this chapter, which will in turn help with technical design decisions.

12.1.1 Start with the problem you are solving

Good product design starts with defining the problem that you are trying to solve. It is a common mistake to start talking about a product in terms of the technology you are creating instead of the problem you are trying to solve. If you are creating autocomplete functionality for an email client, it is too easy to define the problem as "People want their sentences autocompleted in emails." A better way to define the problem is "People want to communicate as efficiently as possible." Starting by focusing on the problem you are solving helps with everything from creating guidelines for annotators to deciding which product features to build or extend next.

It helps to be specific in the problem definition, too. If you are targeting marketing people for your email autocomplete product, you might say, "Marketers want to communicate with their potential customers as efficiently as possible." If you are creating a consumer product, you might say, "People want to communicate with their friends and family as efficiently as possible." This approach will help shape your assumptions when designing the product.

When you have defined the problem you are solving, you can break that general problem into specific tasks that people are trying to perform. For the email autocomplete product example, tasks could include "I want to double the amount of emails I send to potential customers each day" or "I want to clear my inbox by the end of each day without reducing the length of my email replies." Those specific tasks can become some of the metrics for product success. With these product management guidelines in mind, here are the three problems that we are trying to solve as example human-in-the-loop machine learning systems in this chapter:

- Data analysts want to understand the distribution of information in their news headline data.
  - "I want to see how many news headlines are related to specific topics."
  - "I want to track the changes in news headline topics over time."

- "I want to export all the news articles related to a certain topic for further analysis."

- Food safety professionals want to collect data about events in which pathogens or foreign objects have been detected in food.
  - "I want to maintain a complete record of all recorded food safety events in the EU."
  - "I want to track when different food safety events might have come from the same source."
  - "I want to send warnings to specific countries when there are likely to be food safety events that have not yet been detected or reported."

- Transportation researchers want to estimate the number of people who use bicycles on certain streets.
  - "I want to collect information about how often people are cycling down a street."
  - "I want to capture this information from thousands of cameras, and I don't have the budget to do it manually."
  - "I want my model for bicycle identification to be as accurate as possible."

12.1.2 Design systems to solve the problem

For the three use cases, we can start with the problem definitions and design a system that solves those problems. As in chapter 2, we will build a complete human-in-the-loop machine learning system for each example. Think of each of these examples as proof of concept (PoC) for systems that will be made more scalable and more robust later.

Quality control using interannotator agreement

It is not easy to provide a good practical example of interannotator agreement in this chapter, because the examples here need to be stand-alone systems that a single person can work on, assuming that most people are reading this book solo. So this chapter covers most of what was important in the first 11 chapters of this book except interannotator agreement.

To give you an example of interannotator agreement, I'll follow this book with a free article about interannotator agreement that uses the example in chapter 2. That example includes annotating short text according to whether it was disaster-related, using the open-source code that I created for that chapter. The code for that chapter collects annotations that people make and (if they opted in) their identities, allowing us to compare annotations by different people.

So although I can't provide an example of interannotator agreement while writing this book, your own annotations will be contributing to an interannotator agreement study that will help people for years to come!

Notice that two of our systems are similar in terms of the machine learning problem; one is labeling news headlines, and one is labeling images. But because they are supporting different use cases—exploratory data analysis and counting objects—the resulting systems will be different.

The food safety example automates an existing human process, so maintaining the agency of the person doing this work is important. In particular, they should not feel that their work is being slowed now that it is needed to power a machine learning algorithm in addition to being part of their daily task. Model accuracy is least important in this case, because if the assisted text doesn't work, the person can simply type the field value, which they are already doing. Table 12.1 summarizes the factors that are most important in these systems.

Table 12.1 Factors in the design of the three example systems and their relative importance. We are optimizing different factors in different systems based on how the systems are being used, and this information will influence our design decisions.

Example	Agency	Model accuracy	Annotation accuracy
Headlines	Medium	Medium	Low
Food safety	High	Low	High
Bicycle detection	Low	High	Medium

In all three cases, some components can be substituted for more sophisticated components—more active learning sampling methods, more complicated machine learning models, more efficient interfaces, and so on. As you interact with all three examples, think about the most useful next step in each case. Based on the goal of the system, the data, and the task itself, you may have different ideas about what component to expand or add next for each use case.

12.1.3 *Connecting Python and HTML*

We'll build web interfaces for the examples, so we'll need to connect Python with HTML/JavaScript. We will use a Python library called eel that allows us to build local HTML interfaces for Python applications. Many libraries are available for connecting Python to HTML. If you are familiar with another library—flask, kivy, pyqt, tkinter, or some other library/framework for HTML application or Python APIs that can connect easily with HTML applications—that library might be a better choice for you to create a prototype.

We use eel here because it is lightweight and requires little knowledge of JavaScript. If you have not coded in JavaScript but know Python and HTML, you should still be able to follow all the examples in this chapter. We will use eel in a way that puts most of the work in Python for the same reason: this chapter assumes that you are more familiar with Python. If you are more familiar with JavaScript, you can think about which components in this chapter could be implemented in JavaScript.

In each example in this chapter, we'll have three files with code: one for Python (.py), one for JavaScript (.js), and one for the HTML (.html). This format keeps things simple for teaching purposes. Your actual distribution of code should reflect your organization's best practices. You can install eel via pip:

```
pip install eel
```

You can import eel and expose any Python function to the JavaScript in your HTML file with the command @eel.expose before the function:

```
import eel

@eel.expose
def hello(message):
    return "Hello "+message
```

This code allows you to call this `hello` function from within your JavaScript:

```
<script type='text/JavaScript'>

    async function hello(message){

    let message = await eel.hello(message)();  # Call Python function
    console.log(message)
    }
</script>
```

If you call the JavaScript function `hello("World")`, it will print `"Hello World"` to the JavaScript console because the Python function prepends `"Hello"`. Two more lines of code in your Python file ensure that your Python script can talk to your HTML file with the JavaScript:

```
eel.init('./')  # Tell eel where to look for your HTML files
...
eel.start('helloworld.html')
```

In the preceding code snippet, we assume that our HTML file is called helloworld .html and that it is in the same directory as the Python file—hence, the local path `init('./')`. The `start()` call will open a browser window to launch your application, so you typically want this call at the end of your Python script.

Note that although we have named the functions `hello()` in both Python and JavaScript, there is no requirement for this naming convention, because your Java-Script can call any exposed function in Python by name. We follow the convention of using the same function names throughout this chapter to make the code more readable. Similarly, we'll use the same name for our Python, JavaScript, and HTML files in each example to keep things simple, changing only the extensions, even though there's no file naming requirement in eel.

The only additional change in regular Python code is that we need to use eel for thread management, which is a side effect of how the library interacts with HTML. So we'll use `eel.spawn(some_function_())` to call `some_function()` as a new Python thread and use `eel.sleep()` instead of Python's built-in `sleep()` function. These functions perform the same way as the built-in threading and sleep functions with which you may be familiar. We're not going to use threading in complicated ways, but for all three examples, we'll have one thread interacting with the HTML interface while a separate thread retrains the model.

The eel library supports more than the demos here. It also allows you to call the JavaScript functions from within Python, for example. We'll keep our architectures simple and have all operations triggered by the user.

12.2 *Example 1: Exploratory data analysis for news headlines*

Exploratory data analysis (EDA) is one of the most common use cases for quickly developed machine learning systems. Relatively little research on EDA has been cited in the machine learning literature, however, because it does not focus on machine learning accuracy. In industry, data scientists usually want to understand their data in more detail before deciding what models and products to build. EDA in this case allows a data scientist to browse and filter data quickly. For the specific EDA example that we're covering in this section, here is our problem statement and three specific problems that are being solved:

- Data analysts want to understand the distribution of information in their news headline data.
  - "I want to see how many news headlines are related to specific topics."
  - "I want to track the changes in news topic over time."
  - "I want to export all the news articles related to a certain topic for further analysis."

12.2.1 *Assumptions*

Our assumptions for designing this product are

- The headlines are only in English.
- Pretrained language models will help.
- The analyst will have some idea of good keywords to bootstrap.

How does your data determine your architecture decisions?

The data itself can influence your decision about every part of the architecture. We are using the DistilBERT pretrained model, which is trained on English-only data from Wikipedia and a collection of public-domain books. Wikipedia includes titles that are similar to news headlines and includes some headlines of actual news articles. Therefore, this pretrained model is appropriate for our task.

> *(continued)*
>
> That decision could change with slightly different data, however. While I was writing this book, an organization I was helping, Turn.io, wanted to conduct exploratory data analysis on short messages sent to WHO's COVID-19 information service. These messages are in many languages, and the style of writing for direct messages is different from the kind of web data on which most pretrained models are built. In that case, it was more appropriate to use a multilingual model built on more domains of data, such as XLM-R, even though that model requires more processing time than DistilBERT does.
>
> With this in mind, don't take anything in this chapter as being necessarily the best first step for a problem that you are working on. Even a similar task might be better built with different architectures and different pretrained models.

Important considerations:

- *Agency*—The analyst using the system should be empowered to browse the data by keyword and by year.
- *Transparency*—The accuracy of the system should be clear across the entire dataset and also by year.
- *Dense/rich layout*—The analyst should be able to get as much information as possible on the screen, so the layout should be information-dense.
- *Immediacy*—The interface should be immediately useful for helping the analyst understand the data, so the creation of evaluation data should be in parallel with the creation of training data.
- *Stratification*—The analyst is interested in per-year accuracy, so we want to track accuracy per year in addition to overall.
- *Flexibility*—The analyst may want to look at different labels at different times.
- *Extensibility*—The analyst may want to turn this task into a larger-scale task later, so they want to track interesting examples of headlines to add to future guidelines.

12.2.2 Design and implementation

This task is a binary labeling task, so the choice of uncertainty sampling algorithm doesn't matter. We'll use least confidence, and we'll use stratified sampling for real-world diversity to target headlines from specific years. We'll allow the analyst to use keywords to filter the data being annotated.

For annotation, we'll allow the annotator to make a quick binary choice for each headline to optimize for speed. We won't include items sampled by keywords in the evaluation data, as they won't create a balanced sample.

We'll use two machine learning models. One model incrementally updates with each new annotation, increasing the agency of the analyst by allowing them to see the results of their annotations immediately on the model and resulting predictions.

Incremental models, however, are known to have recency biases and to converge on local optimums. The recency bias can be amplified in active learning scenarios because the most recent items are not randomly sampled, especially if they are sampled by keywords. So a second model will be retrained from scratch across all the training data at regular intervals. This model will replace the first model when it is more accurate on the held-out data.

For both machine learning models, we will adapt the model from the DistillBERT pretrained model. DistillBERT is much smaller than BERT but has comparable accuracy. We assume that the faster processing and smaller memory footprint will be net positive even with the small loss in accuracy. This architecture is shown in figure 12.1.

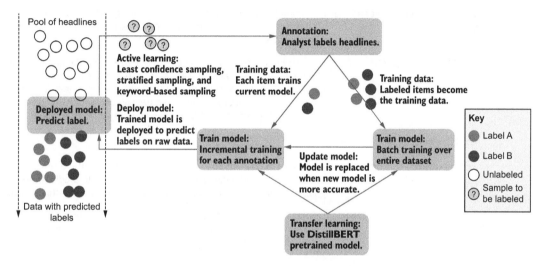

Figure 12.1 Architecture for the example system to classify news headlines

Figure 12.1 is almost identical to the architectures throughout this book but has two models that we can optimize for real-time training in addition to training that aims to maximize accuracy. You can see the code at https://github.com/rmunro/headlines. See the readme file in the repository for more information about the details of the implementation and how to experiment with it.

12.2.3 *Potential extensions*

After playing around with the system for a little while, think about what kind of changes you might make. Table 12.2 offers examples of potential improvements.

Every example in table 12.2 could be implemented in fewer than 50 lines of code, so there are few barriers to implementing one or two of them. But it would be a lot of work to implement all the changes and evaluate which were the most effective. So interacting with the system should give you an idea of the most valuable addition to make first. This example has an element of machine learning assisting a human, which is something that we will double down on in the next example.

Table 12.2   Potential extensions to the example and the sections in which they are covered in this book

Annotation interface	
Batch annotation (section 11.2.1)	Accepting or rejecting multiple annotations at the same time. The set of messages that are already grouped per-year could be a good place to start.
More powerful filtering (section 9.5)	The manual filtering is for string matching, which could be made more sophisticated to allow regular expression matching or combinations of multiple keywords.

Annotation quality control	
Using the model as an annotator (section 9.3)	Cross-validate the training data to find disagreements between the predicted and the actual annotations as potential annotation errors to show the analyst.
Annotation aggregation (sections 8.1–8.3)	If multiple people were using this, strategize about the ground truth and interannotator agreement methods to aggregate that data. You might split the strategy, updating the model incrementally for every annotation in real time, but batch-retraining only with items that have been annotated multiple times and are confidently labeled.

Machine learning architecture	
Self-supervised learning (section 9.4)	Use metadata such as the year or the subdomain of the URL as labels, and build a model over the entire dataset to predict those labels, which in turn can be used as a representation in this model.
Tune the model to the unlabeled data	Tune DistilBERT to the entire dataset of headlines first. This approach adapts the pretrained model to this specific domain of text and will likely lead to more accurate results faster.

Active learning	
Ensemble-based sampling (section 3.4)	Maintain multiple models and track the uncertainty of a prediction across all the models, sampling items with the highest average uncertainty and/or the highest variation in predictions.
Diversity sampling (sections 4.2–4.4)	Explore clustering and model-based outliers to ensure that there aren't parts of the features space that are being oversampled or ignored entirely.

12.3   *Example 2: Collecting data about food safety events*

Many people's daily jobs consist of constructing structured data from unstructured data. These workers include marketing professionals looking for the sentiments that consumers have expressed about certain aspects of a product, whether online or in reviews; health care professionals extracting important information from written electronic medical records; and food safety professionals in our example. Here is the problem statement and three specific problems that are being solved:

- Food safety professionals want to collect data about events in which pathogens or foreign objects have been detected in food.
  - "I want to maintain a complete record of all recorded food safety events in the EU."
  - "I want to track when different food safety events might have come from the same source."
  - "I want to send warnings to specific countries when there are likely to be food safety events that have not yet been detected or reported."

12.3.1 Assumptions

Our assumptions for designing this product are:

- The reports are only in English.
- Pretrained language models will help.
- The food safety expert has the domain expertise needed to extract the information.
- The food safety expert is already performing this task as part of their job.

Important considerations:

- *Agency*—The food safety expert does not want their work processes to be slowed by machine learning integration.
- *Transparency*—The food safety expert should be able to understand how many reports remain, assuming that they want to see every one.
- *Consistency and compactness*—The food safety expert should not have to scroll, use a mouse, or lose track of elements on the screen.
- *Ability to track trends*—The analyst is interested in per-country trends, so we want to track how the information extracted shows trends in movement between countries.

12.3.2 Design and implementation

For active learning, we assume that confusion between two labels is as bad an experience as confusion across all the labels, so we'll use ratio of confidence for uncertainty. The uncertainty score will be used as a threshold to decide whether to display the autocomplete suggestions from the model.

For annotation, if there are no predictions from the model, the interface will use autocomplete suggestions taken from all matching strings of text in the current report. Using the matching strings of text will provide a similar user experience to using the predictive labels for autocomplete even when there are no model predictions.

We'll use one machine learning model adapted from the DistillBERT pretrained model, which is retrained on a regular basis. We could use two models, as in the first example in this chapter, in which one model was incrementally updated. Incremental updates are not as important here, however, because the back-off behavior of matching

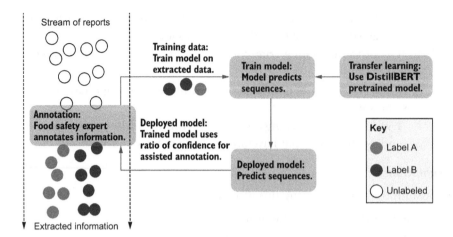

Figure 12.2 Architecture for the example system to extract information about food safety events from text

existing strings is already a good user experience for the food safety professional, so we can keep the architecture as simple as possible and consider this extension after we have a working prototype. This architecture is shown in figure 12.2.

Notice that figure 12.2 has annotation within the stream of information, which makes more sense for a machine-learning assisted task. Otherwise, the loop is the same, with that data powering a model that in turn helps the annotation. You can see the code at https://github.com/rmunro/food_safety. See the readme file in the repository for more information about the details of the implementation and how to experiment with it.

12.3.3 *Potential extensions*

After playing with the implementation for a little while, think about what kind of changes you might make to make the system more efficient. Some possible extensions are summarized in table 12.3.

As with our previous example, all the changes in table 12.3 could be implemented in fewer than 50 lines of code. Any change could be the right next step based on experience with the system.

Table 12.3   Potential extensions to the example and the chapters/sections in which they are covered in this book

Annotation interface	
Predictive annotations (section 11.5.4)	Prepopulate the fields with the predictions when the model is confident in that prediction. That approach will speed annotation but can lead to more errors if the experts are primed to accept wrong predictions.
Adjudication (sections 8.4 and 11.5.4)	Create a separate interface that allows the expert to quickly adjudicate examples that have high value to the model. This approach should be implemented as an optional additional strategy for the expert, not replacing their daily workflow.
Annotation quality control	
Intra-annotator agreement (section 8.2)	Domain experts often underestimate their own consistency, so it might help to give annotator the same task at different times to measure consistency.
Predicting errors (section 9.2.3)	Build a model to explicitly predict where the expert is most likely to make errors, based on ground truth data, inter-/intra-annotator agreement, and/or the amount of time spent on each report (assuming that more time is spent on more complicated tasks). Use this model to flag where errors might occur, and ask the expert to pay more attention and/or give those items to more people.
Machine learning architecture	
Synthetic negative examples (section 9.7)	This dataset comes from templated text that is only about food safety events. This approach will make the model brittle when the text is not about food safety events, like predicting that any word following *detected* is a pathogen. By asking the experts to make the minimal edits to create negative examples with existing contexts such as *detected*, the model is less likely to learn the context erroneously.
Intermediate task training (section 9.4)	If we can create a separate document-labeling model to predict "relevant" and "not relevant," we could use that model as a representation in the main model. If the expert already has a first step where they filter out the relevant from irrelevant reports, that filtering step can become a predictive model in itself. It is likely that such a model will converge on features of detection events such as pathogens and locations, thereby improving overall accuracy.
Active learning	
Reordering based on uncertainty (sections 3.2–3.4)	The system orders by date today. But if the most uncertain items are ordered first instead, that could improve the machine learning model faster and lead to greater speed overall. This order will be an additional change to the current practice of the expert, however, and is likely to feel slower initially as they tackle harder examples.
Other uncertainty metrics (section 3.2)	We use ratio of confidence as the basis for our confidence threshold because it seems to be the best fit for this problem. We can test empirically whether ratio of confidence is the best uncertainty sampling algorithm for this data.

12.4   *Example 3: Identifying bicycles in images*

Whether it's traffic management, monitoring production lines, or counting items on shelves, counting the number of objects in an image is one of the most common use cases in computer vision. In this case, we are assuming that the use case is transportation researchers who want to estimate the number of people who use bicycles on certain streets. Here is the problem statement and three specific problems that are being solved:

- Transportation researchers want to estimate the number of people who use bicycles on certain streets.
  - "I want to collect information about how often people are cycling down a street."
  - "I want to capture this information from thousands of cameras, and I don't have the budget to do it manually."
  - "I want my model for bicycle identification to be as accurate as possible."

"Bicycle" is not one of the 1,000 most common labels in ImageNet, the most popular image classification dataset, so this task is plugging a gap in commonly available models (although "Tandems" and "Mountain Bikes" are in ImageNet). Bicycles are an interesting problem because they are easily identifiable by a human but at different angles will have different feature profiles for a machine learning algorithm. Self-indulgently, I cycle everywhere, so I want this technology to be as accurate as possible. You could adapt this task to some other label, too.

12.4.1   *Assumptions*

Our assumptions for designing this product are:

- The images can be taken from any angle.
- Existing datasets (such as ImageNet, Open Images, and MS COCO) may be useful but might not have coverage of all possible angles and settings for photographs.
- Accuracy of the model is the most important outcome.

Important considerations:

- *Agency*—The transportation researcher does not care about agency in the annotation process; they simply want to build the most accurate and robust model as quickly as possible.
- *Transparency*—Real-time monitoring of the system's accuracy is the most important metric.
- *Diversity*—The transportation researcher wants the model to work equally well (to the extent possible) in different lighting conditions, at different angles, and at different distances from the objects.

12.4.2 Design and implementation

We'll use a machine learning model that relies on two pretrained models built on the ImageNet and COCO datasets, two well-known datasets that have images related to bicycles and so will give us a head start on creating an accurate model.

For active learning, the task is a binary classification task, like the first example. The choice of uncertainty sampling algorithm doesn't matter, so we'll use least confidence. We'll look for corner cases with model-based outliers in which we might have confident predictions but lack strong evidence for that confidence. For annotation, we'll allow the annotator to make a binary choice for each image quickly to optimize for speed. This architecture is shown in figure 12.3.

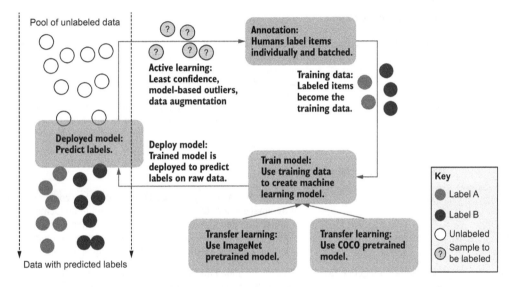

Figure 12.3 Architecture for the example system to label bicycles

Of the three examples in this chapter, figure 12.3 is most similar to the architectures that we have seen throughout the book. The only difference is that we are using multiple pretrained models because we are focused on model accuracy. You can see the code at https://github.com/rmunro/bicycle_detection. See the readme file in the repository for more information about the details of the implementation and how to experiment with it.

12.4.3 Potential extensions

After playing with the system for a little while, think about what kind of changes you might make. Table 12.4 has some suggestions.

As with our previous examples, all the changes in table 12.4 could be implemented in fewer than 50 lines of code. Any change might be the right next step based on experience with the system.

Table 12.4 Potential extensions to the example and the chapters/sections in which they are covered in this book

Annotation interface	
Batch annotations (section 11.2.1)	We could speed annotation by allowing batch annotation interfaces instead of scrolling. An interface with 10 or so images, in which the annotator has to select only images with bicycles in them, might be faster than the scrolling interface.
Bounding-box annotation (section 11.5.2)	For images containing bicycles when the model cannot predict that bicycle correctly, the annotator can annotate the bicycle(s). That image can be used as a cropped training data example to help guide the model on similar examples.
Annotation quality control	
Eliciting subjective judgments (section 9.1)	There are some tough edge cases, such as unicycles, bicycle frames, and bicycles with electric motors. It might be useful to treat these images as subjective tasks and to apply methods like Bayesian Truth Serum (BTS) to find minority but valid interpretations.
Synthetic data (section 9.7)	Can we copy and paste bicycles into some images? Doing so might improve the diversity of contexts. If we include both positive and negative examples, we can help the model focus on the bicycles, not the background.
Machine learning architecture	
Object detection	If the images can be automatically cropped and/or zoomed on the parts of the image where the bicycles are predicted to be located, we could improve the speed and accuracy of the annotation process. This technique could be used in addition to more common data augmentation techniques such as flipping some images during training.
Continuous/contiguous task	The task definition implies that the transportation manager is interested in the number of bicycles, not whether or not one or more occurs, so the model could be more useful with a continuous or contiguous task predicting the exact amount. Note that the annotation will be slower and quality control more difficult to implement.
Active learning	
Ensemble-based sampling (section 3.4)	Maintain multiple models and track the uncertainty of a prediction across all the models, sampling items with the highest average uncertainty and/or the highest variation in predictions.
Representative sampling (section 4.4)	We are using pretrained models from ImageNet and COCO, but we are applying the model to Open Images. So we could use representative sampling to find the images most like Open Images relative to the other sources, as errors are more likely to occur there.

12.5 *Further reading for building human-in-the-loop machine learning products*

Although it is not free, Emmanuel Ameisen's recent book *Building Machine Learning Powered Applications* (O'Reilly, 2020) is a good overview of the factors that you need to take into account when building machine learning applications, such as defining your product goal, setting up the machine learning problem, and building an end-to-end pipeline quickly. Almost all this information applies to human-in-the-loop systems.

Summary

- When defining products for human-in-the-loop machine learning applications, it helps to start with the problem that you are trying to solve and work backward. This approach helps frame everything from the technical design to the interface design and the guidelines for annotation.
- We created a system for exploratory data analysis for short text, giving an analyst the ability to filter news headlines quickly according to different labels so that they can see the changes over time.
- We created a system to extract information from text, helping a food safety expert track information about pathogens and foreign bodies found in food from plain reports.
- We created a system to maximize the accuracy of an image labeling task, assisting a data scientist who is making a bicycle identification model as accurate as possible.

appendix
Machine
learning refresher

This appendix covers the basics of machine learning that are most relevant to human-in-the-loop machine learning, including interpreting the output from a machine learning model; understanding softmax and its limitations; calculating accuracy through recall, precision, F-score area under the ROC curve (AUC), and chance-adjusted accuracy; and measuring the performance of machine learning from a human perspective. This book assumes that you have basic machine learning knowledge. Even if you are experienced, you may want to review this appendix. In particular, the parts related to softmax and accuracy are especially important for this book and are sometimes overlooked by people who are looking only at algorithms.

A.1 Interpreting predictions from a model

Almost all supervised machine learning models give you two things:

- A predicted label (or set of predictions)
- A number (or set of numbers) associated with each predicted label

Suppose that we have a simple object detection model that tries to distinguish among four types of objects: "Cyclist," "Pedestrian," "Sign," and "Animal." The model might give us a prediction like the following listing.

Listing A.1 Example of a JSON-encoded prediction from a model

```
{
    "Object": {
        "Label": "Cyclist",
        "Scores": {
```

```
            "Cyclist": 0.9192784428596497,
            "Pedestrian": 0.01409964170306921,
            "Sign": 0.049725741147994995,
            "Animal": 0.016896208748221397
        }
    }
}
```

In this prediction, the object is predicted to be "Cyclist" with 91.9% accuracy. The scores will add to 100%, giving us the probability distribution for this item.

You can see in the example that "Cyclist" is predicted with a 0.919 score. The scores that might have been "Pedestrian," "Sign," or "Animal" are 0.014, 0.050, and 0.0168, respectively. The four scores total to 1.0, which makes the score like a probability or confidence. You could interpret 0.919 as 91.9% confidence that the object is a "Cyclist," for example. Together, the scores are known as a *probability distribution*.

A.1.1 *Probability distributions*

In the machine learning literature, the term *probability distribution* means only that the numbers across the predicted labels add up to 100%; it does not necessarily mean that each number reflects the actual model confidence that the prediction is correct. For neural networks, logistic regression, and other types of related discriminative supervised learning algorithms, it is not the job of the algorithm to know how confident its predictions are. The job of the algorithm is trying to discriminate among the labels based on the features—hence, the name *discriminative supervised learning*. The raw scores from the last layer of a neural network are the network's trying to discriminate among the predictions it is making. Depending on the parameters of the model, those raw scores in the final layer can be any real number. Although it is outside the scope of this book to go into why neural models don't produce good probability distributions, as a general rule, most models tend to be overconfident, predicting the most likely label with a higher score than its actual probability, but when there is rare data, the models can be underconfident. So the scores that come out of these algorithms often need to be converted to something that more closely approximates the true confidence.

The probability distribution might be called something different in your favorite library. See the following sidebar for more about the differences.

Score, confidence, and probability: Do not trust the name!

Machine learning libraries—open libraries and commercial ones—often use the terms *score*, *confidence*, and *probability* interchangeably. You may not even find consistency within the same library.

I've encountered this situation. When I was running product for Amazon Comprehend, AWS's natural language processing (NLP) service, we had to decide what we should call the numbers associated with each prediction. After long discussion, we decided that *confidence* was misleading, as the outputs from the system were not confidences according to the strict statistical definition of a probability, so we went with *score* instead. An existing computer vision service at AWS, Amazon Rekognition, already used confidence for this same score when predicting the labels of images (and still does to this day).

Most machine learning libraries are built with less consideration to naming conventions than large cloud companies give them, so you shouldn't trust the numbers associated with your predictions based on their names alone. Read the documentation for your machine learning library or service to find out what the numbers associated with each prediction mean.

For generative supervised learning algorithms, like most Bayesian algorithms, the algorithm *is* trying to explicitly model each label, so the confidences can be read directly from your model. These confidences, however, rely on assumptions about the underlying distribution of the data (such as a normal distribution) and the prior probability of each label.

To complicate things further, you can extend a discriminative supervised learning algorithm with generative supervised learning methods to get a truer statistical "probability" straight from the model. Today, generative methods for getting accurate probabilities from discriminative models are not available in the most widely used machine learning libraries. You are overwhelmingly more likely to get a probability distribution generated by the softmax algorithm, so we will start there.

A.2 Softmax deep dive

The most common models are neural networks, and neural network predictions are almost always converted to a 0–1 range of scores by means of softmax. Softmax is defined as

$$\sigma(z_i) = \frac{e^{z_i}}{\sum_j e^{z_j}}$$

The outputs of a neural network will look something like figure A.1.

As figure A.1 shows, softmax is often used as the activation function on the final layer of the model to produce a probability distribution as the set of scores associated with the predicted labels. Softmax can also be used to create a probability distribution from the outputs of a linear activation function (the *logits*).

It is common to use softmax in the final layer or to look only at the result of softmax applied to the logits. Softmax is lossy and loses the distinction between uncertainty due to strongly competing information and uncertainty due to lack of information. We assume that we are using the second type of architecture in figure A.1, but the effects would apply whether softmax is an activation function or is applied to the model scores.

If you are using the second kind of architecture in figure A.1, an activation function in the final layer with negative values such as Leaky ReLU is often better for human-in-the-loop architectures than functions that have a zero lower bound, such as ReLU. For some of the active learning strategies in this book, it can help to quantify

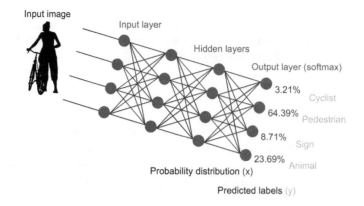

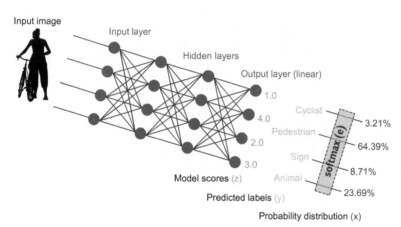

Figure A.1   How softmax creates probability distributions in two types of architectures. In the top example, softmax is the activation function of the output (final) layer, directly outputting a probability distribution. In the bottom example, a linear activation function is used on the output layer, creating model scores (logits) that are converted to probability distributions via softmax. The bottom architecture is only slightly more complicated but is preferred for active learning, as it is more informative.

the amount of negative information for one output. If you know that some other activation function is more accurate for predicting labels, you might consider retraining your final layer for active learning. This strategy—retraining part of a model specifically for human-in-the-loop tasks—is covered throughout this book.

Regardless of the architecture you are using and the range of inputs to softmax, understanding the softmax equation is important because it is lossy (which is widely known) and makes arbitrary input assumptions that can change the rank order of the confidence of predictions (which is not widely known).

A.2.1 Converting the model output to confidences with softmax

Here's an example implementation of softmax in Python, using the PyTorch library:[1]

```
def softmax(self, scores, base=math.e):
    """Returns softmax array for array of scores

    Converts a set of raw scores from a model (logits) into a
    probability distribution via softmax.

    The probability distribution will be a set of real numbers
    such that each is in the range 0-1.0 and the sum is 1.0.

    Assumes input is a pytorch tensor: tensor([1.0, 4.0, 2.0, 3.0])

    Keyword arguments:
        prediction -- pytorch tensor of any real numbers.
        base -- the base for the exponential (default e)
    """
    exps = (base**scores.to(dtype=torch.float)) # exponents of input
    sum_exps = torch.sum(exps) # sum of all exponentials

    prob_dist = exps / sum_exps # normalize exponentials
    return prob_dist
```

Strictly speaking, this function should be called *softargmax*, but in machine learning circles it is almost always shortened to *softmax*. You might also see it called a *Boltzmann distribution* or *Gibbs distribution*.

To get an idea of what the softmax transformation in the preceding equation is doing, let's break down the pieces. Suppose that you predicted the object in an image, and the model gave you raw scores of 1, 4, 2, and 3. The highest number, 4, will become the most confident prediction (table A.1).

Table A.1 An example prediction with the scores (z, logits); each score to the power of the natural exponent (e); and the normalized exponents, which are the softmax values. The normalized vector is called the *probability distribution* because the numbers in a 0–1 range and add up to 1.

Predicted label	Cyclist	Pedestrian	Sign	Animal
scores ($z_1,..z_4$)	1.0	4.0	2.0	3.0
e^z	2.72	54.60	7.39	20.09
softmax	0.0321	0.6439	0.0871	0.2369

The final row, softmax, is each e^z divided by the sum of all numbers in the e^z row. These raw scores,—1, 4, 2, and 3—will be used throughout this section to keep the examples consistent and because they add to 10, which makes intuition easier. The exact range of numbers you get will depend on your activation function. If you are

---

[1] An earlier version of this chapter used the NumPy library instead of the PyTorch library. You can see those examples at http://mng.bz/Xd4p.

using softmax as the final activation function, the exact numbers will be a combination of activation function and weights on the output of the previous layer. Exact integers are unlikely, but the range of 1–4 will be common in a lot of architectures.

As table A.1 shows, "Pedestrian" is the most confident prediction for our example, and the confidence numbers are stretched out from raw numbers; 4.0 out of 10.0 in the raw scores becomes 64% in the softmax. The "Pedestrian" prediction became much bigger in the e^z step, where it is 54.60, $e^{4.0}$ = 54.60, so the most probable label comes to dominate the denominator equation as the largest number.

The benefits of interpretability should be clear: by converting the numbers to exponentials and normalizing them, we are able to convert an unbounded range of positive and negative numbers into probability estimates that are in a 0–1 range and add up to 1. Also, the exponentials might map more closely to real probabilities than if we normalized the raw scores. If your model is training by using maximum likelihood estimation (MLE), the most popular way to train a neural model, it is optimizing the log likelihood. So using an exponential on log likelihood takes us to an actual likelihood.

A.2.2 *The choice of base/temperature for softmax*

As an alternative to changing the base from *e*, you can divide the numerator and denominator by a constant. This technique is called changing the *temperature* of softmax, so it is typically represented by *T*, which is typically 1 in the literature when no number for temperature is reported:

$$\sigma(z_i) = \frac{e^{z_i/T}}{\left(\sum_j e^{z_j/T}\right)}$$

Mathematically, there's no difference between changing the softmax base and changing the temperature; you get the same sets of probability distributions (although not at the same rates). We use softmax base in this book because it makes some of the explanations in chapter 3 easier to understand. If you're using a softmax function that doesn't let you change the base, you might find it easier to experiment with temperature.

Why use base = *e* (or temperature = 1)? Honestly, the reason why *e* is the number we use for normalizing our data is a little shaky. In many areas of machine learning, *e* has special properties, *but this area isn't one of them*. Euler's number (*e*), is approximately 2.71828. As you'll recall from your high school mathematics classes, e^x is its own derivative, and as a result, it has a lot of interesting properties. In machine learning, we particularly like the fact that e^x is the derivative of itself (figure A.2).

The slope at f(x) is f(x) for any given x, the slope of the e^x curve at f′(1) is 1, the slope of the curve at f′(2) is 2, and so on. You may remember this slope written as f′(1) = 1 and f′(2) = 2 in your high school mathematics books; the apostrophe indicates the derivative and is called *f prime*. Or you may have seen the slope written as dy/dx or ẏ. These three notations—f′, dy/dx, and ẏ—come from different mathematicians (Lagrange, Leibniz, and Newton) respectively but mean the same thing. You probably

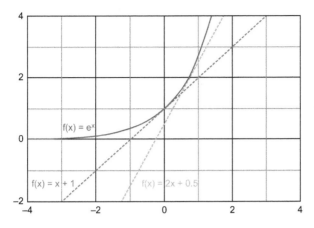

Figure A.2   Graph showing *e* as its own integral. The slope at f(1) = 1 is 1, the slope at f(2) = 2 is 2, and so on.

used Lagrange's notation in high school, Leibniz's in a machine learning course, and Newton's if you come from physics.

The property of $f'(x) = f(x)$ is what we mean when we say that e^x is its own derivative. If you used any base other than e for the exponential curve, you would not get this property. In machine learning, we need to take derivatives of functions to converge them. The *learning* in *machine learning* is mainly converging functions, so when we know the derivative of a function is itself, we save a lot of compute power.

That doesn't necessarily mean that e is the best number for your particular dataset when you are trying to find the best confidence measure, however. From the same input, compare the two graphs in figure A.3, which use e (2.71828) as the exponential base on the left and 10 as the exponential base on the right.

As you can see, the choice of exponent can matter a lot. If we use 10, confidence of "Pedestrian" in our data is now 90%, and the next-most-confident label is less than 10%. Table A.2 shows the scores from using 10 as the exponential base for softmax on our example data.

Table A.2   Repeating the softmax algorithm from the same scores (z, logits) but using 10 instead of e as the power

Predicted label	Cyclist	Pedestrian	Sign	Animal
scores ($z_1, \ldots z_4$)	1.0	4.0	2.0	3.0
10^z	10.00	10000.00	100.00	1000.00
softmax (10)	0.09%	90.01%	0.90%	9.00%

This table gives us a clearer idea of how important the largest number is. With 10 as the exponential base, we get 1 plus 4 zeros (10,000), which is clearly much bigger than any of the other numbers that get pushed down in the final softmax equation as a result:

The higher the exponential base for softmax, the more polarized the probabilities.

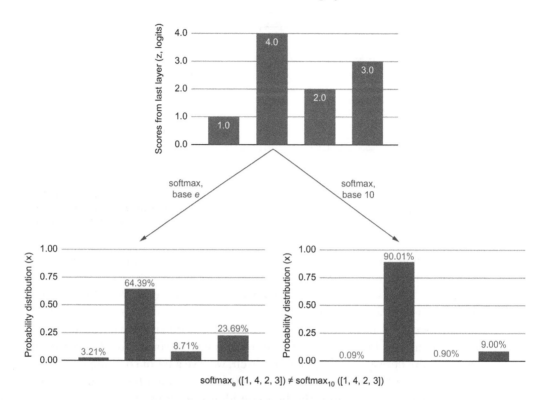

Figure A.3   Comparing two bases for exponentials (*e* and 10) for softmax on the same raw output data from a model. The graphs show that the higher the base, the higher the estimated probability of the highest score, with the highest score dominating the softmax equation to a greater extent at higher bases.

The choice of base won't change which prediction is the most confident for a single item, so it is often overlooked in machine learning tasks when people care only about the predictive accuracy over the labels. The choice of base can change the rank order of confidence, however. That is, Item A might be more confident than Item B under base *e* but less confident under base 10. Table A.3 shows an example.

Table A.3   Two sets of possible inputs to softmax, which will be ranked differently depending on the base/temperature used

Predicted label	Cyclist	Pedestrian	Sign	Animal
Inputs A	3.22	2.88	3.03	3.09
Inputs B	3.25	3.24	3.23	1.45

In both cases, A and B predict that "Cyclist" is the most likely label. But which one is more confident in the correct label? As figure A.4 shows, the answer depends on the base and temperature.

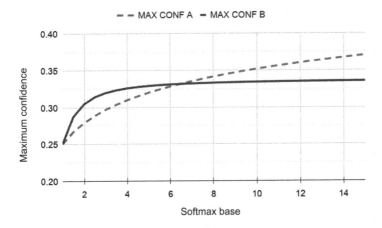

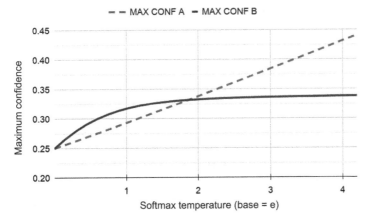

Figure A.4 Comparing the inputs in table A.3 (A = [3.22, 2.88, 3.03, 3.09] and B = [3.25, 3.24, 3.23, 1.45]) with different softmax bases and different temperature, showing either set of inputs could have the most confident result depending on the base or temperature. Strictly, the x-axis in the bottom graph is the *inverse* temperature, which is an valid equally scaling metric, although not as common. We use the inverse here to show both graphs going up and to the right in more or less the same way.

Many people find it surprising that the graph in figure A.4 is possible, including a reviewer of this book, a reviewer at the prominent ICML conference, and a Turing Award winner, which is why I added this figure late in writing this book. Given a random set of inputs (in my experiments), you get the effect in figure A.4 for only about 1% of input pairs. For the least confident predictions when sampling for active learning, however, the samples can vary by up to 50%! Sampling the least confident items is the most common strategy for active learning and is discussed in chapter 3. So this widespread misconception has been widely missed in human-in-the-loop machine learning: changing the base or temperature of softmax has the potential to create more accurate systems by manipulating variables that people previously assumed to be invariant.

Assume that in this text, softmax uses base = e and temperature = 1 in unless explicitly stated otherwise. For now, it is important to get an idea of softmax transforms your inputs into a probability distribution.

A.2.3   *The result from dividing exponentials*

Remember that softmax normalizes the exponentials of the inputs, and recall from your high school mathematics the equation: $c^{(a-b)} = c^a / c^b$. Therefore, when softmax normalizes the exponentials by dividing by all of them, the division of exponentials is essentially subtracting the absolute value of the scores. In other words, only the relative difference among the scores from your model counts with softmax, not their actual values.

Let's plug in our scores of (1.0, 4.0, 2.0, 3.0) to create scenarios in which we add 10, 100, and –3 to each of them, so we are changing the sum of scores but we are keeping the differences between scores the same. As figure A.5 shows, the probability distributions are identical even though the raw scores differ considerably in each of the four sets of predictions because the differences between the four raw scores were identical. The difference between 4 and 3 is the same as the difference between 104 and 103. This limitation is an important one to understand.

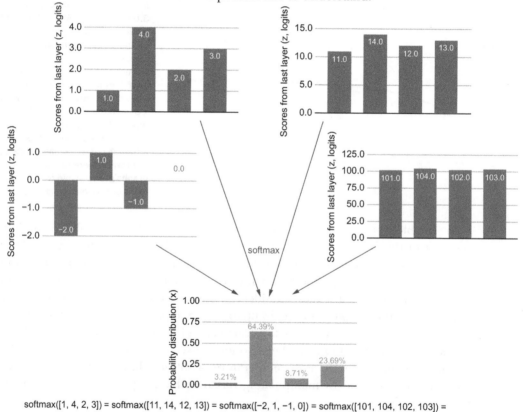

softmax([1, 4, 2, 3]) = softmax([11, 14, 12, 13]) = softmax([–2, 1, –1, 0]) = softmax([101, 104, 102, 103]) =
[0.032, 0.6439, 0.0871, 0.2369]

Figure A.5   Softmax equivalencies: four model scores that give identical probability distributions under softmax. The four softmax probability distributions are identical despite coming from different model scores, showing that only the differences between the scores matter. The scores of (1, 4, 2, 3), for example, give the same probability distribution under softmax as (101, 104, 102, 103).

To see this concept from another point of view, try *multiplying* each of (1.0, 4.0, 2.0, 3.0) by a constant instead of adding a constant, as in figure A.5. Figure A.6 shows the result from multiplying.

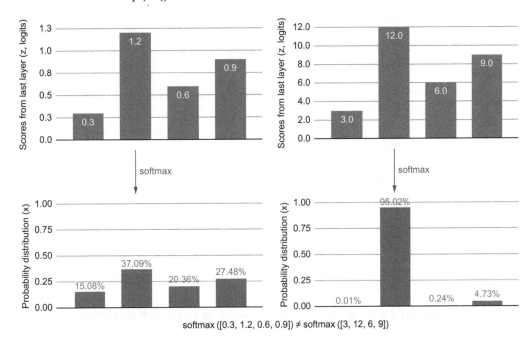

softmax ([0.3, 1.2, 0.6, 0.9]) ≠ softmax ([3, 12, 6, 9])

Figure A.6 Two score distributions are identical except for scale. The right scores are 10 times the left scores. Under softmax, these scores result in different probability distributions. This figure also shows the result of changing the temperature rather than the base. If we start with the values on the left but lower the temperature to 0.1 (effectively multiplying the logits by 10), we get more weight going to the most confident predictions.

In figure A.6, you can see that although the scores from the last layer differ only by the scale of the y-axis, they produce different probability distributions under softmax. For the distributions with lower scores, softmax produced a probability distribution that is a tighter set of numbers than the logits, but with the higher scores, it produced a wider distribution.

Be careful of large inputs into softmax

You run the risk of hardware overflow errors when using softmax with large input values, because the exponent step will produce large values. If you calculate e to the power of 1,000 on your computer, you may see a system error or an infinite value (*inf*), and this result can affect downstream processes. You have two ways to avoid this overflow, and I recommend using one of them if you decide to start experimenting with softmax.

(continued)
The first method is to subtract a constant from your inputs so that the maximum among your inputs is 0. This method uses the phenomena in figure A.5 to your advantage: subtracting a constant gives you the same probability distribution without creating overflow during the exponential step. The second method is to use the log of softmax (PyTorch's default behavior), which keeps the range of numbers contained.

In our examples so far, we have treated softmax as a normalization on the scores from an output layer. You can also use softmax as the activation function of the output layer itself. All the observations about the choice of base/temperature and how that spreads out the data in different ways still applies.

This section and the graphs associated with it are probably the longest description of softmax that you will read anywhere, but this information is important for human-in-the-loop machine learning. Softmax is the most common algorithm used to generate probability distributions from machine learning predictions, yet many people think that *e* as the choice of base has special properties for generating confidences (it does not), or that the choice of base won't change the rank order of uncertainty. So, the ability to truly understand what softmax is doing will help you select the right uncertainty sampling strategy.

A.3   *Measuring human-in-the-loop machine learning systems*

You have many ways to measure the success of a human-in-the-loop machine learning system, and the metrics you use will depend on your task. This section covers some of the most important metrics.

A.3.1   *Precision, recall, and F-score*

For the machine learning algorithm, it is common to use the well-known metrics precision, recall, and F-score. *F-score* is the harmonic mean of precision and recall for a label, where *true positives* are the correct predictions for that label; *false positives* are items incorrectly predicted for that label; and *false negatives* are items that have that label but were predicted to be something else.

$$\text{precision} = \frac{\text{true positives}}{\text{true positives} + \text{false positives}}$$

$$\text{recall} = \frac{\text{true positives}}{\text{true positives} + \text{false negatives}}$$

$$\text{F-score} = \frac{2 \cdot \text{precision} \cdot \text{recall}}{\text{precision} + \text{recall}}$$

If you use plain accuracy and your label is rare, then most of the accuracy will be determined by the large number of true negatives. One method of adjusting for this imbalance is known as *chance-adjusted agreement*, which we'll cover in the next section.

A.3.2 Micro and macro precision, recall, and F-score

The calculations for precision, recall, and F-score are typically for one of the labels in the data. There are two common ways to combine the accuracies for each label into a single accuracy score. *Micro scores* aggregate accuracy at the per-item level, calculating for each item. *Macro scores* calculate accuracy for each label independently.

If you have one label that is much more frequent than the other, that frequency will contribute most to the micro precision, micro recall, and micro F-scores. This result may be what you want in some cases, as it gives you an accuracy number that is weighted by the labels in your test data. But if you know that your test data is not balanced across the labels that your model will encounter when deployed, or if you want your model to be equally accurate in predicting all labels regardless of how frequent they are, macro accuracy scores are more appropriate.

A.3.3 Taking random chance into account: Chance-adjusted accuracy

Suppose that you have two labels, and they are equally frequent. If your model randomly predicts labels, it will still be 50% accurate. Obviously, that result is unfairly positive, making it hard to compare the accuracy with a different model in which more labels may not be balanced. Chance-adjusted accuracy makes the random-chance number 0 and scales the score accordingly:

$$\text{chance adjusted accuracy} = \frac{\text{accuracy} - \text{random chance accuracy}}{1 - \text{random chance accuracy}}$$

So if you were 60% accurate on the task with two labels of equal frequency, chance-adjusted accuracy is (60% – 50%) / (1 – 50%) = 20%. Although chance-adjusted accuracy is not commonly used for evaluating the accuracy of model predictions, it *is* widely used for evaluating the accuracy of human labeling. Chance-adjusted accuracy is more useful when you have big differences in the frequency of different labels. You have multiple ways to calculate random chance; we cover these techniques in chapter 8 when we focus on annotation.

A.3.4 Taking confidence into account: Area under the ROC curve (AUC)

In addition to accuracy over the predicted labels from a model, we care about whether confidence correlates with accuracy, so we can calculate area under the ROC curve (AUC). A ROC (receiver operating characteristic) curve rank-orders a dataset by confidence and calculates the rate of true positives versus false positives.

An example is shown in figure A.7. The ROC curve is created by plotting the true positive rate (TPR) against the false positive rate (FPR) in an order determined by model confidence.

ROC curves can help us decide where we could trust the model's decision and where we want to back off to human judgments. AUC is the calculation of the space under the curve relative to the overall space. You can eyeball AUC to be about 0.80 in figure A.7.

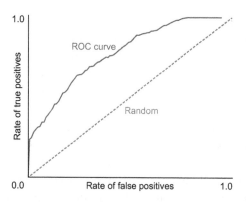

Figure A.7   An example ROC curve, plotting TPR against FPR in an order determined by model confidence. In this example, we see that the line of the ROC curve is near vertical for the first 20%. This line tells us that for the 20% most confident predictions, we are almost 100% accurate. The ROC curve is almost horizontal at 1.0 for the final 30%. This line tells us that by the time we get to the 30% least confident predictions for a label, few items with that label remain.

AUC is the area under the curve generated by ROC as a percentage of the entire possible area. AUC is also the probability that of any two randomly selected items with different labels, the correct label was predicted with higher confidence.

So we can calculate AUC by comparing the confidence of every item with label r with every item without the label (u):

$$AUC = \frac{\sum_{i}^{size(r)} \sum_{j}^{size(r)} \{1 \text{ if } i > j, \text{ otherwise, } 0\}}{size(r) \cdot size(u)}$$

This algorithm compares every item in each set with each other, so it has $O(N^2)$ complexity. You can order the items first and recursively find the ordering position for $O(N \, Log(N))$ complexity if you need to speed this calculation because of a large number of evaluation items.

As we can calculate micro and macro precision, recall, and F-score, we can calculate micro and macro AUC:

- *Micro AUC*—Calculate the AUC, but instead of calculating it for items in one label, calculate it for all items across all labels.
- *Macro AUC*—Calculate the AUC for each label separately, and take the average AUC of all labels.

A.3.5   *Number of model errors spotted*

If you have a system in which a machine learning model backs off to a human when there might be errors, you can count the number of errors found. You might decide that anything below 50% confidence might be an error, for example, and put all those model predictions in front of a person to accept or correct:

$$percent \; errors = \frac{number \; actual \; errors}{number \; sampled}$$

This equation tells you the percentage of items flagged for human review that needed correcting. One variation is to calculate the percentage of all errors, which gives you the total accuracy for humans plus model predictions. Another variation is to calculate the number of errors surfaced per hour or minute, which may make more sense if you have a fixed amount of time for the human component.

A.3.6 *Human labor cost saved*

Another way to calculate the human cost is to measure how much time and effort were saved. Whether you're using active learning to be smarter about which items to label (chapters 3–6) or improving the quality controls and interface for annotation (chapters 8–11), improving the efficiency, accuracy, and user experience of the human component of a human-in-the-loop system may be more important than making small changes in the accuracy of the models. Figure A.8 shows an example.

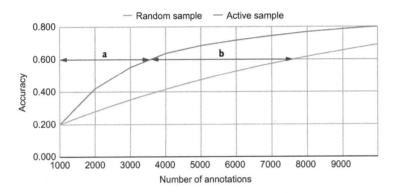

Figure A.8   The reduction in labels is needed. In this example, the strategy that uses active learning (chapters 3–6) reaches the same accuracy as random sampling with fewer than half as many labels. B / (a + b) = 53% reduction in labels needed.

As figure A.8 shows, active learning can reduce the number of labels required by 53% when we look at the x-axis, but if we look at the y-axis, the accuracy difference at that point is about 20%. If you come from an algorithms background, you are probably more accustomed to looking at the y-axis because you typically compare two algorithms on the same data. So if you are comparing the same algorithm on two different datasets, the x-axis has the more important numbers.

A.3.7 *Other methods for calculating accuracy in this book*

This appendix covers the most standard methods for calculating accuracy, but some accuracy metrics that are specific to machine learning are not covered here: bilingual evaluation understudy (BLEU) for language generation; intersection over union (IoU) for object detection; per-demographic accuracies; and chance-adjusted agreement for human annotations. These metrics are introduced at the appropriate places in the book, and so you don't need to understand them yet in this refresher.

The wide variety of sources that ... mean ... has been somewhat hidden ...
certain in the ... ...
described yet not ... the ... to ... in their ...

... ... of the ... ...
where need ... way of ... ... for ... ...
... comparison for ... guide ... ... most ... ...
Figure 4.4.1 allows ... ... the ... ...
... a comprehensive ... ...
... all ... in ... is ... ...

Figure 4.4 ... ... the ... ... it ... ... that
as we ... the ... ... the ... ...
will have ... ... in ... ...

We ... now ... some ... to ... the ... and ... has ... ...
... in ... ... they ... ...
... it is ... ... it ... ... an ... ... for ... ...
... ... In ... of ... ... and ... the ... ...
... in the ... ... and ... ...
the ... ... in ... ...

4.3.7 Other methods for establishing presence in this book

... ... the ... ... the ... by ... ... for ... ...
... ... that the ... ...
... ... (III) ... ...
... ...
... ... (VI ... ... in ... ... the ... ...
... ... and so ... ... to ... and ... ... in ... ...

index